The European Union as a Globa Conflict Manager

In recent years the European Union has played an increasingly important role as a manager of global conflicts. This book provides a comprehensive assessment of how the EU has performed in facilitating mediation, conflict resolution and peacebuilding across the globe.

Offering an accessible introduction to the theories, processes and practice of the EU's role in managing conflict, the book features a broad range of case studies from Europe, Asia and Africa and examines both institutional and policy aspects of EU conflict management.

Drawing together a wide range of expert contributors, this volume will be of great interest to students of European Foreign Policy, the EU as a global actor and conflict resolution and management.

Richard G. Whitman is Professor of Politics and International Relations in the School of Politics and International Relations at the University of Kent, UK.

Stefan Wolff is Professor of International Security at the University of Birmingham, UK, and a Member of the Advisory Council of the European Centre for Minority Issues.

The European Union as a Global Conflict Manager

Edited by
Richard G. Whitman
and Stefan Wolff

Routledge
Taylor & Francis Group

LONDON AND NEW YORK

First published 2012
by Routlcdgc
2 Park Square. Milton Park, Abingdon, Oxon, OX14 4RN

Simultaneously published in the USA and Canada
by Routledge
711 Third Avenue, New York, NY 10017

Routledge is an imprint of the Taylor & Francis Group

British Library Cataloguing in Publication Data
A catalogue record for this book is available from the British Library

Library of Congress Cataloging in Publication Data

A catalog record for this book has been requested

ISBN: 978-0-415-52855-9 (hbk)
ISBN: 978-0-415-52872-6 (pbk)
ISBN: 978-0-203-11503-9 (ebk)

Typeset in Times New Roman
by Cenveo Publisher Services

MIX
Paper from
responsible sources
FSC® C004839
www.fsc.org

Printed and bound in Great Britain by
TJ International Ltd, Padstow, Cornwall

Contents

Tables and figures

Tables

Figures

Notes on contributors

Cornelius Adebahr is a political scientist and entrepreneur, working inter alia at the Research Institute of the German Council on Foreign Relations (DGAP), Berlin. His current research interests include the EU's foreign and security policy as well as international economics. He is the author of *Learning and Change in European Foreign Policy: The Case of the EU Special Representatives* (Nomos 2009) and a frequent commentator in print media and television, including Reuters and the BBC. Since 2000, he has been the owner of Wirtschaft am Wasserturm, a company providing political consultancy, project development and training. He is a lecturer at the Willy Brandt School of Public Policy at Erfurt University, teaching a master's course on European foreign policy, and a member of Team Europe, an experts' network of the European Commission. From 1995 to 2001, he studied Political Science (International Relations), Philosophy, Public Law, and International Economics in Tubingen, Paris, and at the Free University Berlin, where he graduated in 2001 before receiving his PhD (Dr. rer. pol.) in 2008.

Carmen Gebhard is Teaching Fellow of Comparative Politics at the University of Nottingham (UK). She is also a Research Associate at the National Defence Academy of the Republic of Austria. Her research focuses on the role of the EU in international crisis management and conflict resolution, concepts of comprehensive security, and the strategic and operational relationship between the EU and NATO. Recent publications include the journal article 'Making Sense of EU Comprehensive Security' (with P. Norheim-Martinsen, in *European Security* 2: 2011), a co-edited volume *Cooperation or Conflict? Problematizing Organizational Overlap in Europe* (Ashgate 2010, with D. Galbreath), a co-authored book *Global Security – European Capabilities* (German; Boehlau 2010) and a chapter on 'Coherence in the EU's International Relations' in Hill/Smith (eds) *International Relations and the EU* (OUP 2011). She holds a PhD in Comparative Politics (Vienna, Maastricht), a diploma in History (Vienna) and an MA in Political Science (Vienna, Stockholm).

Claire Gordon is Teaching Fellow in East European Politics at the European Institute, London School of Economics and Political Science, UK. Her current research interests include EU enlargement, conditionality, and EU relations with the wider Europe with a special focus on conflict management and minority protection. Her publications include *Europeanization and Regionalization in the EU's Enlargement to Central and Eastern Europe: The Myth of Conditionality* (Palgrave 2004 with James Hughes and Gwendolyn Sasse), 'The Stabilization and Association Process in the Western Balkans: An Effective Instrument of Post-Conflict Management', *Ethnopolitics,* vol. 8, nos. 3–4 (2009) and *Measures to Promote the Socio-Economic Situation of EU Roma Citizens* (European

Parliament, 2011 with William Bartlett and Roberta Benini). She completed her first degree at the University of Cambridge, holds an MSc in Politics and International Relations from the University of Birmingham and a DPhil in Politics from the University of Oxford.

Eva Gross is Senior Fellow and Head of the European Foreign and Security Policy research cluster at the Institute for European Studies (IES), Vrije Universiteit Brussel. An expert on EU foreign and security policy she has published widely on various aspects of European crisis management and international engagement in Afghanistan. Eva Gross holds a PhD from the London School of Economics and has been a Visiting Fellow at the Center for Transatlantic Relations (CTR), SAIS/Johns Hopkins University in Washington, DC and the EU Institute for Security Studies in Paris. In 2005/06 Eva Gross was a fellow of the European Foreign and Security Policy Studies Program of the VolkswagenStiftung, Germany, the Compagnia di San Paolo, Turin and the Rijksbanken Jubilaeumsfond, Stockholm.

James Ker-Lindsay is Eurobank EFG Senior Research Fellow on South East European Politics at the European Institute, London School of Economics, where he works on issues relating to conflict peace and security in the Eastern Mediterranean and Western Balkans. His main publications include *The Cyprus Problem: What Everyone Needs to Know* (Oxford University Press 2011), *Kosovo: The Path to Contested Statehood in the Balkans* (I. B. Tauris 2009), *Crisis and Conciliation: A Year of Rapprochement between Greece and Turkey* (I. B. Tauris 2007) and *EU Accession and UN Peacemaking in Cyprus* (Palgrave Macmillan 2005). He is currently working on a book that examines how states (specifically Cyprus, Serbia and Georgia) prevent the recognition of secessionist territories, which will be published by OUP. In addition to his authored books, he has also edited a number of volumes and has served as the co-editor of *The Cyprus Review.*

Gorm Rye Olsen is Professor of Global Politics and also Head of the Institute of Society and Globalization at Roskilde University, Denmark. His current research interests are mainly directed towards the role of the European Union in global politics including comparing the role of China, the United States and the EU in Africa. A minor research interest is directed towards Danish foreign policy. He has published in a number of academic journals including *Journal of International Relations and Development, Perspectives on European Politics and Society, International Peacekeeping* and *International Politics.* He is the editor (with Ulf Engel) of *Africa and the North. Between Globalization and Marginalization* (Routledge 2005) and the editor (with Ulf Engel) of *The African Exception* (Ashgate 2005).

Nicoletta Pirozzi is Senior Fellow in the European Affairs area at the Istituto Affari Internazionali (IAI) in Rome. She works mainly on CFSP/CSDP, EU civilian crisis management and EU relations with other organisations – particularly United Nations, NATO and African Union – in the field of peace and security. She regularly contributes to the IAI's publication series (IAI Quaderni, IAI Working Papers), both as author and editor, and has published a number of articles and book chapters in peer-reviewed journals and edited volumes. She has been Research Fellow in the European Foreign and Security Policy Studies Programme and Visiting Fellow at the EU Institute for Security Studies in Paris. She graduated in Political Science at the University of Pisa and at the Sant' Anna School of Advanced Studies in Pisa. She also obtained an MA degree in

European Political and Administrative Studies from the College of Europe (Bruges, Belgium). She is currently PhD candidate at the Catholic University in Milan.

Annemarie Peen Rodt is a Postdoctoral Fellow at the Faculty of Political Sciences at the University of Southern Denmark. Her research appraises EU foreign policy and the external regulation of conflict. Recent publications include: 'Taking Stock of EU Military Conflict Management' (*Journal of Contemporary European Research,* June 2011), 'Success in EU Military Conflict Management Operations: What is it?' *(CFSP Forum,* 8 (1) 2010), 'Diffusion of Conflict' (in Gardner, Anne Marie (ed.) *Encyclopedia Princetoniensis: The Princeton Encyclopedia of Self-Determination,* Princeton University Press 2010). Rodt is Associate Editor of the journal *Ethnopolitics,* founding editor of the Ethnopolitics Papers series and co-editor of *CFSP Forum* online. Prior to her academic career, Rodt worked in the Cabinet of the Principal Deputy High Representative of the International Community for Peace Implementation in Bosnia and Herzegovina.

Alistair Shepherd is Lecturer in Contemporary European Security in the Department of International Politics, Aberystwyth University, UK. He obtained his PhD in Political Science at the University of Aberdeen, Scotland, specialising in the EU's security and defence policy. His research interests are in the field of security studies, especially internal and external security in Europe; EU foreign, security and defence policies; Europe's role in conflict management; NATO and transatlantic relations; and national security and defence policies in Europe. Alistair's publications include: '"A milestone in the history of the EU" – Kosovo and the EU's International Role', *International Affairs* (May 2009); a co-edited volume, with David Brown, entitled: *The Security Dimensions of EU Enlargement: Wider Europe, Weaker Europe?* (2007); 'Irrelevant or Indispensable? ESDP, the "War on Terror" and the Fallout from Iraq', in *International Politics* (2006) and a co-authored volume, with Trevor Salmon, *Toward a European Army: A Military Power in the Making?* (2003).

Asaf Siniver is Senior Lecturer in International Security in the Department of Political Science and International Studies at the University of Birmingham, UK. His research interests include conflict resolution, international mediation and the Arab–Israeli conflict, and his work has appeared in various academic journals. He is the author of *Nixon, Kissinger and US Foreign Policy: The Machinery of Crisis* (New York: Cambridge University Press 2008 and 2011), and the editor of *International Terrorism post 9/11: Comparative Dynamics and Responses* (London: Routledge 2010). He is a Leverhulme Research Fellow (2011–13) and an Associate Editor of the journal *Civil Wars.*

Richard G. Whitman is Professor of Politics and International Relations at the University of Kent, UK. His current research interests include the external relations and foreign and security and defence policies of the EU, and the governance and future priorities of the EU. He has published in a variety of academic journals including *International Affairs, European Foreign Affairs Review, Contemporary Security Policy, Journal of European Public Policy* and *Journal of Common Market Studies.* He is the author of *From Civilian Power to Superpower? The International Identity of the European Union* (Macmillan 1998), editor (with Ian Manners) of *The Foreign Policies of European Union Member States* (Manchester University Press 2000), editor (with Alice Landau) of *Rethinking the European Union: Institutions, Interests and Identities* (Macmillan 1997) and (edited with Victoria Curzon Price and Alice Landau) *Enlargement of the European Union: Issues and Strategies* (Routledge 1999). His recent books include *The European Neighbourhood*

Policy in Perspective: Context, Implementation and Impact (Palgrave 2010), co-edited with Stefan Wolff, and he is editor of *Normative Power Europe: Empirical and Theoretical Perspectives* (Palgrave 2011).

Stefan Wolff is Professor of International Security at the University of Birmingham, UK. He specialises in the management of contemporary security challenges and has written extensively on international intervention and conflict management. Among his 15 books to date are *The European Neighbourhood Policy in Perspective: Context, Implementation and Impact* (Palgrave 2010, with Richard Whitman), *Ethnic Conflict: Causes— Consequences—Responses* (Polity 2009, with Karl Cordell), *Ethnic Conflict: A Global Perspective* (Oxford University Press 2006, 2nd edn 2007), *Autonomy, Self-governance and Conflict Resolution* (Routledge 2006, with Marc Weller), *Managing and Settling Ethnic Conflicts* (Palgrave 2005, with Ulrich Schneckener) and *Disputed Territories* (Berghahn 2003). Wolff is also the founding editor of the journal *Ethnopolitics* and an associate editor of the journal *Civil Wars*. He frequently advises governments and international organisations on conflict resolution issues, especially on questions of negotiation strategy and constitutional design, and currently contributes to ongoing settlement efforts in relation to Transnistria. He completed his first degree at the University of Leipzig, Germany, and holds an MPhil in Political Theory from the University of Cambridge and a PhD in Political Science from the London School of Economics.

Acknowledgements

We are indebted to many people for having helped to bring this project to fruition. Starting from an almost casual observation of increasing EU conflict management activity and the lack of a systematic analysis thereof that would marry existing literatures on EU foreign relations and international conflict management, we were exceptionally privileged to have as contributors to this book outstanding scholars who shared this perception and, more importantly, our aspiration to make a theoretically informed and empirically substantiated contribution to enhancing our knowledge and understanding of the EU's role as a global conflict manager.

The contributors to this volume went far beyond the call of duty by offering chapters that are valuable as individual pieces of analysis while at the same time engaging comprehensively with one another and our underlying analytical framework, thus making the volume as a whole larger than the cumulative sum of its individual chapters. Beyond their intellectual contribution, our colleagues' goodwill and enthusiasm for this project has made it a pleasure to develop.

In its four-year genesis, this volume has profited from the financial support of the British Academy, the UK's Economic and Social Research Council, the European Consortium for Political Research, the Specialist Group Ethnopolitics of the Political Studies Association of the UK, the European Union's Sixth Framework Programme, the International Studies Association and the Federal Trust, which enabled us to hold several workshops that were instrumental in facilitating a comprehensive exchange of ideas among contributors and discussants and were crucial in the intellectual maturation of this volume. We are also indebted to the practitioners of national and EU foreign policy and conflict management who were willing to share their insights with us.

Last but by no means least, we would also like to express our thanks and appreciation to Jennifer Gregory for her meticulous copy-editing, and to Craig Fowlie and Nicola Parkin at Routledge for facilitating the publication process with such grace and professionalism. It has been a real pleasure working with you.

Richard G. Whitman and Stefan Wolff
Canterbury and Birmingham
February 2012

List of abbreviations

AA	Association Agreement
AEI	Alliance for European Integration
AIA	Afghan Interim Authority
AKP	Justice and Development Party
AMIS	African Union Mission in Sudan/Darfur
AMM	Aceh Monitoring Mission
ANA	Afghan National Army
ANP	Afghan National Police
ANSF	Afghan National Security Forces
APF	African Peace Facility
ARTF	Afghanistan Reconstruction Trust Fund
AU	African Union
AUP	Aid to Uprooted People
BiH	Bosnia and Herzegovina
CAR	Central African Republic
CCM	Civilian Crisis Management
CEE	Central and Eastern Europe
CESDP	Common European Security and Defence Policy
CFSP	Common Foreign and Security Policy
CHG	Civilian Headline Goal
CIMIC	Civil-Military Cooperation
CIS	Commonwealth of Independent States
CIVCOM	Committee for Civilian Aspects of Crisis Management
CivMil Cell	Civilian–Military Cell
CMC	Crisis Management Concept
CMCO	Civilian–Military Coordination
CMPD	Crisis Management and Planning Directorate
CoE	Council of Europe
COMEUFOR	Commander, European Union Force
COPPS	Coordinating Office for Palestinian Police Support
CPCC	Civilian Planning and Conduct Capability
CRTs	Civilian Response Teams
CSDP	Common Security and Defence Policy
CSTC-A	Combined Security Transition Command–Afghanistan
CTP	Republican Turkish Party
DDR	Disarmament, demobilisation and reintegration

DG	Directorate-General (of the European Union Commission)
DRC	Democratic Republic of the Congo
EAC	External Affairs Council
EC	European Community
ECHO	European Commission's Humanitarian Aid Office
EDA	European Defence Agency
EDF	European Development Fund
EDP	European Diplomatic Programme
EEAS	European External Action Service
EEC	European Economic Community
EGF	European Gendarmerie Force
EIDHR	European Instrument for Democracy and Human Rights
EMP	Euro-Mediterranean Partnership
EMU	Economic Monetary Union
ENP	European Neighbourhood Policy
ENPI	European Neighbourhood Policy Instrument
EOM	Election Observation Mission
EPC	European Political Cooperation
ESDC	European Security and Defence College
ESDP	European Security and Defence Policy
ESS	European Security Strategy
EU	European Union
EUBAM	European Union Border Assistance Mission
EUFOR	European Union Force
EUHR	European Union High Representative
EULEX	European Union Rule of Law Mission in Kosovo
EUMAP	European Union Action Plan for Moldova
EUMM	European Union Monitoring Mission
EUMS	European Union Military Staff
EUPAT	European Union Police Advisory Team
EUPM	European Union Police Mission
EUPOL	European Union Police Mission
EUROFOR	European Rapid Operational Force
EUSR	EU Special Representative
FDD	Focused District Development
FPUs	Formed Police Units
FSU	Former Soviet Union
FYROM	Former Yugoslav Republic of Macedonia
GAER	General Affairs and External Relations Council
GDP	Gross Domestic Product
GFAP	General Framework Agreement for Peace in Bosnia and Herzegovina
NLA	National Liberation Army
GMES	Global Monitoring of Environment and Security
GPPO	German Police Project Office
HDI	Human Development Index
HHG	Helsinki Headline Goal
HQ	Headquarters
HR	High Representative

ICG	International Crisis Group
ICTY	International Criminal Tribunal for the former Yugoslavia
IDP	Internally Displaced Person
IFOR	Implementation Force
IGC	Intergovernmental Conference
IOC	Initial Operating Capability
UNMIK	United Nations Mission in Kosovo
IPCB	International Police Coordination Board
IPRM	Incident Prevention and Reaction Mechanism
IPUs	Integrated Police Units
ISAF	International Security Assistance Force
JEM	Justice and Equality Movement
KFOR	Kosovo Force
LOTFA	Law and Order Trust Fund for Afghanistan
MEPP	Middle East Peace Process
MFAEI	Ministry of Foreign Affairs and European Integration
MINURCAT	United Nations Mission in the Central African Republic and Chad
MoD	Ministry of Defence
MoI	Ministry of the Interior
MoIA	Ministry of Internal Affairs
MONUC	United Nations Mission in the Democratic Republic of the Congo
MoU	Memorandum of Understanding
NAC	North Atlantic Council
NAM	Non-Aligned Movement
NATO	North Atlantic Treaty Organization
NAVFOR	Naval Force
NGOs	Non-governmental Organisations
NIS	Newly independent states
NORDEM	Norwegian Resource Bank for Democracy and Human Rights
NTM-A	NATO Training Mission Afghanistan
OAU	Organisation of African Unity
OHR	Office of the High Representative
OPLAN	Operation Plan
OSCE	Organization for Security and Co-operation in Europe
PA	Palestinian Authority
PCA	Partnership and Cooperation Agreement
PCRU	Post Conflict Reconstruction Unit
PEGASE	Mécanisme Palestino-Européen de Gestion de l'Aide Socio-Economique
PIC	Peace Implementation Council
PLO	Palestinian Liberation Organization
PM	Prime Minister
PRDP	Palestinian Reform and Development Plan
PRTs	Provincial Reconstruction Teams
PSC	Political and Security Committee
RCA	Central African Republic
SAA	Stabilisation and Association Agreement
SALIS	Strategic Airlift Interim Solution
SAP	Stabilisation and Association Process

SCR	Security Council Resolution
SEA	Single European Act
SFOR	Stabilisation Force in Bosnia and Herzegovina
SG	Secretary-General
SHAPE	Supreme Headquarters of Allied Powers in Europe
SitCen	Situation Centre
SITCEN	Situation Centre
SLM/A	Sudan Liberation Movement/Army
SRSG	Special Representative of the Secretary-General
SSR	Security Sector Reform
TEU	Treaty on European Union
TIM	Temporary International Mechanism
TN	Transnistria
ToL	Treaty of Lisbon
TRNC	Turkish Republic of Northern Cyprus
UCK	National Liberation Army
UK	United Kingdom
UN	United Nations
UNAMA	United Nations Assistance Mission to Afghanistan
UNDP	United Nations Development Programme
UNIFIL	United Nations Interim Force in Lebanon
UNOMIG	United Nations Observer Mission in Georgia
UNPROFOR	United Nations Protection Force
UNPT	European Union Planning Team
UNRWA	United Nations Relief and Works Agency for Palestine Refugees
UNSC	United Nations Security Council
UNSCR	United Nations Security Council Resolution
US/USA	United States of America
USSR	Union of Soviet Socialist Republics
WEU	Western European Union
WKC	Watch-Keeping Capability
ZIF	Centre for International Peace Operations

Foreword

Is there scope for the EU to refocus on its role in international security? Can the EU build on its experience as a security actor in the years previous to the Lisbon Treaty and define its ambition for the next decade, both in the civilian and military dimensions of the Common Security and Defence Policy (CSDP)? Is this possible at a time when Europeans are deeply concerned about the future of the Union itself? This book, edited by Richard G. Whitman and Stefan Wolff, not only gives a positive answer to all these questions but concludes that by fully availing of the new institutional and political architecture introduced by the Lisbon Treaty the EU now has a real opportunity to forge 'an institutionalised, well-resourced, global conflict management strategy.' However, this book makes it clear that the Union faces formidable challenges in translating its announced ambition into reality. But it is an ambition of the utmost relevance to international peace in which it is worth investing European resources and capacities, even in a time of budgetary cuts.

Last year's intervention in Libya is a case in point, demonstrating both the capacities and potential of the Union, with most of the operations being conducted by EU member states under the leadership of France and Britain. But Libya also highlighted the Union's difficulties in defining a common policy that would give a distinctly European orientation to the military operation. Not only because the military intervention took place in the framework of NATO, but also because during their involvement as NATO members the EU countries concerned failed to play a role in defining the guidelines for the application of the concept of the Responsibility to Protect (R2P) in Libya. The lack of a clear political orientation undermined the impact of the implementation of R2P in Libya and is today undermining the protection of civilians in Syria.

To be effective as a global conflict manager, the Union needs to develop a comprehensive strategy, bringing together all the instruments of the EU's external action. But even if it succeeds in doing this in a coherent way, it will still need to integrate institutions and member states in the same effort. Such an approach, which could be called an enlarged comprehensive concept, is essential if EU missions are to be able to deal with the causes of a given conflict. In the light of the experience of the post-Lisbon CFSP, this seems to be the major challenge so far.

The basic issue, as the experience of 20 CSDP missions seems to prove, is the need for the Union to formulate common policies that would define the objectives of a given mission. In the first 10 years the criticism was that we had a number of diverse and important missions in almost all continents, but in many cases these missions were not framed by an overarching policy. The clear exceptions were the different missions undertaken in the Balkans, in particular in Bosnia Herzegovina due to that country's perspective of EU accession. This has also been the case in Georgia after the 2008 war with Russia, where the military observer mission was well-integrated in the political objectives of preventing the escalation of the war and maintaining peace.

In the post-Lisbon context European states are clearly more reluctant to become engaged in new missions and we may move to a situation of policies, or at least common positions, without missions, in particular military ones. The impact of cuts in the defence budgets of EU member states will be enormous: in the future cuts in military expenditure may severely constrain their scope for military engagement, making an operation like that undertaken in Libya in 2011 much more unlikely. But the pressure on European states to assume their responsibilities in their neighbourhood will in all probability increase, since their ability to rely on the US, whether inside or outside NATO, is likely to be much less certain in the future. And it is in the European Neighbourhood that the role of the EU as a provider of international security is most needed.

Of course, as this book rightly points out, the EU and the US are not the only players on the global stage and in the polycentric world that is now emerging the Europeans as well the Americans will need to engage with other actors – major powers like China, India or Brazil, middle powers like Turkey, Indonesia or South Africa and many others. Furthermore, in a context of diffusion of power, non-state actors, in particular regional organisations, will become even more important partners. Clearly, the EU has to assume its role as a defence and security actor in the broader context of the international and global community.

In a post-Western world the international agenda, including its security dimension, will be defined not only by the US and the EU and its member states. The global management of conflicts will be dependent on other actors, in particular Russia and China, both permanent members of the United Nations Security Council, but also on India. The current inability of the Western powers to deal with the Syrian crisis and to protect the Syrian population reflects this. In the future, the crisis management policy of the EU will need to take fully into account the need to cooperate with the new global players and engage with them also in a dialogue on concepts and approaches.

The experience of the European Union in the field of conflict management is already quite impressive, as this book shows, but the EU needs to conduct more regular 'lessons learned exercises'. These are essential for the EU to define how to build the next, post-Lisbon, generation of missions. In all this, it must be remembered that civilian missions are as important as the military missions. Shedding new light on the role of the EU in the international arena, *The European Union as a Global Conflict Manager* is a very welcome book, one that should be read by everybody interested in the EU's role as a global actor for peace.

Álvaro de Vasconcelos
Director
European Union Institute for Security Studies (EUISS)

Introduction

1 The European Union as a global conflict manager

Capabilities and context in an interdependent world

Richard G. Whitman and Stefan Wolff

Introduction

> The aim of preserving peace, preventing conflicts from erupting into violence and strengthening international security is an important element of the external action of the European Union as laid down in the Lisbon Treaty. Violent conflicts cost lives, cause human rights abuses, displace people, disrupt livelihoods, set back economic development, exacerbate state fragility, weaken governance and undermine national and regional security. Preventing conflicts and relapses into conflict, in accordance with international law, is therefore a primary objective of the EU's external action, in which it could take a leading role acting in conjunction with its global, regional, national and local partners.
>
> (Council of the European Union 2011)

This bold declaration is the European Union's (EU) latest and most aspirational pronouncement of its intent to play a greater role as an international security actor and bring to bear the whole range of its capabilities for conflict management. The Council Conclusions on Conflict Prevention, from which it is taken, reflect well the broader aspirations that the EU has in this area and how far it has come in developing a more assertive vision for its role in international conflict management. That the Union would arrive at this stage was by no means a foregone conclusion. For more than a decade, the European Union's sole experience of managing intrastate conflict was in the Western Balkans, and it was an experience of mostly abject failure. Only in the early twenty-first century did it seem that the Union had learned the lessons of earlier mistakes: the decisive intervention in Macedonia in 2001, well coordinated with NATO, has rightly been hailed a success. While the ride to stability and security in the Balkans post-2001 was clearly not without bumps in the road, the EU, for the most part, seemed to have gained sufficient control and self-confidence in managing conflicts in its immediate neighbourhood to give rise to a modicum of success. Yet, in February 2008 the unilateral declaration of independence by Kosovo catapulted the Western Balkans back to the centre stage of international security concerns. Despite affirmations to the contrary, the recognition of Kosovo's independence by major Western powers has been seen as a significant precedent in international law and the way in which similar conflicts are handled by the international community. At the same time, it has raised major questions for the stability of borders across the Western Balkans region and beyond, from the Caucasus to South and South East Asia, from Iraq to Somalia and Sudan. At the centre of many of these questions is the role of the international community – defined as international and regional organisations, as well as their powerful member states – in tackling the complexity of interrelated and often internationalised local conflicts, incomplete democratisation processes, growing concerns about the economic viability of conflict-torn states (and their potential successors) and an ever increasing presence of transnational organised crime networks with significant reach beyond their country and region of origin.

Perhaps this is nowhere more apparent at present than in relation to the Arab Spring. From the more-or-less enthusiastic military intervention in Libya, to the difficulties involved with international engagement in the evolving conflict in Yemen during 2011, the blockage, by Russia and China, of decisive action in the case of Syria, and outright rejection of support for the pro-democracy movement in Bahrain, regional and international organisations, including the UN, the EU and the AU, as well as their individual member states, have offered anything but a coherent strategy on how to deal with the humanitarian and security challenges presented by the unrest that has engulfed large parts of the Middle East and North Africa since the end of 2010.

The international community, and the EU within it, has been here before. Take the example of the Western Balkans in the 1990s: finding a unified position on the recognition of the successor states of Socialist Yugoslavia proved a serious problem to the then European Community (EC) in the self-declared 'hour of Europe'. Preventing and containing the bloody disintegration of the country was a task too big for the combined might of the UN, NATO, Organisation for Security and Cooperation in Europe (OSCE), EC and all their member states. Feeble political will in the face of local actors hell-bent on implementing self-serving ethnocentric political agendas allowed the conflict first to escalate and then to go on for three years with around 100,000 people killed in Bosnia alone and millions displaced across the region. Even though the reaction was more determined and swifter in Kosovo in the late 1990s, it took three months of bombing and the credible threat of deploying ground troops before yet another crisis was contained. As noted above, only in the case of Macedonia in 2001 is there a story to be told of a somewhat more successful prevention of violent conflict escalation. Yet, Bosnia, Macedonia and Kosovo remain inextricably linked as three cases in the Western Balkans that, despite superficial stability in the former two, and an apparent 'solution' of the latter, represent unresolved conflicts which all have significant potential to contribute to further regional instability. Similar, and similarly bleak, stories can be told of international (non-)interventions and their outcomes in the South Caucasus, in Africa (e.g. Somalia, Rwanda, Democratic Republic of Congo, Sudan, etc.), the Middle East, Iraq, Afghanistan, Central Asia, Indonesia and so on.

The apparent ineptitude of the international community to manage such conflicts effectively to one side, the management and prevention of conflict remains high on the agenda of many international organisations (IOs), which see this as one of their main security tasks. IOs have indeed become extensively involved in attempts at conflict management and prevention in, for example, the Balkans, Middle East and Africa. Moreover, calls for these organisations to increase their involvement in these areas are frequent. Despite all of this, however, our knowledge and understanding of the impact of IO (or, more generally, third-party) involvement in conflict management is still relatively limited. In particular, while there is considerable case-specific and anecdotal evidence, we lack conceptual frameworks and systematic comparative research on these issues. While offering one possible macro-framework for the study of the EU (i.e. one particular regional organisation with global reach) as a global conflict manager, our approach is informed by two fundamental premises: (i) conflicts, while complex political phenomena, can be prevented and settled and (ii) it is possible to understand different conflict management processes and to discover certain regularities in them that can help us understand the broader notion of conflict management and the role of international organisations, such as the EU, within them.

To be sure, conflict and conflict management are complex processes, but their complexity must not be confused with a difficulty, let alone impossibility, to understand. Rather, what it means is that there are lots of different things to understand. This understanding can be facilitated with the help of an analytical model that allows us to identify, categorise and group a wide range of different factors that are relevant for understanding the success and failure of conflict management efforts. In order to construct such a model, we proceed in several steps. First, we develop the 'shell' of our analytical model, drawing on an existing body of international relations literature where the so-called levels-of-analysis approach has been developed and used since the late 1950s. Second, we argue that, apart from these external factors which are beyond the full control of those who intervene to resolve a particular conflict, there are a number of factors internal to the intervening party that co-determine whether an intervention succeeds or fails. From this perspective, our interest is neither in the causes of conflict nor in the motivations of the EU (or other third parties) to intervene in particular cases of conflict.[1] Rather our interest is in the causes of success and failure of these interventions; that is, in the (external) causes that facilitate or prevent conflict settlement and in the (internal) causes that facilitate or prevent the formulation and implementation of policies of successful intervention.

The development of the EU's activities as a conflict manager has taken place against the background of the development and elaboration of the notion of the comprehensive approach to security.[2] The development of the comprehensive approach has been a guiding idea central to international organisations and individual states in refining conceptions of security and how to manage their security needs. As we indicate in this volume, providing security across all dimensions is a fundamental ambition of the EU, yet at the same time essential to its success as a global security actor, not least in its role as a conflict manager. This presents a formidable challenge in coordinating a significant number of institutional actors and policy domains within the Union, both at the political-strategic level and at the level of planning and operations. From the point of analysts of the EU, capturing the practices of the Union as an actor seeking to engage in a comprehensive approach to security also poses considerable analytical difficulties, including in relation to accounting for success and failure. As we demonstrate in the remainder of this introductory chapter and throughout the contributions that follow, this requires an equally comprehensive analytical approach, and one that looks beyond the Union's own capabilities to the context of specific cases in which these are brought to bear.

Seeking to move to a comprehensive approach has had a considerable impact on how states and international organisations have approached the question of how to coordinate their military and civilian capabilities in ways that are efficient and effective, including in complex conflict management operations (Williams 2011). Conceptually the comprehensive approach intends to inform the organisation of the actors involved to work together from the planning stage to the implementation of activities. It is intended to harness the respective strengths of civilian and military actors in a manner that provides a joined-up approach to all phases of conflict from stabilisation to reconstruction. Consequently in assessing the EU's role in conflict management we are also offering an assessment of the extent to which it has successfully followed through on its ambitions to be a comprehensive security provider.

EU conflict management: a conceptual and empirical clarification

Studying the performance of the EU as a global conflict manager encounters, prima facie, a conceptual difficulty that relates to the very notion of conflict management itself. It is not a term frequently used in EU parlance, certainly when compared with the much more common concepts of conflict prevention and crisis management. These are both distinct notions in terms of both meaning and the policies attached to them. Conflict prevention implies long-term policies aimed at structural changes to eliminate root causes of conflict. Crisis management, in contrast, has a shorter time frame and implies a degree of urgency and immediacy, aiming to stop escalation and/or deal with the consequences of a rapidly worsening situation. In this sense, crisis management can also be seen as short-term prevention, with more limited objectives, such as preventing the spread or intensification of violence, or emergency humanitarian assistance to refugees from an escalating conflict. In our view, conflict management subsumes these two sets of policies, but also covers a third, commonly referred to as conflict settlement or resolution, that is policies aimed at finding a compromise between the parties that will allow them to address remaining and/or future disputes between them by political or judicial means, rather than by recourse to violence. Such policies typically involve various forms of mediation. Compared with conflict prevention and crisis management, they are far less well-developed within the EU institutionally and far fewer actual examples of EU activities exist here.

In view of the different types of policies that we thus conceptualise to be part of EU conflict management, we define this term in the sense of long-term engagement with a particular country or region, an engagement that, over time, will necessitate different conflict management policies, including military crisis management, development and humanitarian aid efforts, and mediation between conflict parties. This is apparent from a number of the subsequent case studies in our volume which indicate that EU conflict management operations involve elements of all three policies, albeit to varying degrees. The Western Balkans, and especially the cases of Bosnia and Herzegovina and Macedonia discussed by Peen Rodt and Wolff in Chapter 10, demonstrate this tendency most clearly. In Bosnia and Herzegovina, the Union was a key player in the early, but ultimately unsuccessful, attempts by the international community to mediate between the conflict parties; it was marginalised in the military operations that helped bring the conflict to an end; and it has played an increasingly, and today dominant, role in the country's post-conflict reconstruction process, including with the deployment of a military and police mission. In Macedonia, alongside NATO, the Union was instrumental in mediating the Ohrid Framework Agreement that has formed the basis of political and institutional reform in the country, and much as in Bosnia and Herzegovina some years later, the EU took over a military mission from NATO and deployed a police mission. In Africa, as discussed by Gorm Rye Olsen in Chapter 5 with reference to the Democratic Republic of the Congo and Darfur, long-term structural prevention in the form of development policy and short-term crisis management in the form of limited troop deployments went hand-in-hand.

In other cases, the EU's involvement in conflict management has been less comprehensive. Cyprus, as discussed by James Ker-Lindsay in Chapter 4, is a case that demonstrates the potential, however limited, of what is often seen as the EU's strongest leverage – accession – as a tool of conflict management. As Ker-Lindsay notes, the EU may not have had much direct involvement in the UN-facilitated negotiations process, but it is difficult to see how this process would have come about without the EU and its promise of membership. Such promise of membership, now a reality at least for the Greek part of Cyprus, is unique to this case and the Western Balkans.

Two other cases – Moldova and Georgia – fall somewhere between the cases with a clear accession perspective (Western Balkans) and those with clearly none (Africa, Afghanistan and arguably Israel/Palestine). In both Moldova and Georgia, the EU had long been on the sidelines of long-standing conflict management processes and had reluctantly accepted a role that would contribute to shaping an environment more conducive to the success of conflict settlement processes dominated by other players. Yet, as Whitman and Wolff argue in Chapter 7, the EU's management of the 2008 crisis of the Georgia–Russia war has been highly effective and the Union now plays a formal role in the Geneva (negotiations) process while having a military observer mission on the ground in Georgia. Importantly, the role the EU played in managing the 2008 crisis was preceded by almost two decades of prior engagement with Georgia, at least partially driven by conflict management 'desires'. In Moldova, the Union does not (yet) have a very prominent role in the negotiations to bring about a settlement of the Transnistria conflict, but, as Gordon shows in Chapter 9, the EU has clearly increased its investment in conflict management over time by bolstering the actual negotiation process and by emphasising political and economic reform in its engagement with Moldova.

This leaves Afghanistan and the Israeli–Palestinian conflict among our case studies. They are similar in the sense that, like Africa, they represent 'out-of-area' cases with no realistic accession perspective. Yet, in terms of impact, the differences are stark. As Siniver argues in Chapter 6, while the EU may theoretically be the most suited third party to mediate in the conflict, it is, despite massive financial commitments and the deployment of a border assistance mission and a police mission to the Palestinian territories, unlikely to be accepted as such unless the US turns its back on the region. In contrast, the case of Afghanistan demonstrates the significant impact that the EU is capable of in post-conflict reconstruction. As Gross illustrates in Chapter 8, the EU's added value, while not always fully successful, is in strengthening Afghan institutions – in this sense, a long-term policy aimed at preventing renewed conflict.

The second difficulty arises from the very fact that conflict management as defined here involves a wide range of different EU policies and institutions with no single 'executor'. While more pronounced prior to the coming in force of the Lisbon Treaty, the very term *EU* conflict management is somewhat misleading, as different policies are the, often jealously guarded, prerogative of different institutions with their distinct competences, resources and decision-making procedures. The capacity of the EU to reconcile these different strands of the EU's conflict management activities is the focus of Gebhard in Chapter 2. As Gebhard illustrates, synergy across EU institutional boundaries is important for the EU's overall performance as a global conflict manager and the EU's institutional nature has affected the progress of its development. Further, the Treaty of Lisbon has re-established, rather than eliminated, divides in the EU's conflict management activities. A clear example of this is the difference between the Common Foreign and Security Policy (CFSP) and the European Neighbourhood Policy (ENP) that is maintained: the former clearly intergovernmental and run by the Council, the latter attached to the Commission. Moreover, as Gebhard demonstrates, the CFSP (and the Common Security and Defence Policy (CSDP) as Shepherd demonstrates in Chapter 3), in terms of resources at least, is much more dependent on cooperation with NATO (principally, under the 2002 Berlin Plus arrangements), while ENP with its 'softer' policies is relatively more independent. At the same time, however, there is clearly a more significant potential for real and meaningful policy coordination in the post-Lisbon era as the joint launch of the ENP review (European Commission 2011) on 25 May 2011 by the High Representative of the European Union for Foreign Affairs and Security Policy and Commission Vice-President, (Baroness) Catherine Ashton, and the European Commissioner for Enlargement and Neighbourhood Policy, Štefan Füle, indicates.

Further, an additional set of institutional actors and processes has emerged alongside the EU's CFSP and external relations in the last decade as the EU has developed a defence policy component. As Shepherd demonstrates in Chapter 3 this has been heavily shaped by the EU's developing conflict management aspirations and especially with the desire to combine military and civilian capabilities for crisis management. This combination of civilian and military capabilities has meant that CSDP, while being just one element of the CFSP, which is itself just one component of the EU's overall approach to conflict management, has quickly become fundamental to the EU's approach to conflict management. The civil–military potential of CSDP, coupled with other instruments from CFSP and across the EU, has left the EU seeking to position itself, at least rhetorically, as a 'unique' and 'comprehensive' crisis manager.

A third difficulty is related to the notion of success. We cannot explain why the EU has or has not succeeded in particular conflict management exercises unless we establish the parameters of success. Peen Rodt's contribution in Chapter 12 on the EU's performance in military conflict management addresses this difficulty head-on in the context of her cases and develops a fourfold notion of success along the lines of internal and external goal attainment and appropriateness. This is a useful framework for a broader definition of the success of EU conflict management as it highlights several aspects of the difficulties associated with the very notion of success. First among them is the fact that we need to judge the level of success against what a conflict management intervention of any kind – civilian and/or military, short-term and/or long-term – was meant to achieve in terms of the mandate that the EU drew up. In other words, did the Union achieve the goals that it set itself? This is clearly an important benchmark in that it allows us to examine the extent to which existing capabilities can produce desired outcomes. Yet, success in conflict management is not only third-party related; in fact, one might argue it is as much if not more about actual impact on the ground. In other words, the question is not only what outcomes the EU produced when implementing a particular conflict management operation but also about whether this operation actually had a positive impact on the conflict as a whole.

This distinction between outcomes and impact is not a merely academic exercise: as a number of our case studies demonstrate, in terms of its goals, the EU has hardly ever failed since its Balkan interventions in the early 1990s. Yet, this is partly due to a more realistic and cautious definition of mission mandates which no longer seek 'peace' but rather more limited goals such as, for example, those defined in relation to the EU missions in the Democratic Republic of the Congo (DRC) as examined by Olsen in Chapter 5. In other cases, goals are vague: supporting, or contributing to, conflict resolution processes – a standard phrase in the definition of tasks for most EU Special Representatives as noted by Adebahr in Chapter 11 – is an outcome that would be difficult not to achieve. However, assessing the role of the EU as a global conflict manager requires us to look further and ask whether these outcomes have actually produced any changes on the ground; in other words, has the EU's (passive) support or (active) contribution actually resulted in a conflict being resolved? It is in this dimension that the picture becomes more mixed and success in terms of, in Peen Rodt's terminology, internal goal attainment needs to be qualified in light of more limited impact on the ground in terms of the actual conflict.

Where does this conceptual exploration leave us? First, it leaves us with a significant, yet diverse number of cases that, in our definition of the term, qualify as instances of conflict management in which the EU has been involved over the past two decades. Second, it leaves us with a range of distinct policies, and institutions that carry them out, within the EU, both of which individually and in relation to each other have undergone important changes over this period. Third, it leaves us with a nuanced definition of success that considers both what the EU has delivered in terms of the goals that it set itself and how much and what kind of impact its policies have had on the ground. Conversely, explaining varying levels of success, then, requires us to consider both EU capabilities and the specific context in which they were brought to bear. In other words, if success is 'measured' in relation to both mandate completion and actual impact, we cannot focus solely on factors that pertain either solely to the EU's existing (or lacking) capabilities or to factors that are specific to the conflict which the Union seeks to manage. Looking at both internal and external factors allows us to avoid 'EU-bashing' at the one extreme and absolving it from any responsibility on the other.

The challenge for us is now to develop a coherent analytical framework that allows us to bring together the study of EU institutions, policies and activity in the field and to explain why the EU in some cases is more successful than in others. We do so by first considering the current state of the field of the study of EU conflict management and then presenting our own approach that has guided the discussion in the chapters that follow this introduction.

The current state of the field

When it comes to the role of the EU as an international security actor, including its role as a conflict manager, much of the literature has, and remains to be, focused on the evolution of the EU's internal processes.[3] Close scrutiny of the development of institutions and policies, their interrelationships, the divergence and convergence of member states' preferences, etc. has long been a primary focus of studies in this area, not least because of a lack of real-world application: after all, the European Security and Defence Policy (ESDP), having been officially launched in 1999, only became fully operational in 2002. This literature, however, is naturally very useful in assessments of EU capabilities. For example, in a ten-year stock-take of ESDP Menon (2009) argues that while the EU has launched 22 military and civilian missions in the first decade of ESDP, these were all limited in size and scope, saying little about actual, especially military, capabilities of the Union. While recognising the overall progress in developing military capability as significant if compared to the pre-1999 era, others are equally sceptical (Cornish and Edwards 2005; Blockmans and Wessel 2009). A similar assessment is frequently made in relation to civilian capabilities: Jakobsen (2006), for example, sees another expectations–capability gap in this area. A third area of concern noticeable in the literature pertains to civil–military coordination (Bird 2007; Cornish and Edwards 2001, 2005; Youngs 2008) and is closely linked to inter-institutional failures of delivering a coordinated, coherent and consistent foreign security policy across the range of available instruments (Bagoyoko and Gibert 2009; Delcour 2010; Gourlay 2004; Olsen 2008) and to do so efficiently (Hardt 2009; Rieker 2009).

Coordination problems, however, are not only a problem of the EU's institutions. In fact, inter-institutional problems are, in part at least, a consequence of often diverging preferences and priorities of the member states. Much of the discussion here is centred on the 'big three' (Germany, France, UK) and their changing relationships with each other and the institutions in Brussels (Gegout 2009; Giegerich 2008a; Gordon 2006; Gross 2007; Howorth 2003a; Irondelle and Mérand 2010; Longhurst and Miskimmon 2007; Mérand *et al*. 2009; Ulriksen *et al*. 2004; Wagnsson 2010). Yet, not everything is dependent on the 'big three' alone. The serious difficulties that the EU has experienced in implementing its Battle Group Concept highlights the crucial role played by smaller member states in an area that remains dominated by intergovernmentalism (Chappell 2009; Jacoby and Jones 2008).[4] Intergovernmentalism, thus, is highly dependent on member states' perceptions of their own interests, including where to spend domestic resources and how to shape the allocation of equally finite EU resources (Youngs 2008) and how they prioritise their other international relationships, primarily with the United States, Russia, NATO and the UN, as well as other significant third-party actors on a case-by-case basis. This latter area raises a final capability issue for the EU: cooperation with partners in the implementation of its conflict management policies within an environment in which the EU itself challenges the existing nature of international organisation (Diez *et al.* 2011). All civilian and military operations undertaken by the EU to date have been carried out in cooperation with third parties. This is a reflection of both the complementary capabilities that such parties bring to an EU mission (or vice versa) and of the EU's strong commitment to multilateral action in the international security arena, which in turn also shapes the nature of many EU operations and arguably their effectiveness. The literature correctly places as much emphasis on bilateral relations in the context of transatlantic links (Giegerich 2010; Howorth and Menon 2009; Posen 2006) and the EU–Russia relationship (Averre 2005, 2009; Piiparinen 2008; Wagnsson 2010; Wilson and Popescu 2009) as on inter-organisational relations, especially with NATO (Duke 2008; Mace 2004; Ulriksen *et al.* 2004), the UN (Charbonneau 2009), the OSCE (Stewart 2008) and the AU (Brosig 2010; Morsut 2009).

Especially in relation to EU cooperation with third parties, this literature has taken a significant turn towards studying the way in which the EU brings to bear its different capabilities to act (i.e., to apply existing policy instruments and deploy civilian and military missions), to provide funding in the short and long term from EU-specific and member state sources, and to coordinate its internal decision-making processes and give them focus and coherence. The related capability to cooperate with third parties in concrete conflict management operations thus provides a crucial link between an analysis focused on EU capabilities and one that examines context-specific factors in relation to a particular conflict when seeking explanations for success or failure of particular conflict interventions. In so doing, part of the literature on EU conflict management recognises, on a case-by-case basis, the significance of the conflict context, albeit in varying degrees of systematisation and generalisability. On the one end of the spectrum, offering a relatively greater degree of systematisation and generalisability, Diez *et al.* (2006), in their work on the impact of the EU on border conflicts, identify a range of factors that determine EU impact in relation to this particular kind of international security challenge. A similarly broad, comparative approach can be found, among others, in the work of Coppieters *et al.* (2004), Emerson *et al.* (2004), Kronenberger and Wouters (2004), Tocci (2005a, 2007a) and Whitman and Wolff (2010b). A mid level of generalisation and systematisation in the literature is represented by studies that focus on particular regions, such as, for example, Sasse's (2008, 2009) work on the former Soviet Union, Gordon's (2009) and Peen Rodt and Wolff's (2010) examination of the Western Balkans, and Olsen's (2002, 2008, 2009) and Gegout's (2009) studies of EU conflict management in Africa. Finally, there is a strand in the literature that offers insights into specific single cases of EU conflict management, including recent work by Knutsen (2009) on the Democratic Republic of Congo, by Ilievski and Taleski (2009) on Macedonia, by Sebastian (2009) on Bosnia and Herzegovina, by Tocci (2009) on the Israeli–Palestinian conflict, and by Yakinthou (2009) on Cyprus. While not easily generalisable beyond the specific case considered, these studies offer valuable case-specific analysis, as well as a broader 'endorsement' of the more general point that context matters in understanding success and failure of EU conflict management.

This more case-specific literature on EU conflict management thus begins to bring together different scholarship on international organisations, on international intervention and on conflict management, and offers comparative insights in relation to other international and regional organisations[5] or examines conflict management as part of other, broader

EU policies, most recently and most significantly enlargement and European Neighbourhood Policy (ENP).[6]

Having thus examined the current state of the field in relation to the study of EU conflict management, what remains is to synthesise the different literatures discussed above into a single conceptual framework that can provide the analytical tools for the study of the EU as a global conflict manager. As we indicated earlier, this needs to incorporate an analysis of factors within the EU, or at least predominantly related to its capabilities, and of factors that are exogenous to the EU yet determine the nature and dynamics of the particular conflict situation the EU confronts. The next two sections of our introductory chapter will outline the main parameters of this framework that then guides the analysis in all subsequent contributions.

The EU's capabilities for global conflict management

If we systematise the preceding discussion of existing analyses of the Union's conflict management capabilities, the EU-internal dimension of our analytical framework comprises three sets of relevant factors; that is, capabilities that the Union must possess in order to succeed in conflict management: capabilities to act, to fund, and to cooperate and coordinate (see Figure 1.1).[7]

Capabilities to act

In terms of capabilities to act, political will is a determining factor for conflict management. State leaders have to agree to be involved as mediators and managers in a conflict. This political will is normally contingent upon state interests and values, and on the type of conflict (limited or widespread), and on the presumed likelihood of the success of any intervention.

This presumed likelihood of success, in turn, is a function of an assessment of how well existing capabilities to act, fund, and coordinate and cooperate are a match for the challenges a given intervention is likely to encounter. Here the EU has made significant progress over the past two decades since the Western European Union (WEU)'s Petersberg tasks were incorporated into the Maastricht Treaty in 1992. Military units of the member states of the WEU could thus be employed for humanitarian and rescue tasks; peacekeeping tasks; and tasks of combat forces in crisis management, including peacemaking. Subsequently, issues of personnel and hardware were addressed by several European Council meetings following the inauguration of crisis management as a distinct policy under ESDP in Cologne in 1999. Specifically, the Helsinki European Council in 1999 agreed the so-called Helsinki Headline

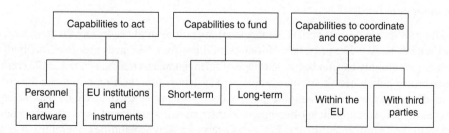

Figure 1.1 The necessary capabilities for EU conflict management

Goal for the development of appropriate capabilities which were defined as forces capable of undertaking the full range of Petersberg tasks up to the level of operations requiring corps strength (50–60,000 persons), deployable at this scale within six days and for the deployment to be sustained for 60 days. At the 22 November 2004 Military Capabilities Commitment Conference, EU member states offered contributions to thirteen EU Battle Groups as part of Rapid Response elements. The Battle Groups reached full operational capability on 1 January 2007 and with two (of now 18 Battle Groups) of 1,500 troops (a battalion-sized force and combat support elements) now on a six-monthly stand-by rotation to undertake Petersberg tasks. The member states failed to realise the Helsinki Headline Goal and the Headline Goal 2010 plan was endorsed by the June 2004 European Council summit meeting held in Brussels with the intention that this would allow the EU member states, by 2010, to 'respond with rapid and decisive action applying a fully coherent approach to the full spectrum of crisis management operations covered by the Treaty on European Union'. However, the intended force was now to be envisioned as only a third as large the original goal.

While there has been some progress in achieving the Headline Goal, a large number of deficiencies remain in areas crucial for EU's ability to pursue more demanding conflict management policies. The development of appropriate institutions and policy instruments, on the other hand, has progressed much faster and more successfully. The Lisbon Treaty's innovations of the new High Representative of the Union for Foreign Affairs and Security Policy, double-hatting as a Vice-President of the European Commission, and the European External Action Service (EEAS) are the culmination of an almost two-decade-long process of institution and capacity building. Pre-dating the Lisbon Treaty, and during the first decade of the twenty-first century, the creation of the EU Special Representatives (EUSRs) has helped diplomatic negotiations with parties in conflict areas. The post of Secretary-General of the Council and High Representative for Common Foreign and Security Policy (CFSP) (and the initial appointment of former NATO Secretary-General Javier Solana to the post) was a significant step forward and indicated that the Union was prepared to follow up on its intentions with substantive commitments. Several other institutions involved in CFSP under the authority of the European Council are also directly relevant to EU crisis management operations, especially the Political and Security Committee (PSC), the EU Military Committee, and the EU Military Staff, all of which were made permanent under the provisions of the Nice Treaty and now fall under the management of Baroness Ashton since the Lisbon Treaty's implementation. Our analysis in this area will thus focus on two related aspects: the extent to which the availability of personnel and hardware (or lack thereof) has stifled the EU's ability to pursue more proactive conflict management policies, and the degree to which the full range of policy instruments was used (or not) in pursuit of constructive conflict management, depending on the ability to back intentions with concrete actions.

Capabilities to fund

Capabilities to fund various crisis management operations in the short and the long term do exist within the EU. The provision of long-term funds for CFSP activities is normally not a problem, it certainly has not been a shortage of financial means that has impeded EU conflict management policy. However, the complicated system within the Union to make the use of its funds transparent and accountable has, until two years into the existence of crisis management as distinct Union policy, often hindered their rapid disbursement. An important contribution to the improvement of the EU's short-term funding capabilities, therefore, was the creation of the Rapid Reaction Mechanism (RRM) in February 2001. Its replacement in

2007 by the Instrument for Stability (IfS) was a further refinement of the EU's capacity to deploy financial resources to deal with issues of conflict prevention, crisis management and peace building. The IfS is intended as a capacity to respond to the need for financial resources for situations of crisis or emerging crisis, when more timely financial resources are not available from other EU sources.

The IfS is more flexible and structured than its predecessor the RRM by being divided into short-term and long-term priorities (the RRM was only intended for activities that did not extend beyond six months). The IfS has a budget of €2.062 billion covering the period of 2007–2013 and broken down between the short-term component of €1,487 million (72 per cent of the total) and the long-term component of €484 million (23 per cent of the total).

The *short-term* component for 'Crisis response and preparedness' aims to prevent conflict, support post-conflict political stabilisation and to ensure early recovery after a natural disaster. It can only be triggered in a situation of crisis or emerging crisis, in order to re-establish the conditions necessary to the implementation of the Community's development assistance under other long-term instruments. The activities under this component include: support for the development of democratic and pluralistic state institutions, support for international criminal tribunals, promotion of independent and pluralist media, aid for the victims of the illicit use of firearms, and support to relieve the impact on the civilian population of anti-personnel landmines.

Under the *long-term* component there are three sets of priorities: fighting and protecting against the proliferation of weapons of mass destruction; strengthening response capacities of non-EU member countries to cross-border threats such as terrorism and organised crime, including the illicit trafficking of weapons, drugs and human beings; enhancing pre- and post-crisis preparedness capacity building.

In this context, our analysis will therefore concentrate on the flexibility of the IfS to address specific crisis situations, the degree to which the ability to have IfS-funded actions implemented by a variety of different actors has enhanced the effectiveness of this mechanism to contribute to EU conflict management, the efficiency of transitioning conflict management policy in specific cases from IfS funds to longer-term financing, and the broader question of whether EU funds made available for conflict management are sufficient, given especially the increasing level of activity that the Union is undertaking in this area.

Capabilities to cooperate and coordinate

Coordination and cooperation capabilities within the EU have two dimensions: a horizontal one (coordination among the strands of the EU's institutions involved in conflict managment) and a vertical one (between the EU as a supranational organisation with its own institutional structures and the EU member states). Thus, our analysis will consider relevant actors' interest structures as well as the opportunities they have to realise these interests on their own or in cooperation with others. The division of labour between institutions in all three pillars and the degree to which this can benefit or frustrate external conflict management policy will be one key focus of analysis, alongside an assessment of the role played by individual member states in the coordination and implementation of EU policies in this area.

At the external level, coordination and cooperation is essential in particular with NATO, at least until the EU has developed robust military capabilities of its own should it choose to do so. Cooperation with third countries (i.e. non-EU and non-NATO members) and international organisations (UN, OSCE, UNHCR, NGOs) is accorded high priority by the Union because of its strong commitment to a multilateral approach and its recognition of the mutual benefits of cooperation, given that different organisations 'specialise' in different crisis management (and conflict prevention) tasks. Our analysis in this area will therefore need to focus on two aspects: to what extent the expected benefits of multilateralism have been realised and in how far the EU's mechanisms and procedures for coordination and cooperation with third parties have been effective on the ground.

All three sets of capabilities are, to a relatively large extent, under the control of the EU.[8] Yet, the effectiveness of the EU's conflict interventions does not only depend on its own capabilities: it is also subject to the dynamics of a situation on the ground in the actual conflict, in particular on the willingness and ability of local conflict parties to submit to, or resist, external conflict management efforts, which in turn is shaped by a wide variety of different factors (of which the EU itself is only one among many). In order to categorise these different factors and understand their interplay and impact on a given conflict – and thus on the EU's ability to manage it successfully – we now turn to adapting a well-known analytical model from international relations theory to our own purposes.

From capabilities to context

The analysis of the causes of success and failure of EU conflict management, however, cannot stop at the assessment of the Union's capabilities alone. Central to our argument and to the subsequent case studies and comparative examination of civilian and military conflict management is the contention that, apart from capabilities, it is the context of a given conflict situation that is crucial to shaping the outcome of any intervention. Thus, our framework requires a substantive component of context analysis in order to offer meaningful explanations for various degrees of success and failure that have arguably characterised EU conflict management operations to date. Here, we draw conceptually on a long-established tradition in international relations (IR) scholarship going back more than five decades to 1961 when J. David Singer published an article in *World Politics* entitled 'The Level-of-Analysis Problem in International Relations' in which he made a strong case for distinguishing between systemic (global) and subsystem (nation-state) levels for the analysis of various processes in the international system (Singer 1961).

While Singer offers good general guidance on the levels-of-analysis approach, his counsel is primarily geared towards deciding which one of the two levels that he identifies should be chosen, rather than giving scholars and analysts a choice of combining the two levels in their analysis. Two years earlier, Kenneth N. Waltz had offered a consideration of three images (i.e. levels of analysis) in accounting for the occurrence of war, and had suggested that neither human nature nor the aggressive behaviour of states alone accounted for war, but rather that the nature of the international system and the expectation of violence within it led to war (Waltz 1959). As Jack Levy has pointed out, the levels-of-analysis approach, in the tradition of Singer and Waltz, was subsequently mostly used in IR scholarship to classify 'independent variables that explain state foreign policy behaviour and international outcomes' (Levy 2001). Levy also emphasises that '[i]t is logically possible and in fact usually desirable for explanations to combine causal variables from different levels of analysis, because whether war or peace occurs is usually determined by multiple variables operating at more than one level of analysis' (Levy 2001). Despite the traditional focus on states and their relations with one another, there is nothing inherently prohibitive in the levels-of-analysis approach to extend its application to non-state actors and structures and to a range of 'issues' that fall somewhere outside the actor and structure dichotomy yet remain important independent variables when accounting for the causes of conflicts within and across, rather than between, states and for the success or failure of specific policies adopted to prevent, manage or settle them.

Implicitly or explicitly, earlier models for the analysis of, in particular ethnic, conflict have drawn on a levels-of-analysis approach (Brubaker 1996; Smith 2002a; Wolff 2003a). Most notably among them, Michael Brown, synthesising the state of the discipline some 15 years ago, suggested a two-stage model accounting for so-called underlying and proximate causes of conflicts. This was in itself a significant advance in the study of internal conflict, as it brought into focus a shortcoming of much of the literature until then which had done 'a commendable job of surveying the underlying factors or permissive conditions that make some situations particularly prone to violence, but [had remained] weak when it [came] to identifying the catalytic factors – the triggers or proximate causes – of internal conflicts' (Brown 1996). Among the underlying causes he identified structural, political, economic and social, and cultural and perceptual factors, individually or in various combinations, as necessary, but not sufficient conditions for the outbreak of conflict. He then used a variation of the levels-of-analysis approach to account for the impact of proximate causes. Presenting a 2-by-2 matrix, Brown (1996) distinguishes between internal and external elite and mass-level factors that he argues are responsible for triggering conflicts.

This two-level approach is consistent with the traditional neo-realist distinction between the system level and the unit level, but it deprives us of a more nuanced analysis. The terminology used by Brown to describe external-level factors ('bad neighbours', 'bad neighbourhoods') emphasises the regional level, which is undoubtedly of great importance, but he does so at the expense of the global level.[9] While Brown makes some reference to broader international developments, such as 'sharp reductions in international financial assistance' and 'sharp declines in commodity prices', more recent literature has identified a range of other factors well beyond a (potential) conflict's immediate neighbourhood. These include diaspora communities (Adamson 2005; Collier 2001; Sheffer 2003), international human rights norms and their use in the justification of outside intervention into internal conflicts (Holzgrefe and Keohane 2003), the moral hazard that intervention precedents create (Crawford and Kuperman 2006), and links between ethnic conflict and organised crime (Goodhand 2004; Kemp 2005, 2004; Williams 2001). Since September 2001, there is also an emerging body of evidence that local conflicts, especially those involving Muslim minorities, have been instrumentalised by al-Qaeda and its local off-shoots in their pursuit of global jihad (Abuza 2003; Frost *et al.* 2003; Smith 2005).

Equally, at the internal level, Brown subsumes national-level and local-level factors into one single category, which is also not unproblematic. For example, it is entirely plausible to attribute a significant share of the blame for the violent escalation of the conflicts in Northern Ireland in the late 1960s and in Kosovo in the second half of the 1990s to bad political leaders (i.e. to internal elite-triggered factors in Brown's terminology). Yet, this glosses over significant and policy-relevant differences, apart from the fact that the United Kingdom was a democracy in the late 1960s, while the former Yugoslavia was at best in a state of arrested transition between communist regime and liberal democratic market economy. The situation in Northern Ireland was very much a local affair between two communities with very different and incompatible conceptions of national belonging exacerbated by economic decline and, at the time, negligible concern by the central government in London. Kosovo, on the other hand, was a conflict primarily between a local secessionist movement and the increasingly repressive institutions of the central government in Belgrade. Thus, while Northern

Ireland in the late 1960s had a realistic chance of effective conflict management and settlement by way of a central government acting as an arbiter,[10] this was an opportunity that did not at all exist in the Kosovo case.

Therefore, we propose an analytical model that disaggregates the traditional two levels of analysis into four (see Table 1.1). At each of these levels, analysis should concern itself with the behaviour and impact of both actors and structures on the onset, duration and termination of ethnic conflicts. The four levels are:

1.   The local (or substate) level: existing scholarship[11] suggests that among state actors and structures, local elites/leaders, authorities and representatives of the central government, established institutional arrangements and socio-economic structures play a decisive role, while among non-state actors and structures it is the locally resident communities/ethnic groups/religious groups and their elites/leaders and locally operating NGOs, rebel forces, private sector interest groups, and criminals whose actions and effects are likely to have an impact. For example, for rebel forces with a clear territorial base in part of the state affected by conflict (e.g. in the South Caucasus, Moldova, and the Western Balkans), specific local dynamics would need to be considered alongside those at the national level of analysis, regardless of whether the overall aim of the movement is secession, control of local resources or state capture. The same holds true for conflicts that are relatively locally contained or where the stakes are of a more localised nature (e.g. in the eastern DRC).

Table 1.1 The levels-of-analysis approach

	State structures and actors	*Non-state structures and actors*	*'Issues'*
Local	local elites/leaders, authorities and representatives of the central government, established institutional arrangements and socio-economic structures	locally resident communities/ ethnic groups/religious groups and their elites/leaders and locally operating NGOs, rebel forces, private sector interest groups, and criminals	
State	national elites/leaders, central government, established institutional arrangements and socio-economic structures	communities/ethnic groups/ religious groups and their elites/leaders and state-wide operating NGOs, rebel forces, private sector interest groups, and criminals	environmental degradation, resource scarcity, energy security, food security, communicable diseases, etc.
Regional	neighbouring states and their institutions, regional powers, and regional IOs, as well as their respective elites/leaders; established structures of political and economic cooperation	cross-border/trans-national networks (ethnic, religious, civil society, business, organised crime, rebel groups, etc.) and their elites/leaders	
Global	powerful states and IOs of global reach and their elites/ leaders	international non-governmental organisations (INGOs), diaspora groups, international organised crime networks, and transaction corporations TNCs, as well as their respective elites/leaders	

2. The state (or national) level: this level of analysis contains essentially the same kinds of actors and structures as exist at the local level and it is difficult to imagine situations in which there would be no relevant factors at the state level of analysis. For example the conflicts in Abkhazia and South Ossetia, as well as in Transnistria, had, at least in the early 1990s, a very clear local dimension, but at the same time could not be fully explained without reference to political, social, economic and cultural dynamics at the state level in Georgia and Moldova – the balance of power and influence of different political parties, the strength of resurgent national sentiment among the titular nations in the wake of the collapse of the Soviet Union, the social and economic impact of independence and of the contested nature of emerging states, etc.

3. The regional level: scholarship on regional security and regional conflict would suggest that relevant neighbouring states and their institutions, regional powers and regional IOs, as well as their respective elites/leaders and established structures of political and economic cooperation, are the key variables to consider among state structures and institutions, while cross-border/transnational networks (ethnic, religious, civil society, business, organised crime, rebel groups, etc.) and their elites/leaders are the relevant non-state equivalents. This is very obvious in the cases of Afghanistan and the breakaway territories in Georgia and Moldova, and equally significant in the case of the eastern DRC and across the conflicts in the Western Balkans and in Cyprus.

4. The global level of analysis: this level benefits from a large body of existing scholarship, suggesting that powerful states and IOs of global reach and their elites/leaders are the relevant state actors and structures, while INGOs, diaspora groups, international organised crime networks and TNCs, as well as their respective elites/leaders, are those worthy of consideration among non-state actors and structures. Most prominently, this is the case with Israeli–Palestinian conflict, but it also applies to most of our other cases, including in particular Afghanistan, Georgia and the Western Balkans.

In addition to structures and actors, we consider it worthwhile to examine the impact on conflicts of a range of issues that cannot easily be classified as either actor or structure related. These include environmental degradation, resource scarcity, energy security, food security, communicable diseases, etc., all of which by their very nature cannot easily be 'assigned' to one particular level of analysis, but rather straddle the boundaries between several levels. For example, energy security is a major factor in the South Caucasus, while environmental degradation, food security and resource scarcity matter significantly in sub-Saharan Africa.

Conclusion

Our chapter began with a brief examination of the state of the field of the EU's role as a global conflict manager, and we found that not only are existing relevant theories of international organisation, international intervention, conflict resolution and of EU foreign policy relatively unconnected but they also do not offer a comprehensive enough framework that could help us understand why the EU might succeed or fail in specific conflict interventions. In order to bridge this gap, we propose to combine an analysis of the EU's internal capabilities to act, fund, and coordinate and cooperate with an analysis of external factors at local, state, regional and global level that shape a specific conflict and thus co-determine the success or failure of a specific intervention.

This approach is reflected in the structure of our book. Following this introduction, the two chapters by Carmen Gebhard and Alistair Shepherd provide an analysis of origins, nature and evolution of the EU's institutions and policies for conflict management. This empirically detailed and conceptual exploration of the actor at the centre of our investigation forms the 'organisational' background to the following seven chapters in which our contributors examine specific cases of EU conflict management in practice, explaining the Union's performance in conflicts in Afghanistan (Eva Gross), Africa (Gorm Rye Olsen), Bosnia and Herzegovina and Macedonia (Annemarie Peen Rodt and Stefan Wolff), Cyprus (James Ker-Lindsay), Georgia (Richard Whitman and Stefan Wolff), the Israeli–Palestinian conflict (Asaf Siniver) and Moldova (Claire Gordon). The three subsequent chapters thereafter offer a comparative analysis of different EU policies, instruments and approaches. Cornelius Adebahr considers the role of the EU's Special Representatives in the making and delivering of conflict management, Annemarie Peen Rodt examines the Union's military conflict management operations to date, and Nicoletta Pirozzi discusses the strengths and weaknesses of the EU's civilian management efforts.

Using our analytical framework that combines internal and external factors, the individual and comparative case studies help us to understand better the dynamics of specific past and present EU conflict interventions and the varied factors that can explain their success and/or failure. On that basis, our concluding chapter then draws some broader conclusions about the effectiveness of EU conflict management, identifies strengths and weaknesses, and makes recommendations as to necessary changes in the EU's approach to conflict management. In other words, the dual focus on EU-internal factors and conflict-specific external factors in the empirical material in our book enables us to identify the causes why some conflicts can be resolved relatively easily, while others become protracted and seemingly resolution-proof, i.e. what issues need to be addressed (in the EU and/or in a particular conflict environment) in order to facilitate more effective conflict management.

Notes

1 Accounts for EU motivations to become involved in different conflicts vary considerably. Compare, for example, Hazelzet (2006), Knutsen (2009), Larsen (2002), Lintonen (2004), Menon and Sedelmeier (2010) and Olsen (2009).
2 For a detailed discussion of the EU's comprehensive approach to security, see Gebhard and Norheim-Martinsen (2011).
3 For early, influential studies setting the standards in this strand of the literature, see Cannizzaro (2002), Dannreuther (2004b), Mahncke *et al.* (2004), Marsh and Mackenstein (2005), Smith (2002b), Smith (2003) and Smith (2004).
4 The role of smaller member states in ESDP/CFSP development and implementation has also been explored, among others by Olsen and Pilegaard (2005) and Gordon (2006) in relation to Denmark, by Ferreira-Pereira (2007) in relation to Portugal and by Devine (2009) in relation to Ireland.
5 See, for example, Lake and Morgan (1997), Thakur and Schnabel (2001), Pugh and Singh Sidhu (2003), Diehl and Lepgold (2003) and Otunnu and Doyle (1998).
6 See, for example, Duke (2003), Diez (2002), Holliday (2004), Sasse *et al.* (2004), von Toggenburg (2005) and Vachudova (2005).
7 In this section, we draw on earlier work, including primarily Wolff (2008), as well as Peen Rodt and Wolff (2010) and Whitman and Wolff (2010a).
8 This EU control is, however, dependent on member state cooperation. In the third area, in relation to cooperation with third parties, EU control is most limited.
9 Another valuable analysis of the regional dimension of (ethnic) conflicts is Lake and Rothchild (1996); see also Cordell and Wolff (2009). For an application of the model developed here to state failure, see Wolff (2011a).
10 The reasons why an initially promising initiative to this effect did not succeed are analysed in Wolff (2001).

11 Here, and below, we draw on a range of original and synthetic sources, including Adamson (2005), Brown (1996), Buzan and Wæver (2003), Carr and Callan (2002), Collier and Hoeffler (2005, 1998), Collier and Sambanis (2002), Cordell and Wolff (2009), Fowkes (2001), Horowitz (1985), Kaufman (2001), Lake and Morgan (1997), Lake and Rothchild (1996), Rotberg (2004), Rubin (2001), Scherrer (2003) and Tellis (1997).

Part 1

Conceptual Perspectives

2 The institutional nature of the EU as a global conflict manager

Carmen Gebhard

Introduction

In recent years, the European Union's (EU) nature as an international actor and global conflict manager has undergone considerable changes – changes in the foundational objectives, the *raison d'être* of its external action as such, and changes in the institutional set-up supporting and enabling it. First it was the formal establishment of a Common Foreign and Security Policy (CFSP) for the EU with the Treaty of Maastricht in 1992 to mark the beginning of a new phase in the history of European Community (EC)/EU external action. Until then, the EC/EU's external portfolio had been mainly composed of its external trade policy, development cooperation, humanitarian assistance and regional cooperation as well as of loose intergovernmental coordination in the framework of the European Political Cooperation (EPC). The CFSP formalized the newly emergent conviction of the then EU-12 to substantiate the Union's external agenda with new institutional arrangements and, not least, with the establishment of a political union. Pushed by the rapidly changing global circumstances, the EU started to develop and assume a more proactive role on the international scene. In 1999, the inception of the European Security and Defence Policy (now Common Security and Defence Policy, CSDP) then added a security and defence political element to this new external profile of the Union, providing the basis for the EU to develop distinct operational capacities for the management of crises and conflicts in its immediate neighbourhood, the European continent and, ultimately, in the world.

The creation of an operational element for the Union's foreign and security policy had a major impact on the internal institutional balance of the EU. As the CSDP started to materialize, the most immediate challenge was to accommodate the newly established set of governing bodies within the wider institutional structures of CFSP, and to administratively enable and prepare the new operational tasks ahead. What proved to be much more controversial and problematic, however, was the functional allocation of CSDP in the broader context of the three pillars of the EU. How should the new policy field relate to and affect other more traditional portfolios of EU external action and, in the first place, the external policy realm governed by the European Commission? If the EU really were to develop genuinely global actorness, which institutional arrangement would be most convenient to ensure optimal performance on the continent and in the world? Which institutional entity would ideally be taking the lead in the newly redrawn external profile of the EU? The enduring divide over these fundamental questions has frequently taken the inter-institutional dialogue away from the actual task at hand – the functional recalibration of the EU's external profile to the service of effective external action, most importantly in the realm of conflict management. As this chapter will show, the respective treaty provisions could not have been more ambiguous and confusing about the relationship and functional ratio between the Community-led and supranational domain of external action covered by the first pillar, and the second pillar of CFSP as its newly substantiated intergovernmental counterpart, then newly featuring CSDP. Preoccupations voiced by the Commission side about a hierarchic order creeping into the single set of institutions and about CFSP/CSDP subtlety infringing on the Community's terrain of external action competences gave rise to considerable inter-institutional frictions, and as such constituted a major challenge to the EU's capability to coordinate its actions internally.

From a conceptual and strategic point of view it was clear from the beginning that the operational elements of external action established within the framework of CSDP were to functionally complement the set of external policy instruments the Community already had at its command. The political and organizational road map to operationalize this idea of complementary agendas, and to complete the inter-institutional task of reconciling the respective portfolios accordingly, however, had yet to be formulated and designed. This chapter seeks to answer why this internal reconciliation exercise between the pillars is so important for the EU's overall performance as a global conflict manager, how the EU's institutional nature has affected progress in this regard, and in what respect there has been progress towards increased synergy across the institutional boundaries at play.

The importance of coherence in the twenty-first century

Conducting security policy in the twenty-first century is a complex challenge for any international actor. Since the late 1980s, the international strategic environment has seen a multiplication of non-conventional types of threat and aggression. Today, international organizations and single nation states alike have to provide for a very broad range of potential security challenges instead of limiting their efforts to the traditional range of conventional security political concerns, i.e. those inherently state-centric and military in nature. Present-day conflict management is an intricate venture in that it demands inclusive solutions and comprehensive approaches that transcend the realm of high politics to cut across various other policy fields. Security is now conceptualised as a matter of environmental balance as much as of economic stability or sustainable development. While the conventional core aspects of security remain relevant, other policy fields are gaining importance and have to be taken into account. Providing security as an international actor has thus become a multifactorial challenge. A set of policy fields is to be coordinated to fulfil this functionally indivisible task, and as it is the case with any combined institutional arrangement, ensuring coherence between the constituent parts is essential.

In order to tap the EU's full security political potential, CSDP as the operational core of its external action profile has to be integrated with the other domains of EU external action. Neither can the comprehensive task of international crisis management and conflict resolution be operated within the limited framework of CSDP, nor can the other structural domains of EU external action be kept strategically and organizationally separate from the CSDP. The traumatic experience of the 1990s, when the EU turned out to be functionally incapable of coping with the Balkan wars, has made it clear that the EU cannot become a credible international player without having any operational assets available. The way the international security landscape has recently evolved, however, also shows that operational crisis management and conflict resolution measures have to be backed by long-term structural efforts to frame the actions on the ground politically, socially and economically. Some of these flanking measures involve diplomatic and political action through the institutional arrangements of the CFSP; in essence, however, the external action instruments governed by the European Commission, such as development cooperation, humanitarian assistance, regional cooperation and external trade are among the most established and thus not least among the most influential policy tools any international actor could have at its command.

The internal institutional tensions that have dominated the EU's foreign and security policy in recent years have severely affected the credibility of the Union as a bilateral and multilateral partner, and reduced the ability of the EU to interact fruitfully with other organizations such as the United Nations (UN), the Organization for Security and Co-operation in Europe (OSCE) and, most importantly, the North Atlantic Treaty Organization (NATO). This is also what makes 'horizontal coherence', i.e. the enhancement of inter-pillar synergy, such a pressing challenge. Despite all internal struggles and the inherent challenge of having to cope with structural complexity, the Union is increasingly perceived as – and not least expected to act like – a coherent if not unitary actor. What has kept the EU and its Member States from overcoming these institutional frictions so far, and why in the first place did they persist despite considerable external pressure?

On various occasions, key figures in EU external policies have underlined the overall conviction of the EU and its Member States to respond to the multiplicity of today's challenges through the broad range of instruments the EU has at its command. It has become much of a rhetorical platitude indeed that the EU is a security political actor of its own kind as it disposes of a uniquely wide array of instruments for the management of crises and conflicts, and thus reflects most ideally the idea of comprehensive security political action. The principal benefit of the EU having both operational and structural capabilities is often rightly emphasised. However, what is frequently being declared as the EU's greatest asset as a crisis manager – its holistic predisposition and the wide range and variety of policy instruments it has at its command – in practice poses enormous organizational and institutional challenges. The institutional set-up that is to enable this comprehensive performance does not exactly match with the political ambitions voiced in these contexts. The EU as it presents itself today is made up of a vertically and horizontally multilayered, and thus complex, system of institutional actors, which in principle would not yet compromise the idea of comprehensiveness. Given this multifaceted and sophisticated structural nature, it actually appears as if the Union was virtually *meant* to act comprehensively. However, the alleged 'array of instruments' is spread across the pillars, and thus divided into different procedural channels of policy development, decision-making, implementation and financing. Therefore, the EU's potential for comprehensiveness in reality frequently constitutes a source of division, and thus, ironically, rather an inherent liability for the Union than a comparative advantage indeed, and this strongly affects the effectiveness and credibility of its actions. It is hence to be noted that the overall success of the Union's performance in the world stands and falls with the political and administrative ability of coping with the very essence of its uniqueness as an international actor: its versatility and comprehensive nature and, thus, its institutional complexity.

The legal basis: root cause of conflict

In public documents and political debates, internal struggles about external action competencies have commonly been referred to as concerns about 'coherence', and the related challenge and ambition to tackle the inherent lack of inter-institutional synergy. As the EU started to prepare for its first crisis management operations within the framework of CSDP, much of the general debate about coherence in external action had started to revolve around the functional role and scope of European security policy, and the way its advancement would affect the internal institutional balance of the EU. The core of this debate lies in the division about which institutional framework – the supranational one of the Commission or the intergovernmental one of the Council – is to provide the primary referent framework for the EU's external action. While, generally, 'coherence' appears to be much of a benign concept for achieving the desirable state of synergy and efficiency, in political terms, however, it bears a very strong power element, which in turn makes it a highly controversial and conflict-prone issue. In a way, establishing coherence is mostly about coordination, and effecting coordination within any administrative system involves the delicate question about who is coordinated and who indeed coordinates. Pointing at a state of procedural or politico-strategic *in*coherence hence often suggests the necessity of some coordinating or structuring hierarchy or institutional prioritization among the structural actors involved (Nuttall 2001). As for the case of EU external action, this coordinating right and responsibility has so far been shared between the two constituent institutional actors – a coordinating and mediating third party has not been provided. According to article 3 of the Treaty on European Union (TEU) (Nice) the Council and the Commission have not only both been entitled and responsible to ensure coherence of external action activities, they have also been bound to cooperate to this end. Article 3 further prescribed that the two institutions would have to ensure the implementation of these policies, 'each in accordance with its respective powers'. The Treaty of Lisbon, which entered into force on 1 December 2009, has brought slight changes to this arrangement by introducing the role of a High Representative (HR), who is also one of the Vice-Presidents of the European Commission. According to article 18 TEU (Lisbon) it is now the responsibility of the HR to ensure the consistency of the EU's external action. In a way, this new HR therefore has to assume a mediating role between the two sides while being representative to both. While it remains to be seen how this institutional set-up will work in practice, it appears clear at this point that coordination between the Commission and the Council will remain controversial. As the following analysis will show, the legal framework that so far was to regulate the conduct of EU external action in an effective and concerted way, provides substantial legal grey zones, which in practice have led to considerable coordination problems and conflicts.

First of all, it is important to acknowledge that the issue of coherence as raised in this specific context of conflict management has been a recurrent matter of dispute in European integration history. In fact, the quest for coherence is – as Gauttier (2004: 24) put it – 'consubstantial with the external action of the EC/EU'. The challenge of having to reconcile supranational structures with intergovernmental elements, or economic with political ones, has probably been in place as long as the desire to have Europe exist as an international entity, and thus, as a political actor on the global scene. Recent debates about coherence in EU crisis management can be seen as yet another episode in a long-standing inter-institutional conflict. The inherent dynamism and the proliferation of operational activities under the aegis of CSDP have added new momentum to old struggles between the EU's main institutional actors, the European Commission and the Council. So far, these struggles have mainly been about (a) conflicts of legal competence and (b) about functional grey zones persistent in the EU's external action profile.

Looking back, the idea of coherent institutional action has been an issue ever since 1965 when the Merger Treaty established a single Council and a single Commission for the European Communities, and thus 'a single set of institutions' to exercise the powers conferred to them by the treaties. Early episodes of the debate on coherence in external action occurred in the course of the 1980s, while the institutionalization of the then informal EPC began to take shape. When the EPC was eventually adopted in the Single European Act

(SEA) in 1987 as a first form of 'political Europe', the issue arose of how these early inter-governmental attempts of giving the internal market a foreign policy dimension could be reconciled with the then established supranational framework of the Community. Nuttall (2001: 2) has a point when stating that today's bifurcation of the EU's external profile originated in this very context, when 'at the insistence of France, the EPC and the Community were kept as far as possible in hermetically sealed compartments'.

The following Intergovernmental Conference (IGC) did not bring any major improvements. The establishment of CFSP in 1992 with the Treaty of Maastricht rather complicated the picture as the institutional background it provided for the political cooperation among the Member States reinforced the pre-established dualism between supranational integration and intergovernmental cooperation instead of removing it (Gauttier 2004), and thus perpetuated the dysfunctional division between the external economic and the foreign political agenda. The choice for a pillar structure and for the establishment of a 'Union' to back the Community politically, determined the course of institutional developments for the years to come. With both consecutive treaty revisions in 1997 and 2000 Member States equally failed to resolve at least part of the problem, and thus left the settlement of institutional fragmentation to practice. The Nice Treaty confirmed the dualist logic, so that the legal basis for the CSDP and its security political portfolio to be functionally integrated across the pillar divide remained weak.

So far, most of the difficulties arising from the existence of legal grey zones in the treaties, i.e. of areas where the competences of the Commission and the Council are not outlined clearly enough to allow the allocation of definitive responsibilities for all instances of external action, have had their root cause in one essential ambiguity, namely the unclear functional ratio or hierarchy between the Community and the Union's legal framework. The legal provisions offered up to the Treaty of Nice left open whether the external aspects of the Community were hierarchically superior to those of Title V TEU, addressing CFSP, and framing CSDP, or how the two domains functionally related to each other. Article 1 TEU (Nice) indicated that the Union was to be '*founded on* the European Communities, *supplemented* by the policies and forms of cooperation established by this Treaty'. This regulation clearly conveyed that the Community framework including the external action elements of the respective policies is superordinate to the intergovernmental dimension of external action as contained in the Union's CFSP. Title V TEU (Nice), in the way it defines the scope of CFSP, however, is said to include and cover *all areas* of foreign and security policy, while in that the role of the Commission remains limited.

As a result of this legal ambiguity, there have been many cases in political practice where factual responsibilities were not clearly defined by the respective legal frameworks, but where also the treaties did not provide any regulations about which entity was to take the lead in certain foreign and even security political matters. As admitted by the treaties, CFSP instruments were often used in a pervasive way: common positions included objectives for political action that infringed on Community competences, like the consolidation of democracies (through development cooperation), or the promotion of human rights. On a couple of instances (see Gauttier 2004 for examples), CFSP measures have challenged the Commission's formerly exclusive competence to act by including operational provisions relating to any of its ongoing Community-financed programmes in a certain country, most importantly in the areas of election monitoring, social and economic reconstruction, the handling of dual-use goods, defence industrial aspects, preventive policies, and external representation.

Further legal grey zones between the Community realm and the CFSP were provided by the legal framework regulating the CSDP. The Treaty of Nice delineated CSDP as including humanitarian and rescue tasks as well as peacekeeping tasks (art. 17 (2) TEU Nice).

These aspects of civilian crisis management were seen by many as pertaining to the Commission's competencies in the fields of political stabilisation, capacity building and technical assistance, mostly in the framework of development cooperation and humanitarian assistance. As the following section will show, the consecutive expansion of the CSDP's civilian agenda, which indeed was largely inspired by functional necessities in complex crisis settings, has aggravated this conflict about legal competences.

The Treaty of Lisbon has been said to enhance horizontal coherence by formally abolishing the pillar structure and by replacing the previous distinction between the political 'Union' and the economic 'Community' with the notion of one 'European Union'. In factual terms, however, the institutional divide between the supranational domain governed by the European Commission and the intergovernmental realm of CFSP has been perpetuated if not reinforced. While outlining the institutional competences of the European Commission, Article 17(1) (TEU Lisbon) states among other things that the Commission is responsible for the EU's external representation 'with the exception of the common foreign and security policy'. This regulation raises a series of critical questions concerning the practicability and functionality of such a distinction. Rather than solving the problem of lacking hierarchy, there seems to be an increased level of ambiguity in how the two realms are meant to interact with each other. By keeping the two strictly separate the Treaty of Lisbon again offers no legal solution for the problem of coherence and coordination between supranational and intergovernmentally governed foreign policies. Title V of the Treaty of Lisbon starts out with 'general provisions' on the EU's external action, which in fact includes both domains and their common objectives. These general provisions, however, are followed by 'specific provisions for the CFSP', which explicitly exclude areas governed by the European Commission but at the same time reiterate the phrase already contained in the Treaty of Nice that the CFSP 'shall cover *all* areas of foreign policy' (art. 24(1); emphasis added). The functional ratio between the two realms remains thus unclear to this day.

Functional overlaps – conflicts in the making

While the legal grey zones outlined above constitute an enormous challenge for inter-institutional coordination as such, these only add up to a set of further inter-institutional unclarities of another source and kind, that is, functional overlaps or areas of alleged duplication between the supranational and the intergovernmental framework of external action. Since the end of the Cold War, 'European' external action has tried to move – albeit at times with considerable delay – in accordance with the newest developments in the international political landscape. While during the Cold War, the (then) EC had kept a relatively low profile in external action matters, the 1990s were characterized by a series of groundbreaking developments in the EU's external policies. Firstly, the EU-12's decision and commitment to install a CFSP as the second pillar of the EU essentially ended the era of non-binding political collaboration in the framework of EPC. The Franco-British agreement of St Malo (1998) on the build-up of autonomous security and defence political capacities then paved the way for the inception of a Common CSDP to frame the EU's operational activities in the area of crisis management, a new field of action, whose visibility and political sensitivity until then has had no parallels in the history of EC/EU external action. Another highly decisive move that changed much about the EU's nature as an international actor was the ambition to reunite the European continent in the course of the 2004 enlargements.

In institutional terms, the inception of CFSP and CSDP considerably strengthened the position of the Member States and the Council. The success of enlargement in turn helped the European Commission to retain a strong status within the institutional triangle, and it actually succeeded in maintaining this relative strength through the launch of the European Neighbourhood Policy (ENP) in 2003, and afterwards in the course of its implementation and advancement. While the geopolitical standing of the EU has certainly been enhanced through this expansion of its sphere of influence on and beyond the continent, the openly voiced ambition to provide operational capacities for civilian and military crisis management in turn increased the outside pressure on the EU to deliver on its own declared goals, and not least, its factual potential as a global player. Generally, in recent years and more than ever, the EU has exposed itself to the world, aspiring openly to perform credibly and effectively to the geopolitical and strategic extent set out in its respective policies. It had to be expected that the resulting pressure to perform also fuelled the internal debates about how to best govern the new functional tasks envisaged.

The ambition to perform comprehensively in international crisis management as such constitutes a functionally expansive task. Performing efficiently in most of today's crisis settings necessitates a holistic view on planning and implementation, i.e. an approach that considers all parts of the conflict cycle and all types of structural impact or operational intervention. With the profound changes in the global political landscape after the end of the Cold War, the dispersion and reallocation of decades-old global power structures, and the multiplication of the faces of threat and aggression, the spectrum of conventional security threats was extended through a range of new challenges. These challenges can no longer be met by way of conventional military means; traditional instruments for establishing peace in the wider sense rather have to be integrated into a broader security political approach.

Today, managing crises and conflicts in a sustainable way demands inclusive solutions, i.e. solutions that cut across all policy fields, which could in some way be deemed relevant for any security political concern or consideration about modelling 'the outside world' towards the better. These new security political demands, which have first challenged the EU's capabilities as a collective actor in the context of the Balkan wars, have been formative for much of the path the CSDP has followed since its inception. While in the first years, the ambition to build up operational assets for crisis management, as agreed on at the European Councils of Cologne and Helsinki in 1999, has largely been a militarily driven project, the CSDP agenda was gradually expanded into the civilian and preventive dimensions of crisis management and conflict resolution in the consecutive years. Although civilian capability development kept lagging behind for a couple of years in terms of public attention and political importance given to it, non-military measures gradually started to take the functional lead within the wider crisis management agenda of CSDP – to the extent that today, eight out of 11 operations currently underway are civilian in nature, and another two have a strong civilian component.

This growing 'civilianization' of CSDP has increased the defensive reflex, which in essence the Commission has shown since the very early years of CSDP development. It could be noted that the mere conviction behind CSDP as such, i.e. the political commitment to turn the EU into an international crisis management actor proper, has had a massive if not doctrinal impact on policy developments in the community areas of external action. Improving the EU's ability to perform visibly, effectively and credibly in the event of a crisis or conflict has become an overarching goal that today dominates or at least appears markedly in most external policy debates within the Community domain, that is about regional cooperation, external trade, humanitarian assistance and development cooperation. Security political considerations and references to the security relevance of certain policy actions are increasingly infiltrating policy areas of the Community, which in past decades used to be distinctly detached from the realm of 'high politics'. This 'securitization' effect could be ascribed to two factors. The first is the general coming into fashion and establishment of comprehensive approaches to security, and the growing consciousness about the functional expansiveness of crisis management as a task. As an argument this would turn the gradual shift of various Community policies towards a broader security-oriented external action agenda more into a conceptually grounded move and a way to acknowledge the functional necessity to provide structural instruments to frame the operational assets becoming available in the framework of CSDP. The second factor is a certain air of competitiveness, provoked by the progressive functional expansion of CSDP, mostly into areas of civilian deployment, where the Community already has some – albeit somewhat limited – competence. In practice, these so-called functional overlaps have mostly been identified and bemoaned in respect to early warning and prevention, situation assessment, fact-finding and monitoring, disaster relief, civil protection, border control and security institutions building.

While neither of the two arguments can be taken as an exclusive explanation, there is supporting evidence for both. Unsurprisingly, the first point appears most legitimate when considering the official argumentation of the European Commission about the increasing relevance of crisis management as a cross-cutting challenge and objective of any external action the EU takes in the world. Most recently, this sort of positive 'securitization' has become evident in the Commission's dealing with the African continent. After decades of viewing Africa solely in the framework of distinctively apolitical action, in the context of the discussions about the joint EU Africa Strategy, which has been launched in 2008, the European Commission has openly adopted a security and crisis management oriented approach to a set of questions that in the past would have traditionally been dealt with within the detached Community framework. Finding evidence, on the other hand, for a fundamentally defensive position of the Commission on many occasions of policy advancement in CSDP is not too challenging an analytical task either. It would go beyond the scope of this chapter to present a full documentation of the Commission's argumentative and rhetoric defensiveness. However, the following general traits in inter-institutional dialogue (or indeed non-dialogue) between the Council and the Commission should offer some insight on the issue. As a matter of fact, a set of decisive and immensely security-relevant innovations within the Community realm of external action have occurred without any profound referencing to parallel policy developments in the Council's domain of CSDP and CFSP, let alone involving any proper or open coordination on new strategic objectives and fields of action. Moreover, the argumentation in Commission documents often assumes a clearly defensive tone. The way policy contents are presented is oftentimes repetitive, and in respect to related CSDP documents, the operational road map for implementation of a policy is largely reactive and virtually counterbalancing. A strong example that covers both arguments is the development and advancement of the Commission's stance on conflict prevention policy, which gained new momentum in 2000, after the CSDP had been installed as a new framework for security political action, and the respective institutional changes within the Council were ongoing and new working structures were proliferating. The defensive position of the Commission must be viewed against the fact that ever since the inception of the CSDP, the division of functional roles in EU external action has been shifted to the disadvantage of the Community's competences.

A legal way out?

Experts are fairly divided about the long-term consequences the Treaty of Lisbon might have for enhancing coherence in EU external action. The limited scope of this chapter will not allow for an in-depth discussion of the probable long-term effects the Reform Treaty will have for the governance of EU external policies including crisis management. However, what appears important to underline in this very context is that the alleged depillarization this treaty reform is said to entail in fact does not hold true for the core provisions concerning EU crisis management. As regards decision-making, and thus, the allocation of hard competences, the existing second pillar will clearly retain its distinct intergovernmental character. Anyway, what could indeed be said to hold potential for sidelining this continuation of old divides in the long run, is the new post of a HR for Foreign Affairs and Security Policy that will integrate the functions of the present EU Commissioner for External Relations and the High Representative for the CFSP. Much has been said about the intricacy of double hatting and will not be repeated here (e.g. Avery 2007). By acting as both Vice-President of the Commission and Chairman of the Foreign Affairs Council, the person in office will certainly become a key figure in external action. Whether the expected benefit of merging these two offices across the old pillar line will indeed translate into factual improvements may be put into question but nevertheless cannot be predicted at this point. As a matter of fact, however, this institutional novelty cannot in itself be presumed to constitute the critical breakthrough that will eventually revolutionize the Union's external action (Wallace 2007). From the point of view of inter-institutional coherence, the new post is indeed more likely to reinvigorate the inter-pillar divide and to fuel the mutual sensation of overlap instead of removing it in the first place. Since the appointment of Catherine Ashton, this has proven to be the case particularly in the context of the build-up of the European External Action Service. Instead of bringing the two realms closer together, there have reportedly been severe internal power struggles concerning the appointment of key positions, and the division of labour and competences between the diplomatic services of the Member States and the Commission delegations.

In the long run, the imposed fusion and amalgamation of pillars that the new double-hatted (non-)foreign minister and the joint diplomatic service actually stand for might have a positive impact on the functional cohesiveness of EU external action. However, the Treaty of Lisbon does not provide the necessary substance to back this sort of integrative leap in legally binding terms (Hofmann and Wessels 2008). Hence again, policy practice in European security and defence is called upon to develop pragmatic solutions that answer the inherent need to compensate for what is not accounted for in the treaties and, thus, to reduce the elements of structural fragmentation that appear most impeding at the moment. It appears legitimate if not indeed necessary to turn to more informal channels of innovation as long as no fundamental reassessment of the Union's division of power is in sight.

Conclusions and outlook

Since the end of the Cold War, the EC/EU has considerably extended the focus of its external policies. The build-up of an operable set of civilian and military capabilities within the framework of CSDP markedly widened the spectrum of instruments the EU now has at its disposal. Regardless of all criticism about the alleged flaws and deficiencies still statable in the EU's foreign and security political conduct, taking this road towards more capable and versatile actorness has certainly increased the overall respectability of the EU as a global player, and not least as an actor in international crisis and conflict management. Quite swiftly in fact, the Union has turned from a mere 'structural factor' to an active – and increasingly proactive – player on the international scene. The recent dynamism – or activism as some might call it – in the area of security and defence has not only changed the EU's profile as a global actor towards the outside; since it has led to the establishment of the CSDP as a new core component of EU external action, it has also had decisive impact on the Union's internal balance of power, i.e. its overall institutional set-up and the question of competence-sharing between its institutions. Following the inception of CSDP as a means to back up the Union with operational assets, the intricate question has emerged of how these new elements could be reconciled with the structural instruments the Community already had at its disposal.

The origins of this contentious issue date back to the early years of the European integration process, when in the 1950s and 1960s it turned out that cooperation in political matters would take a distinct path. Apart from the fact that the creation of the CSDP has perpetuated the 'old divide' between the intergovernmental and the supranational strand in European integration, its subsequent substantiation has also fuelled a long-standing internal conflict between the main institutional players, the European Commission and the Council of the European Union. It has been clear from the beginning to all actors involved in the process that the value added of the CSDP could not be tapped without instantaneously reconciling it with the broader institutional framework of the Union and the Community respectively. Accordingly, recent efforts to enhance the capacity of the EU to deliver on its potential and, thus, to translate its comprehensive profile into effective and credible action, focused primarily on the improvement of institutional coherence.

Beyond all criticism, looking at the current state and recent activities in the field, it must be acknowledged that the EU is performing increasingly well in dealing with its internal division. Many important steps have been taken to enhance coherence on the strategic and – even more so – on the technical and practical level. After fundamental inconsistencies in the very first years of CSDP operationality, day-to-day planning and implementation are now effectively and, by and large, uncontestedly managed by the Council Secretariat. The *ad hoc* working relations between the Council working bodies and with the Community actors have been gradually substantiated through the establishment of a general modus operandi. As a result, the Council–Commission divide is increasingly absorbed by constructive pragmatism, and much of the initial mistrust between the Council and the Commission bureaucracies appears to be incrementally replaced by more goal-oriented coordination. In core CSDP matters, in fact, the Commission is arguably acting like an integrated team member that seems to have accepted its associated role.

As a matter of fact, even with the Reform Treaty, the EU is not yet given the legal preconditions for neat coherence and unity in external action. However, following the necessity of having to grow on demand and without much first-hand experience to build upon, the administrative bodies managing the conduct of EU crisis management have learned quite well to deliver on an *ad hoc* basis. In fact, the external action domain of the Union has proven to be particularly prone to succeed in advancing without effective legal basis. Hence, if perpetuated and pursued systematically, this pragmatic 'ad hocism' and continuous trial-and-error exercise is likely to lead gradually to enhanced effective action, which should do until the next treaty reform will again formalise (at least) part of what will already have become institutional reality.

3 Transforming CSDP for global conflict management

Alistair J. K. Shepherd

Introduction

The Common Security and Defence Policy (CSDP) is fundamental to the European Union's (EU) ambitions in the field of global conflict management. Yet ensuring that CSDP has the coherence and capabilities required and that it is integrated into wider EU conflict management policy remains a largely unrealised goal. A great deal of analysis has been focused on examining coherence across the EU, specifically between the Common Foreign and Security Policy (CFSP) and CSDP in what was Pillar II and the EU's other policy tools in what were formally Pillars I and III. However, less focus has been directed at analysing coherence *within* CFSP and, more specifically, *within* CSDP.

Therefore, this chapter focuses on coherence within CSDP and its implications for the EU's role as a global conflict manager. As the number and variety of EU conflict management operations continues to expand it becomes ever more imperative that *ad hoc* solutions to capability shortfalls and problems of incoherence are replaced by a more systematic approach. If the EU is to live up to its rhetoric of being a 'comprehensive' crisis manager CSDP will be crucial. Hence, the chapter aims to provide a critical analysis of the nature of CSDP. In particular it analyses: (1) the transformation of CSDP from a largely military-driven project to one with a much greater civilian and civil–military focus; and (2) the capability, policy and institutional gaps *within* CSDP that continue to hinder the policy's effectiveness and potential.[1] These gaps undermine the EU's capabilities to act (personnel and hardware and institutions and instruments), to fund conflict management initiatives, whether short- or long-term, and to coordinate its member states, its own institutions and relations with third parties. Understanding CSDP's transformation and overcoming these gaps is crucial to improving the coherence and credibility of the EU's global conflict management ambitions.

The EU has long aspired to a role in global conflict management. Initially, the focus was on conflict prevention through development policy. With the launch of CFSP the EU tried to supplement the largely economic instruments of the European Commission with political and diplomatic ones through the Council of the EU. These approaches drew on the traditions of the EU as a 'civilian power' to develop preventative measures aimed at addressing the root causes of conflict. Efforts to improve coherence in the EU approach increased markedly at the beginning of the twenty-first century, coinciding with the launch of CSDP. Simultaneously the EU became more involved in negotiations to end conflict and in post-conflict stabilisation and reconstruction. The focus on pre- and post-conflict initiatives positioned the EU at either end of the conflict spectrum, leaving it largely absent in the most difficult phase where the polarisation of views leads to violence. With the development of CSDP the EU has the potential to fill this gap and act across the conflict spectrum.

Following its failure to prevent, contain or end violent conflict in the former Yugoslavia the EU sought to complement its existing, largely economic, technical and political instruments for conflict prevention and post-conflict reconstruction with the development of military and, later, civilian crisis management capabilities. The EU (alongside the United Nations) succeeded in negotiating ceasefires and agreements during the Yugoslav wars, but it was undermined by its inability to ensure these were adhered to. This was the key catalyst in the emergence of CSDP. As Elmar Brok, then Chair of the European Parliament's Foreign Affairs Committee, stressed in relation to Kosovo, 'it became clear to the Europeans that no diplomatic action could ever be successful if it could not be sustained, if necessary, by military action' (Brok 1999). Therefore, the initial focus of CSDP was to move the EU beyond its 'civilian power' image by ensuring it had at its disposal military capabilities for crisis management operations. However, as CSDP developed, ensuring that the EU also had the required civilian capabilities for crisis management became just as important. This combination of civilian and military capabilities has meant that CSDP, while being just one element of the CFSP, which is itself just one component of the EU's overall approach to conflict management, has quickly become fundamental to the EU's approach to conflict management. The civil–military potential of CSDP, coupled with other instruments from CFSP and across the EU, has enabled the EU to position itself, at least rhetorically, as a 'unique' and 'comprehensive' crisis manager. The EU claims that this 'distinctive civil-military approach to crisis management was ahead of its time' and that the 'comprehensive approach underpinning CSDP is its added value' (Solana 2009a). These claims suggest that the EU has come a long way from the failure to prevent, contain or end the wars in Yugoslavia and the very public blow those events had on the EU's credibility as a conflict manager. Yet when examining the policies, institutions and capabilities which make up CSDP's crisis management portfolio the degree of comprehensiveness in its civil–military approach is debatable.

Utilising Ramsbotham *et al.*'s (2005: 12) spectrum of conflict resolution responses, the Hourglass Model, this chapter analyses CSDP's potential as an additional tool for EU conflict management. CSDP aimed to enable the EU to undertake more robust peacekeeping operations, which would fill the gap between conflict prevention and post-conflict reconstruction – to enable the EU to use force where necessary to contain and end violent conflict. CSDP could, therefore, contribute 'in areas of heated conflict where violence has become routine and the prevention of violent conflict has failed' (Ramsbotham *et al.* 2005: 133). The military and civilian elements of CSDP need to be able to do this across three crucial phases: containing violence to prevent it escalating into war, containing violent conflict (geographically and in intensity) once it has broken out, and consolidating a ceasefire to enable post-conflict reconstruction.

However, CSDP has seen a gradual transformation away from the initial focus on military capabilities for containing and ending violent conflict. The overtly military focus of CSDP in the early years of its development has given way to a greater civilian and civil–military emphasis. Since its launch CSDP's potential has broadened beyond the ability to resort to the use of force if necessary. Now its capability is aimed at not just containing and ending violent conflict but in missions either side of the outbreak of violent conflict, thereby contributing to the EU's potential in both conflict prevention and post-conflict reconstruction. If CSDP's promise, and more specifically its objectives, are realised it has the potential to become the fulcrum around which EU global conflict management is centred.

Conceptualising conflict management/resolution

Conceptualising conflict management and/or conflict resolution is a controversial and difficult task. Since the emergence of the study of conflict resolution in the wake of the Second World War the field has been united in its desire to search for ways of transforming potentially or actually violent conflict into peaceful processes of political and social change. Yet even at its outset the diversity of the field was evident in the different approaches of John Burton (subjectivist), Kenneth Boulding (objectivist) and Johan Galtung (structuralist) which mirrored the different disciplines within which each was working (Ramsbotham *et al.* 2005: 32–54). In subsequent decades the range of approaches and theories of conflict resolution has multiplied as the field has expanded beyond the state-centric origins to include components below and above the state level (civil society, regional and international levels), with the latest generation of conflict resolution drawing on critical theory, discourse, emancipation and cosmopolitanism (Ramsbotham *et al.* 2005: 33).

Given the diversity of the field, whether the word 'management' or 'resolution' is used and how 'conflict' is understood can have a significant impact on the conceptual approach and empirical focus of any study. In this chapter the focus will be on conflict management within the field of conflict resolution – the overarching term used to describe the entire area of study. Ramsbotham *et al.* (2005: 29) define conflict management as 'the settlement and containment of violent conflict'. More specifically still, the focus is on the utility of CSDP in the field of 'conflict containment' which 'includes peacekeeping and war limitation (geographical constraint, mitigation and alleviation of intensity, and termination at the earliest opportunity)' (Ramsbotham *et al.* 2005: 29). This focus on conflict containment must be embedded within the broader understanding of conflict resolution which covers the entire spectrum of phases of conflict from prevention to settlement/termination, resolution and, ultimately, transformation. These phases of conflict and of conflict resolution are succinctly encapsulated in the Hourglass Model set up by Ramsbotham *et al.* (2005: 12), described as representing: 'the narrowing of political space that characterises conflict escalation, and the widening of political space that characterises conflict de-escalation; as the space narrows and widens, so different conflict resolution responses become more or less appropriate or possible.'

Utilising this model the chapter attempts to map the potential and actual contribution of CSDP during the conflict containment phase, which includes preventative peacekeeping, war limitation and post-ceasefire peacekeeping. The various stages of conflict resolution and conflict and of strategic and tactical responses are neatly summarised in Table 3.1.

It is important to note that the phases are not demarcated as clearly as implied in the model and the approaches and capabilities may not always be deployed best sequentially but perhaps simultaneously, especially in the de-escalation phase (Ramsbotham *et al.* 2005: 12). This means that CSDP's contribution should run simultaneously with other EU instruments to ensure a coherent and comprehensive approach to the conflict management.

The EU's own definitions in the field of conflict resolution are provided by the European Commission (2008) and help further clarify the focus of this chapter:

- peacebuilding: 'actions undertaken over the medium and longer term to address root causes of violent conflicts in a targeted manner';
- conflict prevention: 'actions undertaken over the short term to reduce manifest tensions and/or to prevent the outbreak or recurrence of violent conflict';

Table 3.1 Conflict resolution techniques, complementarity and the hourglass model[2]

Stages of conflict resolution	Stage of conflict	Strategic response	Example of tactical response
Conflict transformation	Difference	Cultural peacebuilding	Problem-solving, support indigenous dispute resolution institutions, CR training, fact-finding missions, peace commissions
	Contradiction	Structural peacebuilding	Development assistance, civil society development, governance training and institution building, human rights training, track II mediation
Conflict settlement	Polarisation	Elite peacemaking	Special envoys and official mediation, negotiation, coercive diplomacy, preventative peacekeeping
	Violence	Peacekeeping	Interposition, crisis management, containment
Conflict containment	War	War limitation	Peace enforcement, peace support and stabilisation
	Ceasefire	Peacekeeping	Preventative peacekeeping, disarmament and security sector reform, confidence building measures, security in community through police training
Conflict settlement	Agreement	Elite peacemaking	Electoral and constitutional reform, power sharing and decentralisation of power, problem-solving
	Normalisation	Structural peacebuilding	Collective security and cooperation arrangements, economic resources cooperation and development, alternative defence
Conflict transformation	Reconciliation	Cultural peacebuilding	Commissions of enquiry, truth and justice commissions, peace media development, peace and conflict awareness education and training, cultural exchanges and initiatives, problem-solving as future imaging

- conflict management: 'actions undertaken with the main objective to prevent the vertical (intensification of violence) or horizontal (territorial spread) escalation of existing violent conflict';
- conflict resolution: 'actions undertaken over the short term to end violent conflict'.

There are clear differences between some of the Commission's definitions and those of Ramsbotham *et al.* However, the conceptualisations of conflict management are similar – limiting the vertical (intensity) and horizontal (geography) escalation of violence. It is in this specific area that CSDP has the potential to enhance EU conflict management capabilities; alongside the United Nations (UN) or autonomously. It is therefore to CSDP that this chapter now turns, analysing its conflict management rationale, the transformation of its military and civilian capabilities and its growing civil–military focus; a transformation that, if carried through, has the potential to make credible the EU's claim to be a unique and comprehensive global conflict manager.

Conflict management: the origin and rationale of CSDP

Several factors explain the emergence of CSDP in 1998–99 including: post-Cold War geo-political transformations; the downgrading of Europe's status in United States (US) foreign policy; the limited influence of the EU in security affairs; changes in United Kingdom (UK) foreign and security policy; French relations with the North Atlantic Treaty Organization (NATO); the completion of Economic and Monetary Union (EMU); bureaucratic pressures within the EU to expand policy competences; and European defence industry manoeuvring. However, CSDP has always been essentially about conflict management. In particular, two drivers emphasise CSDP's conflict management origins and rationale: the violent break-up of Yugoslavia and the emerging notion of an international community with a responsibility to protect.

First, the EU's experience in failing to prevent, contain or end violent conflict has been central to CSDP: 'our experience of the consequences of conflict has been instrumental in the development of civilian and military crisis management capabilities, and is a driving factor in the development of a more effective and responsive common foreign and security policy' (Council of the EU 2000a: 4). The brutal conflicts that tore apart Yugoslavia in the 1990s and the EU's ultimately failed attempts at conflict management during the 'hour of Europe' was perhaps the compelling factor in the emergence of CSDP. If the EU could not resolve conflicts in a region bordered on three sides by EU member states what credibility could it bring when contributing to global conflict management? Milosevic's actions in Kosovo were still reverberating when Elmar Brok argued that diplomatic action, if necessary, needed to be backed up by military action (Brok 1999). The EU's inability to enforce the agreements it brokered meant the warring parties quickly reverted to violence. It eventually took US leadership and military force to bring the conflicts in Bosnia and later Kosovo to an end. Hence, the missing link in the EU's conflict management capabilities was seen to be the credible threat or use of force in support of political and diplomatic efforts.

Second, following the end of the Cold War there was optimism that a genuine 'international community' could emerge, founded on the UN, which should act to ensure a much wider and deeper notion of security for states *and* peoples. This was coupled with an emerging sense of responsibility among many states, especially in Europe, to limit the effects of violent conflict between states and, importantly, within states. This responsibility included protecting and promoting human rights and humanitarianism, even if this meant overriding the primacy of state sovereignty. This shift can be detected in Boutros Ghali's 1992's *Agenda for Peace* which stated that 'the time of absolute and exclusive sovereignty . . . has passed'. Later in the decade, speaking during Operation Allied Force, Tony Blair (1999) spoke of a 'new doctrine of international community' which should be based on the belief that:

> the principle of non-interference must be qualified in important respects. Acts of genocide can never be a purely internal matter. When oppression produces massive flows of refugees which unsettle neighbouring countries then they can properly be described as 'threats to international peace and security'.

As Howorth (2007: 54–5) argues, this notion of transcending state sovereignty fitted easily with the EU's 'multilateral internationalism'. The EU was keen to 'write the new normative rules' of crisis management, 'especially the international legal, institutional, regulatory, interventionist and ethical'. Drawing on this more interventionist approach and seeing itself as an integral part of the international community, the EU needed to transform its conflict management capabilities in support of the new humanitarian objectives being espoused. After all, the EU's CFSP included the objectives: 'to preserve peace and strengthen international security' and 'to develop and consolidate democracy, and the rule of law, and respect for human rights and fundamental freedoms' (European Union 1992).

In December 1998, driven by the EU's failings in the Balkans, the shifting international political environment and the EU's desire to contribute to international security, France and the UK issued a Joint Declaration on European Defence, which proposed that the EU 'must have the capacity for autonomous action, backed by credible military forces, the means to decide to use them, and the readiness to do so, in order to respond to international crises'. The EU, quickly adopting the initiative in June 1999, immediately positioned CSDP as a conflict management tool, linking it explicitly to 'the full range of conflict prevention and crisis management tasks defined in . . . the Petersberg tasks' (European Council 1999a). These tasks, adopted by the EU in the 1999 Treaty of Amsterdam (ToA), include 'Humanitarian and rescue tasks; peacekeeping tasks and tasks of combat forces in crisis management, including peacemaking'. It is clear, therefore, that the central rationale for CSDP was to contribute to preventing, ending and resolving conflict. Six months later, at the Helsinki European Council, new decision and policy-making structures were approved alongside the Helsinki Headline Goal (HHG). The HHG declared that the 'member states must be able, by 2003, to deploy within 60 days and sustain for at least 1 year military forces up to 50,000–60,000 persons capable of the full range of Petersberg tasks' (European Council 1999b). This goal, modelled on NATO's operations in the Balkans (Interviews, September 2008), clearly illustrated that conflict management was the principal rationale for CSDP.

Conflict management and the transformation of CSDP

Since its launch in 1999 CSDP has undergone significant transformation but conflict management remains its *raison d'être*. The range of operations has widened, the military goals have shifted and civilian capabilities have taken on at least equal importance. In terms of the number of operations, civilian crisis management has become the dominant focus, format and function of CSDP. Moreover, the importance of combining the civilian and military capabilities of the EU into a coherent civil–military approach to conflict management has led to a transformation of the character of CSDP. Ensuring this transformation is more than just rhetoric is vital to the EU's ambitions as a comprehensive conflict manager.

Widening the conflict management remit of CSDP

Two key developments have reinforced CSDP's conflict management focus and hastened its transformation: the publication of the European Security Strategy (ESS) and the widening of the Petersberg Tasks. The 2003 ESS highlighted a number of 'key threats', two of which, regional conflict and state failure, are exacerbated by a number of 'global challenges', including: resource competition, global warming, poverty and disease. These challenges, it was argued, contribute significantly to 'political problems and violent conflict' with 'a number of countries and regions caught in a cycle of conflict, insecurity and poverty' (European Council 2003d: 2–3). The ESS adds that:

> none of the new threats is purely military; nor can any be tackled by purely military means . . . in failed states, military instruments may be needed to restore order . . . Regional conflicts need political solutions but military assets and effective policing may

be needed in the post conflict phases . . . the European Union is particularly well equipped to respond to such multifaceted situations.

(European Council 2003d: 7)

An integrated civil–military CSDP is, therefore, crucial to the EU commitment to 'reinforcing its cooperation with the UN to assist countries emerging from conflicts, and to enhancing its support for the UN in short-term crisis management situations' (European Council 2003d: 11). The ESS also devoted considerable space to 'Building Security in our Neighbourhood' highlighting the Balkans, Caucasus, Middle East and Mediterranean as key areas where resolving conflict is central to the EU's foreign policy. The 2008 Report on the Implementation of the ESS returns to this issue highlighting the EU's missions in Kosovo and Georgia and extending the geographical remit for 'building stability' beyond Europe's 'immediate neighbourhood' (European Council 2008a: 6–7). It is clear, therefore, that the EU's growing conflict management ambitions are driving the transformation of CSDP. The EU's ambitions are more explicitly laid out in the revised Petersberg Tasks.

In June 2004 the range of Petersberg Tasks was expanded, and was subsequently included in the 2007 Treaty of Lisbon (ToL), to include: '*joint disarmament operations, humanitarian and rescue tasks, military advice and assistance talks, conflict prevention and peacekeeping tasks, tasks of combat forces in crisis management, including peace-making and post conflict stabilisation*' (European Union 2007).[3] This widening of the Petersberg Tasks correlates closely with Rambotham *et al.*'s hourglass model of conflict resolution capabilities. The broadened remit illustrates that CSDP is being transformed to contribute beyond the conflict containment phase; to do so it will need the capabilities to match its ambitions.

Transforming military capabilities for conflict management

Despite numerous capability commitment conferences, starting in 2000 when over 100,000 troops, 400 aircraft and 100 ships were pledged, the HHG has not been met. Yet the well-documented personnel and equipment shortfalls did not stop CSDP becoming operational in 2003, at least on a limited scale, in Bosnia, Former Yugoslav Republic of Macedonia (FYROM) and the Democratic Republic of the Congo (DRC). The first two EU military missions, in FYROM and the DRC, were significant for the EU's development as a conflict manager and a symbolic shift away from its traditional civilian power image. They also helped shaped the subsequent transformation of the EU's military capability aspirations.

Lessons from the early operations, together with the ESS and elements of the original HHG, drove the transformation of military capability objectives. The HHG was focused on the target of 50-60,000 troops deployable in 60 days, but as part of this member states should 'provide smaller rapid response elements available and deployable at very high readiness' (European Council 1999b). This objective, largely neglected in the early years of CSDP, was revisited in February 2003 at the Franco-British Le Touquet summit. The summit's *Declaration on Strengthening European Cooperation in Security and Defence* (2003) called for improvements in 'European capabilities in planning and deploying forces at short notice, including initial deployment of land, sea and air forces within 5–10 days'. The need for the ability to deploy smaller force packages at shorter notice was highlighted later in 2003 by Operation *Artemis* and became a key element of HG2010.

While the scale, duration and achievements of *Artemis* have been criticised for merely shifting the geographical focus of the violence, *Artemis* fulfilled its mandate by containing the violence within Bunia and ensuring stability until the UN force arrived in September (Ulriksen *et al.* 2004; Faria 2004a). This operation clearly fits into the conflict management role envisaged for CSDP and demonstrated its ability, though still limited, to operate in 'the narrowing of political space that characterises conflict escalation' (Ramsbotham *et al.* 2005: 12). It demonstrated the EU's desire and willingness to contribute to the conflict containment phase as well as the conflict settlement and transformation that it traditionally focused on. It was also an example of the scale and type of CSDP operation that the Le Touquet Summit envisaged when it called for the EU to 'examine how it can contribute to conflict prevention and peacekeeping in Africa, including through autonomous operations, in close cooperation with the United Nations' (*Declaration on Strengthening European Cooperation in Security and Defence* 2003).

The Le Touquet summit and the lessons of *Artemis* shaped the 2004 British–French–German 'food for thought paper' on the Battlegroup concept (EU Institute for Security Studies 2005: 10–16), which was adopted by the EU in June as the military focus of HG 2010. The battlegroups, which became operational in 2007 but have not yet been deployed, are 1500-strong battalion-sized units, deployable within five to ten days and sustainable for 30 days; possibly extending that to 120 days (European Council 2004a). These national or multinational battlegroups are, according to the EU, the 'minimum militarily effective, credible, rapidly deployable, coherent force package capable of stand alone operations, or for the initial phase of larger operations' (EU Council Secretariat 2006a).[4] In any six-month period there are two battlegroups on standby at very high readiness for almost simultaneous deployment to undertake the full range of Petersberg Tasks (Lindstrom 2007). More specifically, the illustrative scenarios for the battlegroups are: separation of parties by force, conflict prevention, stabilisation, reconstruction and military advice to third countries, evacuation operations in non-permissive environments and assistance to humanitarian operations (EU Council Secretariat 2006b). Most of these scenarios correlate neatly with several phases of Ramsbotham *et al.*'s hourglass model.

The other components of the HG2010 included: the importance of the civil–military cell, a European Defence Agency (EDA) to coordinate capability improvements, improved strategic lift (air, land and sea), the availability of an aircraft carrier and its air wing and escort, improved communications and quantitative benchmarks for deployability and multinational training (European Council 2004a). The key elements of strategic lift and civil–military coordination were areas where the lessons of *Artemis* are apparent and will be crucial to CSDP's contribution to an effective EU conflict management approach.

The issue of military capabilities was given renewed prominence under the 2008 French Presidency of the EU, which aimed to 're-launch European defence'. The rationale was to ensure that the battlegroup concept did not become the sole focus of military capability ambitions. While an important development, with the potential to improve interoperability, battlegroups were supposed to be just one element of the EU's military capability. The French Presidency succeeded in raising the profile of capabilities, both military and civilian, resulting in the 2008 *Declaration on Strengthening Capabilities*. On the military side the declaration refocused on being able to deploy 60,000 troops in 60 days and outlined more precisely the types of operations envisaged under CSDP:

> planning and conducting simultaneously a series of operations and missions of varying scope: two major stabilisation and reconstruction operations, with a suitable civilian component, supported by up to 10,000 troops for at least two years; two rapid response operations of limited duration using inter alia EU battle groups; an emergency operation for

the evacuation of EU nationals (in less than ten days) . . .; a maritime or air surveillance/ interdiction mission; a civilian-military humanitarian assistance operation lasting up to 90 days; around a dozen ESDP civilian missions (inter alia police, rule-of-law, civilian administration, civil protection, security sector reform, and observer missions) of vary- ing formats, including rapid response situations, together with a major mission (possi- bly up to 3000 experts) which could last several years.

(Council of the EU 2008a)

In terms of specific capabilities a series of capability initiatives were launched in the areas of force projection, information gathering and space-based intelligence, force protection and effectiveness, and interoperability (Council of the EU 2008a). The declaration also raised, once again, the need to examine the pooling and specialisation of efforts and capabilities, and cost sharing.

The changing military focus of CSDP has, to date, been rather reactionary, often looking at past crises to shape future operations, and significant shortfalls continue to exist (Shepherd 2003; Giegerich 2008). Nevertheless, gradually as various different iterations of headline goals are proposed and amended, the core requirements have been crystallised. Through this crystallisation, EU military capability profile is slowly becoming better suited to the EU's global conflict management ambitions. However, as the ESS points out, the military instru- ment alone is not enough. Therefore, the EU has, with less public attention, also been devel- oping the civilian capabilities it believes CSDP requires to fulfil its conflict management role.

Conflict management and CSDP's civilian capabilities

Despite the military focus at CSDP's launch most operations have been civilian, including police, judicial and monitoring missions. Unsurprisingly therefore, civilian capabilities have become as important as military ones. The HHG was complemented by a less specific, less high-profile statement on 'non-military crisis management of the European Union' which called for an Action Plan for civilian crisis management based on an inventory highlighting EU capabilities in: civilian police; humanitarian assistance; administrative and legal reha- bilitation; search and rescue; and electoral and human rights monitoring (European Council 1999c). The action plan called for enhancing and facilitating EU contributions and activities within other organisations as well as autonomous actions, and ensuring inter-pillar coher- ence (European Council 1999c). The 2000 Feira European Council outlined four priority areas for civilian capabilities: police, rule-of-law, civilian administration and civilian protec- tion, and set a concrete target of 5,000 police officers, 1,000 deployable in 30 days, by 2003 for conflict prevention and crisis management (European Council 2000a). Further targets followed in June 2001: 200 rule-of-law experts to support the police, a pool of civilian administration experts, and civilian protection intervention teams of up to 2,000 personnel available at short notice (European Council 2001a). The June 2004 European Council argued for a civilian headline goal, a capability commitment conference and a broadening of the expertise available for potential CSDP missions (including experts on human rights, politi- cal affairs, security sector reform (SSR), mediation, border control, disarmament, demobili- sation and reintegration (DDR) and media policy). The quantitative side of the civilian equation was met at the November 2004 commitment conference with 5,761 police, 631 rule-of-law experts, 562 administration experts, and 4,988 civil protection personnel pledged (Council of the EU 2004a). These capabilities, at least on paper, increased CSDP's potential contribution to the conflict settlement and containment phases. However, as with military commitments, there have been problems with availability and interoperability, with different national procedures for releasing personnel and differing levels of training and experience.

Consequently, the numerical commitments were complemented by the more qualitative focus of the Civilian Headline Goal (CHG) 2008. The CHG 2008, agreed in December 2004, restated unequivocally CSDP's conflict management rationale describing the civilian dimension as 'part of the EU's overall approach in using civilian and military means to respond coherently to the whole spectrum of crisis management tasks such as conflict prevention, peacekeeping and tasks of combat forces in crisis management, including peacemaking and post-conflict stabilisation' (Council of the EU 2004b) Drawing on lessons from the EU Police Mission in Bosnia (EUPM) and Operation *Proxima* in FYROM, the CHG 2008 also reiterated the need for capabilities in the areas of SSR and DDR. The civilian missions envisaged by the CHG 2008 included strengthening local institutions through advice, training and monitoring and/or performing executive functions (substitution missions) (Council of the EU 2004b). The CHG 2008 also outlined the time frame for deploying missions: decisions to launch civilian missions were to be taken within five days of the approval of the Crisis Management Concept (CMC) by the Council and capabilities were to be deployed within 30 days of the decision to launch a mission. This focus on rapid deployment led to the development of Civilian Response Teams (CRTs) which consisted of integrated packages of experts to: make fact-finding assessments in crises or imminent crises; provide a rapid initial operational presence; and reinforce existing EU mechanisms for crisis management (Council of the EU 2005a). Finally, the CHG 2008 highlighted the growing civil–military focus of CSDP, emphasising the need to be able to 'deploy civilian means simultaneously with military means at the outset of an operation' and that 'close cooperation and coordination with the military efforts have to be ensured throughout all phases of the operation. When necessary, civilian crisis management missions must be able to draw on military enabling capabilities' (Council of the EU 2005a).

The need for coherence, the further development of civilian capabilities and, in particular, greater synergies between civilian and military crisis management was the focus of the new CHG 2010 which built on the CHG 2008. The key goals of the CHG 2010 are to ensure that: sufficient qualified personnel are available for civilian crisis management; capabilities, planning, equipment, training, procedures and concepts are strengthened; the EU can draw on all its means, including civilian and military CSDP, coherently; the political visibility of civilian capabilities is enhanced; and coordination and cooperation with external actors is improved (Council of the EU 2007a). The growing civil–military potential of CSDP is highlighted later in the document, stressing the need for synergies to be 'identified and fully exploited between civilian and military ESDP . . . with a view to maximizing coherence in the field as well as in Brussels', and the need for 'a common stocktaking event on civilian and military ESDP capabilities' (Council of the EU 2007a). These objectives were reiterated in the 2008 *Declaration on Strengthening Capabilities*.

A tool that could assist in the civil–military interface has been the establishment of the European Gendarmerie Force (EGF), which is at the disposal of the EU and should help fill the gap between military and civilian personnel in the field. The *Treaty Establishing the European Gendarmerie Force* (2007) authorises a 3,000-strong EGF with 800 personnel deployable within 30 days for substituting or supplementing local police in crisis management operations. The use of Gendarmerie forces may facilitate a smoother transition from the military to civilian phase of an operation and limit the problem of combat soldiers undertaking civilian police missions (Hills 2001; Lutterbeck 2004) in conflict management.

While these capability and institutional developments were evolving several civilian CSDP missions were under way in Europe, Africa, the Middle East and Indonesia. This rapid rise in the number, scope and geographical variety of missions demonstrates the growing importance of the civilian elements of CSDP and, therefore, the importance of making a reality out of the civil–military potential of the EU in global conflict management. CSDP was launched due to the EU's inability to back up its political, diplomatic and economic weight with the credible threat of force when conflicts became violent. Yet, it was quickly realised that civilian capabilities were equally as important and in several respects just as deficient. While it has not been as easy as first thought to put together the civilian capabilities (Jakobsen 2006; Korski and Gowan 2009) there has, arguably, been more progress on these than on military capabilities, and it is clear that civilian operations are currently the predominant conflict management role for the EU. Nevertheless, there is still a great deal of progress required to overcome the remaining gaps within CSDP and in the EU's overall approach to conflict management.

Bridging the gaps in CSDP: a comprehensive approach to EU conflict management?

Despite the progress outlined above it is well known that there are still significant gaps to be filled in the EU's capabilities to act, as well as to fund and coordinate its own and its member states' conflict management operations. As outlined earlier, there are two broad areas that need to be addressed: (a) the continuing gaps *within* CSDP; and (b) the gaps that continue to exist *between* CSDP and the EU's other key tools for global conflict management (such as aid, development and civil protection). This chapter focuses on the gaps *within* CSDP. These gaps occur in two key areas: those *within* the specific military and civilian components of CSDP; and those *between* the military and civilian elements. Furthermore these gaps can be broken down in terms of capabilities, institutions and policies (specifically concepts, doctrines and procedures).

Identifying and rectifying CSDP's military gaps

The list of military shortfalls in CSDP is well known, yet few have been overcome. The 2006 *Capability Improvement Chart* (the last publicly available) showed that since 2001 just eight shortfalls had been solved, four improved and 52 remained unchanged (Council of the EU 2006a). A Report on EU capabilities highlighted three broad areas which have consistently been the most debilitating military shortfalls: deployability, standardisation and interoperability, and strategic intelligence (International Crisis Group 2005c). The report focuses on air and sealift and aerial refuelling as the crucial deployability gaps. The EU's long-term airlift solution is the A400M military transport aircraft. However, the project has been mired in delays, technical problems and cost overruns with several countries, and even Airbus, contemplating scaling down, pulling out of, or scrapping the programme (Lemer 2009; Wilson 2009; Evans-Pritchard 2009). While the project was reconfirmed in 2010, the delays have led to the delivery date for the first aircraft slipping from 2007 to late 2012 at the earliest, with multiple clients not taking deliveries until the second half of the decade. The temporary (NATO-led) solution is the 2006 Strategic Airlift Interim Solution (SALIS), in which 15 EU and NATO states have a renewable contract to charter Russian and Ukrainian Antonov AN124-100 transport aircraft; two on a permanent basis, two more on six days' notice and a further two at nine days' notice (NATO 2006a). This should help overcome some of the airlift problems encountered during Operation *Artemis* when third state aircraft were chartered for parts of the deployment. In the area of aerial refuelling the EDA has launched an initiative to monitor requirements and look at future possibilities. However, with the number of EU operations continuing to grow and their range extending, the upgrading of the relatively small and aging capability across the EU is growing in urgency. Sealift is also a crucial deployability capability that is still lacking, despite the UK's procurement of roll-on, roll-off ferries and other chartering arrangements. The EU needs to develop longer term solutions for these deployability capabilities and ensure some coordination in procurement. However, the EU's experience in developing the A400M does not bode well for future capability improvements.

With the move to largely multinational battlegroups interoperability and availability of personnel become of even greater importance. Ensuring interoperability is a difficult task and it is one where the EDA has a crucial coordinating role to play across all equipment areas from weapons to communications. On the issue of availability of military personnel the EU states are also performing poorly. While the number of troops deployed has increased they are only a small fraction of overall armed forces, with only 30 percent of European military personnel able to operate outside their national territory (Whitney 2008: 22). It is now imperative that national armed forces are structured, trained and authorised for rapid deployment on overseas conflict management operations. Finally, strategic intelligence is a key requirement for peace-enforcement operations (International Crisis Group 2005c). There is a need for virtual real-time human and technical intelligence, yet the politics and sensitivity of the intelligence means an EU capability is likely to be difficult to develop. The Galileo system and the Global Monitoring of Environment and Security (GMES) initiatives may prove useful but more important is the sharing of intelligence between member states and this is currently limited. Even more limited is the nature of the intelligence that member states are willing to give to EU bodies such as the Joint Situation Centre (SitCen); which is supposed to be the hub of intelligence collection in the EU (Interviews 2007). With defence budgets squeezed and resources likely to diminish further across the EU, the most cost-efficient and coordinated approach to solving many of these military capability gaps is pooling and/or specialisation. While this is politically sensitive for the larger and more capable EU states, economic and military necessity has led to renewed Anglo-French efforts to share and pool key resources linked to aircraft carriers, nuclear weapons technology, submarines, aerial refuelling, and logistics and training, as well as developing a non-standing Combined Joint Expeditionary Force (British Prime Minister's Office 2010). This sort of collaboration is also a necessity in the area of civilian capabilities.

Identifying and rectifying CSDP's civilian gaps

Overcoming the civilian capability gaps has seen a little more progress than on the military side but gaps persist. The final report on the CHG 2008 highlighted that the process had 'revealed considerable potential shortfalls in certain police and rule of law categories; in particular judges and prosecutors, prison personnel, junior and middle ranking police officers, and junior level border police' (Council of the EU 2007b). A European Parliament Report concurred, noting 'continued shortfalls in the areas of police, rule of law and civilian administration' and, worryingly, added the 'lack of use of the valuable Civilian Response Team instrument' (European Parliament Committee on Foreign Affairs 2008). While the CRT instrument was used in 2008, in Georgia and the Palestinian Territories (Council of the

EU 2008b), more recent reports have continued to provide disappointing assessments of the EU's civilian capabilities. A 2009 report argues that the 'supposed civilian power' of the EU is 'largely illusionary' and that 'the EU struggles to find civilians to staff its ESDP missions, and the results of its interventions are often paltry' (Korski and Gowan 2009: 11). The report identifies and analyses three key reasons for the failings: 'the weakness of the concepts governing ESDP interventions, the absence of civilian capacity in almost all 27 EU member states, and institutional wrangles in Brussels' (Korski and Gowan 2009: 24).

These reports highlight the continuing problem of getting the required number and type of personnel and the more strategic problem of the training, coordination and integration of those personnel, many of whom may never have envisaged deploying overseas for conflict management operations. These problems were illustrated in the fluctuating availability of the personnel pledged in 2004/5 with five states raising the number of personnel available but three decreasing their commitment, while nine states' commitments remained stable (Council of the EU 2007b). The CHG 2008 was meant to address these availability issues, but despite the pledges made and the targets being met on paper (as with the military headline goals) the CHG process has not led to an improvement in the availability of deployable civilian personnel and capabilities. EULEX, the EU's high-profile civilian mission in Kosovo, has struggled to reach full strength and is operating with 250 fewer international personnel than its authorised maximum of 1,950 (EU Council Secretariat 2010a), while the EU's police mission (EUPOL) in Afghanistan is 99 international personnel short of its 400 target three years after its launch (EU Council Secretariat 2010b). This uncertainty is highly problematic for conflict management where rapid availability of the appropriate personnel and capabilities is crucial across all phases of activity (from preventative through containment to resolution).

Problems beyond the availability of personnel have also been apparent in EU's operations in the Balkans. The International Crisis Group (2005c) highlighted the weakness and inappropriateness of the European Union Police Mission (EUPM)'s mandate and the low levels of experience among some experts. Juncos (2007) finds further problems, including: the fragmentation of the EU's presence on the ground, the complexity of EU decision-making and the lack of resources. Ioannides (2007) blames the complexity of the EU's pillar structure for coherence problems during operation *Proxima*. Examining the same operation Merlingen and Ostrauskaite (2005) questioned the usefulness of co-location at management, rather than operational, levels of policing. A final problem emanating from the Balkan operations, identified by Emerson and Gross (2007) is the lack of institutional learning within the EU. The underlying critique across the commentaries was the lack of integration and coordination across the various components of conflict management. Separating rule of law from police from civil administration may be useful for databases but not when in the field. This is partly where the push for CRTs came from but, apart from the two missions in 2008, these CRTs have often been ignored, with individuals used on an *ad hoc* basis instead.

Identifying and rectifying CSDP's civil–military gaps

In addition to gaps *within* the military and civilian components of CSDP there are significant gaps *between* the military and civilian components, further undermining the EU's conflict management strategy. When analysing the civil–military potential of the EU there are two distinct elements: Civil–Military Cooperation (CIMIC) in the field and Civil–Military Coordination (CMCO) at the political level (Kohl 2006). According to the EU, CIMIC focuses on 'co-operation and coordination, as appropriate between EU military forces and the independent external civil organisations and actors (international organisations, NGOs, local authorities and populations); while CMCO 'covers internal EU co-ordination of the EU's own civil and military crisis management instruments' (Council of the EU 2009d). This chapter focuses on CMCO and here the EU's experience is mixed at best. Positively, when a plan has to be devised and an operation deployed very quickly, drawing on the capabilities of both civilian and military assets, the EU has demonstrated it can succeed, such as in Aceh. However, without the pressure of having to find a solution within a short space of time relations can be strained, even suspicious, and coordination and cooperation are often weak (Interviews 2007). This severely undermines the integrated, comprehensive approach to crisis management that the EU promotes.

At the heart of the EU's approach to CMCO is the need to develop a 'culture of coordination' (Council of the EU 2003e). One of its key objectives is to ensure synergy between civilian and military capabilities in crisis management and post-conflict reconstruction and is, therefore, vital to the EU's comprehensive approach. CMCO within the EU refers to both inter-pillar and intra-pillar coordination. Within CFSP the Political and Security Committee (PSC) has political control of CSDP operations and coordination. However, below this level the civil and military components of CSDP are, to a large extent, separated both conceptually and physically. At the heart of efforts to improve coordination between the civilian and military components of CSDP is the Civilian–Military Cell (CivMil Cell). The CivMil Cell emerged largely as a compromise in negotiations on a CSDP operational headquarters, but also partly from EU missions in the Balkans revealing the need for a far more integrated civil–military approach. As the CivMil Cell was an alternative to an operational headquarters it was compromised in its civil–military balance. Despite having roughly equal numbers of civilian and military staff it is seen to have a military bias, illustrated by its location within the EU Military Staff (EUMS) (Gordon 2006). The CivMil Cell's potential to improve CMCO has, therefore, been compromised, particularly as there is still little sign of a genuine culture of coordination emerging. The military believe civilian planning is overly optimistic about the environments into which the EU deploys and the civilian elements are wary of militarising EU policy (Interview 2007). The CMCO culture is clearly not yet engrained.

The CivMil Cell also encompasses the ability to establish an Operations Centre at very short notice to run civil–military missions. This became ready for activation in January 2007 but has yet to be tested beyond exercises. The Operations Centre also illustrates a military bias in its organisation, consisting of mostly military divisions and with its civilian component still being under the control of the Council's DG E IX (civilian crisis management directorate). The mere co-location of civilian and military personnel does not provide for integrated operational planning (Norheim-Martinsen 2009: 17). The final addition to the CivMil Cell was the Watch-Keeping Capability (WKC), which became operational in mid-2008 and was also supposed to be available to both military and civilian operational planning, giving them a similar basis for mission planning. The central problem for the CivMil Cell is that there is no comprehensive crisis management concept that incorporates both civilian and political–military elements (Norheim-Martinsen 2009: 17).

Instead of ensuring the CivMil Cell developed into a truly integrated operational planning facility for military, civil–military and civilian operations, the EU decided to set up the Civilian Planning and Conduct Capability (CPCC) as a civilian operational headquarters in all but name.[5] The CPCC, reporting to the PSC, was the civilian equivalent of the EUMS and clearly enhanced the EU's civilian crisis management capabilities, yet it also entrenched the quite distinct and parallel planning structures and chains of command. While the military and civilian pillars within CSDP are linked at the level of the PSC and the CivMil Cell, the problems in setting up a truly integrated mission persisted. According to one official a better solution would be to merge the CPCC with the Operations Centre (which should be a standing military HQ) but politically this is not feasible given the position of states such as Sweden, Germany and the UK (Interviews 2007).

A central problem raised by policy-makers and commentators has been the lack of a 'unity of command' (Interviews 2007), exacerbated by overlapping competences and poor communication. On the military side of conflict management the unity of command is relatively straightforward with the Council having overall political control and the PSC effectively taking the lead. The Commission has no role in decision-making, but does have an input into aspects of planning. However, as the ESS states, none of the threats can be tackled by purely military means and this is true for conflict management. Therefore, the civilian components of a conflict management operation have to be factored in from the start. The setting up of the CivMil Cell did not produce the integration between civilian and military planning that was envisaged and while the CPCC, reporting to the PSC, did establish a clearer civilian chain of command it seemed to entrench rather than moderate the civil–military divide within CSDP. This has meant that the civil–military coordination within CSDP has, up to now, been problematic. The limited coordination and coherence is exacerbated further outside of CFSP when inter-institutional coordination and cooperation is required. Similar problems can be found on the finance side of EU conflict management. CFSP's budget is far too limited for the rapidly expanding number of conflict management missions and while the Commission has a bigger budget for non-CFSP items the funding streams undermine coherence across pillars.

Nevertheless, the EU manages through pragmatic ad hocism, bending the rules slightly and finding solutions when under pressure to launch an operation quickly. While this means the EU is able to contribute to global conflict management it is not making the most of its potential. However, more recent developments suggest that it may, finally, soon have the potential to be able to contribute to global conflict management with greater coherence and move towards becoming a comprehensive conflict manager.

A more coherent EU approach to conflict management?

Modifying some existing structures and instruments, the addition of new structures, and some of the reforms in the ToL, such as the establishment of the High Representative for Union Foreign and Security Policy and the European External Action Service, may be the foundations for a more coherent EU approach to conflict management.

The push for greater civil–military cooperation and coordination within CSDP illustrated by the CivMil Cell may not yet be functioning optimally but there were some successes suggesting it, and other structures, may have the potential to overcome the gaps *within* CSDP and *between* CSDP and other EU institutions. The Aceh Monitoring Mission (AMM) was an early example of how the CivMil Cell can add to the EU's capability to act and to coordinate, both within CSDP and between instruments and institutions. After initial Commission-Council rivalry over the funding and leadership of the AMM, the operation was seen as a real success. The mission deployed (on an interim basis initially) in just 12 days and was on the ground exactly when the peace agreement came into force (Schulze 2007; Feith 2007). Within CSDP the AMM demonstrated the EU can act quickly, as well as its ability to find innovative ways of funding and coordinating conflict management when its back was to the wall (Interviews 2007). The mission also illustrated the usefulness of having access, through the CivMil Cell, to military planning capabilities even for largely civilian missions, with up to 60 per cent of the planning done by military personnel (Interviews 2007). The CivMil Cell was also used in the planning for the EU support mission to the African Union Mission in Sudan/Darfur (AMIS) in which the EU 'provided a consolidated package of civilian and military measures' (EU Council Secretariat 2008a). However, critics argue that these missions were not classified as integrated missions, instead being run out of DGIX, and that the CivMil Cell has not been used for missions since then (Norheim-Martinsen 2009: 18; Korski and Gowan 2009: 58).

Realising the continuing lack of a coherent and coordinated civilian–military planning structure, in late 2008 the European Council called on the Secretary General/High Representative for CFSP to 'establish a new, single civilian-military strategic planning structure for ESDP operations' (Council of the European Union, 2008g). This new structure, known as the Crisis Management and Planning Directorate (CMPD), will merge the strategic planning functions of DG E VIII (military crisis management) and DG E IX (civilian crisis management) as well as incorporate elements of the Civ-Mil Cell (Drent and Zandee 2010). The CMPD will be led by a civilian with a military deputy, countering the military bias seen in the EUMS, with further staff drawn from across CFSP/CSDP structures (Gebhard 2009). The CMPD should improve the coherence of planning civilian and military ESDP operations and, importantly for the EU's comprehensive approach to conflict management, realise the potential for genuine and coherent civil–military crisis management. However, in the first half of 2010 criticisms started to emerge about the potential re-emergence of a military bias within the CMPD. Deletroz claims that only 20 per cent of personnel for the 'so-called "integrated strategic planning unit" seem to have civilian planning expertise' and that civilian experts are left out of decision-making structures (Deletroz 2010).

The potential these developments hold should be enhanced by some of the reforms outlined in the ToL. In particular modifications to the scope of CSDP and how it can operate, the new post of HR representative of the Union for Foreign Affairs and Security and Vice-President of the Commission (HR/VP) and the European External Action Service (EEAS) all have the potential to improve the EU's capabilities to act, fund and coordinate, thereby improving the EU's effectiveness and credibility in conflict management.

First, the ToL formally widens the Petersberg Tasks, as outlined earlier, giving the CSDP a remit across the entire conflict management spectrum. Second, the treaty allows smaller groups of member states that have the political will and capabilities, with the agreement of the other EU states, to undertake an operation on behalf of the EU. Third, the ToL establishes 'structured cooperation' which allows an 'advanced' group of willing and able states to further integrate and enhance their military capabilities, even if other states do not wish to do so (European Union 2007). This may help in driving forward the military capability improvements required for conflict management. In a Union of 27 states these seem practical solutions that should contribute to a more capable, rapid and coherent conflict management approach.

The position of HR/VP has significant potential to ensure greater coherence and strengthen leadership *within* CFSP/CSDP and improve coordination *between* the Commission and the Council in conflict management. While this position entails a massive portfolio it may present the unity of command that has been absent thus far. Acting as High Representative for CFSP and as Commissioner for External Relations the post should provide the holistic view required for conflict management. However, the remit is huge, leading Missiroli (2008) to usefully suggest that the HR/VP role may have to be supported by a number of deputies, including one for 'crisis management proper'. However, CFSP will still have separate decision-making and funding rules, complicating the coordination role of the HR/VP in ensuring coherence. Another possible difficulty is the relationship between this post and the new European Council President when representing the EU overseas (where the Commission President also has a role). Despite these problems, the HR/VP creates the possibility of a unity of command that was not previously achievable. With some institutional streamlining of agencies, committees and units and the good use of deputies and delegation, the potential for greater coherence in drawing together all the relevant tools for conflict management is significantly enhanced. This would be even further enhanced if the HR/VP had, as Missiroli (2007: 22) suggests, some responsibility or authority over DG Development and Europe Aid Cooperation Office (AIDCO) as well.

This potential could be even greater with the addition of the EEAS. The EEAS was rather vaguely mentioned in the Lisbon Treaty and a great deal of work was done in the first half of 2010 to map out the functions and organisation of the new body that will be crucial to the EU's role in conflict management. The details were formally finalised with the Council Decision of 26 July 2010 establishing the EEAS. As stated in the ToL its overall role is to assist the HR/VP. Within Brussels, Missiroli's (2008: 11) hopes for the EEAS to become a 'functional interface between all the main institutional actors of European foreign policy' may be met. The Council decision details all the departments and functions to be transferred to the EEAS including: the Policy Unit, all CSDP and crisis management structures (civilian and military), Directorate General E from the Council Secretariat as well as the Commission's Directorate General for External Relations, the Directorate General for Development and the External Service (Council of the European Union 2010). Bringing these various directorates and experts together could be the basis for eliminating the duplication of Commission and Council expertise and representatives and increase the possibility of improved coherence between civilian and military policies and capabilities. In third countries unified EU delegations may provide a unified point of contact and more coherent information on developments within those countries; as was done in FYROM and with the African Union where one person fulfilled both the Council and Commission representation roles (Adebahr and Grevi 2007).

Conclusion

The EU has the ambition to be a 'unique' and 'comprehensive' global conflict manager and its rhetoric on this has generated a clear expectation among other states and international organisations that it can and will act to prevent, contain and end violent conflict. At the heart of the comprehensive approach is the effective coordination of the whole range of instruments at the EU's disposal; within CSDP this means a coherent and coordinated use of both civilian and military tools. However, to date, the EU continues to suffer from a number of capability, institutional and policy gaps that undermine coherence and the comprehensive nature of its conflict management.

Despite some progress and the ongoing transformation of CSDP there are continuing and significant capability gaps on the military and civilian side with both personnel and equipment shortfalls. The institutional gaps continue across the EU and within CSDP; perhaps best illustrated within CSDP by the parallel chain of commands for civilian and military crisis management operations despite the introduction of the CivMil Cell and CMPD. Similarly, in the policy domain the civilian and military approaches are rarely developed in an integrated fashion (partly due to the institutional division).

However, developments through 2009–10 including the setting up of the CMPD, the entry into force of the ToL and, most recently, the decision to establish the EEAS mean that the EU may finally have the institutional and policy, though not yet capability, advances it needs for comprehensive conflict management. Yet, it is not enough to simply add to the structures and instruments that are in place. A streamlining of structures within CSDP and CFSP (and across the Commission) for conflict management tools is required. As Howorth and Le Gloannec (2007: 31) point out, as CSDP developed 'very few institutions were replaced by new ones, very few were actually discarded'. With the impending introduction of the CMPD, it seems sensible to reassess the roles and added value of the CPCC and the EUMS and other planning structures across CSDP. Similarly, the number of 'intelligence' gathering, 'early warning', 'monitoring' and 'watch-keeping' units within the Council, not to mention the Commission, should be reassessed with a view to consolidation and hopefully greater coherence. With streamlining and coherence as the guiding principles for the transformation of CSDP it may well be transformed into a genuine civil–military instrument with the potential to be at the heart of a coherent, effective and comprehensive global conflict management policy for the EU.

Global conflict management requires a balanced and integrated set of civilian and military instruments *within* CSDP and *between* the EU institutions to ensure a coherent and comprehensive approach. This chapter has provided a preliminary examination of the civilian and military capabilities, and the increasing importance of generating a genuine civil–military nexus, *within* CSDP for the EU's wider conflict management ambitions. Integrating CSDP into the broader conflict management tools of the EU is complex and, for some, controversial. Yet, harnessing the potential of CSDP's transforming civil–military capabilities is vital for the EU in fulfilling its unique potential as a comprehensive global conflict manager.

Notes

1   The gaps *between* CSDP and the EU's other pillars are covered elsewhere in this volume.
2   Adapted from Ramsbotham *et al.* (2005: 14) (first column added by author from Hourglass Model, p. 12).
3   Italics denote new elements of Petersberg Tasks.
4   This has been questioned by some – see Lieutenant General Fry in House of Commons Defence Committee, *The Future of NATO and European Defence* (London: HMSO, March 2008), Q. 177.
5   Again the UK objected to the idea of an operational headquarters even though it was explicitly civilian.

Part 2
Case Studies

4   The role of the EU as a conflict manager in Cyprus

James Ker-Lindsay

Introduction

In many ways, Cyprus can be regarded as the most significant recent example of the European Union's (EU) potential to resolve conflict in its neighbourhood. The process that led to the referendum on the island's reunification in 2004 was directly attributable to the EU decision to accept Cyprus as a member. However, as will be seen, this power had little to do with the EU's active intervention or involvement as an overt and specific actor in the process. Unlike its role in other areas, such as the Balkans or Africa, it did not send peacekeepers to Cyprus. Nor did it conduct a formal mediation process or provide a means of communication between parties. Its role in the actual discussions was in fact very limited, mainly confined to providing technical advice to the parties and to the United Nations (UN).

Instead, the EU provided the context for a meaningful reunification process to take place. Its decision to accept Cyprus as a candidate for membership, and its insistence that it could not be held back because of the division, created the political conditions for the parties, most particularly the Turkish Government and the Turkish Cypriot community, to engage in the negotiation process in a way that had not been seen before. It therefore provided a catalyst for a settlement. The problem was that this process of 'incentivisation' was unevenly applied. Steps needed to be taken to ensure that the Greek Cypriot community could not play the system. This, perhaps more than anything, highlights the fact that while the EU can indeed be a 'game changer', this role requires it to be more active than many assume. It is not enough to think that the mere prospect of accession can help parties reach a solution to a long-standing dispute. The EU must continually ensure that the political incentives and conditions are managed to ensure full engagement by all sides. In other words, when one is considering the ways in which the EU can act as a catalyst for conflict resolution, even the power of attraction – the desirability of EU membership that draws countries closer to the Union – needs to be managed.

Background

On 16 August 1960, Cyprus became an independent state after 82 years of British colonial rule. For many Greek Cypriots the hoisting of the new flag of the Republic was not a moment for celebration or joy. Instead it was greeted with disappointment, even resentment. Five years earlier, in April 1955, they had launched a military campaign to end British rule and bring about the union (*enosis*) of the island with Greece. For their part, the Turkish Cypriot community, which represented just 18 per cent of the island's population, had strongly opposed any attempt to unite the island with Greece. Instead, they wanted to see Cyprus partitioned (*taksim*) with the northern part ceded to Turkey.[1]

Fearing that a full-scale civil war could break out between the two communities, which could then lead to a wider conflict between themselves, Greece and Turkey had agreed at the start of 1959 that the island should become an independent sovereign state. This new Republic of Cyprus would be based on a complex power sharing agreement that would ensure the political equality of the two main communities. At the same time, Greece, Turkey and Britain would act as the ultimate guarantors of the sovereignty, independence and territorial integrity of the new state, with all three maintaining a military presence on the island. Union with either Greece or Turkey would be barred, as would any form of partition. Likewise, Cyprus would be banned from joining any organisation that had only Greece or Turkey, rather than both or neither, as a member. Adhering to this principle, following independence the island quickly became a member of a number of international organisations, including the UN, the Commonwealth and the Non-Aligned Movement.[2] In December 1962, Cyprus formally applied for an association agreement (AA) with the European Economic Community (EEC), as the EU was then called. However, the effort was short-lived. The following year the application was abandoned when Britain's efforts to secure membership of the EEC were vetoed by France (Sepos 2008: 34).[3]

Despite early hopes that the new state would eventually succeed, by the middle of 1963 problems were already emerging. In addition to disputes over taxes and the establishment of separate municipalities in the main towns, as envisaged under the constitution (see Markides 2001), both communities continued to show a greater loyalty to their respective motherlands of Greece and Turkey than to the new state. The necessary component of goodwill was all but absent. This ensured that the numerous problems festered and served to create the conditions for yet more disagreements. In order to break the deadlock that had arisen from this situation, Archbishop Makarios, the Greek Cypriot President, proposed a series of constitutional amendments that he argued would facilitate the smoother functioning of the state. Despite earlier warnings from Greece that this could have grave repercussions, not only between the Greek and Turkish Cypriot communities, but also between Greece and Turkey, Makarios nevertheless went ahead and presented a package of 13 proposals in November that year. These included proposals to limit the right of veto of the Greek Cypriot President and the Turkish Cypriot Vice-president. The Turkish Government rejected the suggestions out of hand and, in the weeks that followed, tensions grew between the communities.

On 21 December 1963, fighting finally erupted in Nicosia, the island's capital. Within days the fighting had spread to other towns and cities on the island and reports were emerging that Turkey was mobilising its armed forces in preparation for an armed intervention. This in turn would lead to a response from Greece, which could ultimately spark a wider regional conflict. Faced with this, Athens and Ankara agreed to jointly form a peacekeeping force under British command. At the same time, a peace conference was convened in London. When this failed, the matter was referred to the United Nations Security Council. On 4 March 1964, the Security Council passed a resolution creating a peacekeeping force (UNFICYP) for the island, a mission that remains in place to this day, and instructing the Secretary-General to appoint a mediator.[4] Over the next ten years, efforts would be made to try to broker an agreement between the two sides, but with little success.

In the meantime, following Britain's decision to reapply for EU membership, which was eventually successful, the Cypriot Government once again reactivated its application for an association agreement (Sepos 2008). Despite the ongoing political problems on the island, the agreement was signed on 19 December 1972. According to the terms of the agreement, the process would consist of two stages. In the first phase tariffs on a range of goods would be reduced. This would then lead to the second stage, a full customs union between the two. This was due to occur ten years later, in 1982.

However, just 18 months later these plans were thrown into disarray. On 15 July 1974, Makarios was overthrown in a *coup d'état* directed by the military government in Greece. Fearing for the safety of the Turkish Cypriot population, the Turkish Government approached Britain to stage a joint intervention under the terms of the 1960 Treaty of Guarantee. London declined. Five days later, Turkey invoked its rights under the 1960 constitution and invaded.[5] Within days, the military government in Greece had fallen and a peace conference was hurriedly arranged in Geneva. However, the two rounds of talks failed to produce an agreement. Therefore, on 14 August, Turkey began the second wave of its invasion. By the time a cease-fire was called three days later, 36 per cent of the island was under Turkish control. The humanitarian impact of the fighting was enormous. In addition to the several thousand Greek and Turkish Cypriots killed or wounded, over two thousand were missing and 200,000 Cypriots had been forced to flee their homes. For the Greek Cypriots, especially, the economic effects were devastating. Many of the most agriculturally fertile parts of the island, for example the citrus-growing areas around Morphou, had been lost. In addition, the important port city of Famagusta, including the Greek Cypriot suburb of Varosha, was now in Turkish hands. Although the EU decided not to suspend the association agreement (Sepos 2008: 34), it was nevertheless obvious that its implementation would be delayed.

In the years after the invasion, the UN remained the principal actor in efforts to broker an agreement between the two sides. In 1977, the leaders of the two communities signed a high-level agreement stating that a future solution would be based on a bizonal, bicommunal federation. This was reconfirmed in 1979. However, on 15 November 1983 the Turkish Cypriot leadership, capitalising on the transition from military to civilian rule then taking place in Turkey, took the opportunity to unilaterally declare independence. Although the new state, the Turkish Republic of Northern Cyprus (TRNC), was quickly recognised by Turkey, the move was roundly condemned by the international community, including the ten members of the EU, who issued a joint statement condemning the move and noting that 'they continue to regard the government of President Kyprianou as the sole legitimate government of the Republic of Cyprus' (Embassy of the Republic of Cyprus in Washington DC 2010a). Likewise, UN Security Council Resolution 541(1983) stated that the declaration of independence was 'legally invalid' and called on all member states not to recognise 'any other Cypriot state other than the Republic of Cyprus'. Despite this development, the UN unsuccessfully continued its attempts to help the sides reach a solution. However, its efforts were continually frustrated by the growing intransigence of the Turkish Cypriot leader, Rauf Denktash, who was strongly supported by successive Turkish governments, and came to be widely regarded by the international community as the main obstacle to a solution (Hannay 2005: 17–21).

EU accession and the catalytic effect

By the start of the 1990s, hopes that the island would be reunified appeared to be receding. In addition to the hard-line policies of the Turkish Cypriot leadership, the Turkish Government appeared to have little interest in reaching a solution. Although the Cyprus issue was certainly a nuisance for Ankara, it did not pose a major problem for Turkey on the international stage. It was in this context that the European Union, through the joint actions and decisions of its various institutions, would become a vital component in efforts to resolve the island's division.

Commission approval for candidacy

Following several extensions to the association agreement, in May 1987 an additional protocol was signed paving the way for a full customs union between Cyprus and the EU by 2002. By now, however, Cyprus was becoming more ambitious in its aims. On 4 July 1990, and acting with the support of both Britain and Greece, which had become a member in 1981, the Republic of Cyprus formally presented its application for membership. Three years later, on 30 June 1993, the Commission published a favourable opinion (*avis*) on the application. By now, the Cold War had ended and the EU was already starting to consider the possibility of a major expansion in the future and Cyprus was certainly seen to be a part of Europe. As the *avis* noted:

> Cyprus's geographical position, the deep-lying bonds which, for two thousand years, have located the island at the very fount of European culture and civilization, the intensity of the European influence apparent in the values shared by the people of Cyprus and in the conduct of the cultural, political, economic and social life of its citizens, the wealth of its contacts of every kind with the Community, all these confer on Cyprus, beyond all doubt, its European identity and character and confirm its vocation to belong to the Community.
>
> (European Commission 1993)

In terms of the economic requirements for membership, and the need to conform to the *acquis communautaire*, the EU's body of laws, the Commission envisaged no 'insurmountable problems'. As the report noted, 'the economy of the southern part of the island has demonstrated an ability to adapt and seems ready to face the challenge of integration provided that the work already started on reforms and on opening up to the outside world is maintained, notably in the context of the customs union'.

As expected, the opinion also paid considerable attention to the question of the division of the island and how this might affect Cyprus's application. On this question, it noted that the process of accession would both shape and be shaped by efforts to reach a comprehensive solution, not least of all because 'the leaders of the Turkish Cypriot community are fully conscious of the economic and social benefits that integration with Europe would bring their Community'. However, in overall terms, the report also seemed to be predicated on a belief that a settlement would form the basis for accession, but nevertheless left the door open to other eventualities.

> 47. This opinion has also shown that Cyprus's integration with the Community implies a peaceful, balanced and lasting settlement of the Cyprus question – a settlement which will make it possible for the two communities to be reconciled, for confidence to be re-established and for their respective leaders to work together. While safeguarding the essential balance between the two communities and the right of each to preserve its fundamental interests, the institutional provisions contained in such a settlement should create the appropriate conditions for Cyprus to participate normally in the decision-making process of the European Community and in the correct application of Community law throughout the island.
>
> 48. In view of all the above and in the expectation of significant progress in the talks currently being pursued under the auspices of the Secretary-General of the United Nations, the Commission feels that a positive signal should be sent to the authorities and

the people of Cyprus confirming that the Community considers Cyprus as eligible for membership and that as soon as the prospect of a settlement is surer, the Community is ready to start the process with Cyprus that should eventually lead to its accession.

51. Lastly, the Commission must envisage the possibility of the failure of the intercommunal talks to produce a political settlement of the Cyprus question in the foreseeable future, in spite of the endeavours of the United Nations Secretary-General. Should this eventuality arise, the Commission feels that the situation should be reassessed in view of the positions adopted by each party in the talks and that the question of Cyprus's accession to the Community should be reconsidered in January 1995.

(European Commission 1993)

Member state support for membership

The Commission opinion was a major step forward inasmuch as it clarified that the island was inherently eligible for membership – even if predicated on a solution being found. The key problem at this stage concerned the reactions of the member states. While there may have been an understanding that Cyprus was European, Cyprus would not be able to pursue accession without a clear say-so from the members. In the end, this did not pose a problem. Despite some earlier French concerns about the implications of opening the way for Cyprus to join the Union, the members were united in their agreement that Turkey could not be granted a veto over who could and could not become a member of the Union. On 25 June 1994, at the Corfu European Council, the member states officially confirmed that Cyprus would be included in the next wave of enlargement discussions, along with Malta.

Although the Cypriot Government was delighted with the Corfu announcement, the Turkish Government and the Turkish Cypriot leadership were furious.[6] As far as they were concerned, any attempt by Cyprus to join the Community would necessarily harm reunification talks. In large part, the response was driven by a stark realisation that Cypriot accession could have a profound effect on Turkey's own EU accession course. Following its own association agreement, which had been signed in 1963, the Turkish Government had submitted an application for full membership three years before Cyprus, in 1987, but had thus far been rebuffed by the Union. If, as seemed possible, Cyprus were to join first, there was a real danger that it could then block Turkey's membership. However, rather than act as a catalyst for a settlement, as many had hoped, it appeared as though the decision would drive the communities further apart. The pace of integration between Turkey and the TRNC now began to quicken and Denktash became increasingly hard line. Nevertheless, the EU remained committed to Cypriot membership.[7] On 6 March 1996, the General Affairs Council of the EU announced that it had been decided that accession negotiations would begin six months after the conclusion of the intergovernmental conference (IGC) taking place that year.

A year and a half later, on 13 December 1997, at the Luxembourg European Council, the member states officially announced that membership talks would begin between the EU and six prospective members, including Cyprus, on 30 March 1998.[8] This time, the Turkish reaction was even more heated, not least of all because its own application for membership had been rejected at the same meeting. An effort to try and ease Turkish concerns by announcing that another partnership meeting would be held in London in March had little effect. Meanwhile, the Turkish Cypriots continued to argue that any effort to start negotiations would mark a violation of the 1960 Constitution of the Republic of Cyprus, which specifically prevented the Cypriot state from joining any organisation that had either Greece or Turkey, but not both, as members. The EU, as they saw it, quite clearly fell into this category, as Greece had been a member since 1981. However, after exhaustive legal analysis, this argument was rejected by the EU, as well as by Britain, the third Guarantor Power. Instead, various outside actors argued that Turkey and the Turkish Cypriots, rather than threaten to retaliate against the island's EU accession, should instead seize the opportunity to bring about reunification of the island. Indeed, under pressure from the EU, the Cypriot Government offered the Turkish Cypriots the opportunity to send a delegation to participate in the talks. Much to the disappointment of the European Union, Denktash refused the offer point-blank. Indeed, he now called for the abandonment of a federal model for a settlement, calling instead for a confederal solution.[9]

UN negotiations, 2002–2004

By late 2001 it was clear that Cyprus was well on the way to full membership. Already it was the star candidate and led the pack in terms of the number of chapters closed. Realising that time was running out to prevent the island's accession, Turkey increased its threats. In early November, Prime Minister Ecevit even went as far as to announce that if the Greek Cypriots joined the EU, Turkey would annex Northern Cyprus. While such an idea had been mooted many times, this was the first time that it had been so openly presented by a head of the Turkish Government (*Turkish Daily News* 2001). However, it seems as if there was also a growing realisation that threats alone might not be enough to force Europe to step back. Therefore, in a move that surprised observers (Hannay 2005: 155), Denktash wrote to President Glafcos Clerides, the Greek Cypriot leader, asking for a direct meeting to discuss the implications of the island's EU accession. At first the meeting was expected to be a one-off. However, the two leaders decided to hold further meetings to discuss the question of missing persons. This in turn led to the announcement that formal negotiations would resume. These started in January 2002. Naturally, there was considerable excitement at the prospect of a settlement, especially as the two sides had suggested that they were aiming to reach an agreement by June of that year. However, the initial optimism withered within weeks. It soon became clear that Denktash had initiated the process in the hope that the EU would then decide to delay Cypriot accession in order to give the talks a chance to develop. This would not happen. Quite apart from the fact that Greece was adamant that there could be no enlargement without Cyprus,[10] the Commission and the other member states were also opposed to any moves to prevent the island from joining at the same time as the other candidates.[11] Indeed, keeping the deadline was seen as the best spur possible to ensure that the Turkish Cypriots and Turkey remained seriously engaged.

The initial June deadline to reach an agreement therefore came and went with little sign that a breakthrough was likely. In fact, hopes of an agreement appeared to be further off than ever. A political crisis in Turkey, coupled with the failing health of Bulent Ecevit, the Turkish Prime Minister, effectively gave Denktash a free hand. However, it was also this situation that was to open the way for an eventual breakthrough. In November 2002, following the collapse of the previous coalition government, Turkey went to the polls to elect a new government. The election produced a stunning victory for the Justice and Development Party (AKP), led by the charismatic former mayor of Istanbul, Recep Tayyip Erdogan. Although he was banned from taking a seat in parliament, and therefore ineligible to take up the post of prime minister, few doubted that Erdogan would be the real power in the new government. It was therefore significant that on the night of his victory, Erdogan set out three foreign policy goals: to push ahead with Turkish EU accession, to continue efforts to improve relations with Greece and to solve the Cyprus problem.[12] This announcement opened the way for the UN Secretary-General, Kofi Annan, to present the Greek and Turkish Cypriots with a comprehensive plan to reunite the island. The hope was that the two sides would be able to agree to the deal ahead of the Copenhagen European Council, which was due to be held in December 2002, and where a final decision on Cypriot accession would be taken.

Despite frantic efforts by the UN and the EU to secure an agreement before the summit,[13] Denktash again stood in the way of a settlement. Departing for the Council meeting, the Greek Cypriot delegation was quite clearly ready to reach an agreement. However, the Turkish Cypriot leader, who was still recovering from major surgery, instead chose to avoid the talks and instead sent along his most hard-line representative. It was obvious to all observers that a deal would not be reached. After almost a day of intense efforts to bring the two sides to the table, the UN was forced to give up its effort. As a result, EU leaders announced, on the afternoon of 13 December 2002, that Cyprus would join the EU on 1 May 2004. Although an agreement had not been reached at Copenhagen, as many had hoped and expected, reunification talks quickly resumed at the start of 2003. This time, the hope was that an agreement could be reached before the formal Treaty of Enlargement was signed in Athens, on 16 April. In order to reach this deadline Annan visited the island at the end of February. However, once again, the Turkish Cypriot leaders refused to engage in discussions. Annan therefore played his last card. He called on Denktash and Tassos Papadopoulos, who had recently been elected as President, to meet him in The Hague on 10 March. There he asked them whether they would be prepared to put a peace plan to a direct vote. Although Papadopoulos grudgingly agreed to hold a referendum, Denktash rejected the idea out of hand. In view of this, Annan announced that he saw no further point in continuing peace talks. The UN process now appeared to come to an end.[14]

On 16 April, just over a month after the collapse of the talks, Cyprus signed the Treaty of Accession at a lavish ceremony of EU leaders held at the foot of the Acropolis, in Athens. The signing of the Treaty of Accession appeared to mark the last stage in Cyprus's accession to the EU. With peace talks now off the agenda and with the threat of Turkish retaliation now diminished, the expectation was that the next year would see the island continue its preparations for accession on 1 May 2004. However, by autumn 2003, the possibility of a last-ditch attempt to reach a settlement prior to accession began to emerge. In mid-December of that year, the Turkish Cypriots went to the polls to elect a new parliament. As expected, the pro-settlement Republican Turkish Party (CTP) won the polls. This presented the Turkish Government with the opportunity it needed to reactivate the process. In January 2004, Prime Minister Erdogan asked Annan to restart talks (*Washington Post* 2004). Following consultations with the parties, the UN Secretary-General called Papadopoulos and Denktash to New York for talks. On 13 February, following three days of talks, it was announced that a new process of negotiations would start in Cyprus the following week. These would last for one month. If, at the end of that period, the two sides had not reached a final agreement on the text of a settlement, a further week of talks would take place abroad. This second round would include representatives from the Greek and Turkish Governments. If at the end of that further period of time no agreement had been reached, the Secretary-General would fill in the blanks and present it to the two communities in separate but simultaneous referendums. The intention was to ensure that all this took place before 1 May.

At first it appeared as thought the two sides might just be able to make some progress. However, within a short period of time it became clear that neither side was truly engaged in the process. Denktash continued to remain wedded to a confederal settlement. Meanwhile, it was also obvious that Papadopoulos had little interest in seeing the talks succeed. Rather than try to hammer out a better agreement, the Greek Cypriot side became increasingly obstructionist. For instance, those involved with the talks noted that Greek Cypriot representatives refused to present the UN with a clear set of positions. What paperwork they did present was deliberately prepared to hide their main concerns. Such tactics were not only seen in the main political talks between the two leaders, but also in the technical committees, which were discussing a whole range of associated issues, such as the creation of federal laws and the management of international agreements. As a result, the first phase of talks ended without progress.

Hopes that the second phase, which was held in the Swiss mountain resort of Burgenstock, might lead to a breakthrough were also short-lived. Although the Turkish Cypriot team was now free of Denktash, who had decided to boycott the second phase, the Greek Cypriot side refused to engage in meaningful negotiations. Despite the presence of the Greek and Turkish Prime Ministers, the week failed to see even one direct discussion between the parties. Indeed, the process was disrupted as Papadopoulos left for several days to attend an EU meeting in Brussels. However, even at this late stage European leaders sought to persuade the two sides to reach an agreement. In a communiqué at the end of the meeting in Belgium, the EU leaders communicated their 'strong preference for the accession of a united Cyprus to the EU and reiterates its readiness to accommodate the terms of such a settlement in line with the principles on which the EU is founded' (Council of the EU 2004c). It was to no avail. On 31 March, the UN Secretary-General was forced to conclude the agreement and present it to the two sides.

The referendum campaign

With just over three weeks to go before the referendum, campaigning quickly got under way in earnest on the island. Very soon it became obvious that the agreement was likely to pass among Turkish Cypriots. Although Denktash vehemently opposed the plan, the Turkish Government had come out in favour of the deal. In contrast, within the Greek Cypriot community there was considerable opposition to the agreement. Although the plan was endorsed by both Clerides and Vassiliou, President of the Republic of Cyprus, and also received the backing of the Greek Government, as well as senior officials from the European Commission and various leaders from EU member states, Papadopoulos came out against the agreement. On 7 April, in a 50-minute televised speech, he blasted the agreement and called on Greek Cypriot voters to reject the plan. Among the various reasons why he called for a vote against the agreement was the argument that Cyprus could secure a better agreement after the island joined the European Union, just over three weeks later.[15]

In the weeks that followed a sustained onslaught was launched against the plan. In addition to failing to correct obvious misrepresentations of the plan, the Cypriot Government did little to set the record straight on areas of ambiguity. Indeed, an effort was made to create confusion and doubt. For instance, a letter was sent to civil servants indicating that the Government was trying to secure the same salaries and pension rights for those working in the new federal administration. The implication being, of course, that these were at risk. At the same time, the Government appeared to take no interest in trying to promote a balanced debate. A decision by the state broadcaster to prevent both Alvaro de Soto, the chief UN official responsible for the Plan, and Gunter Verheugen, the EU Commissioner for Enlargement, who had been a long-standing advocate of the island's accession, from appearing on television was not challenged by the Government. Even though there is no evidence to suggest that the order to prevent them from appearing on television came from the presidential palace, the hope was that the Government would have sought to create an open forum for debate and ensured that all views were given equal air time.

Financial support

In addition to trying to persuade the two communities of the merits of the reunification plan, the EU undertook other initiatives to try to encourage a settlement. One key element of this effort included financial measures. For example, in an attempt to ensure that the financial costs of a settlement did not overburden the new state, a major donor conference was convened in Brussels on 15 April. There the United States (US) pledged to give $400 million towards a settlement in the event that the two sides voted for the deal. The UK offered a further $37 million. All this was on top of $300 million that had already been promised by the EU to the Turkish Cypriot community as part of a package designed to encourage them to take a more positive view of reunification and EU accession (*Cyprus Mail* 2004).[16] While this may have served to encourage the Turkish Cypriots to take a more positive view of the EU, it seemed to have no effect on the Greek Cypriots. Indeed, they all but boycotted the event, sending a low-level delegation to the meeting.

EU instruments

Furious at what was happening, the Commission tried to find other ways to shape the process. It even explored possible ways in which the island's accession might be delayed or prevented. However, it became clear that this would not be possible. The problem was that once the Treaty of Accession had been signed the previous year, there was no way in which to extricate Cyprus. Either every country joined or none would. Besides, even if they had managed to find a way to put the brakes on Cypriot accession, Greece would have stepped in to veto enlargement. Attention therefore turned to ways in which the EU could ensure a more democratic referendum campaign. Again, there was very little that could be done. Although it was destined to become a member, until such time as it formally joined on 1 May 2004, Cyprus remained completely sovereign and was not subject to rules of membership. In other words, Cyprus was in a strange state of limbo. It was guaranteed membership and yet it was not yet subject to any rules.[17] Within reason, it could effectively do as it liked. It could not be coerced or threatened in any way. To be sure, there would be serious recriminations in terms of its overall standing and it might face a slap on the wrists. However, nothing more serious could happen. For example, the EU could not, and would not, recognise the TRNC – in part due to obvious Greek opposition, but also because of the Security Council Resolution in place preventing this. At most, it could try to open up more direct relations with the Turkish Cypriots; an idea put forward by many EU officials.[18] But even this would be limited. The EU was therefore forced to sit back and watch with a mixture of concern, frustration and anger as the campaign unfolded.

Referendum and accession

On 24 April the two communities voted on the peace plan. As expected, the Turkish Cypriots endorsed the agreement by a margin of two to one. In contrast, the Greek Cypriots came out firmly against the settlement. The final results showed that 76 per cent had rejected the plan. The outcome of the referendum was a bitter blow for most of the international community.

Within EU circles, both in member states and within the Commission, there was a deep sense of disappointment at what had happened. In fact, many were positively furious at the behaviour of the Cypriot Government. At a meeting of EU foreign ministers held just days after the vote, George Iacovou, the Cypriot Foreign Minister, was heckled by his counter-parts.[19] Despite his efforts to justify the Greek Cypriot decision, it was a humiliating moment that betrayed just how frustrated the EU was about what had happened.

The unwritten agreement that had been reached between Cyprus and the EU was that the island would be allowed to join on the condition that the Greek Cypriots would agree to accept any settlement that broadly met the terms of a bicommunal and bizonal federation. In the eyes of most observers, the Annan Plan met those criteria. Therefore, by calling on the Greek Cypriots to reject the agreement, Papadopoulos was seen to have broken the compact. Indeed, in a statement that summed up the feeling of many, Verheugen told the European Parliament that he personally felt betrayed by the way in which the Cypriot Government had behaved. As he explained, 'the political damage is large . . . there is now a shadow over Cypriot accession' (*Turkish Daily News* 2004). There were many others who fully agreed with this sentiment. In reply, Papadopoulos responded by stating that such an agreement had been made with the previous administration and could not be expected to apply to his gov-ernment. This went down extremely badly and in fact served to make matters worse. The issue of a settlement was not some trifling matter. Nor were the conditions of Cypriot acces-sion simply applicable to one government, rather than another. The whole basis of Cypriot accession had been built on the argument that the Greek Cypriots should not be punished for Turkish actions and that they would remain reasonable and amenable to reaching a settle-ment. It was a compact made with the Greek Cypriot people as a whole, irrespective of the particular administration in power. As most observers saw it, Papadopoulos had therefore indeed fundamentally betrayed the trust that the member states and the Commission had placed in Cyprus when they agreed to open negotiations. It was therefore little wonder that, on 1 May 2004, just one week after the referendum, the Republic of Cyprus entered the Union under the darkest cloud possible.

Epilogue: the EU and peace efforts after accession

As expected, EU accession has not led to the end of peace efforts. These continue. But the expectation that the EU would fundamentally change the parameters of a settlement, an argument put forward by many Greek Cypriots rejectionists in 2004, has proven to be lim-ited, at best. To be sure, any agreement needs to be in broad accordance with the *acquis communautaire*. However, the view that there can be absolutely no derogations is patently false. By all indications, the EU remains committed to a settlement and would be willing to show a high degree of flexibility on a final settlement. In this regard, while EU membership has necessarily changed certain aspects of how a settlement is discussed it has not proven to be the 'game changer' that many expected. Likewise, the view that the EU could take over from the United Nations as the key mediator has also proven to be incorrect. The EU has remained steadfast in its conviction that talks must be handled by the UN. The member states and the Commission have readily recognised the fundamental paradox of trying to mediate a conflict that involves one of its own members. It cannot be impartial or neutral in such a process – and certainly would not be seen as such by the Turkish Cypriot community or the Turkish Government.

Where the EU can still play a major part is in regards to the degree to which Turkey still wishes to pursue EU membership. Just as the process leading up to the referendum in 2004 was driven by the wish of the Turkish Government to pursue membership, so it is the same today. But even here there are signs that things are changing – in rather curious ways. There are distinct signs that the Turkish Cypriots are moving in a more nationalist direction and seem to be less enamoured of the EU. In part this is because many of them have Republic of Cyprus passports and so gain most of the key advantages of EU membership in terms of free movement in and around Europe. At the same time, the failure of the EU to end their isolation – all efforts to do so have been blocked by the Greek Cypriots – has led to a lot of disillusionment. Meanwhile, although Turkey remains keen to pursue EU membership, there are also signs that it wishes to solve Cyprus as part of a fundamental reorientation of its external relations – the so-called 'Zero Problems' foreign policy agenda being pursued by Ahmet Davutoglu, the Turkish Foreign Minister. The one area where the EU is likely to remain a key actor is in the post-settlement reconstruction phase. But even here there are questions about how much the EU could put into the pot given the straitened financial picture that exists across much of Europe. Thus, while the EU still remains a significant factor, if not actor, in the Cyprus talks, even after the failure of 2004, its influence is less than many might have imagined. Indeed, for a variety of reasons one could even argue that it could actually be waning.

Conclusion

In the run-up to enlargement in 2004, many observers, both within the institutions of the EU and outside of them, came to see Cyprus as an example of the ways in which the EU can fundamentally transform conflicts within Europe and provide the impetus for a solution to long-running disputes. The EU quite clearly showed a real commitment to the solution of the Cyprus Problem and the results were, in their own way, significant. However, the EU's role was not as obvious as one might have expected. For example, the EU did not take a lead role in the actual mediation process. The UN remained the main actor in the attempts to reunite the island. Nor did it involve much by way of active EU support to the UN process. The EU had little overt role in the negotiations. The most significant input of the EU in this regard was the technical assistance provided by the European Commission to the UN team. Even then, it can be argued that this was less about ensuring a settlement was reached and more about making sure that the agreement was compatible with the *acquis*. Still, in terms of its ability to coordinate with external actors, in this case the United Nations, the EU proved to be more than able to do so.

Likewise, the EU's role in terms of providing a financial incentive to the parties was important, but not as great as it could have been. Certainly, the financial package presented to the Turkish Cypriots was welcome and appeared extremely generous given the small size of the Turkish Cypriot community. However, as many Turkish Cypriots argued, the sum was still less than the amount given to the Turkish Cypriots every year by Turkey. Equally, the EU did not perhaps do enough to persuade Greek Cypriots of its commitment. This was seen particularly clearly as regards the question of reconstruction following a settlement. Would the EU have been willing and able to make the massive financial commitment necessary to help facilitate a smooth reunification? The answer seems to be yes. However, this was never obviously tested in any meaningful manner. It seems unlikely that the EU could have afforded, politically and economically, to allow a settlement to fail. Nevertheless, there were doubts and concerns about this very question.

While the EU may have played a relatively small role in terms of its input into the UN-led settlement process, its role in terms of providing the conditions for that process to take place was enormous. There is absolutely no doubt that the EU provided the key impetus for moves towards a meaningful negotiation process. Had it not been for the prospect of EU membership there would have been no move towards a settlement in 2004. For Turkey, the prospect of having a Republic of Cyprus in the EU, which could then veto its own application, was an extremely worrying prospect. This was the sole reason why the Turkish Cypriot leadership, rather than the wider Turkish Cypriot population, sought to re-engage with a UN process that it had treated with disdain for many years. Meanwhile, for the Turkish Cypriots, the EU was seen as offering a new beginning for their isolated community. The lure of the EU membership was not the money on offer. It was the opportunities it could provide. Thus there was a double incentive for Ankara and the Turkish Cypriot community to engage in the UN process in a way that had not been seen before.

In this sense, the EU – both the Commission and the member states – had a profound effect on the conflict. Although the EU played little part in the actual process of conflict resolution, it was the vital catalyst that allowed the negotiations to develop. This started with the Commission's decision to give Cyprus a positive opinion, despite the island's division. It was then followed by the agreement of the member states to accept Cyprus as a candidate and pursue accession despite Turkish opposition. It was precisely because the EU was united across its institutions and among its members in its commitment to the island's accession – albeit in the latter stages shaped by Greece's threat to block the enlargement project as a whole if Cyprus was left out – that the EU was able to provide the impetus for a serious conflict resolution process, which eventually helped the UN reach the situation it did in 2004. Given that Turkey and the Turkish Cypriots were long regarded as the primary impediments to a settlement, and that they subsequently supported the Annan Plan, it is clear that the EU certainly provided the vital element needed to break the deadlock that had existed for many years.

The problem is that the EU, in exercising its ability to provide the conditions for a settlement *vis-à-vis* one party, did not work to ensure that this influence was equally applied to all actors. While it may have created the incentives for the Turkish Cypriots and Turkey to reach a settlement, it also provided the conditions whereby the Greek Cypriots had less reason to be reasonable. This has served to emphasise the intrinsic institutional weakness within the EU in this case. Once the final process of enlargement has started, it cannot easily be stopped. As of the moment the Treaty of Accession was signed in Athens there was no feasible mechanism by which to prevent Cyprus from joining without stopping all the other nine members-to-be from being able to join as well. If there is a flaw in the accession process, at least in instances where the membership of several states is bundled together, then this has to be it. However, solving this problem is not as simple as just signing various treaties. In this case, it is likely that Greece would have been able to hold up the process of ratification of all the treaties for the other new members until it was sure that Cyprus was included in the final line-up.

Since 2004, many observers have argued that allowing a divided Cyprus to join was a deep mistake. This is a harsh judgement. The mistake was not that the EU decided to allow Cyprus to join. Had it not done so, Turkey would not have changed its position. Rather, the error was that it did not take steps to ensure that the incentives for the Greek Cypriots to reach a settlement were just as great as those for the Turkish Cypriots. Steps should have been taken to ensure that the Greek Cypriots could not play the system, thereby guaranteeing membership come what may. Herein lies perhaps the most useful lesson Cyprus can offer. While the EU certainly has a part to play in the management of conflict in its neighbourhood, and can promote and directly affect the course of discussions between states that are actively seeking membership, this power must be exercised in a far more intelligent and engaged manner. Support for an externally managed peace process is important. So too are financial incentives. However, the EU must also take active steps to ensure that the parties are equally bound to find a solution. In the case of Cyprus, the incentives created for one side of the dispute were not matched with hard and fast steps to ensure that the other side felt compelled to engage in the talks in a constructive manner throughout the process. This needs to be considered seriously as the EU attempts to use its influence elsewhere.

Notes

1 This period is covered by inter alia Holland (1998), Hatzivassiliou (1997) and Crawshaw (1978).
2 The decision to join the Non-Aligned Movement (NAM), of which it was a founder member, was linked with the opposition to joining NATO, which was one of the few instances that saw the Greek Cypriots and Turkey in alignment during the early years of the Republic of Cyprus – albeit for very different reasons. Whereas Makarios felt that NATO would always favour Turkey, the Turkish Government believed that if Cyprus joined the organisation then its ability to intervene would be limited.
3 As is noted, the decision to apply for the agreement was shaped by the close trading relationship between Cyprus and Britain. Nicosia was fearful that if the UK joined the EEC, its privileged trading rights deriving from Commonwealth membership would be curtailed.
4 For an analysis of this period, see James Ker-Lindsay (2004).
5 For an account of these events see Birand (1985), Drousiotis (2006) and Asmussen (2008).
6 The situation was made worse by the fact that less than two weeks later, the European Court of Justice issued a rule that effectively barred direct imports from Northern Cyprus. This had a crippling effect on the Turkish Cypriot economy. For more on this see Talmon (2001: 727–50).
7 The decision to included Cyprus in the next wave of enlargement was confirmed at the next European Council meeting, in Essen, at the end of 1994, and again at Cannes, at the start of 1995. It was also endorsed by the European Parliament (1995).
8 The other five were the Czech Republic, Estonia, Hungary, Poland and Slovenia. A further five countries would form a second wave: Bulgaria, Romania, Latvia, Lithuania and Slovakia. Malta had by this stage frozen its application. For a discussion on Malta, see Pace (2002: 24–42).
9 For a discussion of this in the context of EU accession see Oguzlu (2001: 89–100).
10 For instance, Apostolos Kaklamanis, the Speaker of the Greek Parliament, warned that Greece would not allow EU expansion without Cyprus (Macedonian Press Agency, 18 April 2002).
11 Nevertheless, a row broke out between the EU and Cyprus when Javier Solana, the European Union's High Representative for CFSP, stated that if a solution was not found by the time of enlargement then only the Greek Cypriot side would join the EU (*To Vima tis Kyriakis*, 21 April 2001). The Greek Cypriots were furious, insisting that all of Cyprus would be joining the Union but that the occupied areas would not be subject to the terms of the *acquis*. Solana, who appeared to have made a genuine mistake, and was surprised at the extent of Greek Cypriot anger, soon retracted the comment and confirmed that the whole of Cyprus would indeed be considered to be a part of the European Union after accession (Athens News Agency, 23 April 2002).
12 Macedonian Press Agency, 5 November 2002.
13 *United Nations Security Council Document*, S/2003/398, 1 April 2003, para. 45.
14 *United Nations Press Release*, SG/SM/8630, 11 March 2003.
15 Declaration by the President of the Republic Tassos Papadopoulos regarding the referendum of 24th April 2004, Press Release, Press and Information Office, Republic of Cyprus, 7 April 2004.
16 The pledges made were welcomed by the Security Council (*United Nations Press Release*, SC/8061, 16 April 2004).
17 EU official, discussion with the author, April 2004.
18 Gunther Verheugen stated that he 'would find it rather unfair that the Greek-Cypriot community would enjoy benefits of membership, Turkey would enjoy benefits of entering the pre-accession phase, and only the Turkish Cypriots would get nothing' (Reuters 2004).
19 Reuters, 26 April 2004. It was reported that the attacks were led by the foreign ministers of Britain, Germany, the Netherlands and Luxembourg. The reports were denied by the Cypriot Government.

5   Sub-Saharan Africa

A priority region for EU conflict management

Gorm Rye Olsen

Introduction

Following the end of the Cold War, a significant number of civil wars, regular interstate wars and general instability appeared throughout sub-Saharan Africa. As early as in 1993, the European Commission started to scrutinize the new security challenges facing the African countries in the new international system (Landgraf 1998: 103–17). The 1994 genocide in Rwanda gave additional push to the debates within the European Union (EU) on how to prevent a recurrence of such tragedies in Africa. At several Council of Ministers meetings during the 1990s, security issues were discussed and declarations were adopted stating the EU's concern for the lack of stability in many African countries. At the European Council meeting in 1997, a 'Common Position' was issued making it clear that conflict prevention on the continent was an EU priority (Landgraf 1998: 110).

Not only did it become an EU priority to manage violent conflicts in Africa, but also the promotion of peace and stability became a crucial element of the Common Foreign and Security Policy (CFSP) and of the Common Security and Defence Policy (CSDP) aimed at Africa. The St Malo summit between France and the United Kingdom (UK) in December 1998 opened the way for a new and more active European policy towards Africa as the two former colonial powers agreed to cooperate more closely on Africa in the future. The joint visit by the British Foreign Secretary Jack Straw and his French counterpart Hubert Vedrine to the Great Lakes Region in January 2002 was of subsequent strategic and symbolic value for strengthening the so-called 'spirit of Saint Malo' which implied the possibility of France and the UK exerting pressure in Africa either on an individual basis or collectively via the EU (Hoebeke *et al.* 2007: 12; Chafer and Cumming 2010: 1132–4).

No doubt, conflict management has been on the EU's Africa agenda for a number of years. This chapter shows that the EU has pursued an active conflict management policy in Africa with the deployment of no fewer than three military missions on the continent and with very handsome financial and logistical backing of conflict management operations carried out by the African Union (AU). It is the argument that the active European Africa policy has to be explained by a merger of interests between the two main European colonial powers, France and the UK, and the growing interests within the EU in promoting the EU as a significant global conflict manager. For historical reasons, it was natural for the EU to choose Africa as a main geographical area for developing its capabilities for conflict management.

The chapter starts by scrutinizing the capabilities of the EU to carry out its declared policy within the field of conflict management. Then follows the analysis of two geographical areas in Africa where the EU has been actively involved either by having its own troops on the ground or by proxy, i.e. by the AU. The two conflict areas are the Democratic Republic of the Congo (DRC) and the Darfur–Chad region where it is the aim to show the concrete societal circumstances in which the EU has actively been managing conflicts.

A short history of the relations between Europe and Africa

Due to the European colonization of Africa, there has been a close relationship between the two continents ever since the 1870s. Great Britain and France were the dominant colonial powers but there were significant differences between the two empires as far as colonization and decolonization policies are concerned. Irrespective of the decolonization, France maintained a remarkably close relationship with its former colonies and it is striking how little the relationship has changed since the days of colonialism (Médard 2005: 44–6; Charbonneau 2008; Chafer and Cumming 2010: 1130–31).

In spite of the continuity in French Africa policy, a cautious adjustment has taken place since the mid 1990s. One of the characteristics of the 'new' French Africa policy has been a very reluctant attitude towards getting directly involved with military forces in African conflicts, with Rwanda 1994 and Côte d'Ivoire from 2002 as some very significant exceptions to this pattern. Irrespective of the attempts to readjust its Africa policy, Paris continues to have a very strong interest in stability and crisis prevention in Africa (Médard 2005: 38–54; Charbonneau 2008). When it comes to conflict management in Africa, there are fundamental continuities between the Cold War and the post-Cold War situation. It makes Bruno Charbonneau interpret France as 'the gendarme of Africa [which] has simply put on a cloak of multilateral humanism [. . .] a French colonial tradition of military intervention [that] is not necessarily incompatible with a (European) multilateral approach to African crises' (Charbonneau 2007: 22–3). Under the rubric of increased multilateralization, France has worked in favour of increasingly involving its EU partners in Africa. It makes Tony Chafer argue 'cooperation with other EU member states in Africa makes it possible to retain more influence on the continent than unilateral intervention would, a lesson that both France and Britain, but also Belgium when it held the EU presidency, have learnt' (Chafer 2002: 361).

British Africa policy is characterized by a strong sense of responsibility towards its former colonies. Under the Tony Blair governments, the policy increasingly gave priority to strategies aiming at reducing poverty through economic development. Closely related to this was the understanding that achieving peace and security were key conditions for advancing development on the continent (Ramsbotham *et al.* 2005: 325–39). When it came to the policy instruments, the British were pragmatic as they could be bilateral or multilateral as long as they served what the decision-makers perceived as British interests. Within this general policy approach, it is possible to identify two interlinked policy trends in the policy towards the former colonies. During the past 15 years or so, one trend has been favouring a 'multilateralization' of the traditional bilateral links with Africa by strengthening the relations between the EU and Africa. The other policy line has shown itself in a growing propensity for the UK to intervene bilaterally in Africa's internal affairs. In the post-9/11 context, both trends have intensified because of London's increased security concerns on the continent (Cumming 2005: 55–73).

During the current millennium, France and Britain have been cooperating much more closely than was the situation before the 1998 St Malo summit (Chafer and Cumming 2010). The two powers have developed a common understanding of the need for a multilateralization of their former bilateral links to Africa. It has led to common positions on concrete general policy guidelines and policies as well as on concrete initiatives towards Africa. Only a few years after St Malo, the first EU–Africa summit was held in Cairo in 2000. The summit adopted a joint communiqué establishing that security was a core priority of both the EU and the African countries (Olsen 2006). Increasingly, a new understanding of the security challenges of Africa developed among the EU institutions stressing that there is a close link between conflict and development.

The official recognition of a close connection between development on the one hand and peace and stability on the other was clearly demonstrated in the 'European Africa Strategy' adopted in late 2005: 'Without peace, there can be no lasting development. [. . .] it is now universally recognised that there can be no sustainable development without peace and security. Peace and security are therefore the first essential prerequisites for sustainable development' (European Communities 2005: 10, 26). The second EU–Africa summit in Lisbon of 8–9 December 2007 established that making peace and security was a key dimension of the new EU–Africa joint strategy (EU–Africa 2007). A concluding document described the relationship between the two regions as a 'Strategic Partnership' locating peace and security as the key issues on the agenda, along with immigration, trade, human rights, development and climate change. The third Africa–EU summit held in Tripoli in November 2010 once again confirmed 'peace and security remain a cornerstone of our cooperation' (www.africa-eu-partnership.org/site/default.fil, accessed 21 December 2010).

The capabilities of the EU

This section will look at the three conflict management operations to date where the European Union has deployed troops on the ground in Africa. First is Operation *Artemis* which took place in the Ituri province in the DRC during the summer months of 2003. Second is the somewhat bigger operation which also took place in the DRC, aimed at stabilising the situation in the capital, Kinshasa, during the election campaign in 2006. Third, the section will look into the mission that took place in Chad from March 2008 until March 2009. Finally, the section will scrutinize an EU initiative which can be described as conflict management by proxy. The proxy is the AU which has carried out a number of conflict management missions that have only been possible thanks to handsome support from the EU.

Capabilities to act

Within the framework of the European Common Defence Policy (CSDP), the EU Council of Ministers in June 2003 adopted a resolution which, for the first time, deployed EU military forces outside Europe and without using North Atlantic Treaty Organization (NATO) facilities under the Berlin Plus Agreement (Gegout 2005: 427–43; Chafer and Cumming 2010: 1134). The aim of Operation *Artemis* was to stabilize the security situation in the crisis-ridden Ituri province in the DRC and to improve the humanitarian situation in and around the main town Bunia (Faria 2004a: 20–40, Ulriksen *et al.* 2004). Many observers warned that a new outbreak of violence could threaten the international process aimed at reaching a negotiated settlement (Ulriksen *et al.* 2004: 509–11; Faria 2004a). In that situation, the UN Secretary-General asked for the establishment of a coalition willing to bring an end to the humanitarian crisis in Ituri. Moreover, the coalition should secure an interim solution until it was possible to deploy an effective United Nations (UN) force in the province.

France acted as the so-called framework nation for the operation and several EU countries plus some future EU members and non-European countries provided personnel for the operation amounting to almost 1,400 soldiers (Chafer and Cumming 2010: 1134; Faria 2004a: 43ff.). There are several interpretations as to why the EU was willing to launch

Operation *Artemis*. One is that the intervention had its background in the deep division among the European member states caused by the war on Iraq in the spring of 2003. The Ituri mission was an attempt by the European powers to prove that they could still cooperate and that the CFSP/CSDP was still alive (Salmon 2005: 375–9; Menon 2005: 631–48).[1] Also, it appears that the French president Jacques Chirac found it pertinent for the EU to prove that it could act autonomously from NATO. *Artemis* was a way for France to be recognized politically as an effective military actor (Gegout 2005: 347; Ulriksen *et al.* 2004: 512). The UK 'go ahead' to *Artemis* was mainly to prove that London was still interested in developing a European defence dimension (Gegout 2005: 438). In effect, the launch of *Artemis* was motivated by the interests of two former colonial powers, in particular France, which shared an interest with the UK in continuing the development of the CSDP.

In December 2004, the Council adopted a Joint Action to deploy European police officers to the DRC. This so-called EUPOL–Kinshasa mission was the EU's first civilian crisis management operation in Africa, which, remarkably, fell within the framework of the CSDP. The next element in the EU's engagement in the DRC was the launch in June 2005 of an advisory mission for security sector reform to promote policies compatible with human rights, democratic principles and good governance (Howorth 2007: 229). During the election campaign in the spring of 2006, maintenance of order in Kinshasa was recognized by the UN as a key element for the success of the electoral process. Therefore, the EU's Foreign Affairs Council decided temporarily to strengthen the EUPOL mission by adopting a Joint Action on a military operation in support of the UN mission (MONUC) already in the country. The EUFOR DRC was conducted within the framework of the ESDP and was assigned to support MONUC in stabilizing the situation during the election process, protecting civilians and protecting the airport in Kinshasa. The military deployment with the operational headquarters provided by Germany included an advance element of almost 1,000 soldiers in and around Kinshasa. The EU also had available almost 1,200 troops on-call 'over the horizon' in neighbouring Gabon from where they were quickly deployable if necessary (Council of the EU 2006g).

The motives of EU decision-makers launching the EUFOR DRC mission seem to have been mixed. Richard Gowan finds that there was 'little real enthusiasm for the mission in the EU. Many were also unconvinced by the mission's rationale' (Gowan 2007: 75). It was argued that the launch of the mission in the DRC had

> to do with French-German cohesion and with the EU's desire to bolster the credibility of the ESDP after the fiasco over the European constitutional treaty's rejection in the referendums in France and the Netherlands. The actual situation on the ground in the DRC is only a secondary factor.
>
> (Haine and Giegerich 2006)

Howorth (2007: 239ff.) points at 'accusations that it was primarily intended to get some good coverage for the EU', though 'consciously framed as part of the EU's comprehensive approach to the DRC which, taking the different missions together, do amount to a sizeable measure of assistance'. In a discussion paper, the Congo crisis was described as 'a political testing ground for the EU to design forms of intervention' (SDA 2007: 9, 13, 34).

Soon after the UN Security Council in September 2007 passed a resolution authorizing the deployment of a military force for one year in Eastern Chad and in the north-eastern part of the Central African Republic (CAR), the EU signalled it was ready to take on the responsibility for deploying the troops. After months of negotiations and discussions among the member states and the EU institutions, the Council of Ministers on 28 January 2008 finally decided to launch a military operation of up to 3,700 troops to support and protect refugees from Darfur and internally displaced people from the region (Council, Background 2008; Dijkstra 2010: 398ff.). The mission had the objective of facilitating the delivery of humanitarian aid and the free movement of humanitarian personnel. Obviously, the initiative was to be understood as an integral element in the EU's effort to contribute to solving the crisis in Darfur (Council of the EU 2009g).

There is general agreement among observers and EU civil servants in Brussels that France played a remarkably strong role in relation to making the decision on the EUFOR Chad/CAR operation (Dijkstra 2010; Chafer and Cumming 2010: 1136).[2] The initial idea was French launched by the Minister of Foreign Affairs, Bernard Kouchner. In less than a week, Kouchner was able in public to pose the question: 'What can the European Union do in Chad?' Because there was already a UN resolution covering Darfur, for the French it was mainly an issue of revitalizing the existing plans (Dijkstra 2010: 397ff.).[3] Facing serious problems in supplying sufficient soldiers to the mission, France announced that it would 'plug the gaps' and promised to fulfil logistical requirements, including helicopters and transport aircraft. France was expected to supply about 2,000 soldiers or half the total number for the CSDP mission and a general as force commander (Dijkstra 2010: 399–402).

Summing up, the three military missions launched between June 2003 and March 2008 show that the EU has both the capacity and the political will to act on military conflict management in Africa. Having concluded this, it has to be noted that France stands out as a remarkably active actor more or less openly allied with the UK. It is highly likely that the strong French involvement in the EU decision-making processes reflects the French political priority of demonstrating that the EU can act as an independent international conflict manager, at least in Africa. In this context, it appears that there was an identity of interests between the French and British – and the EU.

Capabilities to fund

The funding issue involves both a long-term as well as a short-term perspective. The long-term perspective is in a number of respects surprisingly positive. In November 2003, the General Affairs Council approved a draft decision to use the European Development Fund (EDF) to create a so-called 'Peace Facility of Africa' in line with the request made by the AU (Faria 2004a: 36). In March 2004, it was officially announced that the African Peace Facility (APF) was established. The APF was a 250-million-Euro instrument aimed at conflict management but financed by 'development money', which meant the funding came from the EDF. The novelty with the Fund was that resources originally allocated for economic and social development were now redirected at supporting African peacekeeping operations. The initial €250-million facility was replenished several times, including through additional voluntary contributions from the member states, reaching almost 440 million euros by the end of 2008. By October 2008, it had supported the AU's AMIS mission in Darfur with at least 500 million euros (Council, Factsheet 2008). Also, the EU disbursed a significant amount of money to humanitarian assistance including food aid to Sudan as well as funding political initiatives aimed at solving the crisis in Darfur (Council, Factsheet 2005).

The willingness to finance this particular conflict management instrument is reflected in the new contributions to the APF which were decided upon when the Cotonou agreement was revised in 2005. As part of this second generation of the APF, it has been opened for the individual member states to contribute directly to the APF on top of the contributions that go via the EDF.[4] The military mission in Chad/CAR had a preliminary budget of around 120 million euros whereas the non-military measures were financed within the strategic framework of the tenth EDF, allocating considerable sums both to Chad and to CAR over a five-year period (EU@UN 2008).

The biggest innovation of the APF was in reality that conflict management now became an integrated element of development activities and thereby became located within a policy domain where the Commission plays the predominant role. Until the adoption of the Cotonou Agreement, conflict management and peacekeeping were formally located in the intergovernmental realm where the member states play a predominant role (ECDPM 2006: 8). Both a mid-term evaluation in late 2005 and a lesson learned conference held in mid 2007 concluded the APF was a successful and highly relevant instrument for funding 'African peace and security efforts' (Council of the EU 2009g). By mid 2010, figures put the EU funding in support of the so-called 'African Peace and Security Agenda' at 1 billion euros for the years 2008–2010. In comparison initiatives within trade and regional integration were expected to receive 1.5 billion euros for the years 2008–2013 (European Union 2010).

The launching of the Peace Facility was clearly motivated by a strong desire to have the AU taking responsibility for African security and thereby avoiding direct European military involvement on the continent[5] (Howorth 2007: 217; Biscop 2005: 133). It contributed to specifying two core concerns of the EU towards Africa. One was to avoid deploying European troops on the continent by offering financial contributions to African peace and conflict management operations. The other aim was to contribute to capacity building with the African partners, which included a whole range of activities such as training of African troops to perform peace and security operations (Chafer and Cumming 2010: 1134ff.).[6] There is no doubt that the Facility was instrumental in buttressing the EU's ambition for having a highly profiled conflict management policy in Africa.

Turning towards the short-term perspective on the funding situation, it has to be stressed that the countries participating in the missions described here obviously were willing to finance the national expenses involved in the operations in the DRC and in Chad. On the other hand, it is equally obvious that the participating countries were only prepared to bear the cost for a short period of time. In this context, the bridging concept was a crucial precondition for many member countries to accept the launching of the operations as the end date was clearly indicated during the decision-making processes. The statement: 'I am sure that the member states will not wish to send troops to Africa for longer periods of time'[7] seems to summarize the general attitude among many decision-makers in Brussels towards the end of 2008.

Cooperation and coordination

The capabilities to coordinate and cooperate have two dimensions. On the one hand, it is about the EU institutions in Brussels and the member states, and on the other hand, it is about the European Union's cooperation with the UN and the AU. Both the Council of Ministers directing the CFSP/CSDP initiatives and the Commission having the responsibility for the huge development assistance programme are involved in conflict management in Africa. The 'EU Strategy for Africa' set out the first framework for addressing the political goal of improving coordination, coherence and consistence of the Union's policies and instruments aimed at Africa (European Communities 2005).

In spite of the explicit political goal of improving cooperation among the different EU policy instruments and thus between the two main institutions, there were numerous indications that there were significant problems in making this work when the policies such as the military missions were to be implemented.[8] Also, it is recognized that bureaucratic conflicts and conflicts of interests have disturbed decision-making and implementation of the conflict management policies in Africa (SDA 2007: 11). Nevertheless, an evaluation states that despite 'different policy debates and the number of institutions involved, the policy consensus on how to promote conflict prevention between member states and the Commission and internally between the Development Ministers and Foreign Ministers or between DG Development and DG Relex is remarkably solid' (ECDPM 2006: 26). The assessment is confirmed by an SDA report stating the existence of 'a large degree of common interests between the EU institutions and the bilateral policies pursued by member states' (SDA 2007: 34, 35.).

Turning towards the EU's cooperation with third parties on conflict management in Africa, two organizations are of particular importance, namely the UN and the AU, which represents the most important local partner when it comes to conflict management. The UN is important insofar as the Security Council has to agree on a mandate for deploying troops in peacekeeping missions. It is an explicit precondition for the EU to have such a resolution backing the deployment of EU troops. Also, cooperation with the UN on the ground in Africa is important because the EU either has to take over a UN mission for a period or because the EU has to strengthen a UN mission already in place and, finally, because the EU has to hand over the responsibility to the UN after a mission is completed. The available information on the cooperation between the UN and the EU confirms that it has been good indeed (Morsut 2009).

When the AU was established at the July 2002 summit in Durban, it was clearly stressed that the AU was going to have the primary responsibility for maintaining international peace and security on the continent. In addition, the European Commission and the AU decided to develop cooperation between the two regions with respect to promoting peace and security (Siradag 2009: 38). Since 2002, the EU and the AU have cooperated to prevent and resolve a number of conflicts in Africa (Cilliers 2008; Siradag 2009: 2ff., 28ff.). Among these can be mentioned Darfur, the biggest, most comprehensive, but also the most difficult one. The AU's Peace and Security Council has stressed that the AU should play a more active role in resolving the Darfur crisis and also that it should work closely with the EU in this context. Therefore, the AU has deployed troops under the AMIS I and AMIS II operations in Darfur protecting civilians and carrying out peacekeeping activities. By means of the APF, the EU has handsomely supported the AU with financial, humanitarian and logistical resources, etc. (Murithi 2008: 76–8; Siradag 2009: 43–59). On the other hand, it has to be mentioned that the situation where the EU is relegated to the role of a mere payer of the AU's initiatives does not supply the answers to the complex situations in Africa (Pirozzi 2009: 42). Moreover, the EU has not been successful reinforcing the capabilities and the leadership of the African Union. The implementation procedures, the financial instruments and other mechanisms need to be improved (Pirozzi 2009: Sherriff *et al.* 2010: 15ff.).

The AU has been involved in activities related to promoting peace, security and stability in the DRC where the EU has supplied economic resources via the APF and advice including support of disarmament and support of the general elections (Siradag 2009: 59–66). Between 1993 and 2005, Burundi was ravaged by a civil war between Hutu rebels and the Tutsi-dominated army. Since 2003, the AU has been engaged in maintaining peace and security in the country as it decided to deploy 3,000 troops in the country with support from the EU (Murithi 2008: 74–6; Siradag 2009: 66–73; Daley 2006). It also has to be mentioned that the AU has deployed troops in Somalia which Paul Williams describes as 'an ill-conceived mission deployed to the wrong place at the wrong time by an institution incapable of meeting its grandiose statement of intent' (Williams 2009: 515, 526–7). From the start, it was obvious that the African Union could not pay for the mission, therefore it relied on financial assistance from the EU and several Western states, and later the UN (Williams 2009: 519–20). In conclusion,

> in fact, without the African Peace Facility it is unlikely that the AU would have been able to undertake any of these missions. Since implementation of the African Peace Facility, the relationship between the AU and the EU has developed quite strongly, resulting in the EU strategy for Africa and recently the extension of the joint EU-Africa strategy in December 2007.
>
> (Cilliers 2008: 12)

In conclusion, the EU has been willing to pursue an active conflict management policy in Africa. It has been willing to deploy troops even though this has been for fixed periods. The Union and its members have been willing to fund the operations and there has been a remarkable capability to coordinate and cooperate both within the EU itself and in this case with the UN and the AU. It appears that the explanation to this surprising situation has to be found in the merger of interests between on the one hand France and Great Britain and on the other hand groups, institutions and individuals which all seem to share an ambition to turn the EU into a significant international conflict manager (Chafer and Cumming 2010: 1143ff., 1137).

The conflict context

The EU's military conflict management operations in Africa have been focused on two geographical areas, the DRC and Chad–Darfur. Here, the background to the two Congo missions is scrutinized and then the regional context of the Chad/Darfur missions is looked into. It is done based on one assumption, namely that the dynamics of the two conflict complexes are so intimately interwoven that it makes good sense to treat them as one even though they both involve several separate EU interventions.

The issues in the Congo crises

Since the early years of the 1990s, the DRC has been characterized by continuous political instability. From 1996 till 1997, there was a war mainly affecting the eastern provinces of the enormous country. From 1998 until 2003, most parts of the DRC were ravaged by a bloody war involving a number of African countries such as Uganda, Rwanda, Angola and Zimbabwe (Nest 2001; Taylor and Williams 2001; Clark 2001). It was described as 'Africa's world war'. The situation is summarized by Chivvis (2007: 21–2), who states:

> In the late 1990s, the DRC was in an anarchic, Hobbesian state of war. The challenges to nation building were very great. [. . .] By 2000, the DRC had imploded as foreign armies and rebel groups fought in support of [President] Kabila, against him or among themselves.

At the turn of the century, the Congo had almost collapsed because of these bloody wars. Because of the increasingly chaotic situation, it was obvious to the outside world that something had to be done to stop the anarchy that was threatening a total collapse of the

Congolese state. Because of massive international pressure negotiations on a peace settlement were initiated. They took place in South Africa and resulted in late 2002 in the Sun City/Pretoria peace agreement for the DRC. The agreement provided for demobilization of the Congolese army, integration of rival factions and the establishment of a democratic government. In separate agreements in 2002, Rwanda and Uganda agreed to withdraw their troops from the Congo (Chivvis 2007: 22–3).

The local actors

In the wake of the Sun City agreement, the first challenge was to establish a minimum of security in the country. However, large parts of the country remained lawless and were outside the control of the government in Kinshasa. The situation was especially serious in Ituri and in the two Kivu provinces. Vlassenroot and Raeymaekers (2004: 387) argue strongly that the outbreak of violence in Ituri was the result of 'exploitation, by local and regional actors, of deeply rooted local conflict over access to land, economic opportunity and political power'. The result was a struggle between informal networks linking local warlords and rebel leaders to their external sponsors, mainly Uganda and Rwanda.

The root causes of the conflicts in the region are old tensions between two ethnic communities over land and over the access to land. The two groups are the Hema who are traditionally pastoralists and the Lendu communities which are traditionally agriculturalists (Pottier 2008: 331-5). If access to land was the starting point of the violence, it seems as if the continuation of the conflicts was the result of the interplay between local and national actors. In particular from 1996/97, different local and foreign militias began to operate in Ituri (Vlassenroot and Raeymaekers 2004: 388ff.; 412).

The different local elites in Ituri sought to exploit the situation by strengthening their respective positions in the local power struggle by allying themselves with foreign as well as national army commanders. With the Ugandan army openly supporting one of these warlords, Lubanga, affiliated with the Hema groups, the civil war escalated. In May 2003, the Ugandan forces withdraw from Ituri in compliance with the peace accords. Following the retreat of the Ugandan army, the humanitarian and security situation in the region degraded with heavy fighting between Hema and Lendu militias (Hoebeke *et al.* 2007: 8). The fighting jeopardized the peace and also the UN force on the ground appeared to be in danger. 'Observers feared a repeat of Srebrenica', Chivvis (2007) states.[9] Vlassenroot and Raeymaekers (2004: 397) mention that the local radio, 'Radio Candipas', was particularly disturbing in this context as it had 'worrying resemblance to the upbeat of the Rwandan genocide [. . .] [with an] agenda of apparent ethnic purification'. The propaganda of the radio had a clearly anti-Lendu dimension.

Operation Artemis

In the spring of 2003, many observers warned that a new outbreak of violence could threaten the national peace process aimed at reaching a negotiated settlement (Ulriksen *et al.* 2004: 509–11; Faria 2004a). In that situation, the UN General Secretary Kofi Annan asked for the establishment of a coalition willing to bring an end to the humanitarian crisis in Ituri. At the same time, the coalition should secure an interim solution until it was possible to deploy an effective UN force in the province. Operation *Artemis* was launched in June 2003 with the aim to stabilize the security situation, improve the humanitarian situation in and around the main town of Bunia (Faria 2004a: 2040; Ulriksen *et al.* 2004) and if possible to prevent a possible genocide.

The superior European force clearly resulted in pacifying the regional capital Bunia within a few days. Thus, evaluated against the declared objective, the mission was fairly successful. But stabilizing Bunia was not the same as stabilizing the region as the violence moved into the countryside (Pottier 2008: 438). Ituri remained unstable following the retreat of *Artemis* and the handover of responsibilities to the UN force, MONUC. A major reason for the continued instability was the slow Disarmament, Demobilization and Reintegration (DDR) process (Hoebeke *et al.* 2007: 8ff.). From late 2004, the situation in Ituri began to deteriorate again resulting in an increase in the number of conflicts both among the militias and between the UN forces and militias. The growth in violence was in part an expression of the resistance to the gradual extension of the authority of the central Congolese state (Chivvis 2007: 29f.).

Irrespective of the problems following the ending of Operation *Artemis*, the operation was important as it had a positive impact on the DRC peace process. The high priority given to establishing peace and stability in the DRC by promoting democracy explains the following involvement of the EU in the peace process which, according to the Sun City agreement, in part predicated on the promise of democracy (Chivvis 2007: 25). Democratization was seen as a necessary part of the process promoting security and stability. Concretely, the EU's support focused on the reforming and rebuilding of the Congolese national police. During the years 2005–06, the main efforts were put into preparing a police force large enough and sufficiently well trained to handle responses arising from the upcoming elections (Chivvis 2007: 31; Gegout 2007: 6–8). Towards the end of 2005, the UN launched a request to the EU for assistance in securing the DRC elections scheduled for the summer of 2006. The EU responded positively to this request and as mentioned, it deployed around 1,000 troops in Kinshasa during the election campaign.

To sum up, no doubt the EU has been actively involved in promoting peace and stability in the DRC. Evaluated against the narrow aim of Operation Artemis, it was a success. It was also the case with the stabilization mission in Kinshasa in 2006. Taking a more general perspective on the two interventions, it is doubtful if it is possible to maintain that the two missions have contributed to the long-term stability of the DRC. On the other hand, it is highly probable that the two missions have contributed to establishing the EU as a global conflict manager and, thus, they have also served European interests.

The issues in the Darfur–Chad conflict

For many years, the conflicts in Chad and Darfur have been closely interlinked. 'The Chadian civil war is often described as a "spill over" from Darfur. This is a simplification. Darfur's war actually began as a spill over from Chad more than 20 years ago and the two conflicts have been entangled ever since,' it is emphasized by de Waal (2008: 1; Marchal 2008: 429ff.). It is not only a question of the entanglement of the two conflicts. There is also an internal Chadian conflict and several internal Sudanese disagreements adding to the complexities of the overall picture. Moreover, the involvement of a number of African states as well as non-African actors such as France and the United States (US) add both a regional and an international dimension to the conflict (De Maio 2010: 28f.).

The Chadian actors

Boggero (2009: 21) argues that the Chadian society de facto is portioned into several sovereign zones 'even if the fiction of their juridical integration is maintained'. It is characteristic of Chad that there was never a single dominant ruling elite but rather a lack of hegemony. The political scene was characterized by numerous and competing elites and thus a high level of factionalism. Therefore, politics in Chad has not much to do with political ideology or political principles. Instead, the ethnic elites rely on personal affiliates and personal charisma (Boggero 2009: 22). Each of the so-called zones belongs to a different ethnic group or clan. President Idriss Déby belongs to the Zaghawa clan which shows a mosaic of different players, sub-clans and sub-interests. The Zaghawa is a semi-nomadic tribe with ties on both sides of the Chad–Sudan border and it is one of the three original indigenous populations of Darfur in Sudan (Boggero 2009: 1).

When in 1990 Idriss Déby assumed power, it was with the support of the Sudanese Zaghawa as well as the Sudanese security apparatus. It was characteristic that the Sudanese Zaghawa was strongly represented in the military and security apparatus of Chad (Marchal 2008: 431) and many of the Sudanese Zaghawa were promoted through the ranks of these institutions. Apparently, these promotions carried an implicit commitment, namely that the Chadian Zaghawa, if needed, would support their kinspeople in Darfur.

As soon as he was in power, Idriss Déby purged the ranks of his supporters. From then on, Déby relied heavily on a very narrow circle of close kinsmen. By using state finance as his personal property and distributing largesse, in return he received loyalty from these individuals and groups (de Waal 2008: 1). In the years following his takeover of power, Idriss Déby was increasingly faced with mounting discontent both among his own ethnic group and also in the Chadian society at large (De Maio 2010: 33ff.; Marchal 2008: 433). Therefore, President Déby relied on the Darfur groups for his own security and these groups played a significant role in defending the President against the Sudanese offensive both in 2006 and in February 2008 (de Waal 2008: 1; De Maio 2010: 32ff.).

The discontent resulted, in May 2004, in an attempted coup against the President and during the following retaliation Idriss Déby further alienated his own Zaghawa sub-clan, the Bideyat. With the growing factionalism in the country, the coup represented an alarming sign. 'It was felt like a clearly visible signal of a disintegration of Déby's main constituency, a breakdown of the usual ethnic politics into even smaller units' (Boggero 2009: 22). In February 2008, a new coup was mounted against the President. This time, the capital came close to falling into the hands of the rebels, who were openly supported by Sudan. It appears that France was far from passive during the attack on the capital. Paris was deeply worried and was concerned by the possibility of a regime change in N'Djamena initiated and coordinated by Sudan, not least in the middle of the Darfur crisis (Marchal 2008: 434). It is important to note that since 1986, France has had troops stationed in Chad and the French army has assisted the Chadian army with intelligence and logistics, etc. Thereby, the French forces have been a key factor in the country's civil war.

The Darfur conflict

There is also an internal Sudanese dynamics adding to the cross-border conflict. Since independence from Britain in 1956, Khartoum has been discriminating against Darfur in economic, administrative and political respect, meaning that the life of 'the Darfurians remained desperately poor and underserviced' (de Waal 2007: 1039; Cobham 2005). The basic pattern of grievances was that Darfur has been denied its share in political power and national wealth while the government at the same time used divide-and-rule tactics allowing local militias to destroy people's livelihoods. 'In retrospect, the mystery is not why the war in Darfur broke out, but why it took so long to do so' (de Waal 2007: 1040).

The civil war was initiated by the attacks of the two rebel groups, the 'Sudan Liberation Movement/Army' (SLM/A) and the 'Justice and Equality Movement' (JEM) against government installations. It appears that the two insurgency movements were primarily motivated by the lack of development in the Darfur region. From the outset, both the SLM/A and the JEM aimed at obtaining support from all people not just selected groups because the large majority of the population was negatively affected by the Khartoum government's policy of marginalization (Grawert 2008: 599ff.; Almeida 2008: 100f.). It appears that the government deliberately used ethnicity as a means to redirect the insurgency's grievances. Using the Janjaweed militia as an ethnic card, the government was able to pit the 'African' tribes against the 'Arab' tribes. By portraying the conflict as a 'tribal war' and by denying the political movement behind the insurgency, Khartoum has been able to gain time (de Waal 2005: 197ff.; Almeida 2008: 82ff.).

The government was so successful at manipulating ethnicity in Darfur because of the years of drought in the mid 1980s which exacerbated the competition for resources in the region (Almeida 2008: 63ff.; de Waal 2005). The occurrence of droughts and desertification in Darfur strongly affected the vital migration patterns in the region. When land and resources were abundant, 'Arab' nomads and 'African' agriculturalists used to have an accord of collaboration. As the resources became more and more scarce, the greater became the friction between nomads and agriculturalists (Almeida 2008: 52–81).

As the situation in Darfur deteriorated in the early 2000s, a number of the Sudanese Zaghawa officers represented in the security apparatus of Chad moved back to Sudan to set up the Darfur insurgency (Marchal 2008: 431ff.). Nevertheless, during the first years of the conflict in Darfur, the Sudanese government in Khartoum provided President Déby with funds to divide and weaken the Darfur insurgency, notably the JEM (Boggero 2009: 22). In the summer of 2005, JEM and Déby concluded a gentlemen's agreement allowing the JEM to use Chad as a sanctuary (Marchal 2008: 432). It is no coincidence that since then, Khartoum has emphasized the strong connections between the Darfur field commanders and N'Djamena and the Sudanese government has responded by backing Chadian rebels (de Waal 2008: 2). From 2007 and onwards, a number of the militia groups including the JEM received a dramatic increase in military supplies from their sources in Chad, allowing them to conduct more armed operations in Darfur. The renewed military operations in turn provoked acts of retaliation by Khartoum, also hitting civilians (Marchal 2008: 435).

EUFOR Chad/CAR

The February 2008 attack on the Chadian capital N'Djamena was seen as yet another attempt by the Sudanese government to delay or prevent the deployment of a foreign military force in the region (Marchal 2008: 429f.). The February 2008 situation seems to have convinced the French government that Chad without Déby was a worse proposition than with him and Paris therefore swung back behind the President, it is argued by de Waal (2008: 2). With the election of Nicolas Sarkozy in 2007, French policy shifted towards focusing on using Chad as a launch pad for humanitarian action in Darfur including military support of a UN protection force (de Waal 2008: 3f.).

EUFOR Chad/CAR mission had the objective of facilitating the delivery of humanitarian aid and the free movement of humanitarian personnel. Therefore, the initiative was obviously to be understood as an integral element in the EU's effort to contribute to solving the crisis in Darfur (Council of the EU 2009g). As most of the French troops deployed as part of the EU military operation came from the troops already in the country, not only the rebels operating in Chad but also French NGOs expressed concern that there was a hidden agenda behind the activist French policy (Dijkstra 2010: 397–402). While EUFOR's mandate was for impartial civilian protection, it was a substantially French initiative and it was seen by all political actors in the region as a military protection for President Déby and a non-neutral force (de Waal 2008: 1).

Summing up, it is difficult to evaluate what the actual impact of the EUFOR Chad/CAR mission has been and to measure its humanitarian impact (Vines 2010: 1095). 'It is probably more accurate to credit this EUFOR operation with increasing European learning and coordination on how to conduct such a bridging exercise successfully than with fulfilling a meaningful humanitarian mandate' (Vines 2010: 1096). The bottom line seems to be the combination of the remarkably active French role in relation to making the decision to deploy the EU troops and the obvious French interests in stabilizing the regime of Idriss Déby, which raises serious doubts about the motives as well as about the derived consequences of the mission (Dijkstra 2010: 404–5).

Darfur: EU support to the AU mission – AMIS

The Peace and Security Council of the African Union stressed that the AU should play a more active role in resolving the Darfur crisis and also that the organization should work closely with among others the EU to maintain peace and stability in the region. Therefore, the AU has deployed troops under AMIS I and AMIS II operations in Darfur in order to protect the civilians. By means of the APF, the EU has handsomely supported the AU with financial, logistical and human resources (Murithi 2008: 76–8; Siradag 2009: 43–59).

The EU supported the political, military and police efforts of the AU aimed at addressing the crisis in Darfur. The EU made available equipment, provided planning and technical assistance and deployed military observers. It trained African troops, helped with tactical and strategic transportation and provided police assistance and training. The Council appointed a Special EU representative, Torben Brylle, to the region with the responsibility to coordinate the EU's contributions to AMIS. In addition to the EU assistance, EU member states made substantial bilateral contributions taking the overall EU contributions to AMIS to some 500 million euros for the period 2004–2007 (Council, Factsheet 2008). In summary, even though part of the motivation for the significant support via the APF was to avoid deploying European troops in Darfur, it is worth stressing that AMIS I and AMIS II would have been impossible without the support from the EU and the member states.

Conclusion

The chapter has shown that the EU has pursued an active conflict management policy in Africa. It was the argument that this policy has to be explained with reference to a merger of interests between, on the one hand, France and the UK and, on the other, interests within the EU. The merger of interests has its background in common concerns for Africa and interest in giving the EU a status as a global conflict manager. The combination of these interests has manifested itself in a capacity to act in a number of situations. Also, it has shown itself in a capability to fund conflict management operations in Africa. Finally, the EU has shown its capability to cooperate both among the European institutions and also closely with both the UN and the AU.

The chapter has analysed the conflict management policies in two concrete conflict areas, namely the DRC and Darfur–Chad. On a short-term basis, the EU interventions analysed can be described as relatively successful. The EU deployments were successful so far as they functioned effectively as short-term 'bridging' stabilization missions until the UN could take over. Having established that, it has to be stressed that the long-term effects of the European conflict management operations have been limited, at best. One possible explanation why the effects have been so limited is that the interventions were never intended to do anything about the root causes of the conflicts (Vines 2010). The background to the conflicts appears to be the social structures which in all the cases are characterized by divisions and conflicts along ethnic lines. Thus, the conflicts were at sub-state level between groups with fairly narrow loyalties which, at least in the Chad case, but also in the Congo, includes the political leadership in the country.

It would be naïve not to assume that the policy- and decision-makers in Brussels, London and Paris have been aware of these circumstances. If that assumption is correct, it explains a number of things. It explains why the fixed time limits have been so important in the cases where the EU deployed soldiers on the ground in Africa. It explains why the EU intervened based on the expectation that the UN would continue the operations when the European soldiers had left. It also explains the willingness of the European member states, and not only of France and the UK, to vote in favour of launching the conflict management operations. These three circumstances point towards a conclusion stressing that the launch of the highly profiled military missions in the DRC and in Chad was much more about the EU and about its status as a global actor than it was about Africa.

Notes

1 Confidential interviews, Council Secretariat, Brussels, December 2005.
2 Interviews, Council General Secretariat, Brussels, October 2008.
3 Interview, Council General Secretariat, Brussels, October 2008.
4 Personal interview, Brussels, October 2008.
5 Personal interviews, Brussels, October 2008; personal interviews, Brussels, December 2005.
6 Personal interviews, Council Secretariat, Brussels, October 2008.
7 Interviews, Council Secretariat, Brussels, October 2008.
8 Personal interviews, Council Secretariat, October 2008.
9 Personal interview, Brussels, December 2005.

6 The EU and the Israeli–Palestinian conflict

Asaf Siniver

Introduction

Since the early 1990s the European Union (EU) has actively supported a two-state solution to the Israeli–Palestinian conflict via a multitude of bilateral agreements with the two parties, the facilitation of regional frameworks for dialogue, financial assistance to the Palestinian Authority, and participation in the Quartet, alongside the United States (US), Russia and the United Nations (UN). However, given the long-established diplomatic, political and economic links with both Israel and the Palestinian Authority on one hand, and in the absence of a viable peace 'process' for several years now on the other, the EU is invariably caught between its promising rhetoric on the desirable peaceful ending of the conflict and its lack of clout to turn words to tangible actions on the ground. This chapter begins with a brief background of the Israeli–Palestinian/Arab conflict and the role of the EU and other third parties in trying to bring it to a peaceful resolution. The analysis of EU capabilities and the context of this conflict show that ultimately the EU has failed to make the necessary transition from rhetorical commitments to peace and stability in the conflict to meaningful actions on the ground which could change the stakes or impact on the disputants' positions.

A brief history of the Arab–Israeli conflict

Since its inception more than six decades ago, the Arab–Israeli conflict has been undoubtedly one of the most protracted and intractable conflicts in the twentieth and twenty-first centuries. It encompasses competing religious, ideological, ethnic and historical claims by Jews and Muslims, Israelis and Arabs, each group with its own constructed narrative about the trajectory of historical events that ultimately resulted in the independence of the Jewish state in 1948 and the subsequent outbreak of the conflict.

Mapping the history of the conflict is therefore incredibly difficult since both parties claim historical provenance in the land of Palestine that dates back hundreds and thousands of years. In modern times, however, roots of the conflict are commonly traced back to the migration of Eastern European Jews to Palestine in the late nineteenth century. In the face of increasing persecution and state-sponsored anti-Semitic attacks in Tsarist Russia, Zionism emerged as the ideological answer by calling for a homeland for the Jews in their ancestral 'Land of Israel'. Invariably these waves of Jewish migration to Palestine, accompanied by the purchase of land from indigenous Arab groups, led to cycles of violent skirmishes, which only seemed to increase when the land became a British Mandate at the end of the First World War. Unable to control the situation in Palestine, the British government referred the matter to the United Nations, and in November 1947 the General Assembly passed Resolution

181, calling for the partition of the land to a Jewish state and an Arab state (with Jerusalem awarded international status). Whilst the Arabs rejected the partition plan, the Jews accepted it and in May 1948 declared the establishment of the State of Israel, leading to the first Arab–Israeli war. The nature of the conflict changed dramatically following the Six Day War of June 1967, with Israel now occupying the West Bank and East Jerusalem (previously controlled by Jordan), the Gaza Strip and the Sinai Peninsula (taken from Egypt), and the Syrian Golan Heights. Adding to the territorial dimension of the conflict was the rise of the Palestine Liberation Organization (PLO) in 1964, which by methods of terrorism and international diplomacy brought to the fore the plight of the Palestinian people and their struggle for recognition and self-determination. Peace treaties between Israel and Egypt (1979) and Israel and Jordan (1994) significantly reduced the prospect of further conventional Arab–Israeli wars, though the Israeli–Palestinian question remained largely unanswered until the launching of the Oslo peace process in the early 1990s. Nevertheless, despite the omnipresence of mediation in this period, a significant gap remains between the parties on the following core issues: Jerusalem, borders, Israeli settlements in the occupied West Bank, and the fate of the Palestinian refugees.

Third party involvement in the conflict

During the first two decades of the Arab–Israeli conflict (between 1948 and 1967), third parties rarely engaged in sustained efforts to bring about a peaceful resolution, with the UN leading the most notable efforts. Following Israel's territorial expansion in the Six Day War and the passing of UN Security Council Resolution 242 in 1967 (setting the formula of 'land for peace' as the basis for future Arab–Israeli settlement), the conflict gradually became an arena for superpower competition by proxy, with successive American administrations maintaining Israel's qualitative military superiority, whilst the Soviets backed radical Arab regimes in the region, most notably Egypt and Syria. Diplomatically, too, the US had gradually become the dominant player in the region, by presenting its own peace initiatives outside the UN framework and successfully pushing the Soviets to the sidelines of Middle East diplomacy. Accordingly American mediators helped to produce three disengagement agreements between Israel and Egypt and Syria in 1974–5, and an Israeli–Egyptian peace agreement in 1979. These successful mediation efforts not only cemented the US role as the principal mediator in the region, but they also effectively prevented any prospects of other third parties presenting alternative proposals or peace plans to the disputants. Thus American hegemony (together with local and regional contexts) accounts for much of the ebb and flow in diplomatic activity in the conflict in the past 30 years, with the most important case of non-US mediation in this period (the Norwegian-sponsored Oslo talks) being one of providing 'good offices', rather than formulating proposals and leading the negotiations.

The first attempt at a collective European position on the conflict came in 1973 in response to the Yom Kippur War. Recognising their vulnerability to the emerging Arab oil embargo, the nine members of the European Council called for a resolution of the conflict based on UN Resolution 242, and, most significantly and in a clear shift from the American position, recognised the rights of the Palestinian people (Altunisik 2008: 106). The European Council's position on the conflict was later crystallised in the June 1980 Venice Declaration. This document is still considered the cornerstone of the European approach to the conflict, primarily for its explicit call for Palestinian self-determination, the recognition of the PLO as the legitimate representative of the Palestinian people in future negotiations, and the illegality of Israeli settlements in the Occupied Territories (Venice Declaration 1980). These statements and others have precluded the possibility of European mediation in the conflict due to strong feelings in Israel of anti-Israeli bias in Europe (Yacobi and Newman 2007). Even with the end of the Cold War and the 1991 Gulf Crisis, which created new geopolitical opportunities for the region, European involvement remained marginal. Importantly, however, the American-sponsored 1991 Madrid Peace Conference and the beginning of a 'peace process' between Israel and the PLO following the signing of the Oslo Accords in September 1993, served to vindicate Europe's earlier visions for Arab–Israeli peace. Moreover, with Israel and the PLO recognising each other's existence and legitimacy, and their acceptance of the 'land-for-peace' formula as established in UN resolutions 242 (1967) and 338 (1973), there was now scope for the EU to capitalise on its normative commitment to international law, human rights and democracy promotion. With the US still in charge of mediating and managing negotiations between Israel and the PLO, the EU assumed the role of the largest financier of the peace process through bilateral agreements with the parties as well as broader frameworks such as the 1995 Euro-Mediterranean Partnership (EMP). However, not content with its important, though limited role as financier of the process, the EU continued in this period to promote its normative vision in the conflict. Accordingly, in its 1999 Berlin Declaration the EU further advanced its support for Palestinian self-determination, calling for a viable and democratic Palestinian state alongside a secure Israeli state – a vision which at the time was rejected by both Israel and the US. With the adoption of the 2003 road map for peace, however, the EU once again felt vindicated.

Despite the EU's remarkable vision and important financial support for the peace process, it nevertheless remains a marginal actor, certainly as far as power mediation is concerned. As the following sections will show, the EU's modest involvement stems from external contexts as well as internal deficiencies. However, in assessing the EU's performance in this conflict, one must be aware of the very limited room for manoeuvre it can operate in, given the American hegemonic grip of the diplomacy of the conflict, as well as Israel's reluctance to consider non-US initiatives.

EU capabilities

Since the signing of the Oslo Accords between Israel and the PLO in September 1993 the EU has sought various ways of engagement with the parties, under the pillars of democracy promotion in the Middle East at large, promotion and protection of human rights and international law, and the right to self-determination of both parties to the conflict (Tocci 2007). Substantively, however, the EU has struggled to act upon these noble principles and bring about a meaningful change on the ground. Therefore the following assessment of EU capabilities demonstrates significant shortcomings in the EU's capabilities to act as well as its capabilities to coordinate and cooperate. On the other hand, the EU has consistently displayed capabilities to fund, both short-term and long-term. In its capabilities to act, the EU has sent two missions to the region, one to monitor the Rafah border crossing between the Gaza Strip and Egypt (EUBAM), and the other to train Palestinian police forces (EUPOL COPPS), both with mixed results, whilst continually supporting institution building in Palestine through various initiatives. Undoubtedly the EU's most significant capability in this conflict is its willingness to commit vast amounts of money to short- and long-term projects designed to advance the EU's three normative pillars (international law, human rights and democracy promotion). Concerning its capabilities to coordinate and cooperate, the EU has been consistently compromised in its efforts to manage the conflict by its cumbersome organisational structure and the lack of consensus between member states, not only on how to cooperate with other external actors, such as the US, but also on how to present a unified and coherent European approach to resolution of the conflict.

Capabilities to act

During the first years of the Oslo peace process the EU was largely excluded from any major diplomatic efforts, not least because it had not put in place effective foreign policy mechanisms in the first years following the 1993 Maastricht Treaty. Since then, however, several political frameworks have been developed, including the Common Foreign and Security Policy (CFSP), the Common Security and Defence Policy (CSDP), the European Neighbourhood Policy (ENP) and the Quartet (together with the UN, US and Russia), all bearing important elements or instruments of engagement with the conflict. As the following analysis will show, notwithstanding the marginal contribution of such frameworks to isolated areas, overall they have failed to bring about a positive and tangible change in the EU's ability to leave its mark on the peace process.

The CFSP was established in 1992 and its main objectives were spelled out in the Amsterdam Treaty five years later. They include the safeguarding of the common norms and interests of the EU, preserving peace and strengthening international security, promoting international cooperation and developing and consolidating liberal-democratic values (Aybet 2000). To this extent common strategies have been developed for potential hot spots such as Russia, Ukraine and the Middle East. More specifically to the Israeli–Palestinian conflict, regular mechanisms of dialogue between the Middle East parties and European officials on various levels have been put in place. In addition a special representative to the Middle East was appointed to provide a direct link and to enable constant engagement with developments in the region (including the Syrian and Lebanese tracks). In order to improve effectiveness and credibility, the key post of High Representative for the CFSP was created in 1997, for the purpose of assisting the Presidency and working closely with the Commission and individual member states. One area where the High Representative has been particularly active is the Middle East peace process. Javier Solana, who held the post from 1999–2009, was respected by all parties in the region, and was viewed as a 'real asset' for the EU (House of Lords 2007: 36), whereas his successor, Catherine Ashton, has been criticised for lacking the necessary gravitas to help the EU achieve a greater global impact.[1] While some see the appointment of the High Representative for the CFSP as a positive step towards improving the performance and impact of the EU on the Middle East peace process (Soetendorp 2002: 294), others argue to the contrary and point to the increasing compartmentalisation of the EU's external relations (Sjursen 2003: 38).

An important operational arm of the CFSP is the CSDP which was established in 1999 for the purpose of providing effective and credible military and civilian capabilities to undertake a full range of conflict prevention and crisis management tasks (Europa 2010a). In recent years this attempt by the EU to provide the CFSP with more coherence and additional substance by creating its own military capabilities has put into question the future of its relations with NATO, as EU member states continue steadily to pursue an autonomous political–military capacity (Howorth 2003).

EUPOL COPPS and EUBAM

With relation to the Middle East peace process, the CSDP has been particularly active by setting up two civilian crisis management missions to address specific areas in the Palestinian

Territories: the European Coordinating Office for Palestinian Police Support (EUPOL COPPS) and the EU Border Assistance Mission (EUBAM) Rafah. The first mission started in January 2006 with a three-year mandate, its main aim being to contribute to the establishment of sustainable and effective policing arrangements in Palestine in accordance with the highest Western standards. Some of the projects undertaken by the mission include the training of police officers, providing equipment, and organising joint workshops with Palestinian and Israeli police officers (EU Council Secretariat 2006c). In 2009 the mandate of the mission was extended further, and its budget for 2010 was €6,650,000, employing 41 EU staff and 25 local staff (EU CSDP 2010). The EUBAM Rafah mission was launched in November 2005 following Israel's unilateral withdrawal from the Gaza Strip. The mission's mandate is to monitor the border area of Rafah border crossing between Egypt and the Palestinian Authority, contribute to Palestinian capacity for border control, and assist with liaisons between Israel, Egypt and the Palestinian Authority. However, following the Hamas takeover of the Gaza Strip in June 2007 the EU mission was temporarily suspended. The mission's budget for 2009–10 stood at €1,120,000, employing 19 EU staff and eight local staff (EU CSDP 2009). Indeed, although the Rafah mission can be understood as an important confidence-building measure between Israelis and Palestinians, some question the value of such limited missions under conditions of occupation and with little linkage to high-level political engagements. As one senior Palestinian observed, these small tokens were simply not enough: 'I do not think that our main problem is that of not having enough policemen' (House of Lords 2007: 47). While one should not disregard altogether the potential benefits of such limited initiatives, it is hard to escape the conclusion that overall, and given the EU's economic weight and the varied resources collectively at its disposal, it has failed to leave a meaningful impact on the Middle East peace process.

Capabilities to fund

One of the key reasons for the gap between rhetoric and reality stems from the EU's failure to use as political leverage its financier status in this conflict. This is particularly evident within the context of the ENP, the EU's most visible initiative to facilitate bilateral relations with Israel and the Palestinian Authority. At least notionally, this framework held greater potential for influence on the parties due to its direct bilateral nature (Kronenberger and Wouters 2005). EU's contractual ties with Israel began in the 1960s and have been gradually upgraded to cover extensive areas such as free trade agreements, scientific and technical cooperation, and other social and cultural collaborations. In 2007 the EU exported to Israel €14 billion of goods, and imported Israeli goods worth €11.3 billion. Under the terms of the ENP, Israel also receives €2 million per year between 2007–2013 from the EU in bilateral allocation, primarily for technical and institutional cooperation (European Commission Trade 2010).

Bilateral trade ties with the Palestinian Authority are understandably more modest due to the Israeli occupation and the absence of statehood status (overall trade in 2006 amounted to €52 million), and as such have focused more on aid to address the humanitarian situation in the occupied territories and to support state-building. Some examples include the restarting in 2007 of a three-year, €4 million project to support the Palestinian Ministry of Finance through staff training and development in the Internal Audit and Internal Control departments; a two-year, €2.7 million project designed to help the automation of Palestinian customs systems; the issue of guarantees to small businesses totalling more than €5 million (Europa 2008). Another aspect of the EU's support for institution building and democracy promotion was the participation of an observer mission of 260 members to the Palestinian presidential elections in 2005, and a similar mission for the Palestinian parliamentary elections in January 2006, costing €2.5 million and €3 million respectively (Altunisik 2008). In 2008 the EU introduced PEGASE (*Mécanisme Palestino-Européen de Gestion de l'Aide Socio-Economique*), a three-year mechanism designed to channel European and international assistance to institution and state building and Palestine, to replace the Temporary International Mechanism (TIM), which has been in place since 2006. Through PEGASE, the EU has responded quickly to the humanitarian crisis in Gaza following Operation Cast Lead. In 2009 EU member states had pledged €440 million, more than half of which (€233 million) was directed to the three-year Palestinian Reform and Development Plan (PRDP), €168 million for recurrent expenditure, and €65 million for other development projects. The same year the EU also pledged €67 million to support UNRWA (the United Nations Relief and Works Agency for Palestine Refugees), and a further €61 million in humanitarian and food aid through the European Commission's Humanitarian Aid Office (ECHO). Through PEGASE the EU also pays the salaries and pensions of more than 28,000 public service providers and pensioners, as well as social allowances for nearly 25,000 vulnerable households (CIDSE 2009).

The underlying principle of the EU in its bilateral relations with its neighbours through the ENP framework is one of conditionality or legal obligations embedded in agreements, in order to promote long-term political, economic, social and structural changes to bring about peace, democracy and respect for human rights and international law (Sasse 2008: 295). However, in the application of this policy to offer incentives for domestic reform, the EU has failed to demand the appropriate reciprocal action from Israel and the Palestinian Authority. In particular, the EU has adopted a rather compromising approach towards Israel's continuing abuse of human rights and violation of international law in the occupied territories. Thus, much to the chagrin of several member states, the EU has failed to use the upgrade in EU–Israel relations as leverage against Israeli cooperation on relieving the humanitarian crisis in Gaza. The failure to use the incentive of upgraded relations to get Israel to lift the blockade of Gaza is yet another example of the widening gap between EU's rhetoric on human rights and international law, and its abilities to pursue these noble principles. The EU has also failed to demand the implementation of political and judicial reforms in the Palestinian territories. The message thus coming from the EU appeared to be vague in terms of the enforcement structures linked to the conditionality-based bilateral ties. Israel continued to enjoy unprecedented benefits from its special association with the EU despite its controversial policies against the Palestinians, and the Palestinian Authority continued to receive generous financial aid from the EU, the largest donor to the Palestinian Authority, with an estimated €2 billion of financial assistance between 1994 and 2006 (Tocci 2007: 124), while showing limited commitment to carry out various reform programmes.

To some extent the root causes of this failed policy lie in the EU's (and particularly Germany's) yielding to Israel's pressure to separate the political from the economic spheres of interaction, and to obvious post-war historical and political sensitivities to Israel's accusations of anti-Israel policies (Tovias 2003), as well as the understanding that the Palestinian government sometimes had to take strong and undemocratic actions to counter the rising power of opposition forces (Le More 2005). The inevitable loss of EU credibility was demonstrated following the electoral victory of Hamas in January 2006. Toeing the Israeli and American line, the EU decided to boycott the militant Islamism movement and refused to engage in a political dialogue. However, while boycotting the democratically elected Hamas government in the Gaza Strip, the EU continued its support for the unelected Fatah government in the West Bank. The inevitable result of this policy was that the EU had lost whatever incentives it originally had to promote reconciliation between the warring factions. By heralding the promotion of democracy in the Middle East as the cornerstone of EU normative power (Pace 2007), only to then refuse to acknowledge the outcome of elections which the EU's own election observation mission described as 'open and fairly contested' (EU Election Observation Mission 2006), the EU displayed once more the inherent inconsistencies between its rhetoric and its actions.

Capabilities to coordinate and cooperate

In many ways the EU's failure to deliver on its normative promises and to effectively use its financial muscles as leverage, particularly against Israel, can be explained by the organisational and structural shortcomings. As a French diplomat recently conceded in a round table on EU policies in the Middle East, 'it is hard to talk with one voice when there are 27 different member states' (Herrera 2008). The foreign policies of most EU countries can be summed up by their relations with the big powers (US, China, Russia), their immediate neighbours, and their former colonies. The majority of EU members do not have real interest in, or knowledge of, the intricacies of the Israeli–Palestinian conflict, beyond the obligatory rhetoric about their commitment to a just and lasting peace in the region. This reality was evident in the EU's failure to adopt a coherent response to Israel's offensive in Gaza in 2008–09. Whereas the Czech presidency of the EU described Israeli actions as 'defensive, not offensive', the British officials responded that 'it is not the position of the British government', whereas President Sarkozy of France condemned the 'dangerous military escalation'.[2] Indeed this oft-cited failure to present greater unity and coherence is a recurrent concern raised by EU member states themselves. A report published by the United Kingdom (UK) House of Lords in 2007 about the EU and the Middle East peace process has found that beyond the obvious divergent national priorities, there are some other constraining factors on the ability of the EU to speak with one voice. Cases in point are the six-month rotational presidencies, which have undermined 'the ability of the EU to act as singular, coherent actor'; the sheer number of EU members, which makes it harder to find 'a common policy which has an impact on the ground', and the visits of 'individual EU member State foreign ministers [which] did not enhance the image of the EU as a unified force' (House of Lords 2007: 31). In this respect the conclusion of Javier Solana, the High Representative for the EU's CFSP, could not be taken more seriously: 'I will tell you frankly what we should do: firstly we must maintain unity amongst ourselves' (House of Lords 2007: 32). The problem of internal cohesion invariably affects the EU's ability to communicate effectively its policies, beyond the normative dimension, to other parties in the conflict, including the disputants, the US and other government and non-governmental organisations. This failing is the result of the two main weaknesses of the EU with relation to the Middle East Peace Process (MEPP), namely its cumbersome structures and limited capabilities.

The structural problem is one of vertical and horizontal coherence – the first addresses the need for the member states to present coordinated policies, and the second deals with the reciprocal compatibility of the various EU external activities with each other (Sjursen 2003: 38). An acute problem here is the multitude of foreign policy sources which feed into the CFSP. These include, among others, the European Council (which lays down the general principles), the Council of Ministers (decides over external relations issues, including the CFSP), the Presidency of the Council (the driving force in the legislative and political processes), the High Representative for CFSP (assists the presidency in representing and implementing policies), the Special Representative for the Middle East Peace Process (provides direct link to developments in the region). In addition there are also separate EU delegations in Israel and the Palestinian Authority, and various committees and working groups for the purpose of facilitating the ongoing dialogue with the parties. The problem of limited resources and capabilities is understandable given the difficulty in building strong common institutions and developing efficient foreign policy mechanisms to translate words into action; however, it does not make the EU's failure to follow statements with concrete commitments on the ground more acceptable. As the report by the House of Lords concludes, 'the question now arises as to whether the EU has the capacity in place . . . to assist the peace process' (House of Lords 2007: 37).

The conflict context

After two decades of active engagement with the Middle East peace process the EU has very little to show as achievements, beyond the impressive financial commitment to the advancement of humanitarian, social and communal projects in the Palestinian Occupied Territories. However, the EU cannot be blamed for all the illnesses of the Israeli–Palestinian conflict and for the succession of diplomatic failures in recent years. The ultimate responsibility for these must lie with the parties themselves. Even the most powerful third party cannot force a solution upon the disputants if the right incentives or motivations to compromise are not present, as demonstrated by the failure of successive peace plans presented by the Bush Sr, Clinton, Bush Jr and Obama administrations. Nevertheless, while the ultimate power to negotiate and agree a settlement lies with Israel and the Palestinian Authority, it is the role of external actors to persuade, formulate and indeed manipulate (when necessary) the parties into viewing the status quo as one of a mutually hurting stalemate (Zartman 1985, 2001). In such situations the continuing costs of the present situation (as measured by loss of human lives, damage to the economy, losing face, threat perception, etc.) are no longer tolerable and a diplomatic solution is viewed as a preferred alternative.

Indeed, viewed from a rather charitable position one may argue that through its various political and economic programmes, the EU contributes to the Middle East peace process more than it should. Moreover it would be unfair to offer such a sober conclusion within a narrow analysis of EU engagement with the MEPP, while ignoring EU involvement in many other hot spots around the world at a time when it is still adjusting to the dramatic institutional and structural changes it has experienced since 1993, including the integration of Eastern Europe into the EU and the formulation of new security and defence policies against the background of a new global security environment. There is no doubt then that 'a more substantive role is certainly constrained by strategic deficiencies, lack of a compelling vision for the region, political disunity and institutional weaknesses' (Dannreuther 2004a: 153).

Global/regional levels

The context of the Israeli–Palestinian/Arab conflict, in its various dimensions, is largely independent of the efforts of the EU to make a difference. Domestic Israeli and Palestinian politics, Israeli-Palestinian relations, the disputants' relations with the Arab world, and the omnipresent role of American diplomacy must also be taken into account when assessing the EU's contribution to the management of the conflict. Starting with the global level, by the time the EU entered the arena in the early 1990s, the US was firmly positioned as the principal third party in the conflict and had no interest in letting other – let alone new – actors join in. With the end of the Cold War, the demise of the Soviet Union and the triumph in the Gulf War, the US found itself in the propitious position of devising a 'New Middle East' vision, which had effectively eliminated any alternatives to its approach to the conflict and style of diplomacy. Thus with the US firmly in control of managing the peace process (the secret Oslo negotiations notwithstanding), the EU had to settle for the role of chief financier of the process, though not the coordinator – a role which was assigned to the World Bank by the US (d'Alancon 1994: 47–8). Moreover, during the past decade the global and regional situations have been predominantly shaped by the US-led wars in Iraq and Afghanistan, as part of the Global War on Terror. As a result the Bush Jr administration failed to engage with the peace process in a more effective and consistent manner, and apart from the establishment of the Quartet and the launching of the failed road map for peace, left little mark on the diplomatic history of the conflict. With the contribution of several European countries to the war effort in Iraq and Afghanistan, and the EU's membership in the Quartet, the EU lacked both the capacity and the will to present a more vigorous alternative to the mothballed US-sponsored road map, as it has done in the past with the Venice and Berlin declarations. At a regional level too, the EU has failed to make a difference, beyond the various trade agreements and aid programmes to the Palestinian Authority through the ENP. Moreover, the peace treaties between Israel and Egypt (1979) and Jordan (1994) had significantly reduced the risk of the Israeli–Palestinian conflict escalating into a regional war, while negotiations between Israel and Syria during the 1990s were taking place under the auspices of Washington. Finally, security and intelligence cooperation between Israeli, Egyptian and Jordanian agencies was developing fast, again reducing the need for third party coordination. A notable exception here is the abovementioned EU Border Assistance Mission at Rafah (EUBAM RAFAH).

The Quartet

Based on UN Security Council resolutions 242, 338 and the principles of the 1991 Madrid peace conference, on 30 April 2003 President George W. Bush set out the Quartet's vision of a two-state solution in its road map document ('performance-based roadmap to a permanent two-state solution to the Israeli–Palestinian Conflict') (US Department of State 2003). Comprising the US, UN, the EU and Russia, it issued its first joint statement on 10 April 2002, expressing a commitment to a coordinated approach aimed at resolving the ongoing conflict between Israelis and Palestinians. The essence of the road map was the gradual progression towards a final and comprehensive settlement of the Israeli–Palestinian conflict by the end of 2005. To reach that destination both Israel and the Palestinian Authority were asked to take reciprocal steps towards the implementation of three phases. However, that noble idea of reciprocity and mutuality of interests proved to be the most disastrous element of the road map, as each side blamed the other for failing to fulfil its respective part of the bargain, eventually leading to stalemate and lack of confidence in the process. Phase I of the road map concerned the ending of terror and violence, normalisation of Palestinian life, and building Palestinian institutions (to be completed by May 2003). This phase required an unequivocal Palestinian statement reiterating Israel's right to exist, and a similar Israeli commitment to a two-state solution. It also included various steps that need to be taken by both sides on issues like security, institution building and civil society, settlements and humanitarian issues. Phase II (Transition, June–December 2003), focused on achieving progress towards an 'independent Palestinian state with provisional borders and attributes of new sovereignty, based on new constitution' (US Department of State 2003). Based on evaluation of the Quartet and satisfactory performance in the two previous phases, the objective of the third phase of the road map (Permanent status agreement and end of the Israeli–Palestinian conflict – 2004 to 2005) was the consolidation of reform and stabilisation of Palestinian institutions, and negotiations aimed at permanent status agreement in 2005, bringing about the end of occupation and an agreed, just, fair and realistic solution to the refugees issue, and a negotiated resolution of the status of Jerusalem.

That the road map failed in its task to bring about just and lasting peace should not be attributed solely to the (in)actions of the Quartet members. Violence on both sides prevented the parties from moving forward, and it could well be argued that nearly a decade since the launch of the road map, the parties are still bogged down in the first phase, squabbling over security requirements, institution building and the need to freeze the building or expansion of Israeli settlements. Still, given the unparalleled political, military and economic resources and expertise at the disposal of the Quartet members, the colossal failure of the road map is quite unfathomable.

In many ways the symptoms here are remarkably similar to the ones evident in the workings of the EU, and in particular the multitude of interests and independent policies of the Quartet members which invariably clash and fail to produce – despite the diplomatic rhetoric – coherent and feasible policies for progress. Future historians may ponder what drove the Bush administration to involve the EU, the UN and Russia in this peace initiative. Perhaps it was the need to reassure Arab concerns of American multilateralism in the era of the 'war on terror', or perhaps the necessity to save face in the event of another failed American mediation effort. On the face of it, each of the other members could complement the American approach to peacemaking in the region. At least notionally, the UN provides the necessary aura of international legitimacy to the process; the EU can offer attractive trade and other economic incentives to the package, while flagging its normative commitment to democracy promotion; whereas Russia's attempts to reassert itself as a regional heavy hitter will counteract America's established bias towards Israel. Nevertheless, while the inclusion of the EU in the Quartet is seen as testament to its growing role and legitimacy on the world stage, few would describe the Quartet as anything but an American-led, face-saving initiative. While historically the EU has been more vocal on the conflict than Russia and the UN, it still toes the American line, despite the fact that politically it probably represents the middle ground of the international community on most issues relating to the Israeli–Palestinian conflict. However, it seems that as long as Israel continues to be suspicious of a European pro-Palestinian bias, chances are that the United States will remain the dominant mediator (though not the honest broker so desperately sought on the Palestinian side). Given the EU's failure to translate words into action through its CFSP and CSDP frameworks, and the continuing gap between expectations and capabilities, it is not surprising to see that within the context of the Quartet as well, the EU has failed to make a meaningful impact by taking a coherent and distinguished direction away from the American-led stalemate.

State/local levels

At the state and local levels, domestic politics are also unfavourable to a more active EU engagement in the area of conflict management, particularly on the part of Israel. While the political leadership as well as the general public in the Palestinian territories welcomes a more direct European intervention in the peace process as a counterweight to the pro-Israeli bias of the US, many in Israel are critical of Europe's policies, even though they are largely identical to those advanced by the United States. Like the US, the EU is a member of the

Quartet and supports a two-state solution based on the pre-1967 borders. Both demand a freeze on Israeli settlements and the construction of the separation wall, as well as an end to violence and provocative policies on both sides. Yet the political elite in Israel as well as public opinion are traditionally hostile to the prospect of a greater European role in the conflict. The reasons for this antagonism are numerous, and range from the Jewish collective memory of the Holocaust, which leads many Israelis to still refuse to travel to Germany or to purchase German goods; Britain's alignment with the Arabs of Palestine during its mandate rule in the aftermath of the First World War, and its subsequent refusal to support Jewish statehood at the end of the Second World War; France's cooling off of relations with Israel following the Six Day War; and, more recently, the calls for the boycotting of Israeli goods and academics in some European capitals. Thus despite Israel's favoured trading status with the EU and the fact that culturally Israel sees itself firmly rooted in Europe rather than the Levant, European diplomatic overtures are often met with suspicion and dismissal not only by the Israeli public, but by the government as well. A most recent example came in December 2009, following the news of an EU draft policy paper which would recognise East Jerusalem as the capital of a future Palestinian state. Israel's foreign ministry has in turn criticised such a step which would harm the EU's 'ability to take part as a significant mediator in the political process between Israel and the Palestinians'.[3] Indeed as long as one of the parties to the conflict refuses to accept the EU as a legitimate mediator in the peace process, the EU is likely to remain a marginal actor in this conflict. Perhaps most worryingly for the EU, however, is not the failure to upgrade its role in this conflict from a financier to a manager, but the insignificant impact its financing of the peace process has had on Israelis and Palestinians as a means to change their behaviour and attitude towards the process and each other.

On the Palestinian side, the EU has lost much of its credibility following the Hamas victory in the 2006 parliamentary elections. As noted above, the EU's bilateral agreements with Israel and the Palestinian Authority are rooted in the concept of conditionality, meaning the suspension of agreements in the event of poor performance in areas such as human rights, good governance, the rule of law and political corruption. However, the EU preferred to ignore numerous violations of these conditions on both sides, and used negative conditionality only once, following Hamas's electoral victory in 2006. Even though the EU announced that the elections were open and fairly contested, it joined forces with Israel and the US and refused to acknowledge the Hamas government until it recognised Israel's rights to exist, renounced terrorism, and accepted previously signed agreements with Israel. The result of this policy was disastrous for the EU, as by refusing to negotiate with Hamas it undermined its own normative crusade of democracy promotion in the Palestinian Territories. Moreover, the embargo imposed on the Hamas government by the EU and the US led to the further radicalisation of Hamas and the rise in tensions between the Fatah and Hamas factions, which inevitably resulted in de facto two Palestinian governments, one led by Hamas in the Gaza Strip and the other led by Fatah in the West Bank. The EU's refusal to deal with Hamas while continuing to support the Fatah government in the West Bank has been criticised by many in the region as a demonstration of the Union's double standards and loss of credibility in the eyes of the Palestinians (Khatib 2009).

Conclusion

The EU is viewed by many in the international community as potentially the most suited third party to mediate between Israelis and Palestinians, not least due to its favourable trading relations with Israel and its generous aid to the Palestinian Authority. However, the EU is unlikely to assume the role of conflict manager as long as the US maintains its interests in the Middle East and Israel refuses to accept it as a legitimate third party with real leverage. With the addition of European disunity and its organisational shortcomings, the EU is destined to remain a marginal actor. Thus notwithstanding its important financial aid for the Palestinian Authority, the EU has failed in terms of its own declared mandate in this conflict, and will continue to be thwarted by the realities of the conflict context. Perhaps the EU's most resounding failure was its inability to transform the nature of trade-offs in this conflict by rewriting the stakes and their associated risks and rewards for both sides. Importantly, this failure is not the result of exogenous factors such as the US role in the conflict, rather the EU institutional set-up. Even with the ratification of the Lisbon Treaty in December 2009, which provided the EU with policy mechanisms such as the European External Action Service (EEAS) in order to promote greater coherence and efficiency within the EU, there is still no consistent approach to conflict management for the various hot spots in the European neighbourhood. Within the context of the Middle East peace process, the challenge for the EU remains how to leverage its commendable efforts on the ground (mostly via support for institution building in the Palestinian territories) over the high diplomacy of conflict management and peace negotiations, which remain largely an American prerogative. Ultimately, the EU has been least successful in the area of policy, which it had promoted the most via financial and institutional support for nearly two decades, namely a viable Palestinian state as part of a two-state solution to the conflict. Whereas the onus for the failure to resolve the Israeli–Palestinian conflict should lie primarily with the disputants as well as the US, the principal mediator in the conflict, nevertheless the EU has failed to capitalise on its favourable trade relations with Israel and its generous aid to the Palestinian Authority in order to influence their approach to the conflict and to each other. For the EU to be more successful in the application of its normative principles in the Israeli–Palestinian conflict, it must close the gap between expectations and capabilities, while making its contribution to the peace process both distinct and complementary to that of the US. Failure to do so will cement the EU's role as a financier of the peace process and drive it further away from a more active management of the Israeli–Palestinian conflict.

Notes

1   *The Economist*, 'Catherine Ashton and the British Problem', 15 December, 2009. http://www.economist.com/blogs/charlemagne/2009/12/catherine_ashton_and_the_briti (accessed 20 January 2010).
2   *Reuters*, 'Europe at Odds over Israeli Land Offensive in Gaza', 3 January 2009. http://www.reuters.com/article/idUSL3562581 (accessed 20 January 2010).
3   *The Independent*, 'EU Palestine Move Enrages Israelis', 2 December 2009. http://www.independent.co.uk/news/world/middle-east/eu-palestine-move-enrages-israelis-1832238.html (accessed 20 January 2010).

7 The limits of EU conflict management in the case of Abkhazia and South Ossetia[1]

Richard G. Whitman and Stefan Wolff

Introduction

This chapter explores EU conflict management in the case of the two separatist conflicts that have plagued Georgia and Georgian–Russian relations for most of the post-Soviet period. The focus on these two cases is justified in that it offers an excellent case study on the dangers associated with unrecognised statehood left poorly managed in a region of significant geostrategic importance. It also illustrates vividly the fundamental premise of this book, namely that in order to explain the effectiveness of EU conflict management, we need to look to EU capabilities and the specific conflict context to which they are applied. We proceed in three steps. The chapter begins with a brief background on the two conflicts and then provides an overview of EU–Georgia relations from the early 1990s to the aftermath of the Georgia–Russia war of August 2008. It then examines the EU's capabilities and how they were brought to bear in relation to Georgia's two separatist conflicts, and the multilayered context of the two separatist conflicts that forms the background against which the EU sought to play a role in managing them. In conclusion, we offer some brief thoughts about the balance of factors that account for the ultimate failure of conflict management efforts in this case.

The background to EU conflict management in Georgia

The conflicts in Abkhazia and South Ossetia

The conflicts related to the two separatist regions in Georgia – Abkhazia and South Ossetia – have their origins in Soviet and pre-Soviet politics in the (South) Caucasus. In total, over 80 ethnic groups live in Georgia, the largest, and politically most significant, ones being Georgians, Armenians, Russians, Abkhaz and South Ossetians (Cornell 2002: 63). Since 1988 and before August 2008, Georgia has experienced two violent ethnic conflicts, as well as a short two-phase civil war (Cornell 2002: 75). The latter was between different political factions struggling over control of the Georgian state, while the former were essentially the result of increasingly aggressive Georgian nationalism during, and after, the dying days of the Soviet Union. Both Abkhazia and South Ossetia had enjoyed substantial autonomy throughout the Soviet period and even though the population of both regions was ethnically mixed, it was not until the intensification of Georgian nationalism from the late 1980s onwards that tensions emerged. The nationalist movement in Georgia became further radicalised after Soviet troops crushed a demonstration in April 1989. Calls for independence, the legal proclamation of Georgian as the only official language in August 1989, and a Georgia referendum on independence and the subsequent election of nationalist leader

Zviad Gamsakhurdia in May 1991 provide the background against which these tensions escalated into full-scale violent conflict: Abkhaz and South Ossetians wanted to preserve, and remain within, the Soviet Union, considering their survival as ethno-cultural communities distinct from the Georgian majority to be in acute danger in an independent Georgian state (cf. Cohen 2002, Coppieters 2007, Wennmann 2006).

South Ossetians belong to the same ethnic group as the people of North Ossetia (now an autonomous republic of Russia, which is considered to be the indigenous homeland of Ossetians). A (South) Ossetian presence in contemporary Georgia only dates back a few hundred years (Cornell 2002: 96) and this is often used by Georgian nationalists to dispute any rights of South Ossetians to the territory in which they live. In 1989, South Ossetians made up just over two-thirds of their autonomous region's population, roughly 65,000 out of a population of 98,000. Yet, at that time there were around another 100,000 Ossetians in other regions of Georgia. Tensions grew in the last years of the Soviet Union and escalated initially into full-scale conflict between November 1989 and January 1990. Prompted by the 'March on Tskhinvali', the South Ossetian capital, of between 20,000 and 30,000 Georgian nationalists in August, supposedly to protect the city's Georgian population, the violence which ensued led to the death of six people and the injury of an additional 140. Subsequently, South Ossetians not only boycotted the political process in Georgia, including the September 1990 elections, but also declared their region's independence, while Georgians effectively abolished South Ossetia's autonomy with the proclamation of Georgia as an independent, unitary state with no internal borders.

Tbilisi initially only responded with an economic blockade, but 1991 saw a significant escalation of hostilities, leading initially to the Georgian occupation of South Ossetia's capital, Tskhinvali. On several occasions in March, June and September, Gamsakhurdia, who tried to use South Ossetia to strengthen his own grip on power in Georgia, failed to restore full Georgian control over South Ossetia in the face of well-organised, highly motivated and Russian-backed resistance. The conflict lingered on for another year, but with the disposal of Gamsakhurdia in December 1991 and former Soviet foreign minister Edvard Shevardnadse's ascent to the Georgian presidency in March 1992, it took only one final defeat of Georgian forces to pave the way towards the OSCE-mediated Sochi Agreement of June 1992, which established a permanent ceasefire and a military exclusion zone. It was followed by the deployment of an OSCE Observer Mission and a Russia-led CIS peacekeeping force, as well as the creation of the so-called Joint Control Commission, meant to facilitate cooperation between the sides on a day-to-day basis.

This arrangement worked relatively well during the presidencies of Edvard Shevardnadse, driven primarily by pragmatic considerations that assured all sides of benefits as a result of relative stability based on an acceptance of the status quo. Saakashvili's ascent to power in 2004 changed this configuration significantly as the new president had made restoration of full sovereignty across the entire territory of Georgia a key campaign promise. The success he had in reining in Adjara (the autonomous republic located in the southwestern corner of Georgia) in April 2004 emboldened Saakashvili to move on to South Ossetia in summer that year, under the pretext of abolishing the Ergneti market. While there is little doubt that trading on this market was connected to smuggling, it also presented one of the few opportunities for direct interaction between Georgians and South Ossetians. The violence during and after the closure of the market destroyed much of the confidence built between both sides and threw into jeopardy peace talks taking place at the time. In fact, violence got so bad in early August that a formal ceasefire was agreed between Georgian and South Ossetian authorities, only to be broken within days. Violence continued through much of the summer, with Georgian forces making some strategic gains but eventually withdrawing its military forces and agreeing a further round of formal demilitarisation measures with South Ossetia in Sochi in November. Nonetheless, the 2004 events contributed to further polarisation and radicalisation on all sides, increasing the frequency and intensity of clashes along the cease-fire line-up until the full-scale war in August 2008.

The conflict in South Ossetia led to around 1,000 people being killed, 100,000 being forced to flee, and extensive damage done to homes and infrastructure (International Crisis Group 2008: 4). In addition to ethnic Georgians and South Ossetians leaving the region for Georgia proper and North Ossetia respectively, a very large number of South Ossetians were also driven from their homes in Georgia proper. Within South Ossetia, segregation between the two communities increased significantly as a result of the conflict, with members of each ethnic group taking refuge in the areas controlled by 'their' side.

Historically, the Stalinist period saw the persecution and destruction of the political and cultural elites of the Abkhaz population in Georgia. During this period, Abkhazia addi-tionally experienced a massive influx of Georgians, decreasing the share of ethnic Abkhaz among the resident population to around one-third from the late 1930s to the early 1950s, eventually declining to under 18 per cent by 1989. This policy of Georgianisation continued after the Stalin years, and triggered several short spells of violence in 1957, 1967, 1978 and 1981. The resurgence of Georgian nationalism under Georgia's first post-independence leader Zviad Gamsakhurdia could not but be seen as a precursor of worse things to come by the Abkhaz and led them to conclude that establishing their own state was all the more nec-essary to ensure their ethnic survival.

Following Georgia's declaration of independence in 1991, and the simultaneous abolition of Abkhazia's autonomy, the Abkhaz immediately reinstated their 1925 constitution, defining it as an independent state united with Georgia on the basis of a special union treaty and pro-ceeded to declare their desire to leave Georgia and remain part of the Soviet Union/Russian Federation. This quickly escalated into open violence with Georgian forces taking over the Gali region in August 1992 and cutting Abkhazia off from Russia. However, the pretext of the attacks was alleged abductions of Georgians by supporters of Zviad Gamsakhurdia who had been ousted in a coup in December 1991 by three Georgian warlords who subsequently asked Shevardnadse, a native of Georgia, to lead the country through this difficult period.

As a result of Georgian advances, the Abkhaz leadership was forced to retreat from Sukhumi but immediately regrouped and organised guerrilla-style resistance. Backed by North Caucasian, in particular Chechen, fighters, as well as Russian air support, the Abkhaz quickly recaptured most of the territory initially lost, with Georgian control reduced to the Khodori Gorge and Gali. Ceasefires were agreed and broken time and again until May 1994 when the Moscow Agreement established a permanent ceasefire line with military exclusion zones on either side. In parallel, the UN Security Council passed Resolution 854 establishing the UN Observer Mission in Georgia (UNOMIG). The Russia-dominated CIS also dispatched a peacekeeping force to the region. Since then violations have been rare, even though the general security situation, especially in the Kodori Gorge, a Georgian-held area in Abkhazia, deteriorated sharply in 1998, 2001, 2006 and 2008, bringing both sides to the brink of a new war. Around ten thousand people are believed to have been killed in total in the fighting; in addition, around a quarter of a million Georgians have been displaced from Abkhazia.

The EU's engagement with post-independence Georgia

EU efforts to engage with Georgia over the country's two separatist conflicts date back to the early 1990s and were initially focused on humanitarian assistance: more than half of all

ECHO funding to Georgia prior to the 2008 war and its aftermath was spent between 1992 and 1995, two-thirds of all food aid (from DG Agriculture funds) and all exceptional human-itarian assistance. From 1997 onwards, the EU also begins to commit funds to rehabilitation programmes in the two conflict zones.[2]

A major boost in the amount of EU funding received by Georgia and a significant diver-sification of programmatic areas in which projects are financed occurs after 1999 when rela-tions between Georgia and the EU were put on a contractual footing with the Partnership and Cooperation Agreement (PCA) entering into force. As part of the envisioned political dia-logue to be developed on issues pertaining to security, stability, economic development, institutional reform, and human and minority rights, a hope was expressed that '[s]uch dia-logue may take place on a regional basis, with a view to contributing towards the resolution of regional conflicts and tensions' (European Commission 1999). The Presidency Conclusions of the Cologne European Council (1999: S.93) were even more optimistic, expressing the conviction 'that this will also facilitate . . . the quest for lasting solutions to persisting conflicts in the region'.

In 2001, the European Commission issued a Country Strategy Paper[3] for Georgia which, apart from a gloomy overall assessment of the political and economic situation in Georgia (European Commission 2001a: 4, 7–10), identified the two conflicts in and over Abkhazia and South Ossetia as a major 'impediment to development in Georgia' and a contributing factor to regional instability. Noting the readiness of the EU 'to look for further ways in which it could contribute to conflict resolution, as well as post-conflict rehabilitation', the paper also explicitly committed the EU to the support of 'the principle of Georgian territorial integrity' (ibid.: 5). Less than two years later, the Commission published a revised country strategy, taking account of the deteriorating political and economic situation in Georgia (European Commission 2003c) and restating the commitment to contributing 'to support efforts to prevent and resolve conflicts as well as post conflict rehabilitation' (European Commission 2003c: 4). The latest Country Strategy dates back to 2007 and is generally more upbeat about developments in Georgia after 2003, which included the appointment of an EU Special Representative for the South Caucasus and the deployment of the EU's first-ever Rule of Law mission (EUJUST Themis). While the EU's priorities *vis-à-vis* Georgia— poverty reduction and institutional reform—remain essentially unchanged, the language on Georgia's two conflicts is toned down, merely noting that 'the EU attaches great importance to the resolution of conflicts in Georgia's two breakaway regions of Abkhazia and South Ossetia and is actively involved in ongoing efforts to achieve a peaceful settlement, partly through the offices of the EUSR for the Southern Caucasus and through providing financial assistance for reconstruction and rehabilitation projects in Georgia's conflict zones' (European Commission 2007a: 7). This is quite remarkable in light of the fact that less than a year earlier, External Relations Commissioner Ferrero-Waldner had clearly, and correctly, noted, with respect to the South Caucasus as a whole, that '[t]hree negative strands are coming together, the combination of which is, frankly, alarming', namely the failure of all parties to deliver on conflict settlement, increased defence expenditure, and ever more inflammatory rhetoric. Thus, she warned that '[a]ny further escalation of tension could re-ignite the conflicts with devastating consequences for the entire region' (European Commission 2006b: 1f.).

The 2007 Country Strategy must be seen in the context of the EU's European Neigh-bourhood Policy of which Georgia had become a participant in 2004. As a result, while the 1999 PCA remains the legal foundation of EU – Georgia relations, it is now the ENP Action Plan that provides the framework for EU assistance and it is the ENP instruments (principally,

ENPI and NIF) that are primary implementation tools.[4] In the PCA, the issue of the conflicts in, and over, Abkhazia and South Ossetia only got relatively brief mentions, especially in Article 5 of Title 2 (Political Dialogue), whereas the ENP Action Plan elevated the conflicts and their settlement to a Priority Area (no. 6 among eight priority areas in total). As a consequence, the inclusion of Georgia in the ENP in 2004 saw a general increase in the EU's engagement with the country's two secessionist conflicts. Moreover, the change in government in Tbilisi in 2004 gave the EU greater confidence that its engagement would yield positive results and more quickly so.[5] It is also important to note that this major gear shift in EU engagement in the South Caucasus also reflected a break with previous thinking on the South Caucasus more generally, which now, for the first time, became more differentiated as a region of its own, rather than being treated as a part of the post-Soviet region (Lynch 2004).

Reflected in the policy instruments brought to bear and the funding committed to conflict resolution by the EU is a consistent EU preference for creating enabling conditions for the resolution of the conflicts in, and over, Abkhazia and South Ossetia. The bulk of EU initiatives and funding has gone to rehabilitation projects with the aim to contribute to economic and infrastructural development and thereby also build confidence between the different parties.[6] Being the largest foreign donor, the EU allocated €25m to Abkhazia and €8m to South Ossetia between 1997 and 2006 (European Commission 2007a: 20). In addition, just over €100m were spent on humanitarian assistance under ECHO between 1993 and 2006, primarily 'targeting population groups affected by the conflict' and increasingly concentrating on food security and income-generating activities for internally displaced people and other vulnerable groups (ibid.). This trend continued in 2007 and the first half of 2008 with a further €10m committed to economic rehabilitation projects in the conflict zones of Abkhazia and South Ossetia and to a range of projects catering to the needs of Georgia's still significant number of internally displaced persons (IDPs) from the two conflicts (European Commission 2009b.: 8). Spending on IDPs increased further in the aftermath of the 2008 war which created an additional almost 200,000 IDPs: a total of €61m was additionally allocated under the ENPI and a further €6m, initially committed to the OSCE-administered economic rehabilitation programme for South Ossetia, was reassigned to IDP projects following the closing of the OSCE mission to Georgia (European Commission 2009c: 5, 7).

In addition to these economic and humanitarian programmes, the EU has also been politically engaged in Georgia and in relation to its two secessionist conflicts. Apart from significant funding made available to reforms in the political and judicial institutions of the country, Joint Actions under CFSP have begun to play an increasingly important part of the EU's efforts to contribute to the peaceful resolution of the conflicts in, and over, Abkhazia and South Ossetia. When the first EU Special Representative (EUSR) was appointed in 2003, his mandate in relation to the conflicts in the South Caucasus was merely one of 'assisting' in their resolution. The appointment of the current EUSR, Peter Semneby, in 2006 saw the mandate amended to a more proactive 'contributing' to conflict resolution. This change has been reflected more generally in EU CFSP actions *vis-à-vis* the conflicts in, and over, Abkhazia and South Ossetia.[7] Indicative of this gear change is the first ENP Action Plan, endorsed by the EU–Georgia Cooperation Council in November 2006 and entering into force in 2007 (European Commission 2006a). Under Priority Area 6 (Promote peaceful resolution of internal conflicts), Georgia and the EU commit to a range of specific actions with regard to conflict settlement in Abkhazia and South Ossetia, 'based on respect of the sovereignty and territorial integrity of Georgia within its internationally recognised borders', including confidence building, economic assistance and demilitarisation (European

Commission 2006a: 10). 'Disguised' as action items, the Commission also offers a broader assessment of the state of play at the time, pointing out that there is a 'need to increase the effectiveness of the negotiating mechanisms', that '[t]he work of the Joint Control Commission [for South Ossetia] should be measured by the rapid implementation of all outstanding agreements previously reached and in particular by the start of demilitarisation', that 'constructive cooperation between interested international actors in the region, including the EU and OSCE Member States' is essential for further progress towards conflict settlement (ibid.). This latter point needs to be seen also in conjunction with a reference to the peace plan for South Ossetia, endorsed at the OSCE Ministerial Council in Ljubljana in December 2005. Together with an EU commitment to support the enhancement of the mandates of the UN and OSCE in Georgia, this all clearly underlines the EU's multilateral inclination. Moreover, the EU's explicitly stated intention to '[i]nclude the issue of territorial integrity of Georgia and settlement of Georgia's internal conflicts in EU–Russia political dialogue meetings' (ibid.) reflects the clear realisation that Russia is a veto-player whose support needs to be secured for any conflict settlement to have a realistic prospect of sustainability.[8]

The importance of the EU's capabilities for effective crisis management was underlined in the context and aftermath of the war in August 2008. The French Presidency of the EU, together with the OSCE Chairmanship (at the time held by Finland), was instrumental in brokering the six-point ceasefire plan agreed by Russia and Georgia on 12 August. The follow-up visit by German Chancellor Angela Merkel to both Russia and Georgia between 15 and 17 August further demonstrated that two of the 'Big Three' clearly saw eye to eye on the issue. By the time an implementation agreement was signed by Russia and Georgia on 8 September, after further shuttle diplomacy by Presidents Barroso and Sarkozy, an Extraordinary European Council meeting in Brussels on 1 September had given full backing to the ceasefire agreement and committed the Union 'including through a presence on the ground, to support every effort to secure a peaceful and lasting solution to the conflict in Georgia' (Council of the European Union 2008f). The deployment of a civilian monitoring mission (EUMM) tasked with overseeing the implementation of the ceasefire agreement had its immediate significance in demonstrating the EU's capability to act quickly in terms of decision-making, financing and deployment. Longer-term, the EUMM's significance was further enhanced because it soon became the only internationally mandated presence in Georgia after Russia forced the closure of both the UN and OSCE missions in Abkhazia and South Ossetia, respectively. Moreover, the political weight of the EU in the Geneva settlement negotiations (technically, talks to consolidate the August ceasefire) was considerably higher than the previous roles it had played (observer status in the Joint Control Commission (JCC) for South Ossetia and involvement in the UN Secretary-General (UNSG) Group of Friends for the Abkhazia talks through some of its member states). The EU became, alongside the UN and OSCE, an official co-chair of the Geneva process, in which the European Commission is a co-moderator (with UNHCR) of the Working Group on humanitarian and IDP issues.

The EU response to the August 2008 war between Georgia and Russia also served as a test for the Community Civil Protection Mechanism which was mobilised to facilitate civil protection assistance provided by member states directly to Georgia and the two conflict regions. In addition, the Commission provided €9m worth of immediate humanitarian aid for IDPs and co-hosted with the World Bank the Georgia donors' conference on 22 October where it pledged some €500m for various rehabilitation measures, including further humanitarian assistance (€8m), support of IDPs (€61.5m through ENPI and €15m through IfS), and for the EUMM (€37m for the first 12 months to 30 September 2009).

Following this initial flurry of activity in August and September 2008, there was widespread enthusiasm that the EU had finally made a real breakthrough in its credibility as an international security actor. Since then, however, this perception, which was by and large correct at the time, has required some adjustment. While the humanitarian assistance programmes run by the EU, especially support projects for IDPs, have continued relatively successfully, the political process has stalled and a resolution of the two conflicts in, and over, Abkhazia and South Ossetia is as, if not more, remote than it was at the time of the war in August 2008. Not only has Russia gradually reneged on a number of pledges in the ceasefire agreement and implementation plan, but with its recognition of the independence of Abkhazia and South Ossetia (even though only Nicaragua and Venezuela have so far followed suit) and the consolidation of its political and military presence in both territories, Georgia's territorial integrity and sovereignty are no more than a fiction. Georgia itself has been through a period of heightened domestic tensions seeing a significant, yet ultimately unsuccessful, challenge to the political authority of President Saakashvili and experiencing the consequences of the global financial crisis. In addition to tense relations with Russia, Georgia's ambitions for a more concrete perspective to NATO membership, let alone an accelerated path to it, have not been fulfilled by the alliance to date. Nonetheless, Georgia continues to look to the US rather than the EU for political backing. While relations between the West and Russia have prospects of improving in the wake of a foreign policy reorientation of the US under the Obama administration, little of substance has happened, limiting both EU leverage in the Geneva talks and any incentives for Russia to make compromises. As a result, the EU, for example, had to retract proposals for an inclusion of US monitors into its mission in Georgia, strongly pushed for by Tbilisi, but equally vehemently rejected by Moscow. At the same time, within the EU, the appointment of Jacques Morel as EUSR for the Crisis in Georgia was a concession to the outgoing French EU Presidency, but undermined the role of the existing EUSR for the South Caucasus, Peter Semneby, even though the latter remains tasked with providing political guidance to the EUMM. The EU thus now finds itself between several rocks and hard places in relation to the two conflicts in Abkhazia and South Ossetia: it has not been able to capitalise on its achievements in August and September 2008 by providing clear international leadership for conflict resolution but rather is involved (again) in what has become an almost meaningless settlement process in the shape of the Geneva talks. Where the EU has, however, proven its worth is the broader set of assistance measures from humanitarian aid to support for political, legal and economic reform in Georgia. In other words, the EU has been able to maintain its engagement with both Georgia and the two unrecognised states of Abkhazia and South Ossetia while avoiding the issue of the latter's recognition, arguably by insisting on their non-recognition through the continuing emphasis on Georgia's territorial integrity. While this may have contributed to containing the conflicts, it has done little to resolve them.

Explaining the limitations of conflict management

How can we explain the lack of any tangible progress towards a negotiated settlement of the conflicts over the unrecognised states of Abkhazia and South Ossetia after close to two decades of international involvement, including by the EU? In the case of the Union, the question could also be phrased slightly differently: how can we explain that the EU's impact was close to negligible before the summer of 2008, then for a short period of time very significant, before declining again quite steeply? As we will illustrate in the next two sections, Georgia is a good case to validate our more general assumption that there are two complementary sets of factors at work here – the EU's insufficient capabilities and the context in which the two conflicts are played out at local, state, regional and global levels and their interfaces.

Insufficient EU capabilities

Any third party involved in conflict management must possess three sets of capabilities to have any chance of succeeding in its endeavours: it must have the appropriate policy tools and be able to deploy them in a timely fashion, it must be capable of funding its efforts possibly over extended periods of time, and it must be willing and able to coordinate and cooperate within its own organisational structures and with external actors. While we will assess in the next section whether the actual conflict context was conducive to an externally facilitated settlement, what follows now is an assessment of EU capabilities meant to identify also shortcomings in the Union's overall approach to conflict management and offer some recommendations of what might be done to overcome them. Our focus on EU capabilities and the external conflict context that, together, shape the likelihood of successful EU conflict management also offers a tool for gauging in which situations the Union might be able to succeed given its capabilities and the conflict context and thus to caution against overambitious and unrealistic expectations of what can be expected of the EU as a conflict manager in the case of Georgia, and throughout the Eastern Neighbourhood and beyond.

As noted above, the EU has markedly improved its capabilities to act and to fund. Two EU Special Representatives (for the South Caucasus and the Crisis in Georgia) have been deployed, ENP and the Eastern Partnership have made conflict management one of their priorities, and high-level intervention, such as in the case of the (French) Presidency's shuttle diplomacy during the Georgian–Russian war in August 2008, has left a positive mark. To be sure, Georgia is far from a success story for EU conflict management, but comparing the relative success of the French Presidency's handling of the crisis in summer and autumn 2008 to the considerable difficulties the EU experienced in the Western Balkans throughout the 1990s indicates that the EU has come a long way in achieving some credibility as a conflict manager. Likewise, the various funding instruments available now, such as the IfS and ENPI, are working far more effectively in the short and long term than even the so-called Rapid Reaction Mechanism and other instruments did. Yet, even with improved capabilities, political will to engage *politically* remains a scarce commodity. The main instrument (in terms of duration and funding provided) for EU engagement to date has been the ENP. Yet, as External Relations Commissioner Ferrero-Waldner has already pointed out in 2006, the ENP 'is not in itself a conflict prevention or settlement mechanism', but 'tackles the underlying issues which enable conflicts to fester' (European Commission 2006b: 3). Insisting, as she did at the time, that the example of Western Europe after the end of the Second World War has demonstrated that 'promoting prosperity, stability and security is the ultimate conflict prevention policy' is empirically correct (European Commission 2006b: 3), but not a suitable analogy. Conflicts, such as those in and over Abkhazia and South Ossetia, that are based on incompatible self-determination claims of distinct ethnic groups follow a different logic that is not comprehensively captured and addressed by an approach that seeks 'to contribute to a more positive climate for conflict settlement' (European Commission 2006b: 3). In other words, 'impressive economic growth is not the key mechanism for turning a conflict that springs from issue of identity into a cooperative arrangement' (Coppieters 2007: 26). This is not to say that the EU approach as a whole is flawed, but rather that it lacks a comprehensive vision and strategic follow-through: unlike the UN and OSCE, the EU has significant economic and political instruments that it could deploy in support of a more active diplomatic role in seeking a negotiated settlement (International Crisis Group 2006: 27).[9] Rather than merely supporting existing efforts (which failed to make any progress over more than a decade), the EU should have mustered the political will to take a lead in the settlement process.

That this has not happened either before or after the 2008 Russia–Georgia war is also a reflection of the fact that the most problematic area for the EU is its internal and external capabilities to cooperate and coordinate. As already noted, being a latecomer in the arena of international conflict management, the EU has had significant difficulties finding a role for itself within the broader international conflict management efforts. This has been as much a problem in relation to the EU's internal political dynamics. Especially in the Eastern Neighbourhood, and thus in relation to the conflicts in Georgia, the Union has been unable to overcome different member state preferences on how to deal with Russia and remains fundamentally divided between a more Russia-friendly camp (comprising those, like France and Germany, who prioritise bilateral relations with Russia over a common EU approach) and a more Russia-sceptic camp (including primarily Poland, Sweden and the Baltic states, as well as at times the UK who prefer a much tougher line) (cf. International Crisis Group 2008h: 23f.; Leonard and Popescu 2008: 31ff.). This divide within the EU has meant a repetition of a well-known EU pattern of no or insufficient action until a crisis has fully escalated, rather than the pursuit of a well-conceived, strategic, and properly resourced proactive foreign policy.

Relegated to observer status in South Ossetia and to providing support for confidence-building measures and economic reconstruction in Abkhazia, the EU's role in Abkhazia and South Ossetia was relatively marginal until summer 2008, despite a somewhat higher level of activity from spring 2008 onwards (European Commission 2009c: 7), including a visit by High Representative Solana to Georgia and Abkhazia in June 2008.[10] The Georgian–Russian war in August that year, however, coincided with the French Presidency of the EU and thus with an internationally heavyweight incumbent with an experienced and well-resourced foreign office staff and a president accepted as equal in his national role by Russia. Yet, the EU needs to maintain a careful balance here, as noted by High Representative Solana, between 'unity inside the EU and commitment to our principles' and realising that 'there is no alternative to a strong relationship with Russia' (Council of the European Union 2008f).[11] This was also emphasised in a Commission review of EU–Russia relations in November 2008, acknowledging that 'Russia is a key geopolitical actor, whose constructive involvement in international affairs is a necessary precondition for an effective international community' and observing that the key requirement for successfully engaging Russia in conflict resolution in the common neighbourhood is 'the will and the capacity of the EU to act as one, combining both Community instruments as well as those of CFSP/ESDP' (European Commission 2008a: 4f.).

At the same time, the OSCE chairmanship was held by Finland, another EU member state and one not traditionally perceived as anti-Russian. Seizing the initiative, the French Presidency, in cooperation with the OSCE, brokered a ceasefire and oversaw the swift agreement on, and deployment of, EU monitors to Georgia. While member states remained divided over who to blame, Russia or Georgia or both, the French Presidency of the EU managed these disagreements well enough to preserve the EU's ability to act. While this may be seen as a major breakthrough in the EU's conflict management capabilities, it also indicated some potential weaknesses, as one might wonder whether the same results would have been obtained if the war had happened during the Presidency of a smaller member state anchored in the Russia-sceptic camp within the EU. Moreover, there remain question marks over whether the EU's intervention actually achieved much at all: the EU-proposed ceasefire was agreed by Georgia and Russia, but only after Russia had essentially achieved its aims; Russian recognition of the independence of South Ossetia and Abkhazia happened despite EU opposition at the end of August 2008; and thus far little, if any progress has been made in the Geneva talks, mandated by the ceasefire agreement. Moreover, while the French Presidency managed to keep EU member states in line and on course during the crisis and to get, and implement, an EU-internal agreement on the deployment of monitors to Georgia, the appointment of its own EUSR for the Crisis in Georgia (the existing EUSR for Central Asia, Jacques Morel) did little to dispel perceptions of a specific French national agenda within and beyond the EU.

The conflict context

How did the conflict environment impact on failures and successes of EU conflict management in Georgia?[12] Globally, the EU is a late-comer in the area of conflict management. Throughout the 1990s, the EU was, if anything, focused on the Balkans, with little success. ESDP, the Union's major reservoir of conflict management instruments, only became fully operational in 2003 (a decade after its inception), and continues to lack military teeth. Thus, by the time the EU began to look to the Eastern Neighbourhood (ENP, too, was inaugurated only in 2003) the field of conflict management had already been carved up among other actors, such as the UN and the OSCE, who showed little enthusiasm to let the EU become a major player as well. The Union, thus, remained mostly excluded from political efforts and was relegated to providing economic support and limited confidence-building measures in Abkhazia and South Ossetia where the UN and OSCE, respectively, were the main 'drivers' of peace processes that stalled soon after ceasefire agreements were concluded in the first half of the 1990s (see below). The Union did obtain observer status in the OSCE and Russia-led Joint Control Commission in South Ossetia and appointed a Special Representative for the South Caucasus (as well as after 2008 for the crisis in Georgia). Through the Presidency, held at the time by France, the EU also filled a vacuum created in the wake of the 2008 Russia–Georgia war, and provided, together with the OSCE Chairman-in-Office (Finland at the time), crucial shuttle diplomacy leading to a ceasefire agreement. However, in general, the geopolitical environment offered few concrete opportunities for the EU to play an active, let alone leading, role in managing the conflicts in Georgia. Given their prominence, it is therefore worth briefly exploring here the role of two international organisations – the OSCE and the UN – as part of the broader global conflict context.

As already noted, for most of the period after the outbreak of violence in Abkhazia and South Ossetia, the OSCE and the UN were the most significant external mediators involved in any of the conflicts settlement processes. Their engagement was guided by three principal objectives: to bring active hostilities to an end and to prevent their resumption; to deal with the humanitarian consequences of the two conflicts; and to achieve durable settlements. Yet, with the underlying objective of at least some of the Western members of the two organisations having been to consolidate the independence of Georgia and to effect its integration into European and transatlantic structures, tug-of-war games in which Abkhazia and South Ossetia, as well as eventually Georgia, would become nothing more than pawns, were inevitable: locally between pro-Western and pro-Russian forces, within regional organisations (such as the OSCE and the CIS) and geopolitically between Russia and the West.

This geopolitical dimension of Georgia's contested statehood requires some further analysis of another third-party actor: the United States. US engagement was driven primarily by its own national security and energy agendas. The Baku–Tbilisi–Ceyhan (BTC) pipeline serves major US interests, including diversification of supplies and limiting Russia's (and potentially Iran's) control over Caspian hydrocarbon resources by providing alternative supply lines to world markets. The security of the pipeline, however, remained crucially dependent on stability in Georgia, which established an initial US interest in what was considered Russia's backyard throughout the first half of the 1990s. With the beginning of the Global War on Terrorism, the region rose to higher prominence on the US security agenda because of its strategic location in relation to Afghanistan, Iraq and the Middle East, necessitating the use of Georgian airspace and leading to the establishment of two (joint US–Turkish) airbases in Georgia. In 2002, as part of an effort to widen the coalition of countries supporting the US-led war on terrorism, the Georgia Train and Equip programme was initiated, funded with $64 million and designed to increase the capabilities of Georgia's armed forces by training and equipping four 600 strong battalions of the Georgian army and some additional troops under the command of the ministry of the interior, including border guards. A follow-up to the train and equip programme was the Georgia Sustainment and Stability Operations programme, tied more specifically to Georgian troop deployments in Iraq and providing an additional $60 million in military US assistance in 2005/6.[13] In addition, around $400 million worth of military surplus goods were delivered to Georgia.[14]

While the sustained commitment by the US to Georgia had a significant impact on the country's economic performance, especially after 2004, and arguably contributed to a number of social and political reforms, it also exacerbated Georgian–Russian tensions, especially because of US support for, if not encouragement of, Georgia's aspirations to join NATO. While US policy in the early 1990s acknowledged Russia's claims that Georgia (and other ex-Soviet republics) should be respected as part of its zone of influence, US military and energy security interests over the past decade have turned the South Caucasus into somewhat of a battleground for regional influence. In the context of generally worsening relations between Russia and the West, a perceived US agenda to press ahead with Georgia's NATO membership bid at the Bucharest Summit in April 2008 was at least a contributing factor to the outbreak of violence in South Ossetia over the summer.

These complex strategic configurations of power and the opportunities and constraints they establish for the realisation of the interests of each involved player at least partly explain the failure of international conflict management efforts in facilitating a durable political settlement of the conflicts over Abkhazia and South Ossetia. Much like the EU, the UN, OSCE and US were part of the same conflict context and insufficiently able to shape it to their advantage and thus be in a better position to affect progress towards conflict settlement. Consequently it would be unfair to lay all the blame for the lack of sustainable settlements in the two conflicts in Georgia on third parties alone. Yet, seeing them just as victims of the intransigence of local conflict parties and of the self-interested agendas of other external actors, chiefly Russia, does not tell the entire story of failure either. While the US pursued a predominantly national security agenda in Georgia, which limited the degree to which it could play a more constructive role in conflict settlement, the UN and OSCE were proactively engaged as key players in international conflict management efforts, but proved themselves at the same time extremely protective of 'their' settlement processes, and prevented (for a long time successfully) a more multi-track and multi-actor approach. In the same way that the OSCE maintained its lead role in South Ossetia, the UN had been keen to keep other actors at bay from its efforts in Abkhazia. This exclusion of other third parties from the core conflict settlement processes limited their effectiveness in two ways. On the one hand, it deprived them of capacities that they did not have, or not sufficiently, themselves. For example, the EU's proven track record to facilitate economic reconstruction and reintegration and assist with civilian police and border management has, if anything, been activated only very late. On the other hand, despite the 'protectionism' of the UN and OSCE, the number of external actors on the ground who are keen to contribute to the settlement of these conflicts has steadily increased, but the multiple efforts made by them and the respective key players have not always been sufficiently coordinated, and objectives have at times been contradictory.

Moreover, there were two further factors that added to this unfavourable global context. Kosovo's unilateral declaration of independence in February 2008, and its recognition now by all but five of the EU's 27 member states, created a welcome 'precedent' for Russia, as frequently emphasised by Putin, already in the run-up to February 2008.[15] While Russia's position here is ambivalent, of course, as it also backed Serbia before the International Court of Justice (ICJ) challenging the legality of Kosovo's UDI, this 'successful secession' further strengthened the resolve of the Abkhaz and South Ossetian elites to pursue their course of breaking away from Georgia. The second complicating factor in this respect is Georgia's aspiration to join NATO and NATO's principal openness to this idea, as expressed at the Bucharest summit in April 2008. Unsurprisingly, this was not welcomed by Russia and may well have confirmed to the Kremlin an essentially hostile agenda on the part of Georgia and NATO (in connection also with the then still ongoing US-inspired missile defence shield). The overall worsening relationship between Russia and the West clearly did not facilitate any progress on diffusing ever-increasing tensions in Georgia, thus limiting further whatever conflict prevention and resolution capabilities the EU, alone or in cooperation with other international actors, may have possessed before August 2008.[16] Moroever, as the International Crisis Group argues, defeating Georgia in the August 2008 war served several of the Kremlin's strategic goals in this respect: 'to punish one nation for its NATO ambitions; to warn others, especially Ukraine, not to go down the same route; and to humiliate NATO by showing it to be indecisive and ineffective' (International Crisis Group 2008h: 10).

At the regional level, constraints on EU effectiveness, by and large, also outweighed opportunities. The main factor here is Russia. Russia, at the same time a global player, not least through its status as permanent member of the UN Security Council, has clear security and economic interests in the area considered by the EU as its Eastern Neighbourhood; interests that are often at odds with those of the EU. The Russian military presence in South Ossetia and Abkhazia (in the form of CIS peacekeepers for much of the period after the break-up of the Soviet Union), as well as Russian political influence and economic leverage, makes Russia a veto power when it comes to conflict settlement. Deteriorating relations between Russia and the West, over Kosovo and NATO expansion among other things combined with the limited leverage that the EU has over Russia, have further complicated the task for the EU. EU dependency on oil and gas from Russia and on Russia as a major transit country for energy from the Caspian region has so far outweighed Russian dependency on the EU as a major market. EU efforts to diversify supply and supply routes by investing in pipelines through the South Caucasus have significantly driven increased EU conflict management efforts in this region, and Georgia in particular, but not decreased Russian leverage, predominantly because of the continuing influence that Russia exercises in Abkhazia and South Ossetia.

The regional situation, however, is also characterised by the influence of non-state actors. The fact that, over some 15 years, quasi-state structures have grown in Abkhazia and South Ossetia (to the extent that both regions exhibit key criteria of stateness, such as a permanent government associated with a population and a territory), yet they have remained largely unintegrated into international political and economic networks, has also created opportunities for transnational organised crime that have become entrenched and are closely interwoven with the local political, social and economic structures, and in fact sustain them in many ways financially and militarily. These criminal networks are predominantly involved with drugs smuggling and weapons trafficking and as such are also integrated into global east–west transit routes. Moreover, throughout the 1990s, the conflict zones in Abkhazia and South Ossetia and surrounding areas of Georgia proper provided training and transit opportunities for jihadist fighters joining the Chechen independence struggle, thus also increasing Russian security concerns. While the EU is clearly and negatively affected by this kind of organised criminal activity, it lacks effective instruments to tackle them at their source. Moreover, from a conflict management perspective, such efforts might prove counter-productive by alienating the very local elites that will be essential for achieving a sustainable settlement.

At the state and the local levels, the factors that condition the success or failure of EU conflict management in Georgia are equally unfavourable. Local elites in Abkhazia and especially South Ossetia are deeply dependent on, and controlled by, Russia and involved in organised criminal activity. While they may lack even a minimum of democratic legitimacy in the eyes of the EU, it is difficult to see how any continuing stabilisation, let alone settlement, can be achieved without engaging them. While the EU is keenly aware of this, it remains committed to the territorial integrity of Georgia, which in turn resists any negotiations with the Abkhaz and South Ossetian elites. These elites, heavily dependent as they are on Moscow for political and military backing and for economic lifelines that help them maintain a modicum of local legitimacy for their regimes, thus have very little room for manoeuvre in potential status negotiations. In other words, even though local elites may be able to claim legitimately that they represent the interests of Abkhazia and South Ossetia they have very limited, if any, opportunity in the existing negotiations format to do so effectively because of a regional balance of power that favours Russia from the start. The Russian position, moreover, is clearly at odds with that of Georgia and those among its supporters that insist on the country's territorial integrity. Thus, even though one of the results of the Georgia–Russia war in August 2008 was the creation of a new negotiation format involving both Russia and the EU, these so-called Geneva talks have yet to produce any concrete results. The EU has earned its place in the Geneva talks qua its efforts to broker a ceasefire, but its actual position within them is weak: limited, if any, leverage over Russia is matched by a Georgian preference for the US and NATO as backer. Moreover, the EU's role is constrained structurally.

The current agendas of the immediate conflict parties at the local and state levels in both conflicts have not only created a situation in which the EU is of relatively marginal significance but their perceptions of what their own interests are in relation to security, power and material gain have also meant that their willingness to move beyond the status quo and towards sustainable settlement is at best limited. Security concerns in South Ossetia and Abkhazia remain high for both separatist and Georgian officials. Internal power struggles at the state level continue in Georgia. Repeated election promises by the incumbent president to restore full sovereignty over the entire territory of the Georgian state in its internationally recognised borders from the outset limited the chances of a peaceful settlement of the two conflicts there in light of entrenched positions, and Russian backing, on the other side. Moreover, the material benefits that different sections of the elites on both sides in the conflicts derive from the status quo, and thus the threats they perceive from a negotiated solution, have created significant constituencies who benefit from the lack of a solution and are thus hardly inclined to negotiate in good faith. Abkhaz and South Ossetian leaders cannot even privately contemplate any form of reintegration into Georgia, but differ with regard to their own long-term goals. Abkhaz favour independence and fear increasing Russian dominance, while South Ossetians aim at reunification with the North Ossetian republic in the Russian Federation. Yet, Russia struggles with a restive North Caucasus and is aware of the risk of further destabilisation through continued Ossetian 'reunification' efforts.

Conclusion

The case of the EU's efforts to manage the conflicts in Georgia illustrates the myriad factors that have an impact on the effectiveness of such efforts. While it is clear that the Union had limited capabilities to engage in the whole spectrum of conflict management efforts, it is also evident that the structure of the conflict management process was such that even in those areas where the Union did have appropriate capabilities to make a contribution, it had been marginalised for too long a period by other international actors and did not have the leverage or political will to insist on a more central role. At the same time, one has to be realistic about what the Union could have achieved in a situation where its capabilities had been more developed and its role been more central to the process. Although such an assessment can only be speculative, our analysis of the context factors of the conflicts over Abkhazia and South Ossetia lead us to conclude that there were very clear limits on what any third-party actor would have been able to do in the face of the deliberate escalation policies pursued by all of the immediate conflict parties in the run-up to the 2008 war. However, we have to be careful not to mix the lack of successful long-term structural prevention efforts with the failure to prevent, in the short-term, the violence that ensued in August 2008. Finally, the effectiveness of the Union, and specifically the French Presidency, to broker a ceasefire and deploy a monitoring mission for its implementation, as well as to get all parties to accept the need for engagement in the Geneva talks is a significant success for the EU and emphasises its increasing role and importance as a conflict manager.

Notes

1 This chapter draws, in its empirical part, on previously published works: Akçakoca *et al.* (2009), Whitman and Wolff (2010a), and Wolff (2010).
2 For detailed annual expenditures, see European Commission (2007a : 33).
3 According to the Commission's 2001 Communication on Conflict Prevention, such Country Strategy Papers are 'the instrument for ensuring [...] an integrated approach of conflict prevention' (European Commission 2001: 11).
4 The ENP Action Plan also takes significant inspiration from the PCA and makes frequent reference to it (European Commission 2006a: 5, 6, 11, 19, 21, 25, 34, 40) and clearly states that PCA implementation is the number one priority for future assistance to Georgia (ibid.: 19).
5 Compare for example the EU's assessment of the situation in Georgia in the 2003 Country Strategy with that of the 2007a Country Strategy.
6 Interview with Peter Semneby and Mark Fawcett, Brussels, 16 December 2008, and John Kjaer and Stefano di Cara, Brussels, 16 December 2008.
7 Interview with Peter Semneby and Mark Fawcett, Brussels, 16 December 2008.
8 This manifests itself also in EU–Russia discussions in the framework of the Common Space External Security.
9 This report by the International Crisis Group is overall highly critical of the EU's reluctance 'to take on direct conflict resolution responsibilities' (International Crisis Group 2006: 27).
10 Another high-level visit to Georgia, Abkhazia and Russia was undertaken in July by Frank-Walter Steinmeier in his dual capacity as German foreign minister and coordinator for the five-member Friends of the UN Secretary-General (including also the United States, Britain, France, and Russia). While a peace plan presented by Steinmeier was rejected, further escalation of the conflict over

Abkhazia, seen as much more likely and dangerous than the situation in South Ossetia, was averted at the time.

11 Cooperation with Russia, regardless of how reasonable it may seem from the EU's perspective, has been difficult to sustain at constructive levels. The military escalation in the summer of 2008 and the subsequent recognition by Russia of the independence of Abkhazia and South Ossetia is a clear indication that the Road Map for the Common Space of External Security is barely worth the paper on which it was written, committing the two sides, as it did, to, inter alia, cooperation in crisis management, promoting conflict prevention and settlement, regular consultation, early warning, etc. (see European Commission 2005b).

12 For a more detailed exploration of the dimensions of 'context' and their impact, see Wolff (2008) and Cordell and Wolff (2009). Cf. also Wolff (2011c).

13 Information from www.georgia.usembassy.gov

14 Information from www.state.gov./p/eur/ci/gg/c7008.htm

15 The International Crisis Group notes in this context that soon after Kosovo's declaration of independence, Russia significantly increased the strength of pre-existing links with Abkhazia and South Ossetia (International Crisis Group 2008h: 8).

16 The connection between the escalation of tensions between Georgia and Russia over Abkhazia and South Ossetia, on the one hand, and Kosovo's declaration of independence and the outcome of the Bucharest NATO Summit, on the other, is also emphasised in Independent International Fact-Finding Mission on the Conflict in Georgia (2009: 31).

8 The EU in Afghanistan

Eva Gross

Introduction

The terrorist attacks of 11 September 2001 catapulted Afghanistan into the international spotlight. One of the poorest countries in the world, Afghanistan by 2001 had been isolated during five years of Taliban rule. The international intervention that followed the attacks initially focused on toppling the Taliban regime, but soon came to centre on post-conflict reconstruction. The political, economic and military starting points facing the international community made the task of rebuilding Afghanistan a challenging endeavour. The intervention in Afghanistan has been predominantly led by the United States (US), but engagement in Afghanistan has also been a foreign policy priority for several European Union (EU) member states. The EU, through its political, economic and civilian instruments, has made a sizeable contribution to Afghanistan's reconstruction. Despite the significant international assistance over the past decade, however, the security situation in Afghanistan has progressively deteriorated, and the credibility of the Kabul government has been shown to be weak. These developments have prompted a series of strategic reviews on the part of the US, whose approach since late 2009 has focused on a counter-insurgency strategy with the aim of progressively reducing troop commitments starting in 2011. In political terms, too, Afghanistan and Pakistan have become US policy priorities, which illustrates the transnational and regional dimensions in stabilizing the country.

Within this broader political and strategic context, the added value of the EU's contribution to rebuilding Afghanistan lies in strengthening governance, reforming the police and justice sectors, and emphasizing the rule of law. This chapter analyses EU engagement in Afghanistan over the past decades from two vantage points – one, the EU's ability to affect the conflict and make a positive contribution towards its eventual resolution through its capacity to act; and two, the EU's ability to co-operate with other international actors in Afghanistan both in terms of setting a strategic agenda and of coordinating policy implementation through its capacity to coordinate. Afghanistan's domestic setting but also the broader regional context have made the task for international reconstruction efforts exceedingly complex, and the EU to date has not always had the instruments, policies and indeed strategies in place to have a significant and/or regional impact. The analysis of the EU's engagement in Afghanistan shows that the EU's visibility and effectiveness have suffered from differences among EU member states but also from institutional incoherence. Both have prevented the alignment of the EU's political, economic and civilian crisis management efforts in pursuit of specific policy goals. While the EU has a considerable capacity to fund both short- and long-term measures towards Afghanistan's reconstruction, shortcomings in the EU's capacity to coordinate have negative implications for its capacity to act.

The chapter also shows, however, that the EU has progressively improved and adapted its implementation practices and policy goals in light of the evolving conflict pattern and corresponding shifts in international engagement.

The conflict context

The determinants of the specific conditions under which the reconstruction task facing the international community in Afghanistan has taken place to date include a difficult geo-political context as well as deficits in security, economic development, institution building and governance. Located at the crossroads of Central and South Asia, Afghanistan has long been a target for invasion by regional as well as great powers. The Soviet Union invaded Afghanistan in 1979. The US provided funds and maintained strategic linkages with the Afghan mujahidin who came to occupy the power vacuum after the Soviet withdrawal in 1989. Soon after the fall of the Soviet-backed government in 1992 the various religious, tribal and ethnic factions began a devastating civil war. The Taliban ('religious students') under the leadership of Mullah Muhammad Omar and with the backing of Pakistan (see Rashid 2002) began their ascent to power around Kandahar in 1994, took control of Kabul in 1996 and soon controlled most of the country through a very strict interpretation of sharia or Islamic law (see Roy 2004). Human rights abuses, particularly of ethnic and religious minorities and women, were widespread. Taliban rule resulted in near-complete international isolation, and the country came to serve as a haven for terrorist groups, including al-Qaeda.

Besides the absence of state institutions or domestic elites with the ability and legitimacy to govern at the start of international intervention, in 2001 Afghanistan was also one of the world's worst humanitarian emergencies: over a quarter-century of occupation and civil war had displaced nearly six million people and left an estimated one million dead (UNHCR 2005). Per capita Gross Domestic Product (GDP), estimated at $140–$180, was on par with Somalia and Eritrea (European Commission 2003a). Given these starting points, international engagement in Afghanistan after the fall of the Taliban, apart from the provision of humanitarian relief, initially centred on establishing central state structures and institutions – but increasingly also focused on defeating a growing insurgency.

The Bonn Conference in December 2001 established a transitional process that was to lead to elections of a 'broad-based, gender-sensitive, multi-ethnic and fully representative government' (United Nations 2001). It established the Afghan Interim Authority (AIA) under the leadership of Hamid Karzai, who became the first democratically elected president of the Islamic Republic of Afghanistan in 2004. Following on from the so-called Bonn process, a new partnership was established at the London Conference in 2006. The Afghanistan Compact identified security, governance, rule of law and human rights as well as social and economic development as key pillars of activity. Consequently, the Compact seeks 'to continue in the spirit of the Bonn, Tokyo and Berlin conferences, to work toward a stable and prosperous Afghanistan, with good governance and human rights protection for all under the rule of law' (see NATO 2006b). This agreement was to encourage not only Afghan ownership of the reconstruction process, but also to foster the reliance on domestic governance and security institutions to provide security and stability – a political aim that was reinforced by the 2009 strategic review of US engagement in Afghanistan. Paradoxically, concurrently to the broadening scope of international engagement, US and European publics increasingly withdrew their support for continuing military engagement. Communicating the need for further engagement to the public was made difficult also because there was little by way of success to point to after nearly a decade of international engagement. Instead, the political and security conditions in the country turned ever more complex.

Two challenges in particular complicate international efforts at establishing legitimate, broad-based governance mechanisms. First, a legacy of conflict and large-scale human rights violations, coupled with lack of trust in the political system, have negatively affected local acceptance of government structures. Beyond the government's inability to deliver basic services to the population, the decision to include local militia leaders, many of whom have been involved in past conflict and human rights violations, in the 2005 parliamentary elections further alienated parts of the population (see Ayub and Kouvo 2008). Beyond a fundamental contradiction between the establishment of centralized state structures in what is essentially a decentralized social, political and economic reality, the appointment system of regional government officials reinforces the control of the Afghan President. Accountability and transparency are difficult to establish in a political system where governors are appointed rather than elected. At a time when Afghanistan, and international actors engaged in the country, face increasing security challenges, weak local governance structures are unable to support a self-sustaining political process. EU activity in Afghanistan, therefore, takes place in a conflict setting where development assistance, efforts at establishing the rule of law and political engagement with the host government are overshadowed by ongoing conflict where the Taliban insurgency continually challenges the legitimacy of the government but also the presence of international military forces.

The EU in Afghanistan

Since the fall of the Taliban, the EU has been engaged in Afghanistan in political and economic terms, in addition to the military contributions of individual EU member states to the International Security Assistance Force (ISAF). Significantly, the EU has been a key donor in Afghanistan's reconstruction. In the period from 2002 through June 2009, the EU committed €1.65 billion to Afghanistan (European Commission 2009a) in key areas that include rural development, governance and health. Besides humanitarian aid, Community programmes initially focused on building up infrastructure and on establishing government institutions and public services. In addition, individual EU member states have made substantial contributions to post-conflict reconstruction in financial, political but also military terms. By early 2010, 25 member states were deploying troops to ISAF, with a combined contribution of about 30,000 troops (ISAF 2010).

Formal EU–Afghanistan relations are governed by the 2005 EU–Afghanistan Joint Declaration, which was concluded following the completion of the Bonn process. The Declaration commits the EU to formalized bilateral cooperation and annual meetings at the ministerial level. Key priorities include 'consolidating a democratic political system, establishing responsible and accountable government institutions, strengthening the rule of law, and safeguarding human rights (including the rights of women) and the development of civil society' (Council of the EU 2005b: 2). The 2006 London Conference marked a turning point in EU engagement because it entrusted the EU with additional areas of engagement: reforming the police and justice sectors.

This growing role for the EU in civilian reconstruction and governance through its police mission EUPOL Afghanistan resulted from considerations of consolidating international efforts and the realization that more would have to be done in the area of police and justice reform. European engagement in Afghanistan thus became 'Europeanized' in an effort to both increase the EU's political profile in Afghanistan but also better coordinate

European contributions to the country's reconstruction. As for development, among the priority sectors identified by the European Commission for the 2007–2013 period are rural development, governance and health (European Commission 2009a). Given the large percentage of the population that lives in rural areas, rural development represents a key activity in improving economic development. Together with the provision of primary health care, the two areas serve as important measures that undercut political and institutional reconstruction. In development terms the EU has contributed significantly to infrastructure, technical assistance and capacity building. In the area of health, EU support for the provision of basic health services, infrastructure and the delivery of equipment and medicines has given some 80 per cent of the population access to primary health services (European Union 2009). Similarly, rural development programmes have focused on infrastructure development including building roads to enable farmers to bring their crops to the market or drilling wells. Additional EU aid has focused on social protection, particularly on vulnerable groups, and financial and technical assistance for demining as well as aid to uprooted people (AUP) (European Commission 2009a). This broad support for Afghanistan's development forms an important element in EU assistance to Afghanistan. It also indirectly supports the EU's political involvement as well as its contributions to reforming the rule of law. Finally, election support has emerged as an additional field for the EU to engage in through the launch of an Election Observation Mission (EOM) during the presidential election in 2009. The EU has also made a financial contribution to the election process. It has committed €35 million to the UN fund for electoral support (ELECT), which supports long-term institution building, voter education and civic outreach as well as the preparation of Afghanistan's parliamentary elections in September 2010.

With the launch of EUPOL Afghanistan in 2007 and EU EOM in 2009, EU commitments in Afghanistan have come to span development assistance, governance and rule of law. The EU is represented in the field through the EU Delegation, which is headed by Ambassador Vygaudas Usackas. The ratification of the Lisbon Treaty consolidated the EU's presence in the field through the 'double-hatting' of the position of EU Special Representative (EUSR) with that of the Head of the EU Delegation (European Voice 2010). Double-hatting the two posts was to give the EU more coherence: separating the financial and political competences of the Commission Delegation and the office of the EUSR, respectively, had until then negatively affected both. The EU's capacity to act improved as a result of the Lisbon Treaty but also the expanding number of tasks and policy areas with which the EU engages. The EU's consolidated presence in Kabul notwithstanding, EU activities in Afghanistan continue to be hampered by insufficient linkages between Kabul and Brussels, and between Brussels and individual EU member states. This suggests that the EU's capacity to coordinate, both internally and with other actors engaged in Afghanistan, remains challenging. Analysing EU contributions in the broader context of international engagement in Afghanistan over the past decade not only demonstrates the increase in EU activities but also the shortfalls in international cooperation and the overall direction in reconstruction. The following section presents the broader international context in which EU contributions are located. It is intended to provide a framework for a more detailed analysis of EU contributions that is presented in this chapter's final part.

International engagement in Afghanistan

The past decade has witnessed important shifts in the nature and the focus on international engagement in Afghanistan. During the first five years of international engagement

Afghanistan was considered the 'safe' war, and US and international attention focused on Iraq. The transatlantic rift over Iraq in turn negatively affected transatlantic cooperation in Afghanistan as well (see Rashid 2008). At the same time, the increasing role of the North Atlantic Treaty Organization (NATO) in Afghanistan but also the deteriorating security conditions refocused attention on the country, highlighting the need for cooperation but increasingly also the political, economic and indeed regional dimension to Afghanistan's reconstruction. The advent of the Obama administration with debates over the increase in troop levels and the adoption of a counter-insurgency strategy saw Afghanistan emerge as the top foreign policy priority for the US – and therefore also its allies. Significantly, while the focus remains very much on military involvement and the provision of security, current debates and political initiatives increasingly also take into account the issues of governance as well as Afghanistan's regional dimension. The scope of international engagement, therefore, has significantly broadened. The increasing complexity also reinforces the argument that initial decisions over international engagement continue to haunt international efforts in Afghanistan. Insufficient and fragmented efforts, coupled with a lack of coordination mechanisms, have not been able to prevent the resurgence of the Taliban or to establish self-sustaining, functioning institutions of governance.

Light footprint and fragmentation

Efforts at establishing central state structures initially adopted a 'light footprint' approach, which emphasized a quick turnover of responsibility to the Afghan government. Given the reluctance on the part of the Bush administration to engage in state building, coupled with increasing attention paid to the war in Iraq, emphasis was placed on low visibility and intensity of international engagement. This included the decision not to deploy a peacekeeping force outside Kabul or to engage US troops in peacekeeping tasks (see Dobbins 2008) – this task was left to the Europeans and others through the establishment of the ISAF. ISAF's main role is to assist the Afghan government in extending its authority and creating a secure and stable environment. Concrete aims include the conduct of security and stability operations in coordination with the Afghan National Security Forces (ANSF) and assisting the development of the Afghan National Army (ANA) (see NATO 2009). Military and civilian contributions beyond Kabul in turn have mainly been delivered through Provincial Reconstruction Teams (PRTs). NATO was not initially involved in ISAF, but the organizational requirements for running a multilateral peacekeeping operation, as well as a deteriorating security situation, led to NATO assuming ISAF command in August 2003. PRTs continue to be led by individual nations, operate largely autonomously from one another, and have strong links to respective national capitals, but were formally placed under ISAF command in 2006. ISAF has gradually expanded its geographical and functional reach, in particular in the area of training of ANSF, which also includes police training, with the launch of a NATO Training Mission Afghanistan (NTM-A) in 2009.

   In addition to adopting a 'light footprint' approach, a decision that in hindsight came to be regarded as a squandered opportunity to impose stability, the early period of intervention in Afghanistan also included efforts to include a broad range of countries and institutional stakeholders in the country's reconstruction under the UN umbrella. Designed to signal a broad-based international consensus and commitments to the reconstruction of Afghanistan, this also institutionalized fragmentation of international efforts. Adopting a centralized approach to security, governance and the wider rule of law under the overall authority of the UN was not a politically favoured option. The individualized approach of the PRT concept illustrates this, as does the broader task of security sector reform (SSR), which has become a key activity for the EU in Afghanistan. Following the 2002 Geneva Conference on SSR, the G8 adopted a 'lead nation approach' where individual countries assumed responsibilities for central tasks including the areas of Disarmament, Demobilization and Reintegration (DDR) (Japan), army (USA), police (Germany), justice (Italy) and narcotics (United Kingdom). Varying degrees of financial and personnel commitments on the part of lead nations in pursuit of reform, coupled with the lack of linkages between these individual areas, further reinforced fragmentation, and go some way towards explaining weaknesses in Afghanistan's security sector. The 'EU-ization' of police and justice reform through the launch of the police mission EUPOL Afghanistan in June 2007 and the European Commission taking a lead role in justice reform that same year notwithstanding, Afghanistan's security sector remains weak. As a result, the task of police reform has also been taken up by the US and NATO. This increasing involvement reflects debates and frustration over transatlantic burden sharing, and has overshadowed the role and contribution of the EU. Such multi-faceted engagement affected cooperation and the implementation of reform: differing approaches to training, diverging conceptions of the role of the police in providing security, and different levels of financial engagement on the part of these various actors resulted in overlapping and sometimes contradictory training initiatives (see Gross 2009).

Towards a comprehensive approach

Given the magnitude of the reconstruction task in Afghanistan coupled with the deteriorating security situation the international community increasingly came to realize the detrimental effects of fragmentation and has worked towards creating more coherence and synergies between international efforts. Increasing demands made on ISAF in light of the resurgence of the Taliban gradually shifted the political and operational focus away from the emphasis on a 'light footprint' and towards increased state- and institution-building efforts on the part of the US and its allies. This shift resulted in arguments over burden sharing and a transatlantic division of labour as attention moved from an emphasis on broad-based contributions to the reconstruction of Afghanistan to debates centred on military security. Given the lengthy debates over NATO engagement in Afghanistan, 'going out of area or out of business' also meant that Afghanistan often came to be framed as existential for NATO's future relevance (see Patrick 2009) – which focused additional attention on NATO and the transatlantic alliance rather than European and EU commitments in public discourse but also in political deliberations and decision-making. In operational terms, NATO's experience in Afghanistan also led to the emergence of the notion of 'comprehensive approach' in which military, political and developmental instruments and actors engage in a coordinated fashion. The 2008 NATO summit in Bucharest accordingly emphasized cooperation and contribution of all major actors, including that of non-governmental organizations (NGOs) as well as the host government, and stated that 'it is essential for all major international actors to act in a coordinated way, and to apply a wide spectrum of civil and military instruments in a concerted effort that takes into account their respective strengths and mandates' (see NATO 2008).

These institutional developments reflected the operational lessons from fighting a growing insurgency: emphasizing security without a concurrent emphasis on governance but also economic development was unlikely to yield sustainable results. The deteriorating security situation had several implications, and none too positive, for international engagement in

Afghanistan in general and for implementing a comprehensive approach in particular. On a very practical level, the growing insurgency makes it difficult to administer development programmes across the country, and many agencies cease to operate in those areas of the country that are considered unsafe. This is of particular concern as in purely developmental terms, Afghanistan remains one of the poorest countries in the world: despite receiving close to US$ 36 billion in development contributions over the past eight years, Afghanistan ranks second to last on the UN Human Development Index (HDI). This is reflected in several key development indicators that include low life expectancy at birth (43.6 years) and adult literacy rates (28 per cent), coupled with high fertility rates (7.5) (see United Nations 2009a). Apart from poverty and lack of development, a large rural population that can be difficult to reach poses an additional challenge for development but also for reconstruction tasks. These indicators, but particularly the high rate of illiteracy, also reflect the difficult task of training efforts of military and civilian personnel in the ANA and the Afghan National Police (ANP).

Institutionally, NATO's ability to implement a comprehensive approach remains limited. The organization itself does not possess civilian capabilities although the NATO Senior Civilian Representative is tasked with liaising with representatives of international organizations as well as the Afghan government. Cooperation with NGOs is hampered by the fact that many do not wish to cooperate closely with military forces. This is primarily due to concerns over protecting their independence and neutrality from military and political influence but also to suspicion over being integrated into military plans and agendas (see Jakobsen 2008). Implementing economic development measures, formulating political approaches and engaging in civilian reconstruction requires working with partners, including the UN and the EU. Inter-institutional cooperation has been made difficult, however, by the absence of formalized cooperation mechanisms and the ability to set strategic directions in light of unequal resources extended to Afghanistan's reconstruction. Although the UN through its UN Assistance Mission to Afghanistan (UNAMA) was given a coordinating mandate in the implementation of the Bonn Agreement, in practice it found itself challenged to fill this role. The post of UN Special Representative strengthened UN coordination of international activities. However, limited resources and resulting limited visibility put the UN in a disadvantageous position when it came to assuming its coordinating mandate (see International Crisis Group 2008a).

As for EU–NATO relations, cooperation has been made difficult by the absence of a formal agreement that would permit formal links and cooperation beyond Berlin Plus, which refers only to joint EU–NATO military operations. Afghanistan, therefore, has not been on the agenda of meetings between the Political and Security Committee (PSC) and the North Atlantic Council (NAC) in Brussels. This has obvious consequences for joint strategic agenda setting. In addition, the overwhelming US lead in Afghanistan has also given NATO a more dominant role. This has also negatively affected EUPOL's impact: given the size of the operation, and its approach of civilian policing, the mission has not been able to set or significantly impact on the strategic agenda. As a result, expectations of implementing a truly comprehensive approach – understood as the coordination and cooperation of military, civilian and economic activities across a range of institutions – have proven unrealistic. Efforts at doing so have also exposed to date unresolved inter-institutional differences and political obstacles to cooperation, and have compromised the EU's capacity to coordinate its activities with those of its external partners.

Obama's war: adopting a counter-insurgency strategy

The advent of the Obama administration infused US and therefore also international engagement in Afghanistan with added momentum. The emerging political consensus held that the situation is deteriorating and that a change in strategy towards Afghanistan would be needed. Waning public support for military engagement in Afghanistan in the US and in Europe focused attention on formulating a road map towards an exit strategy. Strategic readjustments (see Woodward 2010) favoured a short-term increase in troop numbers, and this adds pressure on policy makers to produce successful outcomes. Current US strategy towards Afghanistan on the one hand focuses on a more narrow set of interests, namely countering the terrorist threat from the country. On the other hand, following the Iraq template of a temporary 'surge', it advocated a short-term increase of troops, and the build-up of Afghan capacities so as to hand over security responsibility to the Afghan government within a reasonable time period. Politically, the US also placed an increasing focus on Afghanistan's regional dimension, particularly Pakistan. The new military operational culture suggested was that of population-centric counter-insurgency (see ISAF 2009a). Through the adoption of a counter-insurgency strategy in late 2009, the Obama administration refocused its engagement in Afghanistan on increased efforts to train Afghan security forces; a temporary increase in troop levels to fight the Taliban; and has emphasized the importance of governance (see ISAF 2009b).

The current US strategy and indeed the broader international effort in Afghanistan faces a two-fold challenge. In addition to the military challenge facing ISAF troops through the Taliban insurgency, the current Afghan government is weak and there are doubts over whether the Karzai government is a reliable partner for the international community. The 2009 presidential elections did not turn out to be the game changer the international community had hoped they would be. Rather than instilling confidence in the democratic system on the part of the international community as well as the Afghan population, allegations of fraud highlighted corruption, tribal linkages, and a presidential system vested in personal affiliations rather than transparency and accountability. This reinforced concerns, voiced in a leaked cable by US ambassador Eikenberry in Kabul, that President Karzai is 'not an adequate strategic partner' who shuns 'responsibility for any sovereign burden' (quoted in *New York Times* 2010). While the US leadership has since departed from its approach of pressuring Karzai, the conduct of the 2009 presidential elections has highlighted once more the importance of governance but also the essentially political nature of Afghanistan's challenges (see Miliband 2010). When it comes to external coordination, the changing US approach towards Afghanistan has positively affected EU–US relations in the field. US plans of increasing the size of the ANP necessarily calls for greater involvement on the part of all actors involved in police reform in Afghanistan. An increasing emphasis on coordination, therefore, has given more support to EUPOL Afghanistan as an important element in a broader international strategy.

The EU in Afghanistan: analysing impact and accomplishments

Beyond the provision of military security, the multifaceted challenges facing the international community in Afghanistan require political and economic engagement. The EU, with its broad range of instruments and its capability to fund but also to act, in principle is in a privileged position to make an impact in Afghanistan's reconstruction. This section shows that the EU has made significant contributions in terms of economic development as well as governance and the rule of law. The analysis of these contributions also highlights, however, that the EU has fallen somewhat short of its initial goals when it comes to reforming the police and justice sector, and when it comes to wielding political influence. This is due to a number of converging factors. First, EU presence in Afghanistan has suffered from incoherence as far as the application of EU instruments is concerned. Second, the resources extended towards Afghanistan, particularly when it comes to EUPOL Afghanistan, have been insufficient in terms of both personnel and political support. Third, EU member states have often privileged transatlantic or national considerations in their policy-making towards Afghanistan rather than strengthening the EU's position. Finally, the EU has not formulated a strategy or specific policy objectives in Afghanistan. Taken together, these factors have undermined the EU's influence and its capacity to act: the number of largely independent actors and financial instruments that make up the collective European engagement have negatively affected the EU's performance in terms of its coherence and its overall political leverage in the country (see Buckley 2010).

The EU's contribution to police reform

The three weaknesses cited above have also been evident in the EU's engagement in the area of governance and the rule of law. EU activities in this area include financial contributions by the European Commission, political engagement through the EUSR, but also EUPOL Afghanistan. The European Commission makes substantial financial contributions to the Afghanistan Reconstruction Trust Fund (ARTF), but also to the Law and Order Trust Fund (LOTFA) that was established in 2002. LOTFA supports police reform both through the payment of police salaries but also with equipment and facilities, as well as broader institutional development. LOTFA also supports salaries of the personnel of the Ministry of Justice. Since annual costs cannot be covered by tax revenues, LOTFA will continue to finance salaries in the near to long-term future. Far from being self-sustaining financially, an estimated 93 per cent of public expenditures are met by foreign aid (see Maas 2007). Although weak Afghan state structures are largely dependent on foreign investment, this has not necessarily given the international community leverage over governmental authorities. The EU's capability to fund, therefore, does not automatically translate into political influence. Conditionality is difficult to enforce in light of essential expenditures that international assistance supports. Although financial support through LOTFA supports important institutional developments such as pay reform, the recruitment of women, and procurement and maintenance, accountability and transparency with respect to the payment of salaries need to be further pursued (European Commission 2009a).

Contributions to LOTFA link closely to the work undertaken by EUPOL Afghanistan. Beyond the challenge of building transparent government structures at the level of bureaucracy, however, the state of the Afghan police illustrates the difficulty of building public institutions in a developmental and post-conflict context. At the start of reform efforts, most of the estimated 50,000 men working as police were untrained, ill-equipped, illiterate and owed their allegiance to local warlords or militia commanders rather than the central government (International Crisis Group 2007). Initial training initiatives also proved insufficient. Germany as lead nation for police reform through the German Police Project Office (GPPO) contributed €12 million per year for the reconstruction of the police force, including training and equipment (Federal Foreign Office 2007). Germany built the Police Academy in Kabul that was operational as of August 2002, and generally focused on long-term training.

In light of the state of the Afghan police, which required not just the establishment of structures and training procedures but also rapid training of a large number of police officers, the German approach was considered too thorough (International Crisis Group 2007). The US got involved in police training as of 2003 as well, focusing on rapid training, with a view to equipping police with essential skills to take part in counter-insurgency efforts (Gross 2009). In the absence of a transatlantic consensus or indeed coordination between US, EU and national efforts, training initiatives were fragmented, overlapping – and less effective. Still, the increasing focus on police reform, together with the EU's emerging profile in civilian crisis management – including the reform of police and the wider rule of law – led to increasing discussion over a potential EU mission that was eventually decided under the German EU Presidency in the first half of 2007. Significantly, the launch of EUPOL Afghanistan was also influenced by transatlantic pressures on the EU to step up its commitment to Afghanistan, including the use of its civilian crisis management instruments. A Joint EU Assessment Mission report presented to the PSC in October 2006 recommended to 'consider contributing further to support the police sector through a police mission'. The Council approved the Crisis Management Concept for an EU police mission on 12 February 2007. The mission was launched in June 2007. EUPOL Afghanistan is managed in Brussels by the Civilian Planning and Conduct Capability (CPCC), which oversees EU civilian missions. The PSC exerts political control and strategic directions, whereas the role of the EUSR is to provide local guidance – but without being part of the official chain of command.

The main tasks of EUPOL Afghanistan were to

> significantly contribute to the establishment under Afghan ownership of suitable and effective civilian policing arrangements, which will ensure appropriate interaction with the wider criminal justice system [...]. The mission will support the reform process towards a trusted and efficient police service, which works in accordance with international standards, within the framework of the rule of law and respects human rights.
>
> (Council of the EU 2007c).

Rather than a training mission, EUPOL was to contribute to the formulation of an overall strategy, and to mentor staff in the Ministry of the Interior (MoI), as well as police commanders and upper ranking officials. EUPOL's value-added was seen in its subsuming member state and a number of third states' police efforts, and in its potential to improve coordination among the various actors engaged in police reform. A weak link between Brussels and the field, personnel shortages and a vague mandate, however, meant that EUPOL Afghanistan not only got off to a weak start, but also has not been able to meet its stated goals. These shortfalls in the EU's capabilities to act, manifest in the lack of political will to equip the mission with the required personnel, have implications for the EU's capacity to cooperate and coordinate.

EUPOL's current authorized mission strength is 400, and EUPOL staff are deployed in Kabul, the regional commands and the provinces. Deployments through PRTs were slowed down due to the absence of a formalized EU–NATO agreement and the resulting need to draw up bilateral technical agreements with individual lead nations to ensure security for EUPOL staff. The absence of an EU–NATO agreement has also meant that EUPOL officers are not deployed in Turkish- and US-led PRTs. EUPOL suffered not just on account of inter-institutional issues between NATO and the EU. Frequent changes in heads of mission as well as member state reluctance to staff EUPOL with the personnel promised meant that EUPOL could not perform the functions it had set out for itself.

By mid-2010 mission strength was 278 internationals, with 185 deployed at EUPOL Headquarters in Kabul, 89 in the regions, and four providing support within the Mission Support Element in Kabul (EUPOL 2010). This illustrates that personnel shortfalls continue to hamper the mission, even if the objectives and aims of EUPOL have been readjusted to better reflect the capabilities of the mission. What is more, the shortages in personnel are made worse by the fact that EU member states, rather than subsuming their contribution to police reform under EUPOL, continue to conduct separate bilateral police programmes. And the majority of EU member states seconding personnel to EUPOL insist that their national mission staff are deployed in areas controlled by the respective member state. Since launching EUPOL, the size of GPPO has increased – whereas the five countries that make up the European Gendarmerie Force have committed forces to the NATO training mission rather than the EU (see Buckley 2010). This shows that, far from constituting the 'Europeanization' of national contributions to reforming Afghanistan's police, national and transatlantic reflexes continue to be strong. Withholding support for the mission and agreeing to an overly vague mandate on the part of EU member states has undermined EU effectiveness as a result.

In particular, EUPOL's initial objective of assuming a coordination function of existing police reform activities proved unrealistic particularly in light of a financial and political US lead. As a result, EUPOL threatened to decrease both in visibility but also in the value of its contributions to police reform. Two particular challenges facing EUPOL included the internal and external coordination of reform efforts, and the cooperation of Afghan stakeholders in pursuit of institutional reform. The International Police Coordination Board (IPCB), a coordinating mechanism created in 2007, was supposed to facilitate the coordination of international efforts. In reality, however, the relatively low importance assigned to the IPCB (at least prior to the Board's reform in 2009) on the part of the EU and as a result also of the US has weakened this particular coordination mechanism.

Despite EUPOL's growing pains, there are some positive signs as well that point towards improvements in the EU's capacity to act and to coordinate. EUPOL has been able to effectively fine-tune its objectives to support and complement efforts undertaken by the NATO training mission NTM-A. It has also established closer relationships with UNAMA. Improved EU–US coordination has been due in part to efforts at police reform having become increasingly aligned. Rather than working at cross purposes, the US now views EUPOL as value added to its large-scale training efforts. Whereas US training efforts focus overwhelmingly on the establishment of security and are conducted by military personnel, EUPOL focuses on the build-up of a professional civilian police force and is staffed by police and rule of law experts. As a consequence, whereas the training undertaken by NTM-A is largely military focused, EUPOL can contribute civilian policing advice (see Chilton *et al.* 2009).

Beyond a more constructive transatlantic relationship that led to greater alignment between EU and US effort, EUPOL's standing also improved as a result of specific requests made by the Afghan government (see Peral 2009). These included, for instance, the formulation and implementation of an anti-corruption strategy. As a result, EUPOL consolidated its objectives to a limited number of areas in the rule of law and in police. With respect to the rule of law, EUPOL's objectives include the formulation and implementation of an anti-corruption strategy under EUPOL lead; establishing links with prosecutors; and a focus on human rights and gender. Policing objectives include intelligence-led policing, the geographic expansion of the city police project in Kabul and the introduction of community policing through restructuring the Afghan Uniform Civilian Police (EUPOL 2010). Based on an agreement with the UN, EUPOL also trained officers in preparation for the 2010 parliamentary elections, and cooperation with NTM-A on an institutional level is good.

Since its launch in June 2007, therefore, EUPOL has fine-tuned its approach from assuming a coordination function to supporting Afghan-led initiatives and working in support of US efforts. This increasing alignment also reflects the recognition of the security environment in which the ANP operates. In light of deteriorating security, and the need to put police officers on the ground, long-term objectives of civilian policing had to be subordinated to immediate security concerns. While the external coordination in the field has been improved, member states' lack of flexibility in deployment and delays in staffing the mission continue to undermine the EU's credibility as an actor in civilian crisis management.

The EU's contribution to justice reform and public administration

Beyond police reform, the EU through the European Commission also contributes to justice reform. The decision in 2006 to push for greater EU involvement stemmed from the realization that the justice sector had to date not received the attention it had deserved, and that there was a need for improved coordination and a strengthening of the linkages between the police and justice sectors. EU support, including increasing efforts on the part of EUPOL to strengthen the link between police and justice, has made some contributions. This is all the more important because justice reform in general has been neglected in the overall focus on training and reform of the ANA and ANP. There are significant gaps in outreach to parts of the population; low salaries and inadequate training of personnel make the system inefficient and invite corruption; but there is also an inherent contradiction in the Afghan legal system, which is based on mixed civil and sharia law (see International Crisis Group 2010). The EU's assumption of responsibility for reforming the judiciary, together with the former lead nation, Italy, gave the EU a coordinating function. It has also moved justice reform higher up the political agenda. EC contributions consequently focus on support for the 'Access to Justice at District Level' project; provision of technical assistance in the drafting of the National Justice Strategy and National Justice Programme. The overall financial commitment to rule of law in the 2007–13 period is €200 million (see European Commission 2009a). Finally, with respect to the broader rule of law, the Commission also supports Customs and Border Management and Public Administration and Reform. Linking police and justice reform in overall EU engagement has had benefits, particularly since EUPOL Afghanistan has increased its rule of law component to include, for instance, cooperation between EUPOL and the Attorney-General's Office in Kabul, and programmes such as joint police–prosecutor training (EUPOL 2009). The EU has demonstrated its capacity to fund, and to a lesser extent also to act, in carrying out limited activities related to justice reform. However, the fact that other international donors, including the US, have made modest contributions to justice reform, renders the international engagement as a whole less than effective.

Conclusion. The EU in Afghanistan: impact and shortfalls

For the EU, its engagement in Afghanistan has represented a steep learning curve in light of the magnitude of the reconstruction task alone. Its increasing engagement, however, also signaled the external recognition of its increasing role as an international security provider. EUPOL Afghanistan, the Common Security and Defence Policy (CSDP) police mission launched in 2007, came into being in no small part on account of transatlantic pressures for the EU to make use of its civilian crisis management instruments. In this sense, Afghanistan represents a coming of age for CSDP and the EU's ability to contribute to international crisis management. This chapter has highlighted that the EU has had an impact with respect to Afghan stakeholders, its international partners – and in its financial commitments. To be sure, the EU's capability to act and to coordinate has been negatively affected both by the broader fragmentation of international efforts as well as the insufficient political and financial commitments on the part of member states, particularly as far as EUPOL is concerned. European engagement in Afghanistan has thus exposed the weaknesses in the EU's external policy more generally. At the same time, the EU's ability to continually readjust the focus of its policies, and to engage in a growing number of policy areas in light of changing external conditions and in respond to the demands of its partners, also illustrates that the EU has come far in its ability to deliver in post-conflict reconstruction as well as in its growing international reach.

9 The EU as a reluctant conflict manager in Moldova[1]

Claire Gordon

This chapter explores the evolving role of the European Union (EU) as a reluctant conflict manager in the conflict between Moldova and the breakaway region of Transnistria on the Eastern borders of the EU. Since the brief outbreak of violent hostilities between Moldova and the breakaway region of Transnistria in 1991–92 in the immediate aftermath of the break-up of the Soviet Union, no resolution of the conflict has been achieved. Rather a state of frozen conflict has persisted: Transnistria has moved to consolidate its position as a de facto statelet supported militarily, politically and economically by Russia. Meanwhile until recently Moldova's transition had stalled both economically and politically, the country mired in a state of semi-reform, currently the poorest country in Europe vacillating between a geopolitical orientation towards Russia and the EU. In the wake of the violent period of conflict a negotiating mechanism was set up under the chairmanship of the Organisation for Security and Co-operation in Europe (OSCE). This peace-making framework (Moldova, Transnistria, OSCE, Russia and Ukraine) has remained in place since that time albeit with the addition of the United States (US) and EU as observers (hence 5+2) in 2005. In 2006, official negotiations were suspended, but informal talks continued on a fairly regular basis, intensifying in 2010–11, and finally leading to a formal agreement on the resumption of official negotiations in September 2011 (Wolff 2011b).

Up until the early 1990s, both the European Council and the Commission stayed largely on the sidelines of the frozen conflict situation in Transnistria as well as other unresolved conflicts in the post-Soviet space. In the decade following the communist collapse and the disintegration of the Soviet Union, the EU was preoccupied with the process of enlargement to Central and Eastern Europe (CEE), its own ill-fated attempts at conflict management in the former Yugoslavia and subsequently the framing of a policy of post-conflict stabilisation and association in the Western Balkans which intersected with the development of its nascent foreign policy capacities (Gordon 2009). But with the approach of enlargement to CEE in the early 2000s and the recognition of real security concerns linked to the advent of a set of unstable semi-reformed states on EU borders, the EU was galvanised into action. On the surface little progress has been made in the reconciliation of the opposing sides in the Transnistrian conflict, and in terms of negotiating a lasting settlement or committing troops to a restructured peace-keeping force, the EU has purposefully chosen to remain on the margins. Nonetheless there has been enhanced engagement of the EU in other aspects of the conflict management process and, despite continuing shortcomings, these activities may over time support moves towards a final conflict settlement.

Despite requests by the government in Chishinau the EU has remained ambivalent about direct involvement in the settlement negotiations, in part due to the broader geopolitical, energy and economic interests at stake in the EU's relationship with Russia, in part due to the sheer diplomatic obstacles to achieving consensus among 27 EU member states. This reluctance has been reinforced by the evident difficulty for the EU of engaging directly with an unrecognised legal entity and thus being perceived in some way as lending legitimacy to the leadership in Tiraspol when the EU remains formally committed to Moldova's territorial integrity. Rather the EU has focused its efforts on fostering conditions conducive to peace-making by pursuing a dual-pronged approach to conflict management. First, the EU has put in place a set of policies and instruments directed at developing the supporting conditions for achieving a final settlement to the conflict. Since 2003 through the European Neighbourhood Policy (ENP) and actions under the EU Action Plan for Moldova (EUMAP), the EU Border Assistance Mission (EUBAM) and the EU Special Representative (EUSR), the EU has increased its involvement in the country facilitated by the ongoing development and upgrading of its EU internal conflict management capabilities. Second, the EU has sought to contribute to conflict management through a more indirect long-term trickle-down approach under the framework of the ENP. It has done this by encouraging the furthering of economic and political reforms through a process of institutional alignment with EU market regulations and the fostering of shared democratic values and reliance on the soft power of conditionality. The (implicit) objective has been to make membership in that broader economic and political community attractive to people in the breakaway region of Transnistria and thus pave the way to eventual reintegration.

With a rather opportunistic and ineffective Communist leadership at the helm from 2001 to 2009, political and economic advances in Moldova were fitful. Though attracted by the potential geopolitical benefits of closer integration with the EU, the Communist leadership lacked the domestic political will and adequate administrative capacities to commit to this process in practice and to implement the necessary political and economic reforms. Instead throughout this period the Voronin leadership vacillated between Moscow and Brussels. The election of a new EU-oriented coalition government in Moldova in July 2009 and the internal foreign policy institutional reforms post-Lisbon have raised the prospect of increased cooperation between the government in Chishinau and EU institutions on a whole range of issues, including the matter of conflict settlement. But despite increased declaratory willingness on both sides, there has been little evidence to date of an intensification of conflict management activity except at the level of confidence-building measures. The EU's priorities have remained firmly fixed on economic reform and institutional alignment activities as well as continuing to support the maintenance of security along the country's border with Ukraine through the EUBAM mission. Reinforcing this proposition as part of the reform of the EU's foreign policy apparatus post-Lisbon, the appointment of the High Representative of the European Union for Foreign Affairs and Security Policy and the development of the External Action Service (EAS), the position of the EUSR to Moldova was abolished in February 2011, raising the prospect in the short term at least of a downgrading of the EU's role in the diplomatic side of the peace-making process in Moldova (Lobjakas 2010).

Nonetheless despite limited concrete progress in moving towards a final settlement in recent years, the EU has in fact found itself increasingly drawn into a process of procedural and diplomatic entrapment through its increased involvement in different aspects of conflict management in Moldova. The Alliance for European Integration (AEI) government is investing more concerted efforts in meeting the conditionality-lite that lies at the heart of the ENP and other instruments of EU's interrelationship with Moldova. Moreover since its accession to power there has been an increasing level of intensity of interactions and of policy cooperation between Chishinau and Brussels (negotiations are advancing over a new Association

Agreement and a Deep and Comprehensive Free Trade Agreement with Moldova). However, in the area of conflict management cautious optimism must be balanced by a dose of heavy realism.

I have argued elsewhere that key to understanding the efficacy of EU attempts at peace-making in conflict situations is an understanding of the complex multi-level interaction of domestic players with other domestic, regional and international actors and the complex balancing act of costs and interests at play. Thus any assessment of room for progress in moving towards a final settlement in the Transnistria–Moldova situation is coloured by (i) a recognition of the continuing intransigence of the leadership in Tiraspol over any form of compromise power-sharing solution, which is supported in this stance by the not so invisible elephant in the room – the leadership in Moscow, as well as by (ii) an awareness that the relationship with the EU may not hold out sufficiently attractive benefits for the leadership in Moldova particularly if progress stalls in other areas beyond the domain of conflict man-agement. Furthermore though the eight-year long internal struggle to agree on a set of insti-tutional reforms to enable the functioning of an enlarged Union was finally brought to a close with the approval of the Lisbon Treaty, some of the diplomatic challenges which have limited the EU's efficacy as a foreign policy player and conflict manager in particular are yet to be resolved. Finally the period of EU internal preoccupation and retrenchment which set in post-CEE enlargement has continued given the significant economic, regulatory and polit-ical questions which the global economic and financial crisis and the fallout from the bailout of Greece have thrown on the table.

The remainder of the chapter proceeds as follows: first, it provides a brief history of the conflict situation in Transnistria. Second, it considers the evolution of EU engagement in Moldova, including an exploration of existing EU institutional, political and financial capa-bilities that facilitate or constrain its efficacy as a conflict manager. The third part of the chapter turns its attention to the domestic, regional and international context of the conflict dynamic which ultimately holds the key to the likely success of attempts at conflict manage-ment. In a short concluding section the chapter draws the threads of the discussion together evaluating the achievements as well as the shortcomings of the EU's engagement in the conflict situation in Transnistria to date.

Evolution and stagnation of the conflict situation in Transnistria

Unlike the other frozen conflicts in the Former Soviet Union, it is generally accepted that ethnopolitical rivalries do not lie at the heart of the conflict over the breakaway region of Transnistria (Roper 2002). It is clear that political and economic elites in Tiraspol concerned about the potential loss of power and privilege in a newly independent Moldova were the primary driver. Since 1945 Moldova had been one of the 15 union republics of the Union of Soviet Socialist Republics (USSR) made up of Bessarabia, previously part of Romania, and the Western part of Moldavia. In the early 1990s as part of its attempt to embed its independ-ent statehood *vis-à-vis* its former imperial chief in Moscow, the Popular Front of Moldova tried to rally the opposition by underlining the country's proximate relationship to Romania and some voices spoke in favour of unification (King 1999). The severance from Moscow, the loss of political and economic power resources, coupled with concerns about the Romanisation of Moldova sparked a strong reaction among elites in Tiraspol, the capital of Transnistria, west of the River Dniestr. Heavy fighting broke out in 1991–2 between the oppos-ing sides. A peace agreement was finally brokered by the Russian General Alexander Lebed,

Commander of the 14th Division of the Russian Army, which to this day has troops stationed in the region.

Formally the conflict over Transnistria has been frozen since the bilateral ceasefire was agreed between the Russian Federation and the Republic of Moldova in July 1992 with the establishment of a tripartite peacekeeping force comprising Russian, Moldovan and Transnistrian units stationed along the Dniestr valley, on both sides of the river, supervised by the Joint Control Commission. This was swiftly followed by the setting-up of the OSCE negotiations mechanism with the objective of reaching a final peace settlement. Though there have been a number of rounds of negotiations, these have not produced any lasting results. The work of the OSCE has been made more difficult by Russian reluctance to cooperate with the OSCE, claiming on a number of occasions that the organisation is not entirely neutral in its positions on conflict management. Moreover, the OSCE has limited power resources, restricting its clout in the negotiations process. Since 1992 a number of peace proposals have been laid on the table by individual governments including the Russian, Ukrainian and Moldovan leaderships but none of these plans has come to fruition. Most prominent among these have been the Russian-sponsored Primakov Memorandum proposing a common state solution in 1997, the 2003 Kozak memorandum putting forward an asymmetric federal structure for the country together with a continued Russian military presence for a further 20 years – torpedoed at the last minute following the intervention of the EU High Representative (EUHR) Javier Solana – and the April 2005 plan of Ukraine's newly elected President Yushchenko which was primarily important in that it signalled to the EU Ukraine's new willingness to engage in the conflict resolution process in the wake of the Orange Revolution.

However, contrary to the apparent implication of stagnation in the notion of a frozen conflict, the situation on the ground in Transnistria has been far from static. Over the past 20 years, the leadership in Tiraspol has taken steps to consolidate its political and economic hold over the region and entrench its separation from Chishinau. In the course of his presidency, Igor Smirnov put in place a harsh authoritarian regime limiting dissent at all levels of society. The breakaway region was able to benefit economically since the Soviet collapse from the fact that the mainstays of the Soviet industrial complex in the republic were housed in the Transnistrian region and thus it has continued to enjoy certain economic advantages *vis-à-vis* the metropolitan state of Moldova. Though Russia has outwardly supported diplomatic efforts at arriving at a final settlement, it has at the same time bolstered Transnistria economically, politically and militarily throughout this period. Despite the agreement reached with the OSCE in 1999, Russian troops–not to mention equipment–remain in place on the territory of the breakaway region. As long as the leadership in Tiraspol is sheltered and supported by Moscow, this is likely to pose a significant obstacle to a final conflict settlement. The election of Yevgeny Schevchuk, former Speaker of the Supreme Soviet, as President of Transnistria in December 2011, in the process defeating both Igor Smirnov and the Kremlin's favoured candidate, raises the possibility of a new opening in Moldovan–Transnistrian relations, but given the vested elite interests in the breakaway region this remains an open question at best. Early indications suggest that Schevchuk is committed to defending Transnistria's quasi-independent statehood and thus a speedy resolution of the conflict is not likely.

Moldova itself has oscillated between a pro-Russian and a pro-European orientation in its foreign policy since obtaining independence in 1991. European integration was declared as its primary foreign policy objective for the first time in 1999 though this period was short-lived since the Sturza coalition government did not last and the priority of European integration quickly slipped from the top of the political agenda (Buscaneanu 2006: 6). The establishment of the National Commission for European Integration by President Voronin in November 2002 marked a new departure in Moldova's positioning of European integration at the top of its foreign policy agenda though limited actual progress was made.

Since the initiation of the ENP and particularly the commencement of the Action Plan in 2005, Moldova's relationship with the EU has oscillated between disappointment and hope. There was some initial discontent in Moldova over its inclusion in the ENP as a result of the fact that this signalled Moldova's non-inclusion in the Stabilisation and Association Process (SAP) with the accompanying prospect of EU membership. Nonetheless there was also some initial hopefulness among the country's governing circles about what the EUMAP might be able to deliver in terms of increased market access, a visa-free travel regime and increased direct EU participation in the conflict settlement process in Transnistria. Broadly speaking, as Gheorghiu acknowledged, it was still hoped that the ENP and the Action Plan would form 'a bridge towards the following stage – association and integration into the EU' (Gheorghiu 2005, cited by Buscaneanu 2006: 17).

The re-election in early 2005 of the Party of Communists of the Republic of Moldova (albeit dependent on the parliamentary support of members of the Christian Democratic People's Party and the Democratic Party of Moldova) coincided with the agreement over the EUMAP. The new level of EU involvement in the country resulted in a reassertion of Moldova's pro-European foreign policy orientation. The new coalition identified the implementation of the EUMAP and the country's integration into the EU as its top priority (Popescu 2005) though this initial enthusiasm waned due to disappointment with the fruits of this interaction, the rather limited carrots on offer from Brussels as well as the, at best, ambivalent commitment of the Moldovan government to political and economic reform.

Progress with implementing the Action Plan and moving ahead with EU integration was further complicated in the period 2008–2009 with the increasingly inward-looking focus of Moldovan politics shaped by the approach of parliamentary elections in April 2009 and the subsequent rerun of the elections in July 2009. In the period leading up to the elections President Voronin became increasingly focused on attempts to secure his political future at home whatever this might entail, including a renewed rapprochement with Moscow and praising Russia's role in overseeing talks with the Transnistrian region (see Radio Free Europe 2009). As Nicolae Negru, Editor of *Journal de Chishinau*, commented in summer 2009, 'the goal of keeping power is more important than the objective of efficiently approaching Moldova to EU standards'.[2] In the wake of the victory of opposition democratic forces in elections in July 2009, and the further increase in their majority at the elections in December 2010, the new leadership has made a renewed European commitment reflected in the name of the governing coalition, the Alliance for European Integration (AEI). The AEI has concentrated on the internal economic situation as a result of the dire repercussions of the global economic and financial crisis in Moldova as well as strengthening the country's European integration and thus attempts to reinvigorate the conflict settlement process at a diplomatic level have been rather limited until recently.

Finally, from an institutional perspective, despite the signing of the EUMAP in early 2005 and the EU's promotion of policies and instruments directed towards establishing supporting conditions for conflict management, it is noteworthy that throughout the period 2005–2009 the Moldovan government did not take any steps to facilitate institutional join-up or linkages among government institutions dealing with EU integration processes and the implementation of the EUMAP and those bodies working on conflict management and regional affairs. This suggests that the EU is not perceived as a key actor in the conflict management process by those in governing circles in the country. Thus there was no special department dealing with the Transnistrian conflict in the Ministry of Foreign Affairs and European Integration (MFAEI), which is the main ministry with responsibility for the coordination and direction of EUMAP implementation. Before the new government came to power in July 2009, Transnistria and the conflict situation fell under the remit of the Ministry of Reintegration which, though it enjoyed one of the highest levels of allocated budgetary funding, had no input into the preparation of the Action Plan.

With the accession to power of the AEI government the Ministry of Reintegration was disbanded and for a period of time it was unclear where responsibility for conflict management lay, suggesting an initial lack of prioritisation of conflict management in the face of other pressing issues. A Bureau for Reintegration has been established with the task of providing support to Deputy Prime Minister for Reintegration Eugen Carpov, who was appointed to this new position in January 2011, and to a new Commission on Reintegration. Clearly the conflict in Transnistria has moved up the policy agenda. For the time being the Bureau for Reintegration still has rather limited capacities to perform its role and there remains an absence of a comprehensive reintegration strategy. But working groups are being set up in each ministry to develop work in this area and the United Nations Development Programme (UNDP) is funding a capacity-building support project.[3] In an early intervention Eugen Carpov directly linked the need for greater coordination of actions aimed at fulfilling the government objectives set in its 2011–2014 action programme 'European Integration: Freedom, Democracy, Welfare', suggesting a recognition of the close interlinkage between conflict resolution and European integration to which I now turn in the next part of this chapter.[4]

The evolution of EU involvement in Moldova and Transnistria

In the wake of the collapse of the Soviet Union, a number of the newly independent states concluded trade and cooperation agreements with the EU. Moldova's Partnership and Cooperation Agreement (PCA), which came into force in 1998 for an initial period of ten years and post-2008 has been extended on an annual basis, remains the key legal document underpinning relations between EU and Moldova. This is underlined by the fact that

Table 9.1 Time line: Moldova

1994	Agreement reached over EU–Moldova Partnership and Cooperation Agreement (PCA)
1998	PCA entered into force
February 2003	EU travel ban on 17 TN leaders (Council action)
February 2005	EU Action Plan signed (for an initial three years)
March 2005	Establishment of EU Special Representative for Moldova (NB under auspices of Council). Adriaan Jacobovits de Szeged appointed to position
October 2005	Opening of European Commission Delegation in Chishinau
November 2005	Establishment of EUBAM (European Union Border Assistance Mission) to Moldova and Ukraine (currently extended to November 2009)
March 2007	Appointment of Kálmán Mizsei as EU Special Representative for Moldova
Early 2008	Entry into force of visa facilitation agreement
February 2008, 2009	EU–Moldova Action Plan extended on a year-by-year basis
January 2010	Commencement of negotiations on Moldova's Association Agreement
February 2011	Abolition of position of EUSR for Moldova

Moldova's institutional relationship with the EU continues to be structured around the institutions that underpin the PCA framework including the Cooperation Council, Cooperation Committee and Parliamentary Cooperation Committee. The PCA was overwhelmingly concentrated on the development of trade and economic relations with the partnering country as well as at least in declaratory terms on the encouragement of the building of democratic political institutions. But in the case of Moldova no reference was made to the frozen conflict situation in Transnistria in the entire 95-page document (see *Partnership* and *Cooperation Agreement* 1994). The early Cooperation Council meetings steered clear of the topic altogether. The Organisation of Security and Cooperation remained the main intermediary institution attempting to further peace negotiations between the leaderships in Tiraspol and Chishinau together with the participation of Moscow and Kyiv, and the EU played virtually no role in the conflict management process.

In the early noughties the EU finally awoke to the need to increase its involvement in the post-Soviet space, including Moldova, spurred on by the approach of EU enlargement in 2004 and 2007 and, following the accession of Romania in 2007, by the recognition of the presence on its immediate periphery of a poor country with porous borders providing a channel for the trafficking of people, weapons and other goods, beset by the consequences of the unresolved frozen conflict. If enlargement to CEE had been driven both by internal EU interests and the need to protect the security and economic gains of 60 years of Western European cooperation and integration as well as making good on the 'return to Europe' of its CEE neighbours, the new level of engagement with the EU's Eastern neighbourhood was very much driven by internal EU interests. The imperatives to protect the EU, to ensure security and stability on its borders and to put a line under future enlargements to the East for the foreseeable future were paramount.

The first comprehensive proposal 'Communication to the Council and the European Parliament – The Wider Europe – Neighbourhood: A New Framework for Relations with our Eastern and Southern Neighbours', drawn up in the Commission, was presented in March 2003 (European Commission 2003b). While confirming objectives approved by the European Council the previous December, the policy proposal also laid out the parameters of the new set of relationships, stressing the importance of democracy, pluralism, human rights and the rule of law for political stability, underlining the intention to foster regional cooperation, particularly between Russia and the newly independent states, and including a very brief acknowledgement of the negative effects of conflict. The rather general and declaratory tenor of discussion in much of the document, the very cursory mention of Transnistria as a 'magnet for organised crime' and also as derailing 'the process of state-building and state political consolidation' all suggested that in Directorate-General (DG) Enlargement, where the document was drawn up, not only was the issue of frozen conflicts not at the forefront of debate but also that the ENP in its evolution reflected above all the EU's own internal interests – in the case of Transnistria the concern was to avert negative spill-over westwards. In equally general and rather non-committal terms the Commission proposed the following in terms of potential EU involvement in conflict management efforts: greater EU involvement in conflict prevention, crisis management, funding for post-conflict reconstruction and support of the efforts of OSCE and other mediators. The EU's growing concerns with security and stability on its borders had not yet translated into a full-blown recognition of the need for a concerted and coordinated policy effort within the overall framework of the ENP to facilitate conflict management processes in the Eastern neighbourhood.

In May 2004 the European Neighbourhood Strategy Paper was issued (see European Commission 2004b). Compared with March 2003, the May 2004 Strategy Paper gave greater prominence to the EU's contribution to the settlement of regional conflicts. This may have been the result of a degree of learning on the part of the Commission or a reflection of the decision to include in the ENP the countries of the South Caucasus – Armenia, Azerbaijan and Georgia – and as a result their frozen conflicts in Nagorno-Karabakh, South Ossetia and Abkhazia. Though the European Neighbourhood Strategy Paper was more focused on the organisational mechanics of the ENP, some policy areas in the context of broadening dialogue and neighbourhood cooperation were also discussed. However, the areas of concern in the chapter on the Eastern neighbourhood were not fleshed out in any greater detail than in the Wider Europe Strategy Paper.

Building on the recognition of the potential benefits of market alignment in the economic sphere and the spread of democracy, the EU introduced the instrument of Action Plans. Action Plans became the main tool for the translation into policy of the objectives and principles of the ENP. The EU had seen the apparent efficacy of its soft power tools in tying the hands of acceding countries through the CEE enlargement process, thereby inducing the alignment of the economic and political institutions of candidates with EU institutions. In the conceptualisation and design of the ENP it had evidently hoped to repeat this perceived success with the leverage of conditionality, while drawing a line under further enlargement to the East. In the case of the ENP the carrots on offer were aid and technical assistance, integration with the EU in various single market areas but not the ultimate prospect of membership. Moldova signed its Action Plan in February 2005 for an initial three-year period. As far as political issues were concerned EUMAP attached more significance to political change in Moldova than the PCA. Greater attention was paid to democracy and human rights as additional areas of dialogue and potential cooperation including the settlement of the Transnistrian conflict and border management. Moreover there was some attempt to peg progress in political change to future cooperation in other dimensions (this was witnessed again with forthright statements from the Swedish Presidency and its envoy Polish Foreign Minister Sikorski on the eve of the rerun of the elections in Moldova in late July 2009, linking the outcomes of the Moldovan elections with future prospects for EU integration) (see Pop 2009a).

Even so two points are worth making about the actual negotiations process over the Action Plan which reflect the continued primacy of economic issues in the Commission's work and the half-hearted attitude of many Commission officials to assuming an active role in conflict management. First, political issues did not even feature in the first round of negotiations in early 2004. Second, with regard to conflict resolution, it was in fact the Moldovan side that insisted on including a separate chapter on Transnistria in the Action Plan in Brussels in February 2005 (Buscaneanu 2006: 19–20). Nonetheless, in its final incarnation seven out of the ten priority areas in the Action Plan relate to the political dimension of cooperation and there are a considerable number of actions ranging from the general to the more specific enumerated under the priority of political dialogue and reform including actions relating to conflict management in Transnistria (Buscaneanu 2006: 19–20; Gordon and Sasse 2008: 27).

Despite the criticisms which can be levelled about the place of conflict management in the drawing up of EUMAP and the rather general nature of many of the related actions, 2005 witnessed a marked increase in the direct and/or indirect involvement of EU institutions in conflict management processes in Moldova. In March 2005, the institution of European Special Representative for Moldova was established under the EUHR Javier Solana's office in the Council with a mandate inter alia to '[S]trengthen the EU contribution to the resolution of the Transnistria conflict in accordance with agreed EU policy objectives, respecting the sovereignty of the Republic of Moldova within its internationally recognised borders, and in close coordination with the OSCE'. The institution of Special Representative has been used to good effect by the United Nations (UN) in a number of peacekeeping missions and in recent years by the EU in a number of conflict zones (Gordon *et al.* 2008). Given the rather general mandate of the EUSR to Moldova, much rested on the persona and diplomatic behind-the-scenes intermediary skills of the individual occupying the post. The first appointed EUSR for Moldova was Adriaan Jacobovits de Szeged, a highly experienced Dutch diplomat, followed by Kálmán Mizsei, who had previously served as Director of the United Nations Development Programme (UNDP) Regional Bureau in Europe and the Commonwealth of Independent States. (With the post-Lisbon reforms and the development of the EEAS the post of EUSR to Moldova was unfortunately superseded in February 2011.) In October 2005 the European Commission for the first time opened a delegation in Chishinau as a further indication of its increasingly active involvement in the country. The EU also became an official observer in the 5+2 OSCE-chaired negotiations format for the conflict settlement. The latest round of talks, which resumed in October 2005, broke down six months later due to Transnistrian disagreement with new customs rules for Transnistrian exports. Talks have been stalled since then despite various attempts by the OSCE to get the conflicting parties back to the negotiating table (see OSCE Mission to Moldova 2010). Notwithstanding the increase in activity in recent months following the accession to power of the AEI government in terms of the resolution of technical problems between the two sides, the two parties to the conflict have yet to agree arrangements for the resumption of official talks.

The final development in December 2005 was the establishment of the EUBAM as part of the EU's conflict resolution machinery in the framework of the Common Foreign Security Policy (CFSP)/Common Security and Defence Policy (CSDP). EUBAM employs some 200 personnel to supervise the joint Ukrainian–Moldovan 1,222 km border, including the rather porous border with the breakaway region of Transnistria. At the time of the establishment of EUBAM, the Ukrainian and Moldovan presidents also signed a joint declaration on the unification of customs procedures at the Moldova–Ukraine border, including the Transnistrian section. Under this unified customs regime, only goods with the necessary official Moldovan customs documents can cross the border. According to a 2008 report by ADEPT and EXPERT-GRUP on the implementation of EUMAP, 370 Transnistrian-based economic agents had been temporarily or permanently certified in Chishinau. This provision has undoubtedly contributed to the development of their trade relations with EU countries and over the medium to longer term this process could generate support in the Transnistrian region for closer EU integration. It is perhaps worth noting in this regard that the global economic and financial crisis has further increased the dependence of Transnistria on European markets (Popescu 2009: 463). However, the direct role of EUBAM in contributing to the conflict settlement process should not be overstated; rather EUBAM may be seen to be reinforcing the trickle-down dimension of the EU's conflict management agenda.

More direct forms of engagement in Transnistria, particularly with the governing authorities in the breakaway region, have been more problematic for the EU. In general in its actions in the Eastern neighbourhood, the Council, Commission and other EU institutions are faced with the basic predicament of how to deal with breakaway regions. Among the four frozen conflicts in the post-Soviet region the EU is constrained by a fundamental dilemma encapsulated in the following way by DG Relex in 2007, 'how to promote and support human rights in areas whose legal and political status is unclear' without legitimising their claims as independent actors (DG Relex 2007: 22). This dilemma has undermined the meeting of the objectives of a stable neighbourhood in the short to medium term at the very least. In the meantime, as Popescu (2006b) has noted, the gap between the metropolitan states and frozen conflict regions in terms of legislation, standards, values and degrees of reform is likely to increase, at best complicating, at worst excluding the possibility of reintegrating these countries at some point into the overarching state in which they are located. Thus far EU engagement in Transnistria has been limited to the financing of a small number of parallel border and cross-border civil society initiatives through the European Instrument for Democracy and Human Rights (EIDHR) framework and in a number of cases implemented by the UNDP. However, Emerson *et al.* (2007) have suggested that the ENP has suffered a dearth of 'creative thinking' in terms of developing ways to include these regions in some areas of ENP activity such as education, culture, health sector reform, rural development, etc. More recently, Tom de Waal underlined this point by suggesting that the EU and other organisations might consider further so-called 'status-neutral' measures in relation to Abkhazia. The EU could do more 'creative thinking' in this regard in relation to Transnistria as well (see Steele 2009).

By way of a conclusion to this section it is interesting to note that whereas the Commission singled out for praise Moldova's record in cooperation with the EU in the Transnistrian conflict management process and in particular its activities in cooperating with EUBAM in its April 2008 progress report on action plan implementation (in stark contrast to other political areas such as the rule of law and democratic change), it has been more critical of its own contribution to conflict resolution processes in the Eastern neighbourhood, having acknowledged at the end of 2007 that more needed to be done by the EU in addressing regional conflicts (see Europa 2007). Thus before presenting a consideration of the broader contextual dynamics which shape the prospects for conflict resolution in Moldova, I discuss a number of factors which have shaped and constrained the EU's efficacy as a conflict manager in the country, focusing in line with the thrust of this volume on its institutional capabilities to act and fund.

Institutional capabilities to act and their limitations

Insufficient political will among member states

In the 1990s the EU had neither the capacities nor the interest nor political will to engage actively in the newly independent states of the Former Soviet Union of which they knew little. Since the enlargement of the Union into CEE in 2004 and 2007, the EU has been on an intense learning and engagement curve in terms of its Eastern neighbourhood. Nonetheless in the case of conflict management in Moldova, it has been reluctant to get involved in political negotiations over a final settlement and possible power-sharing arrangements. Reluctant to risk confrontation with Moscow, the EU has been rather more willing to assist in building the supporting conditions to embed a possible final settlement and also in preventing further escalation of conflict in the future.

Though for many member states Moldova remains a distant, almost irrelevant state of limited interest (beyond the potential consequences of migrant and trafficked labour and goods), a number of members have been more active. The new member states have generally favoured a more active engagement of the EU and EU CFSP in supporting the newly independent states in the region in their transition away from communism. These have also been supported by some of the older member states (the Netherlands, Sweden and the United Kingdom) which have voiced criticism of aspects of Russian policy in the post-Soviet space and some of which have also developed their own bilateral aid and cooperation programmes in Moldova (Popescu 2009: 464). Member states which contain their own potentially secessionist movements have had rather mixed views about engagement in conflict management processes in general while others have also remained ambivalent about taking a more active role in conflict management – no doubt influenced by the usual suspects of enlargement fatigue, preoccupation with internal EU deepening issues and stalling of Lisbon as well as the prioritisation of relations with other external actors above and beyond Moldova. The current economic and financial crises and its consequences for the EU have further entrenched this inward-looking focus.

Internal institutional divides

Though conflict management is arguably critical to progress in a range of ENP priority areas, foreign policy including EU involvement in conflict management processes remained – at the very least until the enactment of the Lisbon Treaty in December 2009 – a Council-based prerogative and thus was organised on an intergovernmental basis with all the concomitant problems of generating sufficient political will and reaching consensus among up to 27 member states with diverse interests as alluded to above. As Popescu (2005: 10) has stated: 'ENP is a Commission-driven policy, and crisis management is the prerogative of the Council.' Thus for much of the past six years EU engagement in conflict management in Moldova was hampered by the institutional split in policy delivery. Key diplomatic policy initiatives in the conflict management area emanated from the Council. These included the travel ban on 17 political leaders from Transnistria, the establishment of the post of EUSR and the establishment of the border monitoring mission EUBAM. Meanwhile the EUMAP was drawn up and implemented in cooperation with the Commission. This division was also noted by an EU official in Moldova: 'The Commission pursues economic reform, while the EUSR deals with political and conflict resolution issues.' The official highlighted how conflicts and inconsistencies emerge when the Commission refuses to allocate the funds needed for EUSR initiatives.[5]

The above notwithstanding, even prior to Lisbon some mechanisms to facilitate horizontal coordination among EU institutions in the area of conflict management had been put in place, in particular the establishment of Directorate A of DG External Relations, which is responsible for Crisis Platform–Policy Coordination with units focused on crisis response and peace-building as well as CFSP operations but no single unit dedicated to conflict management alone. In a further recognition of the need for cooperation and coordination among EU institutions pre-Lisbon the practice was introduced of inviting a senior official in DG External Relations to attend the meetings of the Council's Political Security Committee. It is too early to say whether the problems of institutional join-up and of horizontal linkage over conflict management-related issues will be further reduced following the location of the newly established Office of the High Representative of the Union for Foreign Affairs and Security Policy inside the Commission, enjoying responsibility for the European External Action Service (EEAS) and continuing to chair key foreign policy councils inside the Council, but evidently the need to bridge these institutional lacunae was among the driving forces behind the treaty reforms.

Dual institutional origins, dual approaches

The dual institutional origins of the ENP may also be reflected in what appears to have been two different (though not necessarily irreconcilable) principles shaping approaches to conflict management in the EU. The former High Representative for CFSP Javier Solana, with his interest in promoting the Union's security objectives and the ambition to enhance the EU's role as an external actor, including in conflict situations on its borders, adopted a more proactive approach to conflict management and supported certain policies directly targeted at addressing the conflict situation. Meanwhile the Commission has favoured a different approach privileging the provision of technical and financial assistance in support of policies designed to facilitate economic and political reform (democratisation, rule of law, human and minority rights protection, etc.) in the metropolitan states and thus increasing the prospects for conflict resolution as a result of the pull factor of economic prosperity and political stability.

Commission's lack of experience in conflict management activities

The focus on domestic politics in the Action Plans underlines the fact that the APs were negotiated between the Commission and the neighbouring state, albeit with some input from the former High Representative for CFSP. The lack of experience and apparent reluctant engagement via the Action Plan of the Commission in conflict management processes is not an entirely surprising reflection of the fact that the form of ENP and the concept and structure of the Action Plans were developed in DG Enlargement, building on the experience of CEE enlargement and in part modelled on the Accession Partnerships. Though there was certainly the potential for ethno-political conflict in CEE and a number of countries have had to address minority-related issues including Slovakia, Hungary, Estonia and Latvia, officials in DG Enlargement, and subsequently DG External Relations and DG Enlargement and Neighbourhood Policy (since February 2010), who have been responsible for the operationalisation of the ENP, had at the outset only limited experience, understanding or capacities for dealing with transitioning countries facing such acute state- and nation-building issues and frozen conflicts as those existent in the EU's eastern neighbourhood. However, DG Enlargement and now DG Enlargement and Neighbourhood Policy's growing experience and knowledge of the Western Balkans since the launch of the SAP in 2000 should have alerted them more to the challenges of and obstacles to political and economic stabilisation in the absence of more direct engagement in conflict resolution processes.

Lack of specificity over EU's role in conflict management via AP

Though EUMAP proclaims the importance of shared responsibility and cooperation between the EU and Moldova in the areas of conflict prevention and resolution and in seeking a viable solution to the Transnistrian conflict, the substance of the Action Plan focuses overwhelmingly on domestic politics with little emphasis on the frozen conflict. Moreover, leaving aside the long list of actions on the Moldovan side, which stands in stark contrast to the number of EU actions and even joint actions, claims of partnership notwithstanding, there is still a lack of specificity in terms of how the EU proposes to participate in the resolution of the Transnistrian conflict.

Funding capabilities and their limitations

Any consideration of the EU's institutional capacity to serve as an effective conflict manager in Moldova cannot ignore the question of available funding levels and instruments. In 2003 the Commission issued a document outlining the financial underpinnings for the new neighbourhood policy. In the initial period from 2004 to 2006 the Commission was to draw on the existing financial framework and instruments (in the case of the Eastern Neighbourhood, Tacis, EIDHR, the Macro Financial Assistance Instrument and Interreg) though it would endeavour to achieve greater coordination between the different instruments.[6] Then in 2007 the ENPI funding instrument was introduced to streamline the disparate funding allocations to ENP countries and to target assistance in line with the key priorities in a particular country's Action Plans. Though on a per capita basis Moldova has received more funding than any other country forming part of the EU's ENP and has received a further increase in funding since the AEI government has been in power, a closer examination of the funding instruments and financing priorities reveals certain shortcomings in the EU's potential to effectively support conflict management activities.

The short-termism of EU funding mechanisms

EU funding mechanisms suffer from both short-termism and a lack of flexibility, restricted by the slowness of the centralised bureaucratic wheel. This makes them ill-suited to many crisis management activities. As Popescu has noted, the funding mechanisms are 'complex, technical, slow to deliver', all of which militates against the capacity for rapid reaction which is often called for in conflict situations (Popescu 2005: 12).[7]

Potential mismatch between Action Plan priorities and National Indicative

In principle ENP Instrument (ENPI) funding is allocated in line with the main priorities laid out in the Country Strategy Paper 2007–2013 and the National Indicative Programme within the ENP framework. It is striking, however, that the different priority areas outlined under ENPI do not map directly on to the priority areas outlined in the Action Plan. Thus EUMAP includes ten priority areas but the National Indicative Programme only identifies three main priority areas. This is vividly reflected in the case of conflict management which is listed as the first priority in the EUMAP but is not accorded an individual listing under the ENPI funding framework (see EU/Moldova Action Plan n.d.).

Absence of separate budgetary lines for conflict management

The fact that Georgia is the only country in the Eastern neighbourhood which has a separate budgetary allocation under its indicative programme for internal conflict resolution underlines the fact that conflict management-related activities are not a priority area of ENPI funding in Moldova. Rather conflict management activities have been subsumed under the designation 'support for democratic development and good governance', which makes it difficult to identify actual levels of funding for conflict management activities, let alone to measure the actual impact of such contributions. Research by Spruds *et al.* (2008) suggests that the EU could have availed itself more of funding opportunities available through the EIDHR which, it concludes, has only provided 'irregular and rather limited financing (200,000 euros in 2007) to Moldova'.

Clear focus on funding for socio-economic reform and market alignment; conflict management and democratisation-related activities relegated to second place

The percentage breakdown of funding allocations in Moldova's indicative programme for 2007–2013 underscores the fact that the key priorities lie in socio-economic reform and administrative capacity-building (with the possibility of up to 75 per cent of funding being directed to these areas) and the underlying Commission emphasis remains market and institutional alignment and a trickle-down approach to conflict management. Out of overall indicative funding for Moldova of 209.7 million euros, the suggested percentage breakdown was proposed as follows: (i) support for democratic development and good governance – 25–35 per cent; (ii) support for regulatory reform and administrative capacity building – 15–20 per cent; and (iii) support for poverty reduction and economic growth 40–60 per cent. According to the European Commission Country Level Evaluation for Moldova, European Commission delegation staff openly stated 'that poverty and the poor social situation took precedence in their strategic planning over political human rights' (European Commission 2007b: 40). This lack of attention to the political dimension and disregard for conflict management issues more specifically was further underscored in an interview with a European delegation official in Moldova in which it was suggested that the Commission had on occasion been reluctant to fund projects proposed by the EUSR.

Conflict management funding concentrated on post-conflict stabilisation and reconstruction

Given the EU's reluctance to take a more proactive role in the peace settlement process, it is hardly surprising that in terms of the actual funding of conflict management projects, to date the EU has directed more resources towards post-conflict rebuilding projects (local infrastructure, public services and social services) rather than focusing on more traditional conflict resolution domains (including demobilisation, disarmament, rule of law, human rights). This reflects the experience and some of the lessons learned from the EU's engagement in the post-conflict environments of the Western Balkans, not to mention its reluctance to lend legitimacy to the breakaway regions, but it also suggests an insufficiently comprehensive understanding of the critical place of conflict resolution in the overall process of political and economic stabilisation (see Gordon *et al.* 2008).

The problem of funding projects in Transnistria

As regards the sponsoring of projects in Transnistria (TN), the EU is faced with the problematic challenge outlined above of not wishing to directly engage with a non-recognised breakaway entity. But leaving TN out of funding allocations altogether runs the risk of further augmenting the separation between Moldova and TN. Some limited funds have been allocated for civil society development projects in the Transnistria region under the EIDHR as well as for parallel projects on either side of the River Dniestr. Though according to Mirimanova no 'specialized peacebuilding cross-conflict projects' have to date received support from the EU (Mirimanova 2010: 23). Moreover, in general the greater part of financial assistance for human rights programmes under EIDHR has not even been allocated to countries in the Eastern neighbourhood.

The Council of Europe (CoE), which opened its Mission in Moldova in 2001, has not been directly involved in the conflict management process. However, through a range of projects in the area of democratisation and a greater willingness to engage in Transnistria, it has made some indirect contribution to creating conditions supportive of conflict settlement. The CoE has been involved in the implementation of several confidence-building measures between the people from both banks of the Dniestr, in the areas of the European electoral heritage, freedom of media and expression and higher education. At the same time, according to the CoE Representative in Chishinau, the impact of its activities has been modest because of the political impediments and lack of financial means to pursue follow-up activities in the region of Transnistria. The small 100,000 euro budget for the Mission in Moldova has in effect remained static for a number of years and considerably constrains the actions of the Mission.[8]

In sum, a combination of internal institutional, political and financial constraints limits the room for manoeuvre of the EU in its role as a conflict manager in Moldova. In addition to the diplomatic obstacles which constrain the EU from taking a more proactive role in peace-making, the EU has not succeeded in delivering its 'transformative' magic through the leverage of soft power (Grabbe 2006). In the case of Moldova a rather different situation emerged compared to that in the CEE countries. The limitations of conditionality when the incentives on offer have not been strong enough have meant that the problems associated with the operationalisation of conditionality have been magnified. Given the rather weak incentives on offer and the problematic leverage of conditionality, the complexities of the domestic context and the broader geopolitical environment have taken on an even greater significance (Gordon and Sasse 2008). It is this dimension which forms the focus of the penultimate section of this chapter.

The conflict context

Ultimately it is the broader context of the conflict and the complex web of domestic, regional and international interactions which shape the interests and willingness to cooperate of the key players upon whom a lasting conflict settlement depends. In this regard the three key players are the leaderships in Moldova, Transnistria and Moscow. It is suggested here that given the complexities of the geopolitical environment in the Eastern neighbourhood, and in the absence of a clear-cut and sufficiently attractive incentive structure in the ENP, that the political and economic conjunctures at home take on an even greater primacy in how the EU's involvement is viewed, brought into play and translated into policy in the Eastern neighbourhood countries.

Up until the elections of July 2009 and the accession to power of the AEI government, Moldova had been mired in a stalled transition for most of the previous 18 years. The country had been led since 2001 by President Voronin's Communist Party of the Republic of Moldova which, while continuing with its half-hearted attempts at reform, sought to steer a course between Moscow and Brussels, preferring rapprochement with different players at different times. The pro-European democratic opposition in Moldova remained rather weak throughout this period, rent by internal divides and on the whole unable to perform the role of a credible opposition.

In terms of relations with the EU, following a period of disappointment upon learning that Moldova's membership in the Stability Pact did not mean that it would also be incorporated into the SAP, the government initially at least welcomed the increased engagement of the EU in Moldova and committed itself to fulfilling the actions laid out in the country's EUMAP, even structuring the government programme to this end. However, rapprochement with EU was treated almost as one of a possible set of geopolitical tools in the country's attempt to forge a viable relationship with its erstwhile imperial chief.

Though the leadership in Chishinau has gone through various shifts in its approaches to Tiraspol, on balance it has been more willing to try to reach a compromise solution compared with the more intransigent leadership in Tiraspol under the authoritarian sway of President Smirnov. Tiraspol has been unwilling to compromise on power-sharing which might reduce its control and sovereignty over its territory and assets. To date Moscow has been prepared to support this position. In a rather defiant demonstration of this position, a referendum was held in September 2006 that approved the breakaway region's secession from Moldova and the goal of joining Russia with an almost unanimous 97 per cent of the vote. Furthermore, the leadership in Transnistria has remained suspicious of any even indirect attempts by the EU at conflict management, given its unambiguous commitment to the territorial integrity of Moldova. Unlike the leadership in Tiraspol, the Gagauz people, a small rural population located along the border with Ukraine, reached an agreement over a rather limited form of autonomy in 1994 (having previously declared its independence in 1990). Though this agreement has since gone through some revision, the Gagauz people have remained largely peaceable. With limited economic assets and the absence of a powerful external economic and political sponsor, the Gagauz people have had no option but to compromise with the leadership in Chishinau.

Though sharing a border with Moldova, Ukraine has been preoccupied with its own extremely difficult post-communist transition and, despite participation in the Joint Control Commission and nominally being part of the 5+2 peace negotiations framework, had shown little active interest in becoming more involved in conflict resolution processes in Transnistria. It was only with the accession to power of President Yushchenko in early 2005 and his positive commitment to a foreign policy of EU integration that the leadership saw that it was in its interest to engage more actively in the processes of conflict management. Involvement in the conflict situation in Transnistria was seen primarily as a way to further rapprochement with the EU. Hence the 2005 Yushchenko plan and also Ukraine's successful participation in the EUBAM mission which has been positively acknowledged in the country's EU progress reports. However, the victory of Viktor Yanukovych in the 2010 elections once again shifted the delicate balancing act between Moscow and Brussels in the corridors of power in Kyiv, with Ukraine adopting a more pro-Moscow orientation and TN slipping further down the policy agenda.

Romania has played a rather clumsy role in its attempts to intercede in the situation in Moldova. At the same time it is in a rather delicate position as any attempt on its part to cooperate or offer some form of support, such as for example visa support to Moldovan citizens, can easily be construed by opponents of conflict resolution as some inherent irredentist agenda on the part of the Romanian government and/or part of a unification agenda on the part of the government in Chishinau. Romania's pending accession to the EU in January 2007 brought hope for increased support for Moldovan integration into the EU, which was, however, dashed. Romania, which at times suffers from a degree of marginalisation among the new member states, has been grappling with inter alia serious internal corruption problems and has found itself subject to a cooperation and verification mechanism on the part of the EU and therefore not particularly focused on its relationship with or the position of Moldova. Furthermore, upon the accession of Romania to the EU, the existing Moldovan–Romanian free trade agreement had to be cancelled (Emerson *et al.* 2007). Nonetheless the accession of Romania did bring heightened EU attention to the conflict in Transnistria.[9] Following a deterioration of relations between Moldova and Romania in the lead-up to the April 2009 elections, the new AEI government has sought to mend fences at the request of the EU – visa restrictions for Romanian citizens have once again been lifted and a new local border traffic treaty has been agreed. However, better relations with Romania may be a double-edged sword potentially stoking fears of renewed conflict potential in TN.

The primary player outside Moldova which will in the end dictate the timing and the willingness of domestic players to compromise over a particular final settlement is the

Russian leadership in Moscow. Since the collapse of the Soviet Union the Russian government's policies towards its so-called 'near abroad' including the breakaway entities in former
Soviet republics have been shaped by the desire to carve out an appropriate post-imperial
role for itself, to retain some form of control and influence over its former territories and to
avoid the encroachment of Western international organisations and states in what it considers its natural sphere of interest. The leadership in Russia has pursued this objective through
a number of means by encouraging economic, energy and security dependencies, acquiring
stakes in key energy sector businesses and pipelines in newly independent states and to
varying degrees stoking the coals of conflict between breakaway regions and their metropolitan states. Given the limited strategic or even economic interest of Tiraspol to Moscow,
it seems possible that a compromise with Russia might be possible – it did seem that embed-
ding Moldova's neutrality in the face of NATO's march eastwards might be a strong bar-
gaining chip. But following the debacle of Georgian President Saakashvili's summer 2008
incursion and the re-escalation of the conflict in South Ossetia, virtually inviting a Russian
invasion in response, the emphasis on NATO expansion which formed part of the Bush
administration's policy has receded somewhat. The Obama administration sees no interest in
stoking the fires of Russian antagonism at the present time. Moreover ripple effects from
other frozen conflicts in the post-Soviet states are keenly felt by the leaderships in the breakaway regions and in the metropolitan states, just as events in Kosovo leading up to and in the
aftermath of its unilateral declaration of independence in February 2008 have been keenly
followed. The leadership in Tiraspol was heartened at the support offered to the secessionist
entities in Georgia in Russia and no doubt governing elites in Chishinau were also somewhat
'chastened' by the response of Moscow.

   Since the early 2000s the EU has gone a long way towards putting in place a framework
for institutional, financial, technical and diplomatic cooperation with Moldova, including
working to create supporting conditions to facilitate the settlement of the conflict over
Transnistria, but ultimately the key axis of Moldova and Transnistria's relationship with
Moscow will determine the timing and shape of the conflict settlement. Moscow is well
aware that many EU member states attach greater importance to their overarching political,
economic and energy interests with Moscow than to reaching a definitive conflict settlement
between Transnistria and Moldova.

Conclusion

This chapter has explored the evolution of the EU's engagement as a conflict manager in
Moldova. Though recognising that the EU has at best been a rather reluctant conflict manager operating under considerable constraints, it has also been suggested that with the exception of taking a more active role in final settlement negotiations, the EU has over time
increased its engagement in the country – in terms of its diplomatic efforts, technical assistance and capacity-building efforts. These efforts have had a dual focus: (i) direct efforts
aimed at bolstering the conflict resolution process as well as (ii) economic and political
reform-facilitating policies constituting a trickle-down approach to conflict management
through the pull effect of working towards economic alignment with market regulations and
the concomitant promise of increased prosperity as well as the fostering of shared democratic values. In fact while the point of departure of the heightened involvement of the EU in
the Eastern neighbourhood in 2003–05 was to protect the security and stability interests
of the enlarged Union, the EU has in fact found itself increasingly drawn into a process of

procedural and diplomatic entrapment – even accepting that more can be done to overcome some of the constraints on the operationalisation of EU policy considered above.

This chapter has also argued that future progress and ultimate success in the area of conflict management depends to a considerable extent on the domestic context in the country. Unlike in CEE where the EU was the only 'game in town' – economically, politically, and from a geo-strategic perspective the same cannot be said for the Eastern neighbourhood countries. Moldova has had a complex post-Soviet relationship with Russia and this must be factored into government calculations in terms of responses to and uses of ENP and other EU policies. In this context, neither the pull factor nor the push factor of the EU may be strong enough to induce institutional alignment, democratic change and norm transfer, let alone to create the conditions in which reaching accommodation with Chishinau would be attractive enough to elites in Tiraspol to build momentum behind a power-sharing solution. At the same time the EU could further its commitment to rapprochement with Moldova and other countries in the Eastern neighbourhood – what is currently on offer in the new Eastern Partnership is still not enough to lock in neighbouring countries and it is too early to say whether Moldova's pending Association Agreement will significantly change this calculation. In addition more will have to be done to create sufficient incentives to encourage Moscow to consider ending its role as supporter and protector of Tiraspol in its current quasi-independent state. From the vantage point of summer 2011 the EU's report card in terms of its role as a conflict manager in Moldova might read: progress has been made but could do more. In terms of the political obstacles to a final settlement the domestic context remains primary and in the case of both Tiraspol and Moscow, a continuation of the status quo seems the most likely short-term outcome. This having been said the coming to power of a new democratic Europe-oriented government in Chishinau may well in due course open the door for another push towards conflict settlement, but for the time being pressing socio-economic issues mean that the AEI's attentions lie elsewhere.

Notes

1   The research for this chapter was supported in part by the EU's Framework Six Project, 'Human and Minority Rights in the Life Cycle of Ethnic Conflicts' (MIRICO).
2   Interview with Nicolae Negru, Editor of *Journal de Chishinau*, July 2008.
3   'Transitional Capacity Support for the Public Administration of Moldova', UNDP, June–August 2011.
4   See http://politicom.moldova.org/news/moldova-to-be-reintegrated-based-on-new-strategy-218699-eng.html?loc=in-tab (accessed June 2011).
5   Interview with EU official, Chishinau, July 2008.
6   Between 1992 and 2006 Moldova received approximately 320 million euros from the EU – mostly under the framework of TACIS and Macro Financial Assistance instrument.
7   See ENPI, Georgia, National Indicative Programme, 2007–2013.
8   Interview with Special Representative of the Secretary General of the Council of Europe, Chishinau, 5 August 2009.
9   Interview with Nicolae Negru, editor of *Journal de Chishinau*, July 2008.

10 EU conflict management in Bosnia and Herzegovina and Macedonia

Annemarie Peen Rodt and Stefan Wolff

Introduction

The failed European attempts to handle the violent disintegration of Yugoslavia in the 1990s were, according to the large majority of Common Foreign and Security Policy (CFSP) scholars, the first real push for European foreign policy makers more actively to seek to develop a common European Union (EU) approach to dealing with violent ethnic conflicts in the Union's near abroad. The atrocities in the Western Balkans had illustrated the inadequacy of the tools available to the Union at the time and left the EU embarrassed. After the North Atlantic Treaty Organization (NATO) came to the rescue of the EU for the second time over Kosovo in 1999, the EU was eager to develop its own conflict management capabilities, and consequently did so with the Yugoslav experience in mind and reflecting past and present failures, as well as a few successes, in the Western Balkans. The EU's approach to violent ethnic conflicts thus arguably being born and bred in the Balkans, the Union's experience in this region is therefore an important aspect of any debate on the EU's potential future global role as a conflict manager. This chapter examines the EU's capabilities and recent track record in dealing with the ethnic conflicts in the Western Balkans and demonstrates how the EU's successes and failures in this respect are a function of its own capabilities as well as the specific contexts in which the conflicts in Bosnia and Herzegovina (BiH) and Macedonia have evolved.

The chapter proceeds as follows. We first discuss the early EU experiences with conflict management in the region in the 1990s. This is followed by a discussion of the EU capabilities brought to bear in the EU's CFSP missions in the Western Balkans and an analysis of the contextual factors of each conflict and the ways in which they have shaped the outcomes of the EU's conflict management efforts.[1]

The EU and its Balkan failures

Based on its principle of respect for state sovereignty and its own experiences of ethnic conflict management, the European Community's (EC) initial response to the Yugoslav crisis was to seek to keep the Yugoslav state intact and in this way to contain the problem. European leaders faced with ethnic conflicts in their own countries expressed fears that if they supported the dissolution of Yugoslavia, this could encourage ethnic minorities elsewhere in the region and beyond to push for independence, ultimately resulting in increasing levels of ethnic violence across Europe. From the beginning of the conflict in Yugoslavia, the EC attempted to take a neutral stance and was reluctant to recognise any one side as the aggressor. Instead, it insisted that the United Nations (UN) impose a general arms embargo on all the Yugoslav republics. This was an approach which meant that not only did the EC fail to send in peacekeeping troops to stop the violence, but also by failing to recognise that the Yugoslav National Army was now effectively the armed forces of Serb nationalists, the arms embargo removed the Croat and Muslim ability to legally defend themselves against the aggressors (Morris 2004; Kintis 1997).

The EC instead supported President Milošević's plan to reconstruct the Yugoslav federation within its existing borders, and attempted to use its power as an economic heavyweight to broker a peace agreement by offering aid to those who cooperated and threatening to withhold it from those who did not. As violence broke out in 1991 first in Slovenia and later Croatia, the EC continued this strategy of attempting to contain the conflict, but by the end of the year the violence had spread to Bosnia. The EC responded to the increasing violence in Bosnia by freezing all financial aid to the region and sending in its troika of Foreign Ministers (later replaced by a single EC negotiator, Lord Carrington) on a number of peace negotiating missions. Following the repeated rejection of these efforts and the increasing humanitarian crisis in Bosnia, the EC, against the advice of its own chief negotiator Lord Carrington (and the UN Secretary General and the United States (US)), in December 1991 declared itself ready to recognise Slovenian and Croatian independence provided that certain conditions on minority protection, peaceful settlement of border disputes and guaranteed government control of their territories, set by the arbitration commission for independence, were met. Germany, however, disregarded the joint EC position and proceeded to recognise the two republics independently, despite the fact that Croatia did not meet the EC conditions. EC recognition of both countries followed shortly after, ignoring not only Croatia's non-compliance but also (and perhaps more importantly in this respect) its own diplomatic negotiator, the independence standards it itself had promoted and thus, effectively, its attempt at a common foreign policy. This undermined the EC's competence and credibility as an international actor not only to its members, allies and observers but also to the warring parties on the ground. The Serbian side especially questioned the EC's credibility as a neutral mediator and when trade embargoes against Croatia, Slovenia and Macedonia were lifted, while the embargo against the Serbs was kept intact, the Serbian delegation withdrew from the negotiations and the EC peace efforts collapsed (Kintis 1997; Silber and Little 1996).

By 1992 full-scale military conflict had broken out in Bosnia. The EU had recognised the country's independence but rejected the request of Bosnian President Izetbegović to send in peacekeeping troops. Instead, the EU and the UN co-hosted another round of peace negotiations, later rejected once again by the Serb delegation. Further sanctions were imposed on Yugoslavia (now consisting of Serbia and Montenegro) and both trade and weapons embargoes remained in force. Under EU pressure, the UN sent protection forces to Croatia, Bosnia and Macedonia, under the assumption that the presence of international troops would calm down nationalist aggression and that the humanitarian purpose of the mission would foster respect for the UN Protection Force (UNPROFOR). The mandate, however, entitled the troops to use force only in 'self-defence', leaving the soldiers on the ground without a mandate to provide the protection the mission's name indicated, or to 'create the conditions for peace and security required for the negotiation of an overall settlement of the Yugoslav crisis', the purpose of the mission according to Security Council Resolution 743 of February 1992. The inability to prevent large-scale disasters such as the 1995 atrocities in 'UN protectorate' Srebrenica, demonstrated yet again the complete failure of the European-led conflict management efforts.[2] Eventually, the US sidelined the EC by sending in the Contact Group of Five to reach an agreement. After NATO's military intervention presidents Milošević,

Tudman and Izetbegović agreed to the US-brokered Dayton Peace Agreement, ending the war in Bosnia (Kintis 1997; Morris 2004; Pentland 2003).

In the beginning of the 1990s the EU was unable to reconcile the conflicting views of its member states, who disagreed not only on what to do and how to do it, but also on the very nature of the problem. France, a historical ally of Serbia and a centralised state itself, favoured keeping the Yugoslav state intact; Italy supported this approach largely due to its strong links with the Yugoslav government; whilst Germany, itself unified only a few months earlier and influenced by a strong public opinion, supported the moves for independence in Slovenia and Croatia and with traditionally strong ties to Croatia through the many ethnic Croats living in Germany, stressed what it called 'its moral duty to help other nations coming out of an era of Communism'. The Netherlands, Belgium, Italy and France favoured an early UN intervention in Yugoslavia assuming that the conflicting parties would then agree to a ceasefire. France pushed for the Western European Union (WEU) to take action, but without support from any other members. The United Kingdom (UK) was reluctant to send in troops, in the light of its recent experiences in Cyprus and Northern Ireland, which had proved the difficulty of withdrawing troops once they were sent in; and Germany was still forbidden from sending troops to any area out of NATO. These are only a few examples of how EU member states perceived the nature of the problem as well as its solution very differently.

The disagreements among its member states left the EU perceived as an indecisive, inconsistent and effectively weak international actor, dismissed by US President Clinton as 'incompetent' in the handling of the Yugoslav crisis. This was at least partially due to the EU's structural deficiencies. It is, however, important to stress that what the EU was lacking more than anything in the early 1990s was the political will of its member states to act – and to act in unison. The EU's early failures in Yugoslavia were arguably because it was not only unable but also unwilling to take the joint decisions required to stop the fighting (Faucompret 2001).

The Dayton Agreement did not put an end to violent conflict in the former Yugoslavia, which culminated in violent clashes between ethnic Albanians and ethnic Serbs in the Kosovo province in 1998–99. The EU, still unable to put weight behind its warnings to President Milošević, was once again sidelined by a US-led NATO intervention. The Kosovo crisis underscored yet again the main structural shortcomings of EC (and later EU) conflict management in the Western Balkans in the 1990s; the EU struggled with its own inexperience in providing 'soft' as well as 'hard' security, it lacked the military strategy and strength to back up its threats and the infant CFSP was simply not ready to deal with a problem as complex as the break-up of Yugoslavia.

The EU did, however, go through a learning process in the Balkans. After the Dayton Agreement the EU gradually began a more coherent and effective response to political stabilisation and economic recovery in the region. The EU assumed a modest role in the first three years of the international protectorate in Bosnia and Herzegovina and contributed significantly in terms of humanitarian aid and assistance in the post-conflict reconstruction in the wider region, but it was not until after the Kosovo campaign that the EU re-emerged with a comprehensive vision for the Western Balkans and a renewed claim to the leadership it had so boldly, yet prematurely, proclaimed in 1991. Today the EU, heavily engaged in conflict prevention, management and resolution, is widely recognised as one of the most, if not the most, important international actors in the region (Cameron 2006; Faucompret 2001; Silber and Little 1996). That this is a reflection of the Union's commitment to the region and its success in managing the conflicts in BiH and Macedonia after the Yugoslav wars is what we demonstrate in the following section when we analyse the capabilities that the EU has brought to bear in the region since 2003. In so doing, we focus on the two police missions and the two military conflict management operations in BiH and Macedonia. We leave out, at this stage, the appointment of EU Special Reprentatives (EUSR) in each country, and also exclude the more recent EU Rule of Law Mission to Kosovo.

Assessing EU conflict management capabilities in the Western Balkans

The EU police mission in Bosnia and Herzegovina

In 2003 the EU Police Mission (EUPM) in BiH became the EU's first ever Common Security and Defence Policy (CSDP) mission. The mission, which is still ongoing, is the longest running CSDP mission so far. It is part of a comprehensive programme of measures aimed at establishing the rule of law in BiH. The mission succeeded the UN's International Police Task Force. It set out to strengthen the operational capacity and joint capability of the law enforcement agencies engaged in the fight against organised crime and corruption in BiH; to assist and support in the planning and conduct of investigations in the fight against organised crime and corruption in a so-called 'systematic approach'; to assist and promote development of the criminal investigative capacities of BiH; to enhance police–prosecution cooperation; to strengthen the police–penitentiary system cooperation; and to contribute to ensuring a suitable level of accountability.

EUPM derives its legitimacy from United Nations Security Council Resolution (UNSCR) 1396 and a decision by the Peace Implementation Council (PIC) to accept EUPM to follow the UN police mission in BiH. The mission personnel comprises staff from EU member and non-member states. EUPM is a crisis management operation and as such has a unified command structure within the single EU institutional framework, comprising the European Council and its Secretary General/High Representative (SG/HR), the Political and Security Committee (PSC) and the EUSR for BiH. The Head of Mission/Police Commissioner, who leads EUPM and is in charge of day-to-day operations, communicates with the SG/HR through the EUSR. Apart from technical and professional assistance and training, EUPM is also involved in the creation and consolidation of new institutional structures. Following an invitation by BiH authorities the EUPM refocused its mission in 2004 to support the BiH police reform process to develop and consolidate local capacity and regional cooperation in the fight against organised crime (European Council 2008c). On 26 April 2010, the Council welcomed a reduction in the mission's mandate and size and a further refocusing of the mission's mandate to primarily support the fight against organised crime and corruption (EEAS 2012b).

Operation Althea in Bosnia and Herzegovina[3]

In 2004, the European Council (2004c) decided to take over responsibility from NATO for militarily securing the conditions for the implementation of the Dayton Peace Agreement. The initial budget for common costs was €71.7 million to be administered through the ATHENA mechanism, which relies on financial contributions by EU member states determined on a Gross Domestic Product (GDP) basis. Both EU member and non-member states participate in this operation. The United Nations Security Council authorised European Union Force (EUFOR) Althea as a legal successor to NATO's Stabilisation Force (SFOR) in the country. UNSCR 2019 extended the mandate of EUFOR Althea until 15 November 2012 (EEAS 2012a).

Perhaps more than any other CSDP operation to date, Operation Althea exemplifies the importance of cooperation among the international organisations making up Europe's security architecture. The EU takeover from NATO was only possible following the work of NATO's Implementation Force (IFOR) and Stabilisation Force (SFOR) and the resulting improvements in the security environment on the ground. Moreover, the EU operation was able to rely on NATO assets and capabilities through the Berlin Plus arrangements between the two organisations. NATO's Deputy Supreme Allied Commander Europe was appointed Operation Commander for Operation Althea, and Supreme Headquarters of Allied Powers in Europe (SHAPE) simultaneously became the EU Operation Headquarters (SHAPE 2004a). The command structure of Operation Althea underlines the close cooperation between NATO and EU: under the political control and strategic direction of the EU's PSC, the EU Operation Headquarters are located at SHAPE in Mons, the EU Command Element at the Allied Joint Forces Command in Naples, and the Headquarters of EUFOR at Camp Butmir in Sarajevo. The EU Command Element at the Allied Joint Forces Command is a particularly crucial element in the coordination process with NATO as it ensures that the EU's operations in the Balkans conform to the EU's regional approach, on the one hand, and cooperate closely with NATO activities in the Balkans, on the other. In addition, the EU closely coordinates its military mission with its police mission. As both are meant to contribute to the implementation of the Dayton Agreement, cooperation is also essential with the PIC, the Office of the High Representative (OHR) and other international actors engaged in the region: primarily, the UN and the Organization for Security and Co-operation in Europe (OSCE).

Operation Concordia in Macedonia[4]

Operation Concordia, launched in 2003, also followed on from a previous international mission, in this case NATO's operation Allied Harmony. The purpose of this mission was to ensure sufficient levels of security and stability in Macedonia to enable the implementation of the 2001 Ohrid Agreement. Concordia derived its legitimacy from a request by Macedonian President Trajkowski and UNSCR 1371. The operation fell within the remit of EU military conflict management operations and was the first ever CSDP deployment of military forces. It comprised 400 soldiers from 26 countries, including non-EU contributor states. Operation Concordia was the first case for EU–NATO cooperation under the Berlin Plus agreements, i.e. the EU made use of NATO capabilities. Initially only expected to last for six months, Operation Concordia was extended at the request of the Macedonian government until December 2003. Command of the operation rested with the EU Force (EUFOR) headquarters. The budget of €6.2 million was contributed by the EU with non-common costs covered by participating states. As part of the day-to-day management structures, a Committee of Contributors had a consultative role in its decision-making procedures.

Operation Proxima in Macedonia

In 2003 Operation Proxima became the second EU police mission in the Balkans. The establishment of the mission followed an invitation from Macedonia's Prime Minister (PM). Its implementation was closely linked to the implementation of the Ohrid Agreement. The mission was extended beyond its initial 12 months following another request by the Macedonian

PM and was completed in December 2005. The mission personnel comprised staff from EU member and non-member states. Operation Proxima was deployed to five locations across Macedonia to monitor, mentor and advise Macedonia's police force and promote so-called 'European policing standards'. The budget was €7.3 million for start-up costs and €7 million for 2004 running costs to be financed from the Community budget. For the 12-month extension a budget of €15.95 million was agreed.

Making sense of context: the Western Balkans as background for EU conflict management in BiH and Macedonia

For a number of reasons, it makes sense to examine the context of the EU's conflict management efforts in BiH and Macedonia together. Both countries have a shared history in Yugoslavia and more generally in a region in which peoples and states share a range of historical, cultural and political experiences. Moreover, the conflicts in both countries are a result, in significant part, of the violent disintegration of Yugoslavia in the early 1990s. Even though BiH and Macedonia were affected by this process in different ways, with different intensity, and at different times, there are nonetheless tangible links between the countries and interdependencies between their conflicts. For reasons of space we focus specifically on the two military operations (Concordia and Althea) and assess the degree to which domestic, regional and international factors proved conducive to their success.

The domestic level

Domestic support for Operation Concordia

When Operation Concordia was launched in Macedonia in 2003 the domestic situation in the country had already much improved since the crisis two years earlier. There had been genuine signs of political compromise. The Ohrid Agreement and the subsequent elections had resulted in the main Albanian political party now being represented in government; and overall, political and security relations between the conflicting parties were improving. The Macedonian authorities, now representing both ethnic Macedonians and ethnic Albanians, fully supported Operation Concordia. The operation was launched upon explicit invitation from the government and the domestic authorities greeted its deployment with enthusiasm (Council Decision 2003/7537/CFSP, 18 March 2003, Council of the EU 2003g; International Crisis Group 2005b).

In his welcoming speech, President Boris Trajkovski explained the government's motivations behind its invitation and its support for the CSDP operation:

> The successful ending of this mission will mark the termination of the last phase of the process of the consolidation of the security. It will mean taking on our own responsibility for the internal stability and fulfilment of one of the preconditions for membership of the Republic of Macedonia in the European Union and NATO [. . .] This mission offers us a chance to develop a particularly close collaboration with the EU Forces from the moment of their establishment, a chance that we do not intend to miss [. . .] Our ambition is full membership in the Union, and I would like to see this mission, and our joint efforts in promoting stability, as a step in that direction. The more of EU we have in Macedonia, the more of Macedonia there is in the EU.
>
> (Trajkovski 2003)

An interviewee from the European Commission delegation to Macedonia confirmed the widespread domestic support for the operation and explained the government's enthusiasm for Concordia in a similar way:

> Concordia was a symbol of Macedonia's ambition to establish tighter links with the EU in all areas, including full membership in the Union. It was one dimension of the European integration of Macedonia and a symbol of an ever-closer union and partnership between the EU and Macedonia. By inviting the EU to launch (the) military mission, Macedonia signalled its willingness and ability to adopt the logic, norms, patterns of behaviour and regulations associated with European integration into its political, security and defence system.[5]

The high level of domestic support for the operation at the state level was shared also at the sub-state level (Mace 2004). The relationship between the EU forces and the Macedonian population was good, as an observer explained:

> In the sphere of improving the social and economic situation of the country, Concordia conducted civil military cooperation projects in the villages of former crisis areas, with the aim of improving the living conditions of people. These projects helped the members of Concordia to establish close relationships with the local population that contributed to improving their mutual rapport.[6]

Colonel Pierre Augustin (2005), the operation's representative from France, has stressed the importance of what he called the operation's 'systematic contact with the ethnic communities'. In particular, he has highlighted that:

> The combination of light and heavy teams performing missions strongly reinforced a palpable deterrence in addition to establishing the perception of the EUFOR as an integrated force dedicated to restoring public confidence. Building this confidence set the foundation for the information collection effort and proved essential to restoring a peaceful environment lost following the events of 2001. EUFOR has become a federating security element in the daily life of the ethnic communities. Immersion and openness of these patrols in the FCA (former crisis area) has been elemental.
>
> (Augustin 2005: 58)

Mace (2004) has suggested that the handover from NATO to the EU and the continuity of the approach between the two operations helped Concordia quickly win the trust and confidence of domestic parties in Macedonia. The following will return to the link between the two organisations at the international level, but it is important to note that this operational connection made Concordia look more robust – both in the eyes of the domestic authorities and the different ethnic communities. Consequently, there was substantial domestic support for Operation Concordia from all the key state and sub-state actors in Macedonia (Cascone 2008; Howorth 2007; Mace 2004).

The high level of domestic support was essential for EUFOR's success in Macedonia. The fact that the EU force had political support from the authorities and communal support from the population made it easier for the operation to achieve its goals in a timely, efficient and effective manner. The fact that there was domestic support also for the wider EU-led international effort to manage the political conflict through the implementation of the Ohrid

Agreement and the Stabilisation and Association Process (SAP) to bring Macedonia on track for EU membership meant that Concordia was able to contribute also to this wider process of managing the underlying conflict. Finally, the fact that the EU troops were never challenged militarily meant that they never decided to apply force. In this way, domestic support proved a necessary condition for the Concordia's overall success. The only spoilers to the operation and limitation to its overall success were a few of its own staff involved in criminal activities in the country.

Domestic support for Operation Althea

In BiH too the security situation when EUFOR was deployed in 2004 had much improved since the end of the war in 1995. However, the legacy of the war had left the former parties to the conflict wary not only of each other, but also of the EU's capability as a conflict manager. There was a shared sense that 'Europe' had failed Bosnia during the war. An International Crisis Group (ICG) report from the time when Operation Althea was launched explains this domestic scepticism: 'Due to its failure to act unanimously and decisively during the war, the EU is still viewed with considerable suspicion in Bosnia' (ICG 2005b: 50).

Unlike the EU, NATO had proved itself as a credible security provider in BiH. The majority of domestic authorities and large parts of the population believed that the NATO presence had played a significant role in preventing the return to war. A new international military deterrent was therefore deemed necessary, but the potential handover to an EU operation raised domestic concern. European troops had a tarnished reputation in the country after the mostly European UNPROFOR had failed to protect civilians on all sides during the war. The wariness of the EU's political commitment and its military capability, although shared across ethnic divisions in the country, was particularly strong among Bosnian Muslims. One interviewee remembered how when British diplomat Robert Cooper attempted to reassure Bosniak PM Adnan Terzić that the EU would make sure the security situation did not deteriorate, Terzić looked at Cooper and said: 'That is what you said last time. I guess I will just have to trust that you will do it this time.'[7]

This initial domestic scepticism about the EU's ability as a military conflict manager, however, must not be mistaken for lack of domestic support for Operation Althea. On the contrary, the domestic fear that it would fail demonstrates a high level of domestic support for EUFOR's purpose: to prevent more violence. The majority of the population and the political leadership wanted peace. Although the political context in the country was difficult, all sides wanted to prevent further violence and therefore supported the operation, once it became clear that it would be NATO's replacement. The Presidency, representing all three constituent peoples of BiH, thus, eventually welcomed the NATO–EU transition and 74 per cent of the country's population supported the EU force, once the troops were deployed (Budin 2006). The domestic-level opposition that the operation has encountered during its deployment has been from a criminal minority and not from the majority of the population or the political leadership.

It is important to make a distinction between domestic support for EUFOR and domestic support for the EU, which have not always gone hand in hand. Whereas EUFOR overall has received a high level of domestic support, the EU has at times been unpopular in the country. It is also important to recognise that the highest domestic authority in BiH is in fact the international Office of the High Representative (OHR), which has effectively run the country since the Dayton Agreement. Because the HR is mandated to sanction any so-called 'anti-Dayton behaviour' and EUFOR's own mandate is annexed in the Dayton Agreement, domestic support for the operation is to some extent institutionalised through the constitutional arrangements of BiH. Although the relationship between the different HRs and EUFOR Commanders has varied over time, the state structures of post-Dayton BiH have by law limited any potential political obstruction to the EUFOR operation. This is not to say that without these structures EUFOR would have met much higher levels of domestic opposition, but rather to underline that domestic support could to some extent be facilitated by the OHR. At the sub-state level EUFOR also enjoyed a good relationship with the local population and has focused much attention on fostering this relationship (Council of the EU 2009b; Friesendorf and Penska 2008; GFAP 1995; OHR 2009). In the same way as in Macedonia, domestic support for the operation has played an important role in the success of EUFOR Althea, which has so far only been compromised by one incident in which it failed to properly coordinate a raid.

The regional level

During the violent break-up of Yugoslavia, the instability affected the entire Western Balkan region. The conflict in Bosnia and Herzegovina, in particular, actively involved regional actors: Serbia (then Yugoslavia) and Croatia (Glenny 2001; Silber and Little 1996). When the Macedonian crisis broke out in 2001, the situation in the region was different. This conflict was for the most part contained within the Macedonian territory and fought out between domestic state and sub-state level actors. Although it is still disputed to what extent the National Liberation Army (NLA), the armed wing of the ethnic Albanian rebels in the conflict, were aided from Kosovo (Mace 2004; Vankovska 2002).

At the launch of operations Concordia (2003) and Althea (2004), unsettled status issues with regard to Kosovo and the Serbia–Montenegro state-union were generating wider concerns about the stability of other borders and geopolitical entities in the region. In BiH, the status of Republika Srpska was (and still is) disputed and in Macedonia there were fears of insecurity, in particular, on the border with Kosovo (ICG 2005a). By March 2009, the regional security context in the Western Balkans had changed. As one interviewee put it:

> In the Western Balkans, regional security is no longer in danger. Serbia and Croatia are focusing on EU accession. They are not interested in interfering in Bosnia. Albania and Montenegro are stable. So are Kosovo and Macedonia, although there may be some isolated violence with regard to Serbia–Kosovo relations regarding the northern part of Kosovo, and this could spill over the Macedonian border. But all in all – the situation is stable. This is not the EU's achievement as such, but the EU has succeeded in changing the focus and priorities on the national political agenda in these countries towards EU membership. This is now the first priority.[8]

Neither Operation Concordia nor Operation Althea has been challenged by any actors at the regional level. The operations have also not been actively supported by regional actors. By and large, both operations have been free from regional interference. As the quote above illustrates, none of the regional actors has had an interest in hindering these operations or indeed interfering with the security situation in Macedonia or BiH during these deployments. The presence of the EU force in both countries was accepted by all the regional security actors in the Balkans. Political support, in the sense that these actors accepted and did not seek to hinder the operations, is indeed widely perceived as a necessary condition for their success. This issue was often raised by interviewees, in particular in BiH, with reference to the way in which regional interference to some extent had caused the failure of the UNPROFOR's attempt to militarily manage the conflict in BiH a decade earlier.[9] These interviews also supported the argument presented in the quote above that the Stabilisation and Association Process, which now offers the prospect of EU membership to the whole region, has changed the political and security agenda in the Balkans. The prospect of EU membership, for which all the countries in the region have a declared desire, has increased the Union's leverage through its conditionality policy. This in turn has positively affected regional security and thus indirectly discouraged actors in the region from interfering with the two CSDP operations.

The international level

For both Operation Concordia and Operation Althea, the most important international security partner was NATO: first, because both operations had operational support from and access to NATO assets through the Berlin Plus arrangements; and second, because both operations took over responsibilities in the field from previous NATO operations. NATO had completed three operations (Essential Harvest, Amber Fox and Allied Harmony) in Macedonia before the EU launched Operation Concordia. Likewise, NATO had undertaken two operations (IFOR and SFOR) in BiH prior to Operation Althea. In both countries, NATO had engaged at the height of the crisis and facilitated a significant improvement in the overall security situation throughout its deployments. At the termination of its operations in both countries, NATO transferred most of its authority and responsibility for security to the EU (and some to local authorities). In this process the EU benefited from NATO's operational experience in both planning and undertaking its many operations in the Balkans, which were not limited to these two countries (Cascone 2008; Howorth 2007; Mace 2004).

The relationship between the EU and NATO was of paramount importance for the preparation, deployment and implementation of both these CSDP operations. Apart from relatively minor turf battles the two organisations worked closely, professionally and well together during both Operation Concordia and Operation Althea. With regard to Concordia, Mace (2004) has argued that the relationship between the two was good, although competitive at times. Cascone (2008) has made the case that these operations were successful and useful tests for NATO–EU cooperation, but he stresses that the coordination between the two organisations in the Balkans was for the most part practical coordination in the field, facilitated more by individual member states of the two organisations pushing for a coherent message than by a genuinely joint EU–NATO approach towards conflict management in the region.

A smaller NATO presence remained in both countries after the official termination of its Peace Support Operations. NATO kept a Senior Civilian Representative and a Senior Military Representative in Skopje to help the government with security sector reform and adaptation to NATO standards for the Partnership for Peace and eventual NATO membership (Mace 2004). The situation was much the same in BiH where NATO opened a new NATO Headquarters (HQ) in Sarajevo when it officially terminated the SFOR operation. The new NATO HQ led by a Senior Military Representative was intended to provide advice on defence reform and assistance to the Bosnian authorities in reforming the armed forces and eventually moving towards a single military force. NATO HQ Sarajevo was also tasked with certain operational tasks in relation to counter-terrorism, intelligence sharing with the EU and ensuring force protection and support to the International Criminal Tribunal for the former Yugoslavia in the detention of persons indicted for war crimes (NATO 2004).

For the purpose of this analysis it is important to recognise that the international presence in both countries was coordinated so that EU and NATO representatives would continue to be in close contact. For example, the two organisations were co-located in Camp Butmir outside Sarajevo for the first few years of Operation Althea. In both countries the respective EUSRs were in charge of coordinating the international community, which also reinforced cooperation. Overall, the coordination and cooperation was good, although to some extent it depended on personalities and personal rapport between specific Heads of Missions. For example, several interviewees pointed out how it benefited NATO–EUFOR–OHR/EUSR cooperation in BiH that EUSR (and HR) Paddy Ashdown had both a political and military background. As one interviewee explained: 'Paddy's military background was helpful. It made it easier for him to cooperate with military people at all levels.'[10]

The role of individuals is often underestimated in the CSDP literature. However, as Friesendorf and Penska (2008) have suggested with regard to EUFOR Althea, personalities and how well different individuals work together are of utmost importance to success. Another important factor with regard to inter-organisational cooperation between NATO and the EU in Macedonia and BiH was the fact that the NATO operations in both countries had large European contingents, which ensured a degree of unofficial institutional memory shared across the official NATO–EU divide. After all, many of the member states of the two organisations and indeed in the two operations were the same. This does not necessarily mean that member states always behave consistently in different organisations (or in different operations), but it has facilitated a greater cooperation in these two cases. For example, the UK, which had played a significant role in IFOR and SFOR, took the lead in Operation Althea. Furthermore, a significant number of NATO staff stayed on under the EU flag in both Concordia and Althea. These important details are sometimes neglected in the literature, which often refers to the two organisations as further apart than they were in reality on the ground.

A final issue which must not be overlooked in the international context of operations Concordia and Althea is the role of the US, both within and outside NATO. The Balkan wars of the 1990s had left the US with a powerful reputation in the region. The US had made it clear that it had the capability to act and that it was willing to use it. Whether one agreed with its actions, America was (and still is) recognised throughout the region as an important actor – in particular, with regards to matters of security. In BiH, for example, the US was long perceived as the only trustworthy guarantor of peace. As the ICG wrote six months before the launch of Operation Althea:

> Most Bosnians – the Bosniaks in particular – see the US as playing a major part in maintaining the peace and unity of the country. Serb and Croat citizens acknowledge that without the US presence, the political and security situation might deteriorate.
>
> (ICG 2004: 6)

The empirical accuracy of this observation was demonstrated in February 2004 (two months into the Althea deployment), when the collective BiH Presidency, which represented all three parties to the conflict, formally asked the US authorities to consider maintaining a base in the country (ICG 2004). However, the Bush administration was eager to downscale its military contributions to the NATO operations in the region (Mace 2004). It had repeatedly expressed its distaste for NATO's involvement in nation-building in BiH. On the other hand, the US needed to 'ensure that its political investments in the region pay off' (ICG 2004: 3). This made the US support the EU takeover in BiH, once the Berlin Plus had been negotiated and successfully tested in Macedonia. For the US, Operation Concordia was in this way a trial run for Operation Althea. The following quote illustrates this:

> EUFOR carried out a 'live fire' exercise there (Macedonia). Here was no threat to a safe and secure environment, and no operations that carried any risk other than traffic accidents or alcohol poisoning by the troops on Friday night. But it offered a benign environment in which the EU could find out the complexities and challenges of mounting a real operation, without any risk of failure. The exercise was successful as EUFOR confronted important issues as communications, logistics and operational mobility and found solutions.[11]

Within the NATO–EU relationship a good relationship between the US and the EU proved essential for the negotiation and successful implementation of the Berlin Plus arrangements and, in effect, to facilitate the necessary operational support for the successful undertaking of the operation at the tactical level. With regard to the relationship between the EU and the US, the UK has played an important part in both these two cases. In negotiating the Berlin Plus and the terms for Concordia, the UK, which had led NATO Operation Essential Harvest, played an important bridging role between the US and the EU (Mace 2004). The fact that the UK had already proved itself to the Americans in IFOR and SFOR helped muster up the necessary US support.[12] These are but some examples of how, in the Balkan operations, the EU often became its own partner, either through EU member states and institutions represented in the field or through their advocacy in international negotiations and arenas. In this way, the EU could affect the international context in which its CSDP military conflict management operations operated.

There were many other international actors involved in conflict management in both Macedonia and in BiH, but NATO, the US within it, was the Union's single most important international security partner in the Balkans. At the tactical, the operational and the strategic levels, NATO's support for these operations was crucial to their success. The UN was important in so far as it authorised the mandates for both operations. Although the UN had deployed peacekeepers in both countries in the past (before NATO), these were withdrawn long before operations Concordia and Althea were on the drawing board. The UN, in operational and tactical terms, did not as such have a direct impact on the success of Concordia and Althea, although it was conducive to the success of both operations that they cooperated and coordinated their activities well with the UN and other non-military international partners in the field.

Conclusion: capabilities, context and EU conflict management in BiH and Macedonia

Current EU capabilities appear to be sufficient to take on tasks of the kind required in the Western Balkans at present. The EU was able to mobilise sufficient personnel, hardware and funds to sustain them. It had the institutional framework and instruments available to make the necessary decisions and proved itself capable of a certain level of cooperation and coordination within its own structures as well as with third parties. This relatively positive assessment of EU conflict management capabilities in the Western Balkans after 1999, however, cannot necessarily be taken as a general indication of the readiness of the Union to manage conflict elsewhere and with a similar degree of success. While it is undoubtedly true that the 'CFSP, through the position of the HR for CFSP, has experienced in a very short time a substantial improvement in its coherence and visibility' (Müller-Brandeck-Bocquet 2002: 278), improved coherence and visibility do not necessarily translate into effectiveness. With respect to the Western Balkans one could question whether the Union has indeed been successful. In Macedonia, for example, it could be argued that early-stage conflict management, despite the mobilisation of significant resources, failed, and that it was only once the violent conflict had erupted that the EU (through conflict management measures) succeeded in brokering a deal between the fighting factions.

Taking into account the complexity of the situation the EU had and has to deal with in the Western Balkans and the intensity of the conflicts it had to manage (in post-Dayton BiH and in Macedonia) the Union has demonstrated that it has developed an institutional framework and a set of policies that enable it to make quicker decisions, provide adequate funds and personnel, and to cooperate and coordinate activities with third parties in ways that enhance its own capabilities and maximise the chances of successful conflict management. It is equally important in this context to bear in mind that since the failure of conflict management in the early and mid-1990s, the Union's capabilities have been improved significantly, enabling it now to undertake both civilian and military operations, i.e. being able to back up its diplomatic efforts with credible threats of force where necessary. This evolution of expertise both at the HQ and ground level demonstrates a significant process of lesson-learning at the institutional and operational level of EU conflict management capabilities.

These constantly improving capabilities of the EU were brought to bear in a context that was overall conducive to success. At the sub-state, state and regional levels, the EU was in a position to elicit sufficient support for its efforts to succeed. While such support, partly based on the experiences in the 1990s, was not always immediately and fully forthcoming, the EU had sufficient capabilities and deployed them adequately to overcome resistance and obstruction. This is clear with regard to managing conflict-related violence: there has been no violence in BiH or Macedonia since the deployment of the EU's police and military missions. State-building efforts more generally have been more successful in Macedonia than in BiH, but even in BiH the 'Dayton state' has so far held together and in fact has seen some key improvements to its functionality. The international context, too, has been one that has been overall supportive of the EU's efforts. Cooperation with US and NATO, in particular, worked well.

Thus, the EU's relative operational success of late in the Western Balkans has its sources not only in improved capabilities. In our view, the Union's experience in the Western Balkans cannot be generalised or exported easily. The distinct advantage that the EU has in this region is that its policy of conditionality is much more effective *vis-à-vis* countries where the promise of closer association with, and potentially accession to, the EU is credible and where both political elites and the general public are ready to make significant compromises in order to attain what many believe to be the only option for a viable future. In other words, the success of EU conflict management in the Western Balkans must be seen in a larger context, in which conflict management is only one element in a comprehensive EU approach to a region. As Javier Solana pointed out as early as 2000,

> [t]he European Union is uniquely placed for comprehensive action in the Western Balkans [and is] the only institution capable of comprehensive action, ranging from trade, economic reform, and infrastructure, humanitarian assistance, human rights and democratisation, justice and police to crisis management and military security.
>
> (Solana 2000)

Without the clear long-term commitment of the EU to the Western Balkans' prospect of EU membership, the incentives for political elites and the various ethnic groups they represent would be less powerful and thus the Union's ability to elicit short- and long-term compliance, which has been a major factor in the success of its conflict management missions so far, diminished.

Notes

1 For background on the conflicts in Bosnia and Herzegovina and Macedonia, see Rodt's Chapter 12 on EU military conflict management in this volume.
2 It is estimated that between 7,000 and 8,000 Muslim men and boys were killed by Serb nationalists in Srebrenica in 1995 (Glenny 2001; Silber and Little 1996).
3 See also Rodt's Chapter 12 on EU military conflict management.
4 See also Rodt's Chapter 12 on EU military conflict management below.
5 Interview, representative from the European Commission delegation to Macedonia, 30 April 2009.
6 Interview, representative from European Commission delegation to Macedonia, 30 April 2009.
7 Interview, representative from the European Commission, 7 May 2009.
8 Interview, representative from the European Commission, 7 May 2009.
9 Interviews, representatives from BiH Council of Ministers, 29 June 2006; Interview, representative from the European Commission delegation in BiH, 30 June 2006; Interview, representative from the OHR, 30 June 2006.
10 Interview, representative from the European Commission, 7 May 2009.
11 Interview, senior Western diplomat, 17 July 2009.
12 Interview, representative from NATO, 2 February 2007.

Part 3

Comparative Perspectives

11 The EU Special Representatives as a capability for conflict management

Cornelius Adebahr

Introduction[1]

For over 15 years, the European Union Special Representatives (EUSRs) have been part of the European Union's (EU) arsenal of foreign policy instruments. They are a very visible expression of the EU's capability to act and to coordinate – the Union's 'face and voice' (EU Council Secretariat 2005: 1) in crisis regions from the African Great Lakes to the Middle East and from the Balkans to Central Asia. Today, the EU has deployed 10 EUSRs to nearly two dozen countries that are of great concern to its broader security interests. In them, the EU has availed itself of a well-established diplomatic instrument that could be seen as a quasi-precondition for international actorness. This makes them a central part of the Union's Common Foreign and Security Policy (CFSP).

Interestingly, EUSRs were not only an expression of the extending reach of European foreign policy, with mutual implications between the deepening of the institutional foundations of CFSP and the evolution of the instrument of EUSRs (Grevi 2007: 29). What is more, as it appears, the EUSRs have consistently been ahead of the institutional and political developments in European foreign policy. The Maastricht Treaty of 1993 had created a foreign policy on paper but failed to provide the Union with the instruments to actually pursue strategic aims or even intervene in conflicts that threatened the stability of the continent. This became most obvious in the wars following the break-up of Yugoslavia, where the system of revolving presidencies – the EU's mechanisms for external representation – had soon shown its limitations. The EU was simply inept at stopping the fighting.

In a situation where the EU had failed the foreign policy test on its doorstep, EU envoys emerged in the African Great Lakes region and for the Middle East Peace Process in 1996. They were dispatched before their function was enshrined in the subsequent Amsterdam Treaty. More substantially, they represented the EU's political approach to a region before there was anything like a common policy. And, not even ten years after their invention, they became a test case for 'double-hatting' long before the Lisbon Treaty put this feature into practice at the level of the new High Representative for Foreign and Security Policy, Catherine Ashton. It is in this sense that they have been breaking new ground for EU foreign policy.

This chapter explores how the EUSRs have contributed to the EU's conflict management efforts by enhancing its capability to both act and coordinate. I will in particular analyse their role in the African Great Lakes, in the Middle East and in Macedonia. These three mandates form a representative mixture of EU engagement in conflict management activities: there is proximity and distance with regard to the conflict zones; the mandates are both regional and country-specific; and there is a varying degree of involvement of other international actors. Particular focus will be on the EUSRs' internal function, coordinating member states, missions, as well as EU institutions.

Based on these observations, I will conclude on two points: first, I will establish a basic profile of the 'envoy instrument', distinguishing more generically between eight different roles that Special Representatives can fulfil. Second, recognising their important internal role, I claim that crisis management as such is not only directed at an external conflict in question but, in the case of the EU, serves a particular function in the broader process of European integration.

Why send an envoy? A common rationale

When in the winter of 1995/96, a political and humanitarian crisis with millions of refugees threatened to destabilise the whole 'Great Lakes region' in Africa, the international community, for want of any better policy, tried to alleviate the suffering mainly by providing humanitarian aid. The flow of money into the region reached a rate of one million US dollars a day, more than half of it emanating from the EU (the Community plus member states) (McLoughlin 1998: 1). It was clear, however, that such aid would not provide a solution to the underlying political problems.

Three insights dominated EU discussions aimed at halting the crisis: first, it was acknowledged that the roots of the crisis were not found in just one state but stretched across boundaries; second, the crisis was seen as another periodic upheaval that was part of a long-term predicament plaguing the region; and third, if the EU wanted to have an impact on the situation itself, it needed a political visibility commensurate with its economic commitment (McLoughlin 1998: 2). While it was clear that, at that time, the EU with its still infant CFSP had little or no influence on the ongoing crisis, the assumption was that any given political presence would be bolstered by the existing economic assistance – and vice versa. In this situation, in March 1996 the Council nominated the former United Nations (UN) Special Representative for Mozambique, Aldo Ajello, as first 'EU Special Envoy' for the Great Lakes region (Council of the EU 1996a).

In the early- and mid-1990s, not only the wars in Central Africa but also the developments in the Middle East were of major concern to the EU. The EU supported the Palestinian democratisation process by sending observers to the 1995 elections to the Palestinian Council, the first democratic elections in the autonomous territories (Council of the EU 1995). However, the assassination of Israeli Prime Minister and Nobel Peace Laureate Yitzhak Rabin in November of the same year stymied most people's hopes for peace. Against this background of rising tensions and growing European involvement, the EU nominated its second Special Envoy in November 1996 (Council of the EU 1996b; see also Dietl 2005: 99–111). Miguel Angel Moratinos, a career diplomat who shortly before had been appointed Spanish ambassador to Israel, became the EU's envoy for the Middle East Peace Process (MEPP).

The motivation to appoint a second EUSR was similar to that of the first one: to achieve political representation proportionate to the EU's economic aid (Council of the EU 1996b; see Soetendorp 2002: 289; Dietl 2005: 102–3; and Ginsberg 2001). In fact, following the Oslo Accord, the EU had taken on the lion's share of the financial support of the Palestinian Authority (PA) (Asseburg 2003b: 175; Soetendorp 2002: 288; see European Commission 2005a: 2). Without this European financial aid, the PA could not have survived for long. To accompany such engagement on the political level was the main task of the EUSR.

At the same time, the idea was to bolster the EU's international standing. The Union should not be disregarded again as it was when the United States (US) failed to consult their European partners prior to the Clinton–Arafat summit of October 1996 (Ginsberg 2001: 149).

However, neither Israel nor the United States welcomed greater involvement on the part of the EU (Dannreuther 2002: 9; see also Regelsberger 1997: 217). While Israelis perceived Europeans as biased against them and preferred the exclusive support of the US, the latter did not see a significant actor in the EU (Dietl 2005: 106–7; Tocci 2005: 13–14; see *Mideast Mirror* 1998). Establishing the EU as a credible partner was conceivably the foremost, though not an easy, task of the EUSRs. That said, just as in the Great Lakes Region, while it joined the mediation efforts of other actors (such as the US or the UN) the EU could not actually contribute to resolving the crisis.

Unfolding events in the Republic of Macedonia in 2001 demanded that the new EU crisis management institutions created under the European Security and Defence Policy (now Common Security and Defence Policy, or CSDP) be put to a test before being solidly established. Once more it was proven that political crises do not wait for mechanisms to be operational. Following violent attacks by Albanian extremists on Macedonian government institutions, the EU engaged in a shuttle diplomacy hitherto unseen: a series of EU emissaries travelled to Skopje, from External Relations Commissioner Chris Patten to the EU Presidency to the (then still fairly new) High Representative for CFSP Javier Solana (Reichwein and Schlotter 2007: 261; Schneckener 2001: 92).

The small and young country of Macedonia soon became a testing ground for the new EU foreign policy instruments, including experimenting with different representatives. A Stabilisation and Association Agreement (SAA), the new bilateral agreement on the road to EU membership, was initialled in April 2001, shortly after the outbreak of the crisis, in order to strengthen the government in power. To uphold its influence, however, the EU held back the SAA's benefits until the government agreed to make concessions to the Albanian side (Piana 2002: 212). To be represented in the crisis mediation efforts, the EU at first nominated, in an ad hoc arrangement, the British ambassador in Skopje as Solana's deputy. This position was upgraded in June 2001 and with a view to having a counterpart to the respective US envoy (Jaanson 2008: 7) by the appointment of former French Defence Minister François Léotard as EU Special Representative (Council of the EU 2001a). His original task was to closely monitor the developments on the ground and to support political dialogue between the parties with the objective of contributing to a settlement (Grevi 2007: 92).

In addition to the three mandates examined here in more detail, other EUSR mandates have been issued to cover the Union's major regions of concern: the Western Balkans and South-eastern Europe, Central Africa and the Middle East, as well as the South Caucasus and Central Asia. Both the rise in numbers and the widening of geographical scope of the EUSRs led the High Representative for CFSP, Javier Solana, to remark on the occasion of the first joint EUSR seminar:

> You as EUSRs are the visible expression of the EU's growing engagement in some of the world's most troubled countries and regions. The list of where we have EUSRs is, in part, also [a] list of where our foreign and security policy priorities lie.
>
> (Solana 2005: 2)

As it thus appears, EUSRs have a common rationale. The initial reasons for sending an EU Special Representative to a given country or region centre on three aims:

1. to achieve political representation commensurate with existing economic engagement, ultimately enhancing the EU's international standing;

2. to gain information about an ongoing conflict and, on this basis, develop a policy towards a given country or region;
3. to influence international mediation efforts with respect to a crisis.

The EUSRs – a capability to act and coordinate

By their mere existence, EUSRs represent the Union in a given country or region. Being a face and a voice of the EU, they (passively) stand for and (actively) inform others about EU policies. Until the entry into force of the Lisbon Treaty in December 2009, the EU did not have any 'embassies' dealing with foreign policy issues. The 130 or so delegations to third countries and international organisations of the European Community (EC), in contrast, could only deal with economic and bilateral affairs (cf. European Commission 2004c). The EUSRs thus increased the EU's visibility and profile, especially compared to the rotating Presidency. Given the establishment of the External Action Service (EAS) under the Lisbon Treaty, Union delegations abroad now cover the full range of the EU's external relations as well as foreign policy. What is of interest here, thus, is the EUSRs' more active role, both towards the conflict (acting) and towards other EU actors (coordinating). I will deal with these two aspects consecutively.

Capability to act

The focus of the EUSRs' work is on security policy and crisis management: they offer advice and support to the conflicting parties with the aim of effectively implementing EU policies and terminating the crisis or conflict. To do this, they have a range of – primarily diplomatic – means at their disposal, e.g. proffering good offices, mediation, facilitation and the like. EUSRs also closely cooperate with third parties, be they states (like Russia or the US) or international organisations (like the UN, the African Union, or the Organization for Security and Co-operation in Europe (OSCE)). More often than not, international crisis management efforts are conducted through a group of friends, as the informal setting bringing together interested states and organisations is often called.

In addition, EUSRs also provide information about and analysis of the current situation in their mandate area to EU decision-makers. Based on their findings, EUSRs can develop policy proposals that they feed into the Brussels policy-making process. Functionally, they could thus also be considered, in analogy to the anatomical metaphor used previously, the 'eyes and ears' of the EU.

The EUSRs are closely linked to all four major players in EU foreign policy – the High Representative, the Council, the Commission and the member states – in all phases of their work. They implement their respective mandate under the authority of the High Representative, Catherine Ashton. The Political and Security Committee (PSC) is the EUSRs' primary point of contact with the Council. It provides the EUSRs with strategic guidance and political direction. While EUSRs may sometimes report directly to the Council, the actual working level contacts are mostly with the High Representative's new EAS. By reporting regularly to the Council working groups, EUSRs also reach the staff in member states' permanent missions and the relevant Commission units. Due to their status as CFSP Advisors paid from Community funds, they are accountable to the Commission for the budget allocated under the financial statement for their missions.

African Great Lakes

The very first mandate ever was simple, broad and open to initiatives on the part of the EUSR (see Council of the EU 1996a). Its objective was to assist the countries of the region in resolving the crisis, complementing rather than competing with existing international initiatives such as those of the UN and the Organisation of African Unity (OAU). Given the inexperience of member states with such an instrument, the EUSR's working mandate was deliberately left broad, if not vague: to support the ongoing crisis management efforts by international and African actors; to establish and maintain close contacts with all parties involved; and to help with the preparations for a peace conference. The mandate also contained an important element with regard to a potentially proactive role of the EUSRs. By stipulating that the envoy 'may make recommendations to the Council on measures which the Union might undertake to fulfil its objectives in the region' (ibid.), it opened the way for providing relevant policy input rather than only reporting to the Council.

Much of the EUSR's work in the Great Lakes region was directed at active conflict resolution, though without being able to pacify the region substantially; at least, it helped the EU gain a place in the international arena. The EUSR intensified his support of international mediation efforts led by UN and OAU after fighting broke out again in 1998. Previously, Laurent Kabila, with support from Rwanda, Uganda, Angola, Burundi and Eritrea, had ousted President Mobutu of Zaire in May 1997 and renamed the country as Democratic Republic of Congo (DRC). Other neighbouring countries were drawn in, turning the conflict into what commentators dubbed 'Africa's first world war' (International Crisis Group 2000: 1; Doyle 1998; CNN 2000).

The Lusaka Peace Agreement of 1999, which EUSR Ajello had helped to negotiate together with a myriad other special envoys both African and non-African (Krause and Schlotter 2007: 362), formally brought a ceasefire and a commitment to withdraw all foreign troops (Moller 2002: 35). The EU supported the follow-up to the Lusaka Agreement with the establishment of a Joint Military Commission. Yet, fighting between different rebel groups, most of them with foreign support, persisted and both the ceasefire and the troop withdrawal were largely ignored (International Crisis Group 2000: 2; Fiedler 2004: 323). When President Laurent Desiré Kabila of Congo was assassinated in January 2001, his son, Joseph Kabila, took over and embarked on a process of national dialogue, democratisation and economic liberalisation. He concluded peace agreements with Rwanda and Uganda as well as the most important rebel groups; in the wake of this effort, a large number of foreign troops left the country (Krause 2003: 166).

In the following years, EUSR Ajello concentrated his efforts mostly on the DRC, and there shifted his focus from conflict resolution to sustaining a fragile peace and a delicate political transition (Grevi 2007: 112–13). His responsibility increased with the EU's first autonomous military operation *Artemis* in Eastern Congo, launched in June 2003 and conceived as a three-month-long 'bridging mission' in preparation for the launch of a UN operation (see Faria 2004b: 47–55). Fourteen hundred troops under French command were dispatched to protect civilians who had fled the fighting in the area bordering Uganda and Rwanda. Ajello's task was to provide political support to the mission, which he did not see as an end in itself but rather as 'the start of something bigger' in the framework of CFSP (Astill and Norton-Taylor 2003: 13). He was right to the extent that soon two more CSDP operations followed, one supporting Congolese police (EUPOL Kinshasa, later extended to EUPOL RD Congo) and another dealing with security sector reform (EUSEC RD Congo), in 2004 and 2005 respectively (European Council 2003d: 12; see Law 2007: 10–11). While these two missions are still ongoing, EUFOR DR Congo was a shorter military operation in support of the UN Organisation Mission in the DRC (MONUC) during the election process in the country (Council of the EU 2006b).

After four successive CSDP missions in the country, it is fair to say that, given the multiplicity of the means employed on the ground, the DRC has become, together with the Western Balkans, 'the largest laboratory for EU crisis management' (Grevi 2007: 114; for the Balkans, see Calic 2008: 27). In all this, it was the permanent presence of EUSR Ajello as a coordinating authority which helped to politically prepare as well as smoothly run these missions (Grevi 2007: 116; Council of the EU 2007d: paragraph 290). Concluding nearly 11 full years in office, Aldo Ajello, the first ever and longest-serving EUSR, handed over, in February 2007, to Roeland van de Geer, a Dutch career diplomat with considerable experience in Africa (Council of the EU 2007e).

Middle East Peace Process

The initial mandate for the Middle East Peace Process broadly included five different tasks: to establish contacts with the parties and other relevant actors; to offer advice and good offices to the parties; to help implement agreements reached by the parties; to develop and pursue the EU's own initiatives; and to monitor compliance (or non-compliance) of the parties with international norms and their possible actions prejudging a final peace settlement (Council of the EU 1996b). Like his colleague of the African Great Lakes region, however, EUSR Moratinos had to carve out a role for himself, usually working quietly but decisively in the background. He did so for example during the successful mediation efforts that took place early during his mandate, in January 1997, aimed at the withdrawal of Israeli troops from Hebron (see Soetendorp 2002: 290; Makovsky 1997: 1). One of the first major achievements of the new EU Special Envoy was to arrange, together with the Dutch presidency, a meeting of the Israeli Minister of Foreign Affairs Levy with the President of the PA Council Arafat, on the margins of the Euro-Mediterranean Conference in Malta in April 1997 (Regelsberger 1997: 217; Nolan 1997). This took place following a long period of frosty silence, when Israelis and Palestinians refused to speak with each other on an official level.

One year later, in April 1998, the EU and the PA adopted, on Moratinos's initiative, an agreement to establish an EU–Palestinian Joint Permanent Security Cooperation Committee, including the installation of an EU security advisor with the EUSR's staff (Ginsberg 2001: 139; see Pelletreau 1998; *The Economist* 1997). This led the Council to modify the mandate in order to include cooperation on security issues with the aim of assisting the Palestinians to meet their commitments on security under the Oslo Accords (Council of the EU 1998). Another important policy contribution of EUSR Moratinos concerned the proceedings of the March 1999 Berlin European Council. At that meeting, the heads of state and government advanced a two-state solution to the Middle East conflict, which made the EU the first international actor to promote this proposal (European Council 1999f: Part IV).

With the outbreak of the so-called second Intifada in September 2000 and the breakdown of the last-ditch effort in Israeli–Palestinian negotiations in Taba in January 2001, the Middle East Peace Process was at an impasse. In a change from the previous desire for a visible political role (in addition to its existing economic importance), the EU now used the presence of its Special Representative to demand a more active and responsible role in the conflict resolution efforts. Simultaneously, trust of the EU among regional leaders grew (Dannreuther 2002: 10), although Israel in particular remained wary (Asseburg 2003b: 184; see Ortega 2003: 56). At the Taba talks, for example, with the lack of any US presence, the EUSR was the only outside observer and 'the resulting Moratinos "non-paper" became the jointly recognised record' (Nonneman 2003: 39; see Moratinos 2002).

The gradual emergence of the Middle East 'Quartet' in 2001 and 2002 gave another boost to the EU's presence in the international arena. It also led the Council to give EUSR Moratinos more freedom to present his own policy proposals, bolstering his role as the Union's representative therein (Dietl 2005: 109–110; Council of the EU 2002b). The Quartet assembled representatives of the US, Russia, the UN and the EU as the main actors mediating the Israeli–Palestinian conflict (Dietl 2005: 242).[2] While initially regarded as a fig leaf for the US administration's unwillingness to deal with the conflict actively, the Quartet soon began to develop its own positive dynamic and policy proposals (Neugart 2003: 284). The group's most important output of that time, other than continuous multilateral meetings and shuttle diplomacy, had been the agreement on a 'road map', in October 2002. The document, which in substance envisioned a peaceful two-state solution and, procedurally speaking, reaffirmed US commitment to the MEPP, clearly bore a European stamp (Asseburg 2003a: 23–24; Tocci 2005: 14).

In July 2003, Ambassador Moratinos handed over his position to Marc Otte, a Belgian diplomat who had previously worked as Solana's advisor on defence and security policy (Council of the EU 2003b). This experience served him well when, in late 2005, following the withdrawal of Israeli forces from the Gaza strip, the EU deployed its first two CSDP missions in the Middle East. An EU Border Assistance Mission was sent to monitor operations of the Gaza–Egypt border crossing point at Rafah (EUBAM Rafah), and an EU Co-ordinating Office for Palestinian Police Support (EU COPPS, headquartered in Ramallah) was established to provide support to the Palestinian Civil Police. In both cases, the head of mission received guidance from High Representative Solana through EUSR Otte, requiring him to build a bridge into the security sector (Council of the EU 2005e). The fact that, with EUBAM Rafah, Israel had accepted the EU as a partner in the field of security policy was in itself considered a success and a sign of the EU's increased international reputation (Neugart 2006: 279; Beatty 2003; Keinon *et al.* 2003).

Victory for the Hamas party in the Palestinian elections in January 2006 put a freeze on Middle East diplomacy, effectively stopping an until then fairly successful EU policy and the EUSR's work (Tocci 2006: 8). As a reaction, the EU resorted to holding back its support funds for the Palestinian territories.[3] Moreover, the war between Israel and the Lebanese Hezbollah in the summer of 2006 severely tested European diplomacy, eventually leading not to a CSDP mission there but to a UN mission with strong European ingredients (United Nations Interim Force in Lebanon, UNIFIL). In this deteriorating situation, EUSR Otte continued to negotiate as a member of the Quartet, as well as to bring about practical improvements in direct talks with the conflict parties, such as the reopening of the Rafah crossing point in July 2006 (see Grevi 2007: 138).

Macedonia

In Macedonia, EUSR Léotard was instrumental in the international mediation efforts, acting both in his own capacity as a respected former politician and in support of the High Representative (Reichwein and Schlotter 2007: 262–5; Finn 2001). A breakthrough was reached in August 2001 when the Macedonian government and Albanian leaders met in Ohrid for negotiations under American and European supervision. The talks eventually produced a Framework Agreement outlining, among other things, a constitutional reform giving more representation to the Albanian minority.

Successful mediation did not bring an end to the EUSR's mandate, though – only a change of guard. At the end of October, Alain Le Roy replaced his fellow countryman Léotard. Given their different backgrounds – one a politician and 'troubleshooter', the other a career diplomat – this change of personnel reflected the progress made on the way to pacifying the conflicting parties. Le Roy's main task was to supervise the agreement's implementation on behalf of the international community, thereby facilitating further progress towards European integration (through the Stabilisation and Association Process, SAP) (Council of the EU 2001b; Grevi 2007: 93–4).

At the end of October 2002, Alain le Roy handed over to the Belgian Alexis Brouhns (Council of the EU 2002a). EUSR Brouhns served in Skopje for a little more than a year, and it was during his turn that CSDP operations *Concordia*, a military stabilisation operation, and its successor *Proxima*, a police-monitoring mission, were deployed to Macedonia (Council of the EU 2003a, 2003c). When the EU police advisory team (EUPAT), successor to operation *Proxima*, terminated its work in June 2006, this concluded five years of CSDP involvement in the country (Council of the EU 2005f). With the European Council having granted Macedonia candidate status (European Council 2005), EUSR Europe Fouéré started to concentrate on supporting important steps on the way to European integration, including reform of the judiciary, and on coordinating the various EU actors on the ground (see Grevi 2007: 96). Not least because of this enormous progress, from the brink of civil war to EU candidacy in only four years, EU action in Macedonia is often hailed as a successful example of, if not conflict *prevention*, then at least crisis *management* in close cooperation with the US and the North Atlantic Treaty Organization (NATO) (Piana 2002: 212–16).

Capability to coordinate

In the realm of foreign policy, the Union has to rely on the consensus of 27 member states and the Commission does not have the policy-unifying role it has in the first pillar. Therefore, EUSRs strive to coordinate national policies of member states and CSDP operations as well as the activities of other EU institutions (i.e. mainly the Commission), aiming to achieve the greatest coherence possible (see Grevi 2007: 46). After a number of years, the Council for-malised this coordinating function in its 2007 guidelines (Council of the EU 2007f: 6).

Member states

The particular function of internal coordination was obvious from the very beginning. Because an EU strategy towards the Great Lakes region simply did not exist (Fiedler 2004: 330; Grevi 2007: 112), the envoy's efforts to narrow the considerable policy differences in EU member states' approaches to this region were of great importance. Especially former colonial powers like France, the United Kingdom (UK) and Belgium had particular, often-times diverging, interests in the region (Fiedler 2004: 318; Krause and Schlotter 2007: 353).

Over the years, EUSRs have learned to fill the intergovernmental coordination role bestowed upon them. This includes the habit of regularly meeting national ambassadors in the field and paying frequent visits to member state capitals in order to discuss policy. Cooperation with national ambassadors had first emerged as an unwritten rule before being incorporated into the guidelines. Non-resident EUSRs hold at least one meeting with national ambassadors (often including the Commission head of delegation) when they embark on a trip to the region. Such an exchange of opinion could also possibly take place twice per trip: to receive local information prior to meeting the national authorities, and to brief ambassadors pursuant to these talks. The 2007 guidelines then specified that the EUSR should provide regular briefings to member states' missions in the field, which in turn should make best efforts to assist the EUSR in the implementation of their mandate (Council of the EU 2007f: 6). In addition, many official meetings are attended in the troika format, bringing together the EUSR, the head of Commission delegation and the Presidency ambassador (the latter function now being taken up by the head of Union delegation). Such coordination is again in the interest of the EUSR and his or her team because they need the ambassadors on board if they want their issues to make it through the Council.

Another instrument is that of establishing a core group of member states with a particular interest in the country or region of concern, which can meet either in the field or in capitals. Aldo Ajello established such an informal group among the national ambassadors in the Great Lakes region. In doing so, he drew on his own experiences from the UN: already as Special Representative of the Secretary-General (SRSG) for Mozambique, he had established what he called a 'mini Security Council' of relevant UN member states whose representatives he met and briefed regularly (Peck 2004: 333). Not only are meaningful policy discussions difficult with 27 people around the table, but also it is particularly important to integrate the more active member states in order to avoid sending conflicting messages. In this vein, it has become a regular activity of EUSRs to travel to the capitals of interested member states in order to explain and discuss the European approach to their mandate area. Enhancing such inclusiveness towards member states is by no means restricted to the big ones, but includes all those with a stake in the respective region.

All in all, such coordination has helped not only to keep member states on board, but more importantly to streamline information flowing from the field into national capitals as well as that of the EU. An explanation by Aldo Ajello may illustrate this effect:

> When I briefed [national ambassadors] each week, I was basically dictating the reports they would write to their capitals – which had two good results. First, I knew they were sending the right information. Second, I knew they were all sending the same information at the same time. So, all the capitals were reacting in the same way.
>
> (Peck 2004: 333)

Such internal harmonisation of positions is important because EUSRs, in dealing with crises, usually work through international coordination formats where more and more often the EU is present in a way in which the member states are not. In these cases, EU core groups headed by the EUSR become the main policy-discussing bodies, helping to develop a unified policy by bringing together the different positions from member states. In the Great Lakes, for example, it was only after the EU had reached internal consensus about its policies, greatly advanced by the EUSR, that it could become active externally (Grevi 2007: 113).

In addition, EUSRs can take a position in the middle ground above perceived national interest: this was particularly significant in the case of Macedonia, where national ambassadors, being based in Skopje and with the government as their main interlocutor, tended to be pro-Macedonian. While they had little understanding of the Albanian revolt in 2001, the EUSR and his team were newcomers with a more balanced view, who could talk to both the Macedonian government and to the Albanian leaders.

Missions

On top of coordinating member states, the EUSRs form a link to CSDP instruments on the ground. In the Congo, the onset of four CSDP missions marked a shift away from building a policy consensus among member states to 'managing the growing EU projection in the field'

(Grevi 2007: 113). Following the *Artemis* mission, the Council mandated the EUSR to provide political guidance to the heads of the EU police and security sector reform missions in
the DRC (EUPOL Kinshasa and EUSEC RD Congo) as well as of the EUPOL COPPS in the
Palestinian Territories (Council of the EU 2005c, 2005e). Likewise in Macedonia, for both
Concordia and *Proxima*, the EUSR acted as the primary interface between the CSDP head
of mission and local political authorities, as well as coordinating the missions with other EU
activities on the ground (Grevi 2007: 93).

By 2006, it was therefore fair to say that a pattern had emerged in EU civilian crisis management where the head of mission reports to the High Representative through the EUSR
with political guidance flowing in the opposite direction, from the PSC through the EUSR to
the head of mission (Hansen 2006: 36). With the creation of a Civilian Planning and Conduct
Capability (CPCC) in the course of 2007, a new civilian command structure was established
in Brussels and EUSRs have formally been removed from the chain of command. Still, the
EUSR is left with providing 'local' (rather than general) political guidance to the head of
mission (Council of the EU 2007f: 7).

Institutions

Gradually, and informally, routines of cooperation between the EUSRs and the Commission
have been established. As a result, there is today much closer regular cooperation between
the two than when EUSRs began their work in the mid-1990s. A visible expression of this
new cooperation was the system of task forces that had been set up to integrate the EUSRs,
the Council Secretariat and the Commission in an effort to draw together all sources of specialised knowledge within the central EU institutions (International Crisis Group 2001: 45;
see Hansen 2006: 41; Grevi 2007: 108). With the establishment of the EAS, this system has
found its logical extension. For liaison in the field, the current set of guidelines stipulates
close coordination, including regular briefings and mutual support (Council of the EU 2007f: 6).
Given their role as somewhat detached from the Council's side, the EUSRs could at times act
as an informal mediator between the Council and the Commission in external representation.

EUSRs usually receive logistical support such as office space on delegation premises for
their political advisors in the field or informational support with regard to country-specific
contacts. In return, the EUSR typically includes the EU head of delegation in his activities.
While much of this cooperation takes place at an informal level, other instances are more
formal. Early on, the EUSR for the MEPP, for example, produced a 'vision paper' as a
longer-term strategy for the region together with the Commission (George 2000). Also the
disbursement of the 'African Peace Facility' requires cooperation between the Commission
and the PSC, thus building a bridge between the two pillars (Grevi 2007: 101).

This notwithstanding, the relationship is not free from competition, although the pre-
Lisbon rivalry of the Commission and the Council for the position of number one European
representative used to be more pronounced in Brussels. Here the legal division with different
competencies in the two Treaty pillars was much more present, generating a widespread
mutual lack of understanding. The illustrious 'two sides of Rue de la Loi' on which the Commission and the Council are located created the institutional reflex where by each side would
start working on its own proposal before coming together and sharing information. The
set-up of the EAS, headed by Lady Ashton as both High Representative and Commission
Vice-President and located in its own building at the Rond Point Schuman at the end of the
dividing Rue, is now meant to overcome this distance, both physical and mental, within the
EU capital.

In the field, there is more room for pragmatism, which will still be needed even under Lisbon given the large array of external competencies remaining solely with the Commission. In the past, the two sides often felt unwillingly caught in a process dictated by the Treaty and sometimes contrary to the actual aims on the ground. When the political line is identical but institutional infighting is about responsibilities in implementation, operational questions become hostages of institutional arrangements and a good part of an outward-oriented project is directed towards overcoming Treaty barriers. For example, the training of the Congolese police ended in permanent makeshift because it had to be devised in parallel projects due to overlapping competences. Even with the EAS, there remains a need for close coordination with Commission activities such as humanitarian aid in crisis regions.

EUSRs have also helped to improve institutional interactions between the Commission and member states. Positively acting as boundary spanners, they have brought the different desks together. As a result, an EUSR 'is currently the most streamlined way in which the Commission and member states can coordinate through a single contact point in a complex crisis that threatens to become a conflict' (International Crisis Group 2005c: 43).

A major institutional innovation was the appointment in October 2005 of Erwan Fouéré, a Commission official of Irish nationality, as the new EUSR for Macedonia and, simultaneously, head of the Commission delegation (Council of the EU 2005d). The two mandates were of course distinct, but intended to be complementary: they both aimed at ensuring a lasting stabilisation of the country and supporting the transition from post-conflict reconstruction to pre-EU accession. This was the first time that such a personal union spanned the first and second pillars of EU policy as they were created under the Maastricht Treaty. This double-hatting was also a real-life test case of the 'EU Foreign Minister' that came with the Lisbon Treaty four years later.

The role of EUSRs in crisis management and EU integration

Summing up the findings of this paper, it is fair to say that the EUSRs have become an all-round instrument that the EU can flexibly deploy anywhere within its political reach (which is, admittedly, still limited to its broader vicinity). In terms of crisis management, there is hardly anything EUSRs do not do, stretching from classic diplomatic activities (like regional and multilateral collaboration, the supervision of human rights and the rule of law, as well as public diplomacy) to active engagement in conflict resolution (including through participation in peace negotiations, supervision of the implementation of international agreements, institution-building and security sector reform). More than just representing the Union abroad and enhancing the EU's standing, they embody the Union's approach to comprehensive crisis management, which is regarded as one of the hallmarks of the EU's international identity as a 'distinct power'.[4]

Despite being deployed on a mission abroad, EUSRs also work on the inside of the EU. Their mere presence obliges member states to devise a policy for a given country or region. They have raised the qualitative level of policy deliberations in Brussels by providing EU-made information, making decision-making bodies less dependent on information graciously given by larger member states (see Grevi 2007: 46). Furthermore, they help establish and consolidate a political position of the EU by internally straddling policy areas as well as institutions. This furthers an externally coherent stance, which again eases the EUSRs' cooperation in multilateral settings. By enhancing the synergy between the instruments and resources at the Union's disposal, in particular by coordinating EU actors such as CSDP missions on the ground, the EUSRs have greatly contributed to building a more integrated EU foreign policy.

This, in fact, can be regarded as the real success story of the EUSRs: they may not have pacified the conflict areas to which they were dispatched (note that other international organisations and powerful states failed in just the same way). But they helped to bring about internal policy coherence, paving the way for further institutional developments such as the EU Foreign Service established under the Lisbon Treaty. And they made a claim for the EU to be recognised as an actor in crisis management alongside powerful states and traditional institutions such as the US, Russia, the UN, the OSCE or NATO.

Before elaborating on this latter point with a view to the broader process of European integration, I will briefly extend the observations about the EUSRs' external as well as internal roles to a more structurally grounded analysis of the various roles they can assume. These roles are not meant to be prescriptive or in any way defining of what an envoy should (or should not) do. They rather serve as a means of illustrating, in more general terms, the many crisis management activities of the EUSRs.

The different roles of EUSRs

In addition to their internal and external dimensions, the roles of envoys can be structured around their degree of activity. The latter is here portrayed in two forms: presence and actorness. The concept of 'presence' was introduced to describe the status of the EC/EU without referring to it being an international actor equal to states or international organisations (Allen and Smith 1990). Or in other words: presence is more about 'being' than 'acting' (Bretherton and Vogler 1999: 33). The 'being' part can be further divided into factual presence as its most basic form and informational presence where the presence is used to either gather or distribute information. 'Actorness', in contrast, builds on concrete 'acting', either individually or intersubjectively.

Based on these categories of presence and actorness in an internal and external dimension, one can distinguish eight different roles that EUSRs can fulfil. Internally, presence refers to the fact that by their sheer existence, envoys oblige their sending institution to provide political guidance for them, i.e. to agree at least on a minimal policy. In addition, their presence on the ground provides information for policy analysis. Their internal actorness finds an expression in the ability to make policy proposals and to coordinate different EU agents. Externally, presence implies that the visibility itself of an actor raises expectations of third parties and, thus, can exert influence. This includes the dissemination of information insofar as it is not intended to have direct effect (see Bretherton and Vogler 1999: 5). External actorness is expressed both by individual activity and by cooperation with third parties. Here again, presence may also lead to a more operative policy (i.e. actorness) simply because there is someone present in the field to execute it (Regelsberger 1997: 221). Table 11.1 summarises the main roles that EUSRs fulfil.

Table 11.1 Eight different roles of EUSRs

	Presence		Actorness	
	Factual presence	*Informational presence*	*Individual actorness*	*Intersubjective actorness*
Internal -In capitals/headquarters -In the field	Obligation	Analysis	Proposals	Coordination
External -Towards conflict parties -Towards third parties	Visibility	Dissemination	Activity	Cooperation

Crisis management as an engine of EU integration

The significant internal dimension of the EUSRs' activity points to a more comprehensive observation of the development of EU foreign policy in general and of crisis management in particular: that it is not exclusively (maybe not even mainly) conceived towards the external world, but just as well to the EU's internal affairs.

From the time when Putnam conceptualised what he called 'two-level games' (Putnam 1988), the domestic relevance of foreign policy has been widely recognised. In the context of European integration, however, the importance of these two levels is a different one: whereas in the world of states the *international* level is about survival (at least in a neo-realist reading), for the European Union survival of the integration project will be determined at the *internal* level. To what extent a growing number of member states ('widening') can continue to integrate their policies ('deepening') will be decisive. Pressure from the international level – for example the weakened weight of member states due to globalisation and the rise of new powers such as India and China, or the demand for European action in what is perceived as a multipolar world (Solana 2008) – so far serves as a welcome line of reasoning rather than an (already) existential threat.

It is therefore reasonable to view the EU's growing global engagement not only as a response to external crises but also as a means to rally member states around a common cause. As early as in the Single European Act of 1986, EU heads of state and government publicly stated the expectation (in Title III, Art. 30, No. 6(a)) 'that closer co-operation on questions of European security would contribute in an essential way to the development of a European identity in external policy matters' (European Economic Community 1986). Hindsight confirms this ambition to create an identity through common action, both in establishing CFSP and by promoting other external policies such as enlargement (Tonra 2001: 15; Smith 2003: 9; Sedelmeier 2003: 6).

By providing a focal point for a given crisis or region and by thus creating the need to give common instructions to them, the EUSRs help create common viewpoints within a multilateral frame of reference (Ginsberg and Smith 2007: 269). A 'habit of coordination', first noticed with regard to the closed circles of foreign ministers and their political directors in the early days of European Political Cooperation (de Schoutheete de Tervarent 1980; Nuttall 1992) and later detected in the group of ambassadors assembling as the Committee of Permanent Representatives in Brussels (Checkel 2005; Lewis 2003) as well as the Political and Security Committee (Juncos and Reynolds 2007), can also be found among those dealing with the EUSRs. The permanent interaction in Brussels over time should create a sense of belonging to a common endeavour and of shared ownership of foreign policy initiatives (Grevi 2007: 33).

The instrument of EU Special Representatives therefore confirms the importance of the internal function of foreign policy. Even though the EUSRs' many internal tasks are not always explicitly spelled out in the mandate, it could be shown that in practice these are at least as important as the external tasks:

- coordinating member states' policies as well as CSDP operations on the ground;
- encouraging the development of common policies by providing information and analysis;
- acting as bridge-builders across institutional and political divides.

Thus, CFSP is rightly viewed as a driver of European integration, just as political integration also furthers closer cooperation in foreign policy. Ultimately, the question of how the EU foreign service would look like or where and how the EU will engage next in crisis management will also be answered with a view to their integration potential rather than by merely looking at the EAS's needs or the EU's problem-solving capacity.

Notes

1   This article is based on research carried out between 2006 and 2008 as part of the European Foreign and Security Policy Studies Programme of Compagnia di San Paolo, Riksbankens Jubileumsfond, and Volkswagen Foundation, whose support is gratefully acknowledged. For an extensive overview of the work of EU Special Representatives and how they have contributed to learning and change in European foreign policy, see Adebahr (2009).

2   The more formal launch of the Quartet took place in April 2002 in Madrid during the Spanish EU presidency with a meeting of the four principals; until then, only the respective special envoys had met as the Quartet.

3   By this time EU funding had reached around 500 million euros a year, over half of which was provided by the EC budget and the remainder bilaterally by EU member states (cf. European Commission 2005a: 2).

4   The term 'distinct' is used here to relate to the various concepts to describe the EU's particular approach to foreign policy that have been developed ever since François Duchêne declared the European Community a 'civilian power' (Duchêne 1972, 1973). Different EU-specific elaborations of Joseph Nye's 'soft power' concept (Nye 1990) propose for example a civilian superpower (Whitman 1998), a normative power (Manners 2002), a smart power (Ferrero-Waldner 2007), a gentle power (Lucarelli 2006) and an ethical power Europe (Aggestam 2008).

12 EU performance in military conflict management

Annemarie Peen Rodt

Introduction

From 2003 to 2010 the European Union (EU) engaged militarily to contribute to the management of conflicts in Macedonia, Bosnia and Herzegovina (BiH), the Democratic Republic of Congo (DRC), Chad and the Central African Republic (CAR). This chapter takes stock of their success. It first develops a definition and a set of criteria for success in military conflict management. It then goes on to evaluate each of the five operations and comparatively assesses the EU's performance in military conflict management to date.[1]

Defining success

EU military conflict management operations are military operations launched under the auspices of the European Union, within the framework of the Common Security and Defence Policy (CSDP),[2] undertaken by EU troops on the ground to facilitate the management of the violent aspect of a conflict. The EU has so far conducted five such operations. An overview of these is provided in Table 12.1.

In order to evaluate the success of EU military conflict management, *success* must first be defined. The definition of success is crucial to the evaluation of military operations, yet it is hardly discussed in the CSDP literature. The scholarly tradition varies considerably with regard to its definitions of success, which are often implicit rather than explicit in the literature. The following develops a definition and a theoretical framework for the systematic evaluation of success in EU military conflict management operations. It facilitates an evaluation, which takes into account both actor and target perspectives on success. It is important to include both EU-specific and conflict-specific perspectives in the definition and evaluation of success in EU military conflict management. The internal EU perspective will evaluate whether an operation successfully achieved its purpose for the Union. The external conflict perspective will assess the operation according to the overall purpose of conflict management; namely, to manage the violent aspect of a conflict. *Internal success*, thus, refers to an operation which is successful from the point of view of the EU, whereas *external success* indicates a positive impact on the conflict situation on the ground. Both of these aspects of success are necessary for an operation to be an overall success.

It is important to consider not only what an operation has achieved, but also how it sought to achieve what it did. Therefore, internal and external success must both be divided further into two separate success criteria. The first criterion evaluates whether the operation achieved its purpose (goal attainment) and the second examines the way in which the operation sought to achieve this purpose (appropriateness). In the following, the EU operations will, thus, be

Table 12.1 EU military conflict management operations: 2003–2010

Completed operations	Ongoing operations
European Union Military Operation in the Former Yugoslav Republic of Macedonia (EUFOR Concordia): 31 March 2003 – 15 December 2003 European Union Military Operation in the Democratic Republic of Congo (Operation Artemis): 12 June 2003– 1 September 2003 EUFOR RD Congo: 12 June 2006 – 30 November 2006 European Union Military Bridging Operations in Chad and the Central African Republic (EUFOR Chad/CAR): 28 January 2008 – 15 March 2009	European Union Military Operation in Bosnia and Herzegovina (EUFOR Althea): 2 December 2004 – ongoing

(Council of the EU 2009a)

evaluated according to four success criteria: (1) internal goal attainment, (2) internal appropriateness, (3) external goal attainment and (4) external appropriateness. Examining success according to these four criteria will allow for a nuanced analysis of success in each operation and a focused and systematic comparison of success across the different operations.

To facilitate the evaluation, a set of indicators has been identified for each of the four success criteria. Internal goal attainment will be evaluated according to whether the key objectives in each operation's mandate were achieved. Internal appropriateness will be assessed according to the timeliness, efficiency and cost-effectiveness of its implementation. External goal attainment will be evaluated according to whether more violence was averted; in other words, whether continuation, diffusion, escalation and intensification of violence were prevented.[3] Finally, external appropriateness will be evaluated according to whether the application of force was discriminatory and proportional.[4] An operation is only a complete success if these indicators are met and all four success criteria are fulfilled. This is illustrated in Figure 12.1.

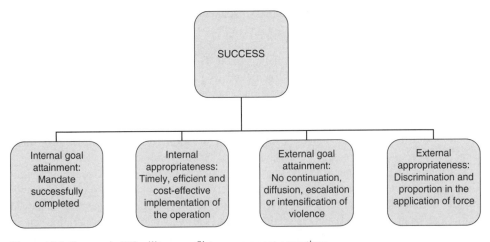

Figure 12.1 Success in EU military conflict management operations

EU military conflict management operations: 2003–2010

According to the definition developed above an EU military conflict management operation is a success overall when its purpose has been achieved and implemented in an appropriate manner from both an internal EU and an external conflict perspective. This section will examine the success of each of the five EU military conflict management operations launched between 2003 and 2010.

Operation Concordia in Macedonia

After its independence in 1991 Macedonia's stability was threatened by animosity between ethnic Albanian and ethnic Macedonian elements of its population. The Albanian minority, which made up 25 per cent of the population, had suffered discrimination under the Communist regime throughout the 1970s and 1980s. Following the country's independence ethnic Albanians remained underrepresented in state institutions and many feared that the discrimination against them was becoming embedded in the new Macedonian state structures (Glenny 2001; International Crisis Group 2005a). In particular, ethnic Albanian communities expressed dissatisfaction with their unequal representation in the police and with the fact that Albanian was not recognised as an official language. On the flipside, many ethnic Macedonians suspected that the Albanian community had a separatist agenda. The mistrust between the two communities continued throughout the 1990s (Mace 2004). In January 2001 the conflict turned violent as the ethnic Albanian National Liberation Army (NLA) and Macedonian state forces clashed in Tetovo. The violence and the popular protests undermined Macedonia's government and led to significant population displacements (Mace 2004). Observers at the time feared that a fully fledged civil war might break out in Macedonia and could potentially destabilise the southern Balkan region once again (Glenny 2001). The EU and NATO with strong support from the United States pushed for a negotiated settlement. A Framework Agreement was reached in Ohrid in August 2001. The Ohrid agreement ended the violent conflict and NATO forces were deployed to keep the peace (Mace 2004).[5]

In January 2003 the Macedonian authorities invited the EU to take over NATO's military responsibilities in the country. The Council expressed the Union's readiness to do so, and on 31 March 2003, as NATO terminated its deployment, the EU launched its first military conflict management operation in its place. The EU operation, code-named *Concordia*, was authorised by United Nations Security Council Resolution (UNSCR) 1371. The Berlin Plus arrangements between EU and NATO, completed just two weeks earlier, allowed *Concordia* access to NATO assets during the deployment.[6] Operational Headquarters were set up at NATO's Supreme Headquarters of Allied Powers in Europe (SHAPE). Admiral Feist, Deputy Supreme Allied Commander for Europe, was appointed Operations Commander and Brigadier-General Maral became Force Commander.[7] France was framework nation for the operation.[8] *Concordia* comprised 350 soldiers from 13 of the 15 EU member states at the time and 13 non-EU countries. The operation was initially mandated for six months, but upon request from the Macedonian President, it was extended until December 2003 (European Council 2003a; Council of the EU 2009a).[9]

Mission accomplished

Concordia was mandated to contribute to a stable and secure environment to allow the Macedonian government to implement the Framework Agreement. The EU's mandate, inherited from NATO, endorsed three main objectives: to support the implementation of the Framework Agreement; to contribute to the security of its observers; and to contribute to a safe and secure environment for its implementation. In terms of its internal goal attainment *Concordia* was a success. Its mandated purpose to further contribute to a stable and secure environment in which the Macedonian government could implement the Framework Agreement was successfully achieved. The EU Force (EUFOR) contributed to its implementation and successfully protected its observers (Augustin 2005; International Crisis Group 2005a: 48–9). EUFOR also supported Macedonian security forces in defusing minor incidents of civil unrest in northern Macedonia in September 2003, and a fully fledged civil war never materialised (Howorth 2007: 231–41). Although implementing the final aspects of the Framework Agreement remains a political challenge for the country, the security environment in which it is attempting to do so is now stable.

Concordia did experience various problems. A senior diplomat based in Skopje at the time has confirmed that some EU officers became engaged with a criminal group in Macedonia. On at least one occasion these officers misinformed the EUFOR Commander, which caused him to make an unsubstantiated public accusation of excessive government use of force against the criminal group. Other challenges resulted from political turf battles between NATO and EU HQ concerning security clearance for non-NATO EU member states, the place of NATO's regional command in Naples (Allied Force South Europe) within *Concordia's* chain of command and how long *Concordia's* command arrangements should stay in place after the operation. These problems were all relatively minor and could be resolved on a case-by-case basis (ISIS 2003; Mace 2004). Despite these minor limitations to its efficiency the operation did successfully achieve its internal goals in a timely and cost-effective fashion. From the EU perspective *Concordia* was by and large a success. The fact that the operation was a military success contributed to its internal political success, because it demonstrated that the EU was now capable of conducting a small-scale military conflict management operation. It also illustrated that the Berlin Plus arrangements worked relatively well. As such, it set a precedent, however small, for subsequent EU military conflict management operations. Moreover, *Concordia* added to the EU's comprehensive approach towards Macedonia and to the Union's striving for political leadership of international efforts in the country and the region. Finally, it added a military dimension not only to the EU's role in the Balkans, but to the CSDP as a whole (Cascone 2008; Dobbins *et al.* 2008; Mace 2004). In other words, the operation was politically beneficial to the EU at a comparatively low cost.

From a conflict perspective the absence of sustained violent conflict in Macedonia during and after *Concordia* demonstrates a great improvement in the security situation since 2001. The violent conflict has successfully been managed and no continuation, diffusion, escalation or intensification of violence has occurred. The question is to what extent these positive developments in Macedonia are attributable to EUFOR. The usefulness of the operation has been questioned in the past, because Macedonia was relatively stable by the time *Concordia* was deployed. It is often stressed that it was NATO, not the EU, which stepped in militarily to manage the 2001 crisis (Cascone 2008). However, the management of the violent conflict in Macedonia as a whole is the joint achievement of the country's political leadership, civil society and population (all, both ethnic Albanian and ethnic Macedonian) on the one hand and the international community on the other. The EU engagement, of which Operation *Concordia* was an important component, played a crucial part in this process. During the 2001 crisis the EU and the US worked together with ethnic Macedonian and Albanian leaders to reach a conflict settlement and prevent more violence. Together they managed to facilitate the signing of the Framework Agreement. Subsequently, NATO completed three military operations in the country before handing over its responsibilities to EUFOR in 2003 (Mace 2004; Ludlow 2003; Robertson 2003). From 2001 to 2003 NATO was indeed the international provider of military security in the country, but since the Ohrid agreement the EU has taken the political lead of conflict management more generally in Macedonia. Under the joint leadership of the EU Special Representative (EUSR) and the European Commission delegation, which now share a joint mission in Skopje, the EU through a combination of political, economic, technical, military (*Concordia*) and police assistance has played a crucial part not only in the securitisation, but also in the stabilisation and normalisation of the conflict. The EU's multifaceted approach towards Macedonia incorporated conflict management within the wider European integration process. This integrated approach was framed within the Stabilisation and Association Process (SAP), which aims at eventual EU membership for the country. Although the US supports this process and the Macedonian authorities and population must be commended for their efforts in this regard, it is the EU that has taken the lead in stabilising and securing Macedonia (Mace 2004).

Although the security situation in the country was more stable in 2003 than when NATO engaged in 2001, the security challenges EUFOR faced must not be underestimated. Ethnic tensions still ran high and there was a perception among international representatives on the ground that violent conflict could resume. The fact that the United Nations Security Council (UNSC) deemed it appropriate to authorise an EU follow-up operation to the NATO deployment is but one indicator of the international community's security concerns in Macedonia at the time. As one aspect of a wider EU approach towards the management of the conflict, *Concordia* played an important part in providing a secure environment in which the implementation of the Framework Agreement and the SAP could take place. By guaranteeing the military management of the conflict it facilitated its political management. This demonstrates the operation's importance within the EU's broader strategy to secure peace and stability in the country. In its role within the wider EU (and international) approach towards Macedonia, and the Balkans more generally, the operation was successful in facilitating the management of the Macedonian conflict and contributing to the prevention of more violence during and after its deployment. In other words, the operation was successful in its external goal attainment.

EUFOR never applied force in Macedonia. Observers disagree on whether it should have been more forceful in its approach. Doubts have sometimes been expressed as to whether EUFOR would have been willing and able to manage the situation if hostilities had recommenced (International Crisis Group 2005b; Howorth 2007). However, it is important to base the evaluation of an operation on actual events rather than hypothetical scenarios. The security situation did not deteriorate. Because the conflict did not return to violence, it was clearly possible to manage the security situation in the country without the application of force. EUFOR's decision not to use force was, therefore, a proportionate response to the challenge at hand. As it did not apply force, EUFOR also ensured that it did not physically target or harm civilians. In other words, it demonstrated due diligence, discrimination and proportion in its military response. Overall, the operation did more good than harm. In effect, it was also externally appropriate. It is important to recognise that other actors helped to ensure that the situation did not deteriorate and in this way added to *Concordia*'s success. This serves as a reminder that a successful operation cannot necessarily be accredited to the EU alone.

Operation Artemis in the Democratic Republic of Congo

Since the mid-1990s the DRC has been engulfed in a myriad of intertwined conflicts. At the local level there are conflicts for land, power and resources. These conflicts, which have been particularly fierce in the east of the country, have often assumed an ethnic dimension. At the state level belligerent parties have struggled for control of the state apparatus since the fall of President Sese Seko in 1997, and at the regional level the DRC conflict is part of a wider conflict formation, which has affected much of central and southern Africa. Within the DRC, regional actors Rwanda and Uganda have been directly engaged in the fighting (Prunier 2009; Tull 2009). In 1999 the Lusaka ceasefire agreement made way for the authorisation of the United Nations Organisation Mission in DRC (MONUC).[10] In late 2002 a further agreement was reached on the withdrawal of 23,000 Rwandan soldiers and most of the 10,000 Ugandan soldiers in the country. However, proxy militias supported by the two governments remained active in the DRC. The 2002 Sun City agreement ushered in a transitional government in 2003, in which President Kabila would share power with four vice-presidents including former rebel leaders Bemba and Ruberwa. The war officially ended in 2004, but the violence continued and the security situation in Ituri, the Kivus and Katanga remained particularly volatile (International Crisis Group 2008f; Prunier 2009; Tull 2009).

The violence in Ituri became the focus of the EU's Operation *Artemis*, the first of two EU military conflict management operations in the DRC. From 1999 to 2003 factional fighting in Ituri had killed an estimated 50,000 people. An additional 500,000 people had fled the district (Homan 2007). At the time of the *Artemis* deployment Ituri and its district capital, Bunia, were engulfed in crisis following the withdrawal of the Ugandan People's Defence Force subsequent to the Luanda Agreement between Uganda and the DRC in September 2002. Ethnic Lendu militias and the ethnic Hema-dominated Union of Congolese Patriots were fighting for the control of Bunia. In search of safety thousands of civilians gathered around the MONUC HQ in the town, where a 700-strong Uruguayan battalion was based. But the fighting continued and large-scale atrocities were inflicted upon the civilian population. Observers warned of another potential genocide in the Great Lakes region. The crisis undermined the Sun City agreement and risked re-engaging Uganda and Rwanda in the fighting. The humanitarian situation was severe. MONUC was unable to cope and the UN called for urgent help from the international community (Tull 2009).

The EU, on French initiative, responded positively to the UN request and on 12 June 2003 it agreed to deploy its first military conflict management operation in Africa. The *Artemis* operation was designed as a stop-gap measure to fill the security vacuum in Bunia pending MONUC reinforcements. EUFOR's mandate was set out in UNSCR 1484. France acted as framework nation and Operational HQ were located in Paris. Major General Neveux was appointed Operations Commander and Brigadier General Thonier became Force Commander. At its peak the operation comprised 2,200 troops. The operation handed over its military responsibilities to the reinforced UN mission in September 2003 (European Council 2003b; Howorth 2007: 231–41).

A flying start, but a disappointing finish

The mandated purpose of Operation *Artemis* was to contribute to the stabilisation of the security conditions and the humanitarian situation in Bunia pending MONUC reinforcements. The operation had three key objectives: to ensure the protection of displaced persons in the refugee camps in Bunia and, if the situation so required, contribute to the safety of the civilian population, UN personnel and humanitarian agencies in the town; to ensure the protection of the airport; and to give impetus to the overall peace process in the DRC and the Great Lakes region (Ulriksen *et al.* 2004; European Council 2003b). In terms of its internal goal attainment *Artemis* was a success. It prohibited the open bearing of arms in Bunia and established checkpoints at the entrances to the city. It secured the airport and the refugee camps in its area of operations. Several militia groups were successfully contained, some were disarmed and the supply chains of several groups were disrupted. An important element of the operation was its presence and show-of-force missions carried out by ground forces patrolling throughout Bunia accompanied by regular French Mirage over-flights. This enabled humanitarian organisations to travel to places outside the town that they had previously not been able to reach. It allowed a daily influx of 1,000–1,500 refugees into the city. It also made it possible for the Interim Administration in Ituri to resume some activities. The operation re-established basic order in Bunia and filled the security gap until UN reinforcements arrived. The improved situation in Bunia had a positive effect on the peace process in the country and the region. According to its operational purpose, the operation was undeniably a success (Gegout 2005; International Crisis Group 2005b: 46–9; Ulriksen *et al.* 2004).

In terms of its implementation the EU responded quickly and efficiently to the UN request. EU soldiers were on the ground in Bunia within seven days of the official decision to deploy. The rapid force projection was an achievement for the EU, although much of the planning had been done by France before the EU had officially agreed to undertake the operation (International Crisis Group 2005b: 46–9; Howorth 2007: 231–41; Ulriksen *et al.* 2004). It is important to recognise the logistical challenges that *Artemis* successfully overcame. The local infrastructure was wholly inadequate and the operation demonstrated a general EU shortage in strategic-lift capacity. *Artemis* was able to meet these challenges through a concerted effort by its engineers and through charter arrangements and strategic lift support from Canada and Brazil (Giegerich 2008; Homan 2007; Ulriksen *et al.* 2004). These issues illustrated potential challenges for future, more ambitious EU military conflict management operations, but for its internally defined purpose *Artemis* was able to overcome them. From an internal EU perspective, *Artemis* was both a military and political success. It demonstrated that the Union could successfully undertake military conflict management operations on a significant scale, on its own and outside of Europe. It bridged the political divide on security and defence matters within the EU at the time and added a military dimension to the Union's engagement in Africa (Hadden 2009: 1–21; Homan 2007; Ulriksen *et al.* 2004). The only limitation to the operation's internal success was misconduct by individual EU soldiers involved in the torture of a Congolese civilian. This incident, which will be investigated in greater detail below, compromised the internal appropriateness of the operation and threw a shadow over the operation's otherwise stellar internal success.

From an external conflict-specific perspective *Artemis*'s success was impressive, yet limited. Upon its deployment EUFOR alleviated the crisis in its area of operations. It regained control and prevented an otherwise expected further deterioration of the security situation in Bunia. Nonetheless, a common criticism of *Artemis* is that it was too limited in the time, scope and geographical area of its deployment (Homan 2007). *Artemis* restored stability in Bunia only temporarily and because it did so by driving the militia out of its area of operations rather than by disarming or dismantling these groups fully it allowed them to continue to operate elsewhere (Giegerich 2008). Operation *Artemis*, like the international efforts in the DRC more generally, left much to be desired in terms of managing the violence in the country. The positive impact that the operation did have on the local Ituri conflict, however, must not be underestimated. It is important to recall that over 50,000 people had been killed in the region between 1999 and 2003. At the time of the *Artemis* deployment the crisis was spiralling out of control and no other international actor was willing and able to provide even a short-term military stabilisation of the situation. The effect that this operation had on the ground was significant both in terms of its direct limitation of human rights abuses inflicted on civilians and indirectly as the lull in violence allowed access to humanitarian aid, movement for refugees and internally displaced people and a recommencement of the political negotiations in Kinshasa (Howorth 2007: 231–41; Keukeleire and MacNaughtan 2008: 174–98; Tull 2009). These were significant conflict-related achievements. Despite its limitations the operation made an important contribution to the management of the violent conflict in the DRC and the protection of civilians in Bunia at the time. However, as with any military conflict management operation and in particular one as limited as *Artemis*, there was a danger that the violent conflict would recommence after the troops withdrew.

The geographical, temporal and functional constraints of *Artemis*'s mandate compromised the sustainability of its positive impact on the conflict. Shortly after *Artemis* handed over its responsibilities to MONUC the security situation in Ituri deteriorated once again. Renewed massacres, just a month after the EUFOR withdrawal, added to the enormous suffering already sustained by the civilian population. The atrocities happened despite MONUC's continued peacekeeping efforts in the area. However, even with its reinforced mandate MONUC had lesser capabilities in Ituri than *Artemis*, and in effect it failed to sustain the positive momentum and prevent more violence (Giegerich 2008).

Although *Artemis* performed well and attained significant achievements in Bunia throughout its deployment, the broader international strategy of securing peace and stability in Ituri, let alone the DRC and the Great Lakes region, was only temporarily advanced by the EUFOR deployment (Giegerich 2008; Homan 2007). Since then there has been another upsurge in violence and the situation in Ituri remains volatile (UN Secretary General 2009). Not even in the specific area in which the EU force was deployed did the operation have sustainable success in preventing more violence. After its withdrawal the violent conflict in Ituri continued and intensified. The deterioration in the security situation was arguably primarily due to the limitations to *Artemis*'s mandate and MONUC's failure to sustain EUFOR's achievements. The EU force was, thus, successful in its external goal attainment during the deployment, but the larger international conflict management effort, of which *Artemis* was part, failed to prevent the continuation and intensification of violence after its withdrawal. With regard to its external goal attainment the operation was, therefore, only a partial success, as its achievements, although significant in the short term, proved short-lived and unsustainable in the longer term. This is not to blame EU soldiers for the actions of belligerent parties or for the failures on the UN in the DRC, but rather to reflect that as part of the wider international conflict management effort *Artemis* did not succeed in preventing more violence in Ituri, in the DRC or in the Great Lakes. In effect, it was only a partial success in terms of its external goal attainment. This once again demonstrates how it is not only up to the EU whether it succeeds in its military conflict management operations.

Operation *Artemis* was the first EU military conflict management operation to come under direct physical attack. EU ground forces were caught up in several violent clashes with local militia. EUFOR killed more than 20 militiamen during its deployment, but the armed confrontations were localised and of short duration (Giegerich 2008). Considering the precarious security situation in which the troops operated, the specificities of the situations in which they engaged in armed battle and their positive impact overall on the security situation in Bunia at the time, the use of force was proportionate to the challenge at hand. Overall, the operation did more good than harm. However, French soldiers tortured a Congolese civilian during the operation (Deutsche Welle 2008b; SVT 2008). Swedish national television, SVT

(2008), broadcast the following account as it was told by the Swedish *Artemis* soldiers, who reported the incident:

> In July 2003 French soldiers captured a young man in his twenties, and took him to the Swedish–French base [. . .] The man was paraded around the base with a snare around his neck by a French Colonel's aide. During the interrogation, which continued several hours in the French section, the prisoner was subjected to mock drowning. The prisoner's screams were heard over the entire base [. . .] The prisoner was bent down against the ground and an officer performed a mock execution by shooting his gun at the prisoner's head without a shot going off [. . .] The torture continued all evening until midnight when the prisoner with a hood over his head was loaded onto a French jeep and driven out of the camp. His destiny is unknown.

Swedish soldiers filed complaints with the Swedish operational chief in the field. Upon their return to Sweden several of them reported it to their superiors there too. The Swedish Armed Forces subsequently undertook an official investigation, which concluded that torture had taken place. The Swedish report was sent to the French Defence Department, which in turn undertook its own investigation and concluded that no criminal offence had been committed (SVT 2008). The data concerning this incident is limited and at times contradictory. However, the accounts and complaints from the Swedish soldiers, the Swedish Army's official report and the independent investigation conducted by the Swedish National Television all concluded that this was a case of disproportionate and indiscriminate use of force against a civilian. Although the implementation of the operation was otherwise successful, this misconduct by individual EUFOR soldiers meant that the operation was only a partial success in its external appropriateness. The torture of a civilian during an otherwise largely successful operation demonstrates why it is important to evaluate not only the achievements but also the conduct of the forces.

Operation Althea in Bosnia and Herzegovina

The violent conflict in Bosnia and Herzegovina started in April 1992. Over the next three and a half years the war, which was fought mainly between factions of ethnic Serbs, Croats and Muslims, claimed at least 97,207 lives (Research and Documentation Centre Sarajevo 2007).[11] By the end of the war more than half of the population had been killed, expelled or fled their homes. The violent conflict ended when Croatian President Tudjman, Yugoslav President Milošević and Bosnian President Izetbegović, representing Bosnian Croats, Bosnian Serbs and Bosnian Muslims (Bosniaks) respectively, agreed to a settlement forced through by the US in Dayton, Ohio, in November 1995 (Chandler 2000; Glenny 2001; Silber and Little 1996). The Dayton agreement, officially named the General Framework Agreement for Peace in Bosnia and Herzegovina (GFAP), was signed in Paris on 14 December 1995. The agreement and the constitutional structures it put in place ended the war in the BiH at the time, but have since been criticised for not ensuring a sustainable peace in the country (Chandler 2000). The GFAP authorised an international High Representative (HR) to facilitate, mobilise and coordinate the civilian aspects of the peace implementation process in the country.[12] The UN endorsed the establishment of a multinational NATO Implementation Force (IFOR) to undertake the military aspects of the GFAP and assume the authority transferred from the existing United Nations Protection Force (UNPROFOR) in the country. After the 1996 elections IFOR was replaced by NATO's smaller Stabilisation Force (SFOR) (NATO 2005).[13]

When NATO decided to withdraw SFOR in 2004, UNSCR 1551 endorsed the launch of an EU operation in its place. On 12 July 2004 the Council decided to launch Operation *Althea* and on 2 December 2004 EUFOR took over NATO's military responsibilities in BiH.[14] As the operation was launched under Berlin Plus, Operational HQ were located at SHAPE and Admiral Feist was appointed Operations Commander. Major General Leakey became the first EU Force Commander in BiH.[15] The EU initially deployed 7,000 troops to the country under a Chapter VII mandate. The force has since been reduced to 1,600 troops (backed by KFOR and over-the-horizon forces). A total of 27 countries including 22 EU member states and five non-EU troop-contributing nations provide the necessary capabilities to carry out EUFOR's tasks at present. The operation is ongoing. The Operations Commander has been preparing a possible evolution into a non-executive, capacity-building mission. However, an official decision on such a transition remains outstanding. Under UNSCR 2019 (2011) the operation retains its executive function and ability to deploy considerable reserve forces to the area at short notice. For the time being *Althea*'s executive mandate has been extended until 15 November 2012 (Council of the EU 2009b; Howorth 2007).

So far, so good

The operational purpose of EUFOR *Althea* is to provide a military presence in order to contribute to a safe and secure environment in BiH. It is mandated to deny conditions for a resumption of violence; to manage any residual military aspect of the GFAP; and thereby to allow EU and international actors to carry out their responsibilities in the country. The operation is explicitly framed as part of the EU's comprehensive approach towards BiH, which also comprises political, economic, social and policing instruments intended to support conflict management, European integration and eventual EU membership for BiH. As in Macedonia, these are all framed within the Stabilisation and Association Process. In the short term *Althea* set out to ensure a smooth transition from SFOR and to maintain a secure environment for the implementation of the GFAP. In the medium term it intended to facilitate the European integration process; to assist BiH in reaching a Stabilisation and Association Agreement (SAA) with the EU; and to move closer towards eventual EU membership. In the long term *Althea*, as part of the wider international approach, hoped to help create a stable and viable multi-ethnic BiH at peace locally, nationally and with its neighbours in the region (European Council 2004c; Council of the EU 2009b; Howorth 2007). In 2007 EUFOR's presence in BiH was reduced to 2,200 troops. Following the peaceful conduct of the recent elections, EUFOR has undertaken a further reduction in forces with approximately 1,600 troops remaining in the country (backed by over-the horizon reserves). *Althea*'s operational focus remains the maintenance of a safe and secure environment in BiH, ensuring compliance with the GFAP and supporting the HR/EUSR.

As the operation is still ongoing it is too early to undertake a conclusive evaluation of its success, but some preliminary observations can be made. *Althea* has successfully maintained a safe and secure environment in BiH throughout its deployment. Its own transition and the improved security situation in the country are both positive indicators of EUFOR's internal goal attainment. *Althea* achieved its short-term military objectives in a relatively smooth transition from SFOR. With regard to the medium-term objectives BiH signed an SAA with the EU in 2007, but its further European integration process has been slow. The long-term political objective of regional stability and cooperation has also only been partly achieved so far. Although the security situation in the Balkans is stable, political dynamics remain challenging (International Crisis Group 2009e; Howorth 2007). Whether the political objectives of the operation and the wider EU approach towards BiH and the Balkans will succeed remains to be seen, but from an internal military perspective the operation has been successful so far. It has provided a military presence in order to contribute to the safe and secure environment in BiH. It has successfully denied conditions for a resumption of violence. It has managed the military aspects of the GFAP and allowed the EU and other international actors to carry out their responsibilities in the country.

In terms of the internal appropriateness of its implementation *Althea* has so far been timely, efficient and cost-effective. This was helped initially by the fact that the EU operation was taking over responsibilities from the NATO operation in BiH. SFOR had been a largely European undertaking and many of the former NATO troops remained in the country under EUFOR command. Much of the initial EUFOR mandate and operation plan also mirrored previous SFOR commitments. The handover and successful implementation of the operation so far were further facilitated by the Berlin Plus arrangements between NATO and the EU and their joint experience in Macedonia (International Crisis Group 2005b: 49–51). The setting up of *Althea* and the transfer of responsibilities was planned by the two organisations in cooperation. Detailed preparation helped them limit misunderstandings and overlap at the practical level and facilitated an internally successful implementation of *Althea* to date. Although there have been political disagreements between the two organisations, these were resolved by the commanders on the ground and did not significantly affect the positive achievements and implementation of the EUFOR operation (Cascone 2008). From an EU perspective *Althea* has been a success so far.

From an external perspective, sustained violent conflict has been kept at bay throughout EUFOR's deployment and the return of violence remains, at worst, a threat rather than a reality; a threat, the seriousness of which is much disputed. What is widely agreed upon, however, is that the current situation in BiH is far from ideal. Ethno-political tensions in the country remain high, but it remains unclear whether the tensions in BiH are of a purely political nature or whether the country is at risk of more violence. On 26 March 2009 the Peace Implementation Council (PIC) announced that the Office of the High Representative (OHR) would remain open and active until the political deadlock was resolved. Alongside the appointment of yet another 'last' High Representative in March 2009, the extended mandates of both OHR and EUFOR illustrate that the PIC does not perceive the situation in the country to be stable enough for the international community to disengage and EUFOR to leave. The PIC, which comprises 55 countries and agencies, has underlined that EUFOR remains crucial to the maintenance of a safe and secure environment in the country (Peace Implementation Council 2009a, b, c).

Operation *Althea* has been and still is perceived to play a deterrent role in BiH. As in Macedonia the security situation in BiH had much improved since NATO engaged immediately after the signing of the peace agreement. However, an authoritative international presence, both military and political, was considered essential in BiH also after NATO's withdrawal (International Crisis Group 2004). Throughout the duration of EUFOR's mandate, the principal challengers to BiH security have been weapons smugglers, war criminals and extremist religious groups. One might be tempted to ask, therefore, whether EUFOR *Althea* is really a conflict management operation. EUFOR was – and still is – deployed in BiH in case the security situation deteriorates. This was a similar line of thinking as in the *Concordia* case, although in Macedonia the threat was perceived to be less perilous. In BiH the return to war was perceived as a very real threat by both many Bosnians and international observers at the time of the initial EU deployment (Black 2003; Harton 2004; International Crisis Group 2004). Nonetheless, the security situation in BiH has remained stable and the country's territorial integrity has not been challenged militarily since the signing of the Dayton agreement. This is attributable in part to EUFOR's presence. National events, such as the ten-year commemoration of the Srebrenica massacre, which divided the population and was widely perceived as a threat to national security, have taken place without major disturbances.[16] This is another indicator that EUFOR, which had principal authority for the military aspects of conflict management in the country, has been doing its job well. Regional events such as Kosovo's unilateral declaration of independence, which it was feared might provoke a deterioration of the security situation in BiH, also did not do so. It had a significant destabilising effect, politically, but militarily BiH has remained safe and secure (International Crisis group 2004, 2008g).

EUFOR is only one aspect of a mammoth effort to consolidate peace and security in BiH. The EU with its efforts to promote European integration and eventual EU membership for BiH provides the political backbone of the international engagement in the country. As in Macedonia the EU has linked – and made the first conditional upon the second – its enlargement process to successful conflict management in BiH. EUFOR contributes to this wider EU effort by guaranteeing a secure environment in which this process can progress should the political leadership in BiH and Brussels want it to (Cameron 2006; Office of the High Representative 2009). Whether *Althea* will continue to successfully manage the security aspects of this process and of the GFAP; and, in effect, successfully prevent more violence in BiH remains to be seen. The operation, as part of the wider EU and international community approach, has thus far succeeded in preventing a continuation, diffusion, escalation and intensification of violence. *Althea* has until now been successful in its external goal attainment.

EUFOR *Althea* only used force on one occasion. This was a shooting incident involving Italian EU officers seeking to arrest a person indicted for war crimes. The Carabinieri came under attack and in the exchange one person was killed. The EUFOR soldiers opened fire only once fired upon. The person who was killed in the confrontation was carrying an automatic weapon at the time (Bassuener and Ferhatovic 2008). Therefore, despite its unfortunate outcome, this incident does not compromise the external appropriateness of the operation. *Althea* meets the external appropriateness criterion both with regard to the proportion and discrimination of its use of force. It is important to stress that the EU troops only used force on this one occasion. Overall, the analysis can conclude that *Althea* has done far more good than harm in BiH and that it was successful in its external appropriateness.

EUFOR DR Congo

In June 2006 the EU launched its second military operation in the DRC. This operation, codenamed EUFOR DR Congo, was deployed to support the UN mission in the country, MONUC, during the period encompassing the DRC elections in July 2006. The mandate was set out in UNSCR 1671. The EU Joint Action of 27 April 2006 appointed Operations Commander Lieutenant General Viereck and Force Commander Major General Damay. Germany was framework nation and Operations Headquarters were located in Potsdam. EUFOR DRC deployed some 400 military personnel in an advance element to Kinshasa and an additional battalion-sized over-the-horizon force on stand-by in neighbouring Gabon. At peak strength in mid-August 2006 EUFOR DR Congo had 2,466 troops in the field, but a maximum of 1,000 were deployed in the DRC at any one time. Twenty-two member states participated in the operation with two-thirds of the troops coming from France and Germany. The operation was concluded in November 2006 (Council of the EU 2006b, c).

Limited, brief, risk-averse and ineffective

The operational purpose of EUFOR DRC was to support MONUC during the elections. To this end the mandate singled out four key objectives: to support MONUC in its efforts to stabilise the security situation in its area of deployment, in case MONUC faced difficulties; to contribute to the protection of civilians under imminent threat of physical violence, without prejudice to the responsibilities of the DRC government; to contribute to the protection of Kinshasa airport; and to execute limited operations to extract individuals in danger (Council of the EU 2006c). The operation was a success in its internal goal attainment. The elections went relatively smoothly and both rounds of the ballots were held in a generally peaceful and orderly manner. Although some violent incidents occurred in Kinshasa, these did not have a significant negative impact on the outcome of the election process or EUFOR's internal goal achievement. Election observers confirmed that the organisation and conduct of the elections under the aegis of the Independent Electoral Committee went well. Scholars have questioned the extent to which this was attributable to the EU's military operation, however (Gegout 2007; Giegerich 2008; Howorth 2007: 231–41). In terms of its contribution to MONUC's efforts to manage the security situation in Kinshasa, to the protection of civilians under imminent threat, to the protection of Kinshasa airport and to the execution of limited operations to extract individuals in danger the operation succeeded. When fighting broke out between supporters of the two presidential candidates in Kinshasa in August 2006, EUFOR supported MONUC, helped separate the fighting factions and re-establish order. It assisted in the recovery of diplomats trapped by the violence and mediated between belligerent parties. EUFOR also airlifted weapons out of areas occupied by groups of demobilised soldiers and participated in humanitarian initiatives (Gegout 2007; Giegerich 2008).

   With regard to the timeliness of its deployment the operation experienced some problems. As the Union did not have permanent planning and control capacities, EU-level operational planning could not start until Operational Headquarters had been designated. No member state was eager to adopt the framework responsibilities for this operation and the force generation process was slow and cumbersome. In effect, the deployment was continuously delayed (Giegerich 2008). It took the EU almost three months to respond affirmatively to the UN's request and six months until the force was operational. This process was very slow compared to *Artemis*'s seven-day deployment three years earlier. The delay was partly due to British and German reluctance towards the operation and their hesitance to deploy troops. The United Kingdom (UK) ruled out participation, given its military commitments in Iraq and Afghanistan. Germany was eventually persuaded to take part on the condition that only 100 of its 780 troops would be deployed in Kinshasa, while the rest would remain as part of the reserve in Gabon (Howorth 2007: 231–41). Once the force was deployed its mission was efficiently implemented. When tensions increased in Kinshasa EUFOR successfully brought in reinforcements and helped calm the situation. Militarily the operation was a success, in part due to its limited mandate (Gegout 2007; Giegerich 2008; Howorth 2007: 231–41). It is important, however, not to underestimate the internal importance of the operation for the EU. Politically and militarily, EUFOR DRC was an achievement for the Union. It confirmed the EU's capacity for autonomous military action outside Europe and it demonstrated once again that the Union could serve as a partner for the UN in difficult situations (Hadden 2009; Olsen 2009). It also added another dimension to the EU's emerging approach to the DRC (Dobbins *et al.* 2008). Overall, the operation was an internal success, albeit limited by its delayed deployment.

From a conflict perspective the operation's success was much more limited. Although it successfully provided support to MONUC in Kinshasa, it contributed little to the management of the violence in other parts of the country at the time. When the EU launched EUFOR DRC the security situation in the country was still dire. The International Rescue Committee estimated that 1,200 people, half of them children, died daily as a direct or indirect consequence of the conflict (UNICEF 2006). The security situation in the east of the country was particularly unstable. In July alone, while EUFOR DRC was being deployed to Kinshasa, 17,000 people fled renewed fighting in Ituri. Despite the increased violence and a need for further international assistance in the east, EUFOR DRC was not deployed there. The EU troops were confined to their area of operations in and around the capital and much of the force remained in Gabon. Except for relatively minor disturbances the security situation in Kinshasa was comparatively stable. Although the operation did successfully support MONUC in the handling of these disturbances the operation's achievements with regard to the management of the conflict as a whole did not constitute an external success (Gegout 2007). At its launch Haine and Giegerich (2006: 1) warned: 'The operation is limited, brief, risk-averse and ultimately ineffective.' In terms of its contribution towards the management of the conflict, EUFOR DRC was exactly that. It did not in any tangible way contribute to the prevention of more violence in the country. The conflict continued and intensified in the east of the country. In terms of its external goal attainment the operation was, therefore, only a partial success. With regard to its external appropriateness the operation was successful, as it did not use force in its handling of any incidents in Kinshasa. Although it did not achieve much in terms of improving the conflict situation in the country, it did still play a deterrent role in Kinshasa. In effect, the operation still did less harm than good.

The security situation in the DRC is still volatile and the humanitarian situation is desperate. Neither Operation *Artemis* nor EUFOR DRC facilitated an end to the violent conflict. However, these two operations, unlike *Concordia* and *Althea*, were not mandated, equipped or intended to operate throughout the country or to manage the conflict as a whole. In both the DRC operations the EU forces were deployed to support MONUC only for a few months at a time. Unlike the situation in the Balkans, where the EU had a lead role in international conflict management during Concordia and Althea, in the DRC the EU and its military conflict management operations played only a supporting role to the much larger UN mission. MONUC, now renamed MONUSCO, is the backbone of the international attempt to manage the violent conflict in the DRC.[17] It is important to keep this in mind, when considering the limitations to the external success of these two EU operations.

EUFOR Chad/CAR

The EU's most recent military conflict management operation, EUFOR Chad/CAR, was launched in the tri-border area between Sudan, Chad and the Central African Republic. A complex conflict formation encompasses the region and within each of the three countries there is a web of closely related internal conflicts. The alarming security situation in the border region is a consequence of local, state, regional and international conflict dynamics. Both Chad and CAR were experiencing domestic conflicts of their own, before the Darfur conflict erupted in Sudan in 2003 (Berg 2008). Despite the domestic problems in Chad and CAR, however, EUFOR Chad/CAR's mandate focused on alleviating the direct consequences of the Darfur crisis on the security situation in the refugee camps in eastern Chad and north-eastern CAR.

In a Joint Action adopted on 15 October 2007 the Council decided to launch the operation. Lieutenant General Nash was appointed Operations Commander and Brigadier General

Ganascia became Force Commander. Operational Headquarters were located at Mont Valérien. The operation was authorised by UNSCR 1778 and launched in January 2008. The mandate authorised an operation of one year's duration from the date upon which it reached Initial Operating Capability (IOC). It reached IOC in March and Full Operating Capability in September 2008. The fully deployed force consisted of 3,400 troops from 25 European states, 19 of which had personnel present on the ground (Council of the EU 2007g, 2009c).

The wrong mission accomplished?

EUFOR Chad/CAR was a bridging operation intended to support the civilian United Nations Mission in the Central African Republic and Chad (MINURCAT), while the UN prepared its military component. The mandated purpose of EUFOR Chad/CAR was to contribute to the improvement of security in eastern Chad and north-eastern CAR. EUFOR had three key objectives: to protect civilians in danger, particularly refugees and displaced persons; to facilitate delivery of humanitarian aid and free movement of humanitarian personnel by helping to improve security in the area of operations; and to contribute to protecting UN personnel, facilities, installations and equipment, while also ensuring the security and freedom of movement of its own staff (Council of the EU 2009c; Hadden 2009: 5–21).

Due to resource shortfalls on part of the EU and instabilities in the Chadian capital at the time, there were minor delays to the launch of the operation (Ehrhart 2008). Once the force was on the ground it constituted the largest, most multinational military operation that the Union has launched in Africa. EUFOR Chad/CAR was undertaken in a vast, remote and inhospitable area of operations and its deployment alone represented an unprecedented logistical challenge for the EU. The construction of the operational infrastructure from brownfield sites to finished camps involved a massive building effort. EUFOR completed six camps with capacity for up to 2,000 people and undertook major work on N'djamena and Abeche airports to facilitate the deployment and sustainability of the operation. Assembling and deploying the force was a great challenge for the Union. The operation required nine major sea moves, 1,500 containers, 540 strategic flights, 150 convoys of over 2,000 kilometres and 365 aviation flights (Council of the EU 2009c; Nash 2008). This is important because, considering the delicate security situation, the vast area of operations, the logistical circumstances on the ground and the Union's relative military inexperience, the deployment represented a great challenge and upon its completion a great achievement for the EU. Once the bases had been constructed, the airports developed and the troops and equipment had arrived safely, EUFOR established a robust military presence in order to deter the persecution of refugees and IDPs in its area of operations. EUFOR was successful in terms of its internal goal achievement. Its presence, regular patrolling and targeted operations had a deterrence effect, which helped increase security in its areas of operations. EUFOR helped protect civilians and facilitated the delivery of humanitarian aid in the time and space that its troops were operating. With regard to its operational objectives to protect the UN presence and also to ensure the security and freedom of movement of its own staff, the operation was also successful. However, it took months before EUFOR could assist the UN mission, because the deployment of the civilian MINURCAT component was continually delayed (Ehrhart 2008; Oxfam International 2008; Pop 2009b).

With regard to its implementation EUFOR Chad/CAR had mixed results. The initial delays to the deployment hindered a timely execution of its mandate in the first half of the operation. EUFOR Chad/CAR was launched in January 2008, but it did not reach Full Operating Capability until September 2008. The first part of the deployment was focused on deployment, building and engineering tasks. The operation, which was initially intended to total 4,000 troops, also had significant problems in acquiring the necessary troops and equipment from EU member states. France, the main instigator of the operation, eventually announced that it would fill the gaps. Once the troops and equipment were deployed, EUFOR Chad/CAR was both efficient and cost-effective in achieving its objectives in the field. From a political-strategic perspective the operation had significant value for the EU. It enhanced the operational experience of the CSDP. It was another autonomous operation in Africa conducted without the help of the US and, as such, it enhanced the Union's role as a military conflict manager. It increased the EU's involvement and influence not only in the region, but also in Africa (Mattelaer 2008; Olsen 2009). This added to the internal goal attainment and cost-effectiveness of the operation. With regard to its internal appropriateness, however, EUFOR was only partially successful due to the deployment delays and the limited capability of the operation during the first half of the mandate. Moreover, the internal appropriateness of the operation was compromised when two EUFOR Chad/CAR soldiers accidentally crossed into Sudanese territory and one was killed and the other wounded. This was a high cost for the EU, which had never previously lost a soldier in combat (BBC 2008; Pineau 2008). Consequently, the operation was only a partial internal success.

The conflict context in which EUFOR Chad/CAR engaged was difficult. Just 24 hours after the operation was launched its deployment was interrupted by a major rebel offensive on Chad's capital, N'djamena. Sources suggest that the rebel alliance consciously decided to storm the city in anticipation of the EUFOR deployment (Fletcher 2008). Both EUFOR Chad/CAR and MINURCAT were initially delayed. EUFOR managed to deploy its forces with much less of a delay than MINURCAT. The problems facing MINURCAT, however, directly affected the success of the EU operation, as it was dependent on effective cooperation with the UN mission. EUFOR's presence, its regular patrolling and targeted operations, nonetheless, contributed to an increased sense of security in its area of operations (Oxfam International 2008). In December 2008 there was a lull in violence in northern CAR (International Crisis Group 2008e). EUFOR had a positive, albeit limited, impact on security in Chad as well, but in both countries its achievements risked being compromised, if the UN follow-up mission did not successfully manage to sustain them. Some observers at the time questioned whether MINURCAT was up to the challenge (Ehrhart 2008; International Crisis Group 2009a). When EUFOR handed over responsibility to MINURCAT in March 2009 the situation in the area was still precarious. The EU operation, which was specifically mandated to protect refugees from the conflict in Darfur, withdrew amid rising tensions resulting from the international arrest warrant against Sudanese President al-Bashir. UN Secretary General Ban Ki-moon and President Obama warned that the situation may deteriorate even further (Pop 2009b). It is clear from the current instability in the area that EUFOR Chad/CAR has not helped to facilitate an end to violent conflict in the region.

Like Operation *Artemis* in the DRC, EUFOR Chad/CAR did have some success in temporarily alleviating the violence in its area of operations (Mattelaer 2008; Oxfam International 2008). However, unlike *Artemis*, which was deployed with remarkable speed, EUFOR Chad/CAR had less impact than its mandate allowed, because of the delays to its own and MINURCAT's deployments (Ehrhart 2008). Moreover, the EU soldiers were not authorised to provide security within the refugee camps. The intention was that this would be provided by Chadian police officers trained by MINURCAT. However, the Chadian police was not fulfilling this role throughout most of EUFOR's deployment and in effect a security vacuum, which was exploited by local bandits and militias, left refugees and internally displaced persons (IDPs) in the camps unprotected (Mattelaer 2006; Oxfam International 2008).

As aid workers in the area were also increasingly threatened, humanitarian efforts were downscaled. This negatively affected EUFOR's ability to support the delivery of humanitarian aid.

Chadian and Sudanese objections to an EU deployment directly on the border between Chad and Sudan also limited the operation's success in managing the regional aspect of the conflict. Consequently, the proxy war between Sudan and Chad continued, while the EU troops were deployed in the region. As the EU force was not operating in the border area, where the instability was worst, the operation had less impact on the humanitarian consequences of conflict in these areas (Ehrhart 2008). It is important to recognise that this operation, like the two operations in the DRC, was not mandated, equipped or intended to operate throughout the three countries involved in the conflict. With significant limitations to its mandate the EU force was unable to successfully manage the violent conflict in the region. The EU forces did not succeed in preventing more violence. In its area of operations, however, the operation did help to improve the situation. From a conflict perspective the operation was a partial success. Where it was deployed, once it was deployed, EUFOR did deter violence and significantly improved the security situation. However, the operation's contribution to the international efforts to manage the conflict was limited by a lack of support from domestic, regional and international actors involved in both the conflict and its management.

EUFOR Chad/CAR repeatedly came under fire and on at least three occasions it fired back. Two of these incidents were confrontations with local armed groups in Chad and the third incident occurred when a single EUFOR Land Rover strayed into Sudan. In Chad both attacks on EUFOR were conducted by unidentified armed groups. EUFOR sustained no serious casualties and there are no reports of its opponents suffering any fatalities. In both incidents EUFOR opened fire only after they were fired upon and on both occasions civilians were helped from the scene by EUFOR soldiers. There are different accounts of what happened when the EUFOR vehicle crossed into Sudan. Both the Sudanese authorities and EUFOR claim to have fired in self-defence and both have reported casualties. France has officially criticised the Sudanese army for its disproportionate response, but the incident could have been avoided, if the troops had not strayed into Sudanese territory (EUFOR Chad/CAR 2008a, b, c; Pineau 2008). The EUFOR soldiers' use of force, however, was proportionate to the armed confrontation they met in Sudan and discriminatory in the sense that it did not target civilians. Throughout its deployment the force did far more good than harm. Consequently, the operation was a success in its external appropriateness.

Conclusion

From 2003 to 2010 the EU launched five military conflict management operations. *Concordia*, *Althea*, *Artemis*, EUFOR DRC and EUFOR Chad/CAR were launched to help manage conflicts in Macedonia, BiH, DRC and the tri-border area between Sudan, Chad and CAR. This chapter set out to examine their success. It first defined success and then evaluated the five EU military conflict management operations conducted to date.

According to the definition developed above an operation is a success when its purpose has been achieved and implemented in an appropriate manner from both an EU perspective and a conflict perspective. To evaluate success accordingly this definition was broken down into four success criteria: internal goal attainment, internal appropriateness, external goal attainment and external appropriateness. The internal goal attainment criterion evaluated whether each operation successfully fulfilled its mandate and key operational objectives.

The internal appropriateness criterion assessed the implementation of each operation with regard to its timeliness, efficiency and cost-effectiveness. The external goal attainment criterion examined the contribution that each operation made to the overall management of the violent conflict. That is, its contribution to preventing continuation, diffusion, escalation and intensification of violence. Finally, the external appropriateness criterion evaluated the implementation of each operation according to the Just War Theory principles governing the appropriate use of force: namely, discrimination between combatants and non-combatants and proportionality in the application of force. A breakdown of the success of each of the operations is illustrated in Table 12.2 below.

The different degrees of success in these operations illustrate why it is important to include both goal attainment and appropriateness criteria for success and why it is necessary to evaluate them from both EU and conflict perspectives. It also demonstrates why it is useful to evaluate success comparatively and to undertake this comparison in a structured and focused way to get a more nuanced picture of the EU's performance in military conflict management.

In terms of its overall performance in military conflict management from 2003 to 2010, the EU has had stellar success in achieving its self-defined operational objectives. It has also been relatively successful in implementing these objectives, although delays in deployment and force generation as well as misconduct by individual soldiers have on occasion limited their timeliness, efficiency and cost-effectiveness. The EU has contributed a great deal to conflict management in Macedonia and BiH, amongst other initiatives, through its military operations. The EU's military operations have been less successful in their efforts to facilitate conflict management in the DRC, Chad and CAR. In reality these operations may very well have saved more lives in the limited time and space in which they operated, due to higher levels of violence in conflict situations in which they intervened. However, their success was limited by the restrictions imposed on them, in large part by the EU itself. Finally, with the exception of the *Artemis* torture case, all five operations have been discriminatory and proportional in their application of force. In sum, the EU's performance in military conflict management has been a relative success from the point of view of the Union, but more humble with regard to the management of the conflict situations on the ground.

The above indicates that the success of EU military conflict management operations is dependent on the context in which they engage. This context encompasses the EU context in which the operations take place and the conflict context in which they operate. In the EU context, the Union's will and ability to act, to fund and to cooperate and coordinate its efforts to accommodate the operation in question influences its chances of success. This in turn depends on the level of active support that the operation enjoys from EU member states and

Table 12.2 Success in EU military conflict management operations: 2003–2010

	Internal goal attainment	Internal appropriateness	External goal attainment	External appropriateness
Operation Concordia	Success	Partial success	Success	Success
Operation Artemis	Success	Partial success	Partial success	Partial success
Operation Althea	Preliminary success	Preliminary success	Preliminary success	Preliminary success
EUFOR DR Congo	Success	Partial success	Partial success	Success
EUFOR Chad/CAR	Success	Partial success	Partial success	Success

institutions. In the conflict context, the support of local, state, regional and international actors engaged in the conflict and its management influences an operation's chance of success. The EU can influence the behaviour of these actors through its efforts to cooperate and coordinate its conflict management efforts with them. In conclusion, an EU military conflict management operation is more likely to succeed when it has sufficient support from the parties involved in the conflict and its management as well as the EU's member states and institutions. The cases examined above illustrate this. *Concordia* and *Althea* enjoyed more active support both from EU member states and institutions and from local, state, regional and international actors involved. None of these parties actively opposed these operations. In effect, they had greater success. In Africa, where the operations engaged in more volatile conflict situations, they enjoyed less support and more opposition both within the EU and in the conflict context. Consequently, their success was limited. *Artemis* and EUFOR Chad/CAR enjoyed more EU support than EUFOR DRC; in effect they achieved more than EUFOR DRC, despite their more challenging operating theatres. In conclusion, without sufficient EU capabilities to act, to fund and to cooperate and coordinate efforts to facilitate its success, an EU conflict management operation cannot succeed.

Notes

1 This enquiry focuses on the EU's track record as a military conflict manager. It evaluates EU military conflict management operations only and does not include civilian or hybrid missions. The operations are assessed from a conflict perspective, thus, the enquiry does not include EU responses to natural disasters or non-conflict related crises. It also does not include missions such as the EU naval deployment off the coast of Somalia or EU support to the African Union Mission in Sudan. Although these are conflict-related operations, they are not strictly speaking EU military conflict management operations.
2 The policy was officially named the *European Security and Defence Policy* until the adoption of the Treaty of Lisbon in December 2009. When this treaty was ratified, the policy was officially renamed the *Common Security and Defence Policy*.
3 Once a conflict has turned violent, the violence may develop in a variety of different ways. Conflicts do not necessarily develop in a linear and logical fashion and may move back and forth between different stages of violence and non-violence. If a conflict becomes more violent, there are four principal processes by which this may take place: namely, through (1) continuation, (2) diffusion, (3) escalation and (4) intensification of violence. *Continuation* refers to the process in which the violent aspect of a conflict continues over time. *Diffusion* describes the scenario when violent conflict in one geographic area directly or indirectly generates violent conflict in another area. *Escalation* occurs when external actors become involved in an already existing conflict within its confined geographic borders (Gleditsch 2007; Lobell and Mauceri 2004: 1–10). *Intensification* refers to the process in which the violence itself increases. This includes both an increase in the number of violent incidents and an intensification in their nature.
4 Proportionality in military response and discrimination between combatants and non-combatants in military targeting are the two fundamental premises of *Jus in Bello,* the Just War tradition's *Justice in War* doctrine (Guthrie and Quinlan 2007: 35–43).
5 NATO had military peacekeepers in Macedonia from August 2001 until March 2003. Operation *Essential Harvest* deployed 4,600 NATO troops to collect and destroy weapons handed over by armed groups as they disbanded. Operation *Amber Fox* roughly comprised 800 personnel to contribute to the protection of the international monitors overseeing the implementation of the Ohrid agreement. Operation *Allied Harmony*, consisting of 400 troops, continued to support the monitors and advise the government on how to take ownership of security throughout the country. NATO also had a significant presence in the form of the Kosovo Force (KFOR) Rear, which would later be identified as a theatre reserve, which Operation *Concordia* could call on *in extremis*. After Operation *Allied Harmony* was completed, NATO kept a small representation in the country to assist the continuation of the disarmament process (Mace 2004; Robertson 2003).

6 An exchange of letters between High Representative for the Common Foreign and Security Policy (CFSP) Javier Solana and NATO Secretary General Lord Robertson, in March 2003, concluded the *Berlin Plus arrangements* for strategic partnership between the two organisations in crisis management. This allows the EU to make use of NATO assets and capabilities in conflict management operations (NATO 2006c).

7 Major General dos Santos took over as EU Force Commander in October 2003.

8 The EU Framework Nation Concept was adopted on 24 July 2002. It allows for the national headquarters of a member state to be multi-nationalised for the purpose and duration of a CSDP military operation (Ulriksen *et al.* 2004).

9 In July 2003 the Council agreed to extend the operation under the previous terms until December 2003. At this point the European Rapid Operational Force (EUROFOR) took over the framework responsibilities from France. When *Concordia* was terminated the EU launched a civilian police mission, code-named *Proxima*, to support the development of the Macedonian police service (Council of the EU 2003f).

10 MONUC was initially established as a small military liaison team in 1999. It has since become one of the biggest and most expensive UN operations ever deployed. Today it is a multidimensional peacekeeping mission with a broad mandate. With 18,434 uniformed personnel deployed MONUC has become the centrepiece of the international efforts to regulate the DRC conflict (United Nations 2009b; Tull 2009).

11 In 2007 an independent study, funded mainly by the Norwegian government, concluded that at least 97,207 people were killed during the war in BiH. Mirsad Tokaca, who led the project, estimated that the total number of dead, which is significantly lower than previous estimates (around 250,000 people), could rise due to ongoing research, but with a maximum of another 10,000 dead. The death toll refers to deaths directly related to military activities and does not include indirect causes of death during war such as death due to starvation, lack of medication or suicide, nor does it include people who died at an earlier age than would normally be expected during peace time (Research and Documentation Centre Sarajevo 2007).

12 The Office of the High Representative was established as an *ad hoc* international institution responsible for overseeing the implementation of civilian aspects of the GFAP. The Peace Implementation Council, the international body guiding the peace process in BiH, oversees the OHR's work. In March 2009 PIC appointed Austrian diplomat Valentin Inzko the seventh High Representative in the country. In June 2009 PIC confirmed that the OHR would remain in place until its objectives and conditions for closure are met. In the intervening period the OHR is working towards transition into an EU civilian mission. At present the HR is also the EU Special Representative to BiH (Office of the High Representative 2009).

13 When SFOR withdrew in 2004, a small NATO HQ remained in Sarajevo to provide assistance to local authorities on defence reform, counter-terrorism, detention of persons indicted for war crimes and intelligence-sharing with the EU (NATO 2004).

14 The idea that the EU might take over from NATO in BiH had first been aired at the European Council in Copenhagen in 2002. However, the handover was not officially agreed until the Berlin Plus arrangements were in place and had been tested in Operation *Concordia* (Cascone 2008; International Crisis Group 2005b: 49–51).

15 Admiral Feist was replaced by General Reith in 2004. Major General Leakey was later replaced by Major General Chiarini (2005), Major General Villalain (2007), Major General Castagnotto (2008) and Major General Bernhard Bair (2009) (Council of the EU 2009b).

16 An estimated 8,000 men and boys were killed by Bosnian Serb fighters in Srebrenica in July 1995 (Glenny 2001: 650).

17 In May 2010 the UNSC extended the MONUC mandate until 30 June 2010 and decided that from 1 July 2010 the mission would become the United Nations Organization Stabilization Mission in the Democratic Republic of Congo (United Nations 2010).

13 EU performance in civilian crisis management

Nicoletta Pirozzi

Introduction

The aim of this chapter is to assess the evolution of European Union (EU) civilian crisis management in terms of its internal effectiveness by looking at institutional coherence, decision-making mechanisms and capabilities development. The EU's capability to act will then be analysed through the experience of its most recently deployed civilian missions in two crucial theatres of intervention: Georgia and Kosovo. These case studies will consider both the functioning of the EU's civilian crisis management machine and its interaction with the crisis context, including local, state and international actors. The final objective is to draw some conclusions on the EU's crisis management system in the civilian field and its impact on conflict scenarios, with a view to elaborate guidelines for further improvement.

Origin and evolution of EU civilian crisis management

The security environment emerging in the post-Cold War era is characterised by complex challenges and threats, which undermine the effectiveness of traditional forms of coercion and policy instruments. These threats have made it necessary for all international actors, including the EU, to be adequately equipped to respond. Attempts to impose security through traditional interventions can generate backlashes which have the potential to create new sources of uncertainty (Cerny 2000). It is now common wisdom that effective external actions in conflict situations must be based on a comprehensive approach to security, which refers to the entire crisis management cycle. This implies the need for an inclusive strategy able to identify the root causes of conflicts in order to prevent them, facilitate the de-escalation of a crisis and its transformation and rebuild stable democratic institutions that can avoid the re-emergence of a conflict. The recognition of this new security scenario by the EU has been followed by the progressive adaptation of its crisis management capabilities.

With the development of European Security and Defence Policy (ESDP), called Common Security and Defence Policy (CSDP) after the entry into force of the Lisbon Treaty, the EU has defined its own specific framework for crisis management that is now in the process of refinement. The adoption of the European Security Strategy (ESS) in December 2003 represented a key step towards the identification of the main challenges and threats the EU must be able to face in order to be a credible actor in a changed international environment (European Council 2003d). However, this process did not result in the elaboration of a coherent strategy for action in the CSDP framework, which is still striking a difficult balance between the need to accommodate national interests and the urge to prioritise allocation of resources to selected areas and sectors of intervention. Against this background, the civilian sector has gained increasing importance in the context of EU crisis management doctrine and practice: it represents the area in which the EU has the most operations today and can be considered to offer the real comparative advantage with regard to other security actors.

From 2003 to 2010, the EU has deployed 17 civilian (or civilian–military) missions, out of 24 CSDP operations, in the Balkans (EUPM in Bosnia–Herzegovina, EULEX Kosovo, EUPAT and EUPOL Proxima in the Former Yugoslav Republic of Macedonia), in Africa (EUPOL RD Congo, EUPOL Kinshasa and EUSEC RD Congo in the Democratic Republic of the Congo, Support to AMIS II in Sudan/Darfur and EU SSR in Guinea Bissau), in the South Caucasus (EUJUST Themis and EUMM in Georgia), in the Middle East (EUPOL COPPS and EUBAM Rafah in the Palestinian territories, EUJUST LEX in Iraq), in South East Asia (AMM in the Indonesian province of Aceh), in Central Asia (EUPOL Afghanistan) and in Eastern Europe (EUBAM Moldova/Ukraine) (see Table 13.1).

Looking at the nature of the crises that have erupted in recent years and the type of interventions required from the EU, it is possible to sketch out some preliminary trends. The complexity of the crises required the development of a comprehensive approach to security which makes use of a vast and differentiated array of instruments and involves a variety of actors and expertise. The EU has established new structures and instruments to implement integrated action, with civilian and military components working in the same crisis scenario. In the civilian sector, the need to intervene in situations of failing state institutions has determined a trend towards multifunctional missions, including different dimensions such as rule of law, police and justice sectors. EU civilian crisis management missions also entail a combination of substitution (or executive) tasks and strengthening tasks such as mentoring, monitoring and advising. Finally, the fact that a number of actors are often present in the same crisis area – including international and regional organisations, non-governmental organisations (NGOs) and local actors – has required the establishment of a series of coordination mechanisms, as well as joint planning and management initiatives.

This constant evolution in the field of civilian crisis management has posed a number of challenges for the EU, in terms of both internal and external effectiveness. On the basis of the experience gained through a number of civilian missions in the past few years, the EU has learned lessons and identified best practices (Council of the EU 2008e). First of all, EU civilian crisis management requires structures that are able to give missions the necessary support for their deployment, particularly as regards administrative and financial matters, logistics and human resources management. The EU's architecture should also be adequately equipped with a capacity for planning and deploying several missions at the same time, as well as envisage a rapid-reaction system. Civilian capabilities need to be constantly developed through improved training and recruitment mechanisms, both at national and EU levels. Effective EU action also calls for an acceptable degree of coherence between CSDP missions and other EU instruments, as well as good cooperation with other players, in particular other international organisations, partner states and civil society organisations. Finally, realistic needs assessments and regular revisions must ensure that the capabilities in the field correspond to both the mandate of missions and the evolving security context in theatre. In the following paragraphs, these maxims of action are assessed against the analysis of recent developments in EU civilian crisis management in terms of institutions, instruments and personnel.

Building an EU civilian crisis management architecture

The EU's institutional architecture for planning and conducting civilian missions is the product of a series of consecutive adjustments, which have developed since the

Table 13.1 EU civilian and civilian–military missions 2003–2010

Mission	Timeframe	Operational area	Joint action		Legal basis and Extension of mandate	Personnel (Max)	Aim and type of mission	Head of Mission
			Initial decision					
EUPM in BiH	01.01.2003–31.12.2011	Bosnia and Herzegovina	JA 2002/210/CFSP of 11.03.2002		JA 2002/210/CFSP of 11.03.02 JA 2003/141/CFSP of 27.02.03 CD 2003/856/CFSP of 08.12.03 CD 2004/837/CFSP of 06.12.04 JA 2005/824/CFSP of 24.11.05 CD 2006/865/CFSP of 28.11.06 JA 2007/749/CFSP of 19.11.07 CD 2007/791/CFSP of 04.12.07 JA 2008/130/CFSP of 18.02.08 CD 2009/906/CFSP of 09.12.09	282	Civilian mission designed to support the police reform process and to develop and consolidate local capacity and regional cooperation in the fight against major and organised crime.	Kevin Carthly (Ireland) (01.03.04–31.12.05); Vincenzo Coppola (Italy) (01.01.06–31.10.08); Stefan Feller (Germany) (from 01.11.08)
EUPOL Proxima	15.12.2003–14.12.2005	Former Yugoslav Republic of Macedonia	JA 2003/681/CFSP of 29.09.2003		JA 2003/681/CFSP of 29.09.03 JA 2004/789/CFSP of 22.12.04	194	Civilian mission designed to support the development of an efficient and professional police service and promote European standards of policing.	Bert D'Hooge (Belgium) (15.12.03–14.12.04); Jürgen Scholz (Germany) (from 15.12.04)
EUJUST Themis	16.07.2004–14.07.2005	Georgia	JA 2004/523/CFSP of 28.06.2004		JA 2004/523/CFSP of 28.06.04 JA 2004/638/CFSP of 13.09.04	10	Civilian mission designed to support the Georgian authorities in addressing urgent challenges in the criminal justice system, assisting the Georgian government in developing a co-ordinated overall approach to the reform process.	Sylvie Pantz (France)

Table 13.1 continues overleaf

Table 13.1 continued

Mission	Timeframe	Operational area	Joint action	Personnel (Max)	Aim and type of mission	Head of Mission
EUPOL Kinshasa	30.04.2005– 30.06.2007	Democratic Republic of Congo	JA 2004/847/CFSP of 09.12.2004	24	Civilian mission designed to monitor, mentor and advise on the setting-up and the initial running of an Integrated Police Unit (IPU) in Kinshasa in order to ensure that the IPU acts following the training received in the Academy Centre and according to international best practices in this field.	Adilio Ruivo Custodio (Portugal)
			JA 2004/847 CFSP of 09.12.04 JA 2005/822/CFSP of 21.11.05 JA 2006/300/CFSP of 21.04.06 JA 2006/913/CFSP of 07.12.06				
EUSEC RD Congo	02.05.2005– 30.09.2010	Democratic Republic of Congo	JA 2005/355/ESDP of 02.05.05	44	Civilian mission designed to provide advice and assistance for security sector reform in the DRC with the aim of contributing to a successful integration of the Congolese army, while ensuring the promotion of policies that are compatible with human rights and international humanitarian law, democratic standards, principles of good public management, transparency and observance of the rule of law.	Pierre Joana (France) (02.05.06–02.08); Michel Sido (France) (01.03.08–30.06.08); Jean Paul Michel (France) (from 01.07.08)
			JA 2005/355/CFSP of 02.05.05 JA 2006/303/CFSP of 25.04.06 JA 2007/192/CFSP of 27.03.07 JA 2007/406/CFSP of 12.06.07 JA 2008/491/CFSP of 26.06.08 JA 2009/509/CFSP of 25.06.09 JA 2009/709/CFSP of 18.09.09				

Mission	Duration	Location	Legal basis	Legal basis	Personnel	Description	Head of Mission
EUJUST LEX	01.07.2005–30.06.2010	Iraq	JA 2005/190/ESDP of 07.03.05	JA 2005/190/CFSP of 07.03.05 JA 2006/413/CFSP of 12.06.06 JA 2006/708/CFSP of 17.10.06 JA 2007/760/CFSP of 22.11.07 JA 2008/304/CFSP of 14.04.08 JA 2008/480/CFSP of 23.06.08 JA 2009/475/CFSP of 11.06.09	45	Civilian mission designed to provide training for high- and mid-level officials from the police, judiciary and penitentiary, in order to contribute to the restructuring of the criminal justice system according to European standards, in particular human rights standards.	Stephen White (UK) (01.07.05–31.12.09); Francisco Diaz Alcantud (Spain) (from 01.01.10)
Support to AMIS II	18.07.2005–01.01.08	Sudan (Darfur)	JA 2005/557/ESDP of 18.07.2005 JA 2007/245/CFSP of 23.04.07 JA 2007/887/CFSP of 20.12.07	JA 2005/557/CFSP of 18.07.05 CD 2005/806/CFSP of 21.11.05 CD 2006/486/CFSP of 11.07.06 CD 2006/725/CFSP of 17.10.06 CD 2007/245/CFSP of 23.04.07	47	EU supporting action including civilian and military components designed to provide assistance to AU mission in Sudan (Darfur).	Douglas Brand (UK) (29.07.05–31.10.06); Åke Rohge (Sweden) (from 01.11.06)
Aceh Monitoring Mission–AMM	15.09.2005–11.12.2006	Indonesia	JA/2005/643/ ESDP of 09.09.2005	JA 2005/643/CFSP of 09.09.05 JA 2006/407/CFSP of 07.06.06 JA 2006/607/CFSP of 07.09.06	From 226–36	Civilian mission designed to monitor the implementation of various aspects of the peace agreement set out in the Memorandum of Understanding (MoU) signed by the Government of Indonesia and the Free Aceh Movement (GAM) on 15 August 2005.	Pieter Feith (The Netherlands)

Table 13.1 continues overleaf

Table 13.1 continued

Mission	Timeframe	Operational area	Joint action	Personnel (Max)	Aim and type of mission	Head of Mission
EU BAM Rafah	30.11.2005– 24.05.2011	Palestinian territories	JA 2005/889/ESDP of 12.12.2005	25	Civilian mission designed to monitor the 'Agreement on Movement and Access' concluded by Israel and the Palestinian Authority and including principles for Rafah crossing (Gaza); to monitor the operations at Rafah crossing point.	Pietro Pistolese (Italy) (01.12.05–24.11.08); Alain Faugeras (France) (from: 25.11.08)
			JA 2005/889/CFSP of 12.12.05 JA 2006/773/CFSP of 13.11.06 JA 2007/359/CFSP OF 23.05.07 JA 2008/379/CFSP of 19.05.08 JA 2008/862/CFSP of 10.11.08 JA 2009/854/CFSP of 20.11.09				
EUBAM Moldova/ Ukraine	01. 12.2005– 30.11.2009	Moldova/ Ukraine	JA 2005/776/CFSP of 07.11. 2005	200	Civilian mission designed to prevent smuggling, trafficking, and customs fraud, by providing advice and training to improve the capacity of the Moldovan and Ukrainian border and customs services.	Ferenc Banfi (Hungary)
			JA 2005/776/CFSP of 07.11.05			
EUPAT	15. 12.2005– 14. 06.2007	Former Yugoslav Republic of Macedonia	JA 2005/826/CFSP of 24.11.2005	30	Civilian mission designed to support the development of an efficient and professional police service based on European standards of policing, by monitoring and mentoring the country's police on priority issues in the field of border police, public peace and order and accountability, the fight against corruption and organised crime.	Jürgen Scholz (Germany)
			JA 2005/64/CFSP of 24.11.05			

EUPOL COPPS	01.01.2006– 31.12.2010	Palestinian territories	JA 2005/797/CFSP of 14.11.2005	JA 2005/797/CFSP of 14.11.05 JA 2008/958/CFSP of 16.12.08 CD 2009/955/CFSP of 15.12.09	Civilian mission designed to advise and closely mentor the Palestinian Civil Police; to coordinate and facilitate EU and member states assistance, and where requested, international assistance; advise on police-related Criminal Justice elements.	Jonathan McIvor (UK) (01.01.06–31.12.06); Colin Smith (UK) (01.01.07–31.12.08); Paul Kernaghan (UK) (01.01.09–31.12.09); Henrik Malmquist (Sweden) (from 01.01.2010)
EUPOL Afghanistan	15.06.2007– 31.05.2013	Afghanistan	JA 2007/369/CFSP of 30.05.2007	JA 2007/369/CFSP of 30.05.07 JA 2007/733/CFSP of 13.11.07 JA 2008/229/CFSP of 17.03.08 JA 2008/643/CFSP of 04.08.08 CD 2008/884/CFSP of 21.11.08 JA 2009/842/CFSP of 17.11.09 CD 2010/279/CFSP of 18.05.10	Civilian mission designed to contribute to the establishment of sustainable and effective civilian policing arrangements under Afghan ownership and in accordance with international standards, by monitoring, mentoring, advising and training at the level of the Afghan Ministry of Interior, regions and provinces.	Friedrich Eichele (Germany) (01.05.07–11.10.07); Jürgen Scholz (Germany) (12.10.07–15.10.08); Kai Vittrup (Denmark) (from 16.10.08)
EUPOL RD Congo	01.07.2007– 30.06.2010	Democratic Republic of Congo	JA 2007/405 CFSP of 12.06.2007	JA 2007/405 CFSP of 12.06.07 JA 2008/38/CFSP of 20.12.07 JA 2008/485/CFSP of 23.06.08 JA 2009/466/CFSP of 15.06.09	Civilian mission designed to support and assist DRC authorities in the security sector reform process, in the field of police and its interaction with the justice sector, in close cooperation with EUSEC RD Congo.	Adilio Ruivo Custodio (Portugal) (from 01.07.07)

Table 13.1 continues overleaf

Table 13.1 continued

Mission	Timeframe	Operational area	Joint action		Personnel (Max)	Aim and type of mission	Head of Mission
EU SSR Guinea Bissau	12.02.2008– 30.09.2010	Guinea Bissau	JA 2008/112/CFSP of 12.02.2008	JA 2008/112/CFSP of 12.02.08 JA 2009/405/CFSP of 18.05.09 JA 2009/841/CFSP of 17.11.09 CD 2010/298/CFSP of 26.05.10	33	Civilian-military mission in support of the national security sector reform process.	Esteban Verástegui (Spain) (from: 01.03.08)
EULEX Kosovo	16.02.2008– 14.06.2010	Kosovo	JA 2008/124/CFSP of 04.02.08	JA 2008/124/CFSP of 04.02.08 JA 2009/445/CFSP of 09.06.09	2,818	Civilian mission assisting the Kosovo authorities in consolidating the rule of law area, specifically in the police, judiciary and customs areas, and in contributing to a safe and secure environment for all inhabitants, regardless of their ethnic origins.	Yves de Kermabon (France) (from: 07.02.08)
EUMM Georgia	01.10.2008– 14.09.2010	Georgia	JA 2008/736/ CFSPof 15.09.2008	JA 2008/736/CFSP of 15.09.08 JA 2008/759/CFSP of 25.09.08 JA 2009/294/CFSP of 23.03.09 JA 2009/572/CFSP of 29.07.09	398	Civilian monitoring mission established to contribute to stability throughout Georgia and the surrounding region, to oversee the deployment of the police and armed forces, to observe compliance of all parties with human rights and humanitarian law and to help build confidence between the parties of the August 2008 conflict.	Hansjörg Haber (Germany) (from: 17.09.08)

Source: EU Council General Secretariat and Italian Permanent Representation to the EU. Compilation: Nicoletta Pirozzi and Sammi Sandawi. Latest update 26 June 2010

Feira European Council in 2000, where priority areas for civilian crisis management were identified for the first time, and the operationalisation of the civilian sector started in 2003 with the first mission in Bosnia and Herzegovina (EUPM). Some innovations have been conceived at the Hampton Court informal summit in 2005 and partly implemented in its follow-up process (Council of the EU 2006f, 2005g). However, these steps forward have been rather timid and have resulted in a limited impact on the development of an effective EU civilian crisis management (CCM) mechanism. Progress is expected on the basis of the new norms of the Lisbon Treaty, mainly concerning the conduct and supervision of EU civilian missions.

The competence for EU CCM has been traditionally shared by the General Secretariat of the EU Council and a series of intergovernmental groups composed of the EU member states' representatives within the EU Council. The main structures responsible for EU CCM are the Crisis Management and Planning Directorate (CMPD) and the Civilian Planning and Conduct Capability (CPCC).

All the CSDP structures, including the civilian ones, have been integrated in the newly established European External Action Service (EEAS), created by the Lisbon Treaty, with the objective of enhancing the coherence of policy planning for crisis management. Hence, the EEAS does incorporate both the strategic planning (CMPD) and operational planning and implementation (CPCC) of civilian missions, under the authority of a Vice Secretary General (Quille 2010).

The CMPD has incorporated former Directorates General E IX, responsible for civilian crisis management, and E VIII, responsible for political–military issues. It is an integrated structure that should ensure the effective implementation of the Civilian–Military Co-ordination (CMCO) concept. The CMPD is divided into three sections: one for the strategic planning of civilian, military and civilian–military missions; one for horizontal issues, including civilian capabilities development, lessons identified and lessons learned, elaboration of the CCM doctrine, civilian exercises and training of personnel; one for partnerships with other organisations and other crisis management actors.

The establishment of the CPCC in August 2007 can be considered an important innovation within the EU CCM structure, even further when compared with other organisations that deal with civilian crisis management. It represents a general operational headquarters for EU civilian missions. Once the Crisis Management Concept has been adopted, the CPCC is tasked with taking the lead for the operational planning and mission support for civilian operations. The CPCC Director, as EU Civilian Operations Commander, is responsible for all civilian EU missions worldwide and acts as a point of contact for all heads of mission serving in the field. Its personnel has different functional and geographical expertise, covering almost the full spectrum of ongoing EU civilian missions.

The main intergovernmental groups devoted to EU CCM in the EU Council are the Committee for Civilian Aspects of Crisis Management (CIVCOM) and the Political and Security Committee (PSC). The CIVCOM discusses the options available for each EU civilian mission at different stages of the planning process, with the view of submitting its recommendations to the PSC. The PSC decides on the mandate and composition of each mission and transmits its recommendations to the Foreign Affairs Council (FAC) for the adoption of the Joint Action. The PSC also exercises political control over and strategic management of all the EU missions, including civilian and integrated ones, under the authority of the High Representative for Foreign Affairs and Security Policy (Article 38 Treaty on European Union (TEU)).

The Lisbon Treaty has upgraded the role of the new High Representative (HR) in this field: from now on, the HR is responsible for the coordination of the civilian and military aspects of crisis management, under the authority of the EU Council and in close coordination with the PSC (Article 43 TEU). A representative of the HR chairs the meetings of the PSC and the HR himself chairs the FAC, having a direct say and impact on the activities of the two main bodies charged with crisis management in the EU. The Lisbon Treaty also reinforces the role of the European Parliament (EP) in security and defence policy. The EP now exercises an enhanced control on CSDP missions, well beyond budgetary oversight, being involved to a greater extent in the adoption of strategies and mandates for CSDP missions, and granted extended access to classified documents and information concerning CSDP missions.

The constant update of the institutional structures has led to difficult interaction and partial overlapping between the actors involved in the EU CCM. The evolution of the EU CCM architecture has also been affected by the divergences among EU member states over the approach and importance of civilian crisis management. While some have traditionally campaigned for enhanced capacities in the civilian sector, others have always pushed for devoting greater attention and resources to a more substantive development in the military field. The result is that the civilian component of CSDP structures is under-resourced and not prepared to cope with growing EU activism in civilian crisis management, which counts several missions deployed in unstable theatres and is tasked with increasingly complex mandates.

Moreover, there are still persistent tensions between the EEAS and the European Commission, due to the attribution of competences to the two institutions in this field. The Commission on the one hand is responsible for the financial and logistical support of civilian missions, and on the other directly conducts some projects which support (not always in a properly coordinated manner) the activities of CSDP missions in the field, i.e. in the framework of programmes for Disarmament, Demobilisation and Reintegration (DDR) and Security Sector Reform (SSR). Among the Commission's tools for crisis management, the Instrument for Stability (IfS) deserves a particular mention. In force since 2007, it offers financial support to short- and long-term actions in crisis situations and has been designed to complement other CFSP and geographic instruments. However, its coordination with other financial means has not always been effective.

EU civilian capabilities in the making

Beyond institutions and instruments, there is also a need for effective operational capabilities to deploy once a decision to act has been made. The EU has made significant progress since the original civilian targets were defined at the Feira European Council in June 2000 (in the four areas of police, rule of law, civilian administration and civil protection) (Council of the EU 2000b). Following the adoption of an Action Plan for civilian aspects of ESDP at the European Council of June 2004, a Civilian Capabilities Commitment Conference was held in November 2004 with the task of reviewing the EU's civilian capabilities (Council of the EU 2004d). At the Conference, the quantitative targets set in Feira were exceeded and additional areas for the EU CCM were identified in the monitoring and other support functions (support to the EU Special Representatives and multifunctional missions), for a total of over 12,000 personnel (Council of the EU 2004a). However, this gave little indication about their actual deployability, readiness and sustainability.

A first development in the EU's ability to foresee future scenarios of crises requiring a civilian response and to assess the appropriate means to address them was represented by the Civilian Headline Goal 2008 (CHG 2008), adopted by the European Council in December 2004 (Council of the EU 2004b). In the CHG 2008, key commitments identified through a needs-based analysis were set out for the first time, using illustrative scenarios to assess the size, type and duration of civilian responses that might be required. In the CHG follow-up process, Civilian Capabilities Improvement Conferences were held in 2005, 2006 and 2007, together with Exercise Studies in 2005 and 2006. Building on the CHG 2008 and on the crisis management experience developed in the framework of ESDP, a new Civilian Headline Goal 2010 (CHG 2010) was adopted in November 2007, with the objective of facilitating the deployment of civilian crisis management capabilities of high quality, with the support functions and equipment required in a short time span and in sufficient quantity (Council of the EU 2007h). This implies the need to meet a series of challenging goals, including improving the quality of civilian capabilities – also through the targeting of training efforts to operational needs – enhancing the availability of personnel, developing practical and technological applications to further support planning and conduct of operations, and achieving enhanced synergies between civilian and military CSDP, European Community and other actors. A Civilian CSDP Capability Improvement Plan was adopted in January 2009 to provide guidance for the CHG 2010 implementation process, reviewing the illustrative scenarios and the strategic planning assumptions (Council of the EU 2009f).

In both the CHGs, EU member states recognised the need for rapid reaction tools in order to ensure a timely and effective EU response to crises. On this basis, work has been undertaken on Integrated Police Units (IPUs) and Formed Police Units (FPUs), in particular to complete the transition of these rapidly deployable police elements from a military to a civilian chain of command and to enhance their coordination with rule of law elements. Furthermore, the instrument of the Civilian Response Teams (CRTs) reached operational status in January 2007. CRTs were conceived as multifunctional civilian crisis management resources in an integrated format to be drawn from an initial pool of roughly two hundred experts nominated by EU member states and to be deployed within five days for up to three months. Examples of CRT members' expertise include border policing, administration of justice, management of public administration services, civil protection, logistics and operational support. However, CRTs' use up to date has been limited to the deployment of a few experts on an individual basis, rather than in the team format originally envisaged. Notwithstanding the fact that civilian CSDP activity in these fields has risen considerably since the establishment of CRTs, it remains to be assessed why their deployment has been so infrequent since 2007.

In general terms, even if the past years of civilian CSDP have been characterised by significant achievements in terms of capability development, it seems these efforts have been mainly directed at addressing the most urgent need of ensuring a presence on the ground, without paying too much attention to the qualitative aspects of it. In general, EU civilian crisis management capabilities remain critically underdeveloped, particularly in comparison with their military counterparts, and the sector as a whole needs to become more professional. In particular, the substantive aspects of interoperability, deployability, sustainability and quality of civilian crisis management capabilities appear to be largely neglected and still represent the main challenges to face if the EU wants to fulfil the new tasks it is called on to accomplish in the near future.

Enhancing training and recruitment of civilian personnel

The possibility of relying on well-trained civilian experts ready for rapid deployment is crucial for enhancing the effectiveness of EU civilian operations. In some functional areas, such as the police sector, training activities seem well established and have resulted in positive outcomes in terms of the preparedness and availability of personnel to be deployed in a field mission. In other areas, particularly those in which the engagement of the EU is comparatively recent, training activities still need to be developed. Among them, rule of law, democratisation and good governance, human rights and gender, civilian administration (including reintegration of combatants, refugees and displaced persons) require particular attention. A relevant initiative undertaken in these areas is the Project on Training for Civilian Aspects of Crisis Management, launched by the European Commission in October 2001. During the implementation phase of the Project, an informal European Group on Training was formed including training institutions from EU member states. The objective of the project was to contribute to the member states' efforts to establish pools of civilian experts for rapid deployment in crisis management operations through the implementation of Core Courses and Specialised Courses. The Project of the European Commission formally ended in 2009: a Europe's New Training Initiative for Civilian Crisis Management (ENTRi) was established under the Instrument for Stability in early 2011.[1]

Another important aspect is to create an effective link between future scenarios for CSDP missions and the EU's capability development process. A system has been put in place to identify the capabilities required for possible CSDP missions in a timely manner. This system mainly relies on a software tool, called Goalkeeper, which has been developed to facilitate the planning of civilian CSDP missions (Council of the EU 2009e). This system automatically incorporates all calls for contributions that the EU produces for civilian CSDP missions, using a catalogue of standard job descriptions covering CCM priority areas. This tool may help the planners at the EU level to identify at an early stage in the mission planning process what specific capabilities the EU needs for a particular civilian CSDP mission; contributors at the member states level would thus have more time to organise the secondment procedures for the personnel concerned. It will also impact on the link between training and recruitment, as it will identify relevant training opportunities across the EU for specific personnel categories. Finally, it is designed to include a list of potential candidates that are available to be deployed in CSDP civilian missions, identified through EU and national channels of recruitment. However, the speed and scope of implementation of this tool will largely depend on the contributions by national governments and their will to share relevant information, especially that related to strategic planning and personnel.

Beyond these significant initiatives, there are still a number of outstanding issues in the field of training and recruitment. Training activities in the EU are currently dispersive and uncoordinated and involve a variety of actors: member states and their training activities at the national level; diplomatic training under the umbrella of the European Diplomatic Programme (EDP); police training under the responsibility of the European Police College; all kinds of training falling under the responsibility of the European Security and Defence College (ESDC); training in the field of civilian crisis management under the auspices of the Commission; and training activities conducted by NGOs. In the current situation, training standards vary considerably among different member states and training institutions. Working out common training standards should therefore be promoted at the EU level, in order to ensure an adequate degree of expertise among the civilian personnel. A higher level of coordination between training actors should also be encouraged, to limit overlap in certain training areas while other sectors are neglected. Proposals have been developed for establishing an EU training accreditation and certification system, possibly working out standards and procedures for an 'EU label'. The certification of training courses would be based on a standardised set of teaching elements and a minimum course duration, while a validating body should be established to effectively monitor and evaluate these various training activities. Thus, training – based on a minimum set of training modules by an accredited training institute – could become a prerequisite for serving in an EU mission.

In terms of recruitment of civilian personnel for civilian CSDP missions, current recruitment mechanisms are decentralised, conducted via contact points in EU member states. Many EU member states have developed pools or rosters of experts who are potentially available for deployment in CSDP missions. Examples include the Post Conflict Reconstruction Unit (PCRU) in the United Kingdom (UK), the Norwegian Resource Bank for Democracy and Human Rights (NORDEM) in Norway, and the Centre for International Peace Operations (ZIF) in Germany. However, pools and rosters developed in EU member states differ widely in terms of range and quality of civilian personnel selected. For example, in some cases the selection of civilian personnel is restricted to civil servants and recruitment practices do not generally reach relevant experts employed in the private, NGO or academic sector. Women are generally under-represented in the nominations of member states. A possible solution could be the creation of an EU central roster, but experience in different contexts (United Nations Department of Peace-Keeping Operations, UN DPKO) shows that such a centralised roster can be difficult to manage. The decentralisation option seems more feasible, but this would call for the harmonisation and standardisation of existing rosters (Gourlay 2006b). Furthermore, effective links between training and recruitment institutions in EU member states should be developed, together with widespread publicity systems to reach suitable candidates and encourage them to apply for vacant posts in CSDP missions.

Deployment procedures also present considerable problems that need to be addressed, especially in terms of the legal, administrative and financial conditions for the secondment of civilian personnel. In order to encourage the secondment of public service employees, new regulations providing incentives in terms of career promotion and competitive salaries should be introduced. Options should be developed and implemented to ensure the inclusion in existing rosters of experts from the private/NGO/academic sectors. This could be done by developing back-up arrangements for identifying suitable experts, including linkages with specialised NGO roster managers, or improving modalities whereby independent civilian experts can be offered a contract directly by the Head of Mission to participate in CSDP operations, including financial provisions.

The European Union Monitoring Mission (EUMM) in Georgia[2]

The EU Monitoring Mission (EUMM) in Georgia was launched on 1 October 2008, in accordance with the arrangements set out in the six-point agreement between Moscow and Tbilisi of 12 August 2008, as supplemented by the agreement reached on 8 September 2008 for its implementation (*Peace Agreement* 2008). On 15 September 2008, the EU decided to deploy a civilian monitoring mission, unarmed and with no executive powers (Council of the EU 2008d). Its mandate ranges from contributing to stabilisation, normalisation and confidence building to informing EU decision-making on the situation in the field. The mission personnel come from a variety of military, police and civilian backgrounds, thus ensuring a mixture of professional skills and experience.

Looking at the EU's capability to act, the recruitment and preparation process was rapid and smooth: in only two weeks, more than 200 monitors from 22 member states were deployed on the ground; 99 per cent of the positions originally foreseen for the mission are occupied. This result is quite impressive if compared with the share of other ongoing civilian missions (i.e. EULEX Kosovo, and EUPOL Afghanistan). The preparation for the deployment of the mission was undertaken by an exploratory team, which was deployed to Georgia on 2 September 2008 with a view to gathering relevant information. The team was composed of representatives from the General Secretariat of the EU Council (notably SitCen and CPCC) and CRTs experts. The preliminary assessment conducted by the exploratory team had to be readjusted over time in accordance with changing conditions of the crisis context, at both operational and political levels (Council of the EU 2008d). The initial number of mission personnel was defined by the political agreement reached on 8 September 2008 between French and Russian presidents: the document clearly states that at least 200 EU monitors should be deployed in the field. Since then, the size of the mission has expanded significantly and counts about 400 personnel. With a view to enhancing the expertise of the personnel deployed, EUMM has initiated an innovative experiment and established a capacity enhancement unit within its headquarters in Tbilisi, which provides in-mission training for local and international staff, including language, monitoring and reporting skills. The mission has been equipped with armoured and soft-skinned vehicles which are designed to allow monitors to operate in all types of conditions.

In terms of presence of the mission in the field, along with the headquarters in Tbilisi, regional field offices were originally foreseen in Tbilisi/Basaleti, Gori, Poti and Zugdidi. EUMM field offices are also located in Mtskheta, Gori and Zugdidi, while three forward offices have been set up in Khaishi, close to Abkhazia's administrative border, Pasanauri and Saghkaere, which are situated respectively on the eastern and western sides of South Ossetia's administrative border. Up to now, the mission still does not have access to the territories of the separatist regions of South Ossetia and Abkhazia: this situation seriously hampers the full implementation of its mandate. In fact, on the basis of the six-point agreement, EUMM's mandate covers the entire territory of Georgia. However, the definition of the territory of Georgia is the object of an unresolved dispute between Russia and the EU. While the EU considers the breakaway regions to be part of Georgia, Russia has recognised them as independent from Tbilisi.

In order to assess the EU's capability to ensure internal coordination and cooperation, it must be underlined that the Union's presence in Georgia was originally ensured by four different actors: EUMM; the EU Delegation in Tbilisi; the EU Special Representative (EUSR) for the South Caucasus, appointed in December 2003 and responsible for the EU's relations with Georgia and the other two countries of the region (Armenia and Azerbaijan); and the EUSR for the crisis in Georgia, appointed in September 2008 to represent the EU at the Geneva talks and facilitate the implementation of the settlement plan between Georgia and Russia (Council of the EU 2006d; European Council 2008d). The cooperation between EUMM and the EU Delegation has worked quite well: joint confidence-building projects have been launched, where the EUMM is responsible for collecting information in the field, the European Commission is the source of project funding and the United Nations Development Programme (UNDP) acts as the implementation agency. On the contrary, the relations between the two EUSRs and the mission itself have been rather problematic, due to overlapping competences and functions. The implementation of the innovations of the Lisbon Treaty should bring some significant changes towards a more coherent presence of the EU in Tbilisi. In the meantime, the High Representative for Foreign Affairs and Security

Policy, Catherine Ashton, has decided to merge the two EUSR positions: Philippe Lefort was appointed EU Special Representative for the South Caucasus and the crisis in Georgia on 1 September 2011.

If we turn to the EU's relations with third parties, the original mandate contained a provision for EUMM coordination with the United Nations Observer Mission in Georgia (UNOMIG) and the Organization for Security and Co-operation in Europe (OSCE) Mission that monitored South Ossetia at the time. The OSCE mission left the country at the end of 2008 and the United Nations (UN) mission ended on 15 June 2009, after 16 years, due to the lack of consensus among UN Security Council members on the extension of its mandate. In fact, Russia has vetoed the continuation of both missions in the Georgian territory. Since then, the EU has ensured the only international presence in the field.

As for the parties involved in the conflict, EUMM should maintain a neutral stance. However, the political context of the mission is not conducive to an effective balance in its relations with the different actors (Fischer 2009). In particular, from its inception, EUMM has been perceived as being very close to the Georgian side. This feeling has been reinforced by the close cooperation established between the EU mission and the Georgian authorities, while the relationships with Abkhazia and South Ossetia remain difficult, although to different degrees. EUMM has concluded a Memoranda of Understanding (MoU) with the Georgian Ministry of Defence (MoD) and Ministry of Internal Affairs (MoIA). In particular, the agreement signed with the MoD in January 2009 provides regulations on the movements of Georgian troops in the territories adjacent to the administrative borders with Abkhazia and South Ossetia and concedes to EUMM the right to conduct inspections of facilities and sites of the Georgian armed forces. A first MoU between EUMM and the MoIA was finalised in October 2008, through which the Ministry agreed to give advance notification of any deployment of police forces in the zones adjacent to the separatist regions. Through an annex to the MoU signed in May 2009, EUMM also has the right to conduct unannounced inspections of all Georgian police facilities in the neighbouring areas of South Ossetia and Abkhazia.

EUMM has tried to achieve closer contacts and mutual confidence-building with the Abkhaz and South Ossetian authorities through the so-called Incident Prevention and Reaction Mechanisms (IPRMs), approved in the Fourth Round of Geneva talks in February 2009. IPRM meetings take place in Abkhazia and South Ossetia separately and involve representatives from the Georgian, Russian and the de facto Abkhaz and South Ossetian authorities, respectively. The UN chairs the Abkhaz meetings, and the OSCE attends the South Ossetian meetings, while the EUMM is involved in both of them. The IPRM is functioning quite well for Abkhazia: meetings take place regularly every three weeks in Gali, where participants exchange information with regard to recent incidents, as well as follow up on incidents reported during the previous meetings. Among the incidents addressed are arrests by Russian forces of Georgian citizens who cross the Abkhaz administrative border. In 2009, IPRM succeeded in solving the dispute over three foreign ships heading to Abkhazia which were confiscated by the Georgian authorities.

As for the IPRM established for South Ossetia, it was inaugurated in February 2009 but has been blocked in October 2009. The main reason for the stalemate has been identified by the EU as the attempt by the South Ossetian authorities to use the mechanism in order to gain de facto institutional recognition. A positive signal towards a normalisation of the relations between South Ossetia and the EUMM came at the beginning of 2010: following the arrest of a South Ossetian citizen by the Georgian authorities, EUMM was invited for the first time to visit Zhimbali in the separatist territory (Government of Georgia 2010). The meetings resumed in Ergneti on 29 October 2010.

In the meantime, a 'hotline' system has been established to allow all sides involved to communicate and hopefully resolve issues in a fast and efficient manner. For example, the instrument has proved to be useful in response to a false alarm launched by a Georgian TV station in March 2010, concerning a new Russian attack on the Georgian territory. EUMM promptly informed the Russian border officers and the South Ossetian authorities of the mendacious news, thus preventing an escalation of tension between the parties. The Georgian government has also approved a 'State Strategy on Occupied Territories: Engagement through Cooperation' as a step towards easing tensions, building confidence and reaching out to the residents of the Abkhaz and South Ossetian regions. In particular, the document calls for the establishment of a status-neutral framework for interaction with Georgian authorities and those of the separatist territories.

It can be affirmed that the EUMM's physical presence and visibility has facilitated a decrease in tensions among the parties on the ground. Enhanced cooperation between law enforcement bodies on all sides of the administrative boundary lines has been a key requirement for the EUMM to build greater stability and security. It should also be acknowledged that the resolution of the conflict between Georgia and Russia is not within the mandate of EUMM, even if the Head of Mission is actively involved in the internationally mediated talks on security guarantees for the two republics held in Geneva. The current mandate of the mission expires in September 2012 and an exit strategy has not yet been designed.

The European Union Rule of Law Mission (EULEX) in Kosovo[3]

EULEX Kosovo is the most ambitious and the largest EU civilian mission ever, with 3,200 staff members expected to be deployed in its three components (police, judiciary and customs area) (Council of the EU 2008c).

Nevertheless, the mission has been affected since its inception by the scarcity of personnel available and qualified to be employed in the field. More than two years after its launch, the mission was not yet fully operational. Among the international personnel, the most difficult experts to recruit were judges, prosecutors and penitentiary police. This was partly due to the unwillingness of EU member states to second highly specialised personnel who could be usefully employed at the national level. Moreover, these categories of personnel are generally reluctant to serve in international missions, especially for long periods of time: the lack of a wide and targeted publicity on the opportunities available in CSDP missions and adequate incentives for national personnel to be deployed abroad are both determinants of this situation. Experts identified by EU member states often do not have the required qualifications – in terms of language knowledge, experience in previous missions or specific skills – to be selected for the mission. This can be linked to both the lack of an efficient training system at the national level and the absence of EU adequate training and recruitment mechanisms for these categories of personnel. Among local personnel, it is particularly difficult to find interpreters and language assistants for Serbian: this is due to a mix of political resistances, lack of widespread publicity and the competition from other organisations present in the field, which often offer higher salaries and better conditions. All these elements had a heavy impact on the functioning of the mission and the full implementation of its mandate.

The mission's start-up phase has been complicated by both internal and external coordination issues. Planned to start on 15 June 2008, Initial Operational Capability (IOC) was only announced at the beginning of December 2008. The divisions among EU member states over the recognition of Kosovo's independence and the status of the mission have delayed its operationalisation. Moreover, the definition of the mission's mandate, together with the uncertainties regarding the timing and modalities of its handover from the United Nations Mission in Kosovo (UNMIK), have hampered a rapid and smooth transition. As an example, the judicial component has suffered from the resistance encountered in obtaining the trial documentation from UN personnel. Most of the tasks included in the UNMIK's mandate are now handled by EULEX and a number of UN personnel have been recruited by the EU mission. The links between the two missions have guaranteed a significant degree of continuity of the international presence in Kosovo. However, EULEX has also inherited criticism and scepticism coming from local authorities and Kosovo's population due to the negative perception of the UN operation, at least in its latest stages.

The planning phase of the mission has been conducted by the European Union Planning Team (EUPT) for Kosovo, composed of experts from the EU Council and the European Commission, as well as experts seconded by EU member states (Council of the EU 2006e). The needs assessment conducted by EUPT in terms of the number and expertise of required personnel has been subject to constant revision, due to the evolving situation in the field but also, to a certain extent, to the inaccurate planning of the mission necessities. The organisational chart of the mission has been reviewed more than once and a new Operation Plan (OPLAN) has been approved together with an extension of the mission mandate until June 2012. The perception of some of the personnel interviewed is that while some units are over-staffed (i.e. the police monitoring component), others are suffering in implementing their mandate due to a lack of appropriate resources (i.e. the justice component, especially in the regional courts). Rigidity in procedures and lack of flexibility in adjusting available resources to actual needs have also been experienced.

Coordination among the different components of the mission is still a work in progress. A problematic aspect is the relationship between the prosecutors and the police: the police personnel have shown some reluctance to accept the leadership of prosecutors in investigations. This is partly due to the differences of status and roles of law enforcement agencies in the various EU member states: in some cases, they enjoy a high degree of autonomy in conducting the investigations and report to the prosecutors only at the end of them. Another source of tensions is the significant level of independence claimed by the judicial component of EULEX with respect to the mission's chain of command.

Cooperation between EULEX and local authorities has developed over time. The judicial system is still unprepared to carry out its functions in an independent and efficient way. One reason is the lack of adequate salaries and structures for judicial personnel. Local judges and prosecutors are also strongly influenced by the volatile political and security context and tend to leave the judgement of the most controversial cases to the EULEX personnel. An example is the trial of Albin Kurti, a political leader of Kosovo's radical movement, for the episodes of violence that erupted in the course of a protest in February 2010. Defence lawyers, including the Head of the Kosovo Bar Association, have repeatedly refused to act on behalf of Kurti, as they consider the prosecution to be politically motivated. EULEX has experienced serious difficulties in finding a local representative available to sit in the trial with two international judges and in securing the collaboration of the local police to bring to court the political leader. The reorganisation of the structure of Kosovo's police has also proved to be difficult and police cooperation with EULEX for investigation activities remains an arduous process (see EULEX Programme Report 2010). A technical arrangement for the exchange of police information concluded between EULEX and the Serbian Ministry of Internal Affairs has produced tensions between the EU mission and Kosovo's authorities.

The core function of EULEX personnel is to monitor, mentor and advise their local counterparts on all areas related to the rule of law, measured in terms of sustainability, accountability, multi-ethnicity, freedom from political interference, and compliance with internationally recognised standards and European best practices. However, EULEX also has an important executive mandate, which distinguishes it from the other EU civilian missions. For example, EULEX justice experts regularly carry out crime investigations, prosecute persons suspected of offences and adjudicate cases in court. The Police Executive Department in EULEX is in charge, with autonomous and direct investigation functions, especially in sectors such as organised and financial crimes, war crimes, criminal intelligence and international police cooperation.

Pending the recognition of the Kosovar state by Belgrade and some EU member states, it is common opinion that the mission has helped to improve the situation in the field, with the exception of the northern regions, where security remains potentially fragile. When the mission was launched, there was consensus within EU political circles that the critical weakness of the justice and law enforcement sectors in Kosovo necessitated that the international community undertake some executive and capacity-building functions. However, the strong presence and mandate of EULEX in Kosovo's judiciary and security sectors raise questions about the future prospects of establishing a self-sustainable system built upon local ownership. The immaturity of Kosovo's political establishment, together with a widespread system of corruption and nepotism, contributes to the persistent fragility of Kosovo's institutions. The lack of participation by the Serbians in the state administration makes the EULEX mandate partial and incomplete.

EU civilian operations: lessons learned and way forward

On the basis of the institutional and operational background outlined above, it is possible to identify some lessons learned and policy paths for further developments in EU civilian crisis management. These include, among others, developing effective planning institutions and instruments, providing adequate personnel and hardware, matching mission mandate with crisis context, and ensuring EU's internal coherence.

Ensuring effective planning

First, it is important to ensure adequate planning of civilian and integrated missions conducted by the EU, both at the strategic and operational levels. This implies a realistic assessment of the situation in the field, the elaboration of a coherent strategic vision and the identification of the most appropriate instruments to conduct the mission. During the first years of operational CSDP, these planning activities have been partial at best. The situation has improved with the recent innovations in EU civilian crisis management architecture, particularly through the establishment of the CMPD as an integrated planning unit, and the practice of deploying preliminary assessment and planning teams which benefit from the expertise of personnel coming from different EU institutions and member states. Nevertheless, a more efficient division of labour among the various EU CCM structures in the framework of the new European External Action Service is much needed, with special attention given to the respective competences of the CPCC and the CMPD. Moreover, the number and expertise of personnel in charge of civilian crisis management should be enhanced, especially in the crucial fields of justice and the rule of law.

Enhancing capability development

A wide availability of human resources, both in terms of quality and quantity, is crucial in order to ensure effective actions in the field. It is a worrying signal that significant interventions such as EU Police Mission (EUPOL) in Afghanistan and EULEX in Kosovo encountered such difficulties in reaching full operability, due to the lack of available and qualified personnel. Thus it is a priority for the EU to put in place efficient recruitment mechanisms, exploiting the potential of Goalkeeper and making the calls for contribution more regular and uniform. Training activities, including generic, specialised and pre-deployment training, should be streamlined at the EU level. Harmonisation of training curricula, standardisation of quality criteria and joint activities among different EU member states should be promoted. The EU should also take the lead in generic training for certain categories of experts (i.e. judges, prosecutors, financial police), for example by reinforcing the civilian component of the ESDC. Procurement procedures should also be improved through a closer cooperation between CSDP structures and the responsible services at the European Commission.

Matching mandate and context

A clear and realistic definition of the mandate is a crucial element for the success of EU civilian missions, which often have to deal with sensitive issues such as institutional reform processes in conflict-affected areas. The mandate of these missions should be the result of a frank assessment of the EU's political interests in intervention, the situation in the field and the availability of resources. The scope of EU civilian missions is usually broad, including different dimensions (from justice to rule of law and human rights) and tasks of a mixed nature (not only monitoring and advising, but also executive responsibilities). This has contributed to delays and shortcomings in the identification of specific parameters for action. As a consequence, in a number of cases the mandates designed for EU civilian missions have been overambitious or unrealistic *vis-à-vis* the characteristics of the theatres of operation (as in the cases of EUPM in Bosnia–Herzegovina, EUPOL in Afghanistan and, to a certain extent, also EULEX in Kosovo). An overall look at the existing missions also raises questions as to the sustainability of the operations and their strategic impact in terms of long-term stability in a given crisis region.

Improving the political dimension

The experience gained in the field through civilian missions suggests that the political dimension is crucial in order to confer credibility on the EU's interventions. A common political stance at the EU level is a precondition for the deployment and management of a mission, but also for the identification of a realistic exit strategy. The lack of a shared position among EU member states on the recognition of Kosovo's independence on one hand and towards Russia and the Eastern Neighbourhood on the other has undeniably compromised the effectiveness of EULEX and EUMM, respectively. The most urgent priority for the EU is therefore to support institutional and operational capabilities with a coherent strategy for projecting its 'civilian power' beyond its borders. In this perspective, the new European External Action Service offers a unique opportunity to reconcile CSDP process and dynamics with the overarching EU foreign policy system.

Notes

1   More information on the European Group on Training and on the Europe's New Training Initiative for Civilian Crisis Management can be found at http://www.europeangroupontraining.eu and http://www.entriforcem.eu/
2   The information contained in this paragraph relies mainly on interviews conducted by the author with personnel of EUMM Georgia.
3   The information contained in this paragraph relies mainly on interviews conducted by the author with personnel of EULEX Kosovo.

Conclusion

14 The EU as a global conflict manager

Reflections on the past, perspectives for the future

Richard G. Whitman and Stefan Wolff

Introduction

Over the past two decades, the European Union has significantly expanded its role as a conflict manager both in terms of the scope of activities and in terms of their geographical spread. Over 20 civilian and military crisis management operations have been conducted by the Union and its member states in Africa, Asia and Europe, in cooperation with other international and regional organisations (including the UN, OSCE, AU, NATO and Association of South East Asian Nations (ASEAN)), and deploying thousands of civilian experts and military personnel. While none of these missions can be classified as a failure, the track record of the EU in terms of achieving a lasting and positive impact on local conflicts, beyond the often narrow mandate that the Union gives itself, is somewhat patchy. This is not surprising given either the complexity of the conflict situations the EU has become involved in or the only gradual development of capabilities to deal with them. More importantly, the unqualified and qualified successes that the Union has had in managing conflict offer important lessons that can enable the EU to become a more effective conflict manager in the future. It is these reflections on the past that we now turn to in our concluding chapter in order to develop credible perspectives for the Union's future role as a global conflict manager.

The EU's performance to date

If nothing else, the preceding case studies clearly illustrate that the EU has become more globally engaged as a conflict manager over the past two decades. It has developed capabilities to act, fund, and coordinate and cooperate, albeit to varying degrees, and brought them to bear in a wide range of conflicts, and mostly successfully so. At the same time, a systematic analysis and comparison of our case studies reveals a number of areas where the EU has room for improvement. Yet, to be fair, there are also obstacles to more effective conflict management that are not of the Union's own making and often beyond its capabilities to remove.

How do capabilities matter?

The availability of relevant capabilities is an essential condition of successful conflict management. In our and our contributors' analysis, the EU does not suffer from a capability gap when it comes to *funding* specific missions and operations, regardless of whether they are civilian, military or hybrid in nature. The EU has also overcome earlier problems in making

funding quickly available. This is particularly obvious when we consider the EU's performance in the Western Balkans in the first decade after the end of the Cold War. Yet, the relatively easy availability of funding for conflict management missions and operations is only
part of the story. The EU's *capability to act*, especially in a military sense, remains curtailed
because of the limited progress that has been made in achieving the Helsinki Headline Goals.
This is, in part, compensated by effective cooperation with NATO and in part by the limited
scope of EU military crisis management operations to date. As the five EU operations
Concordia, Althea, Artemis, EUFOR DRC and EUFOR Chad/CAR in Macedonia, Bosnia
and Herzegovina, DRC and the tri-border area between Sudan, Chad and CAR indicate, their
success is in terms of achieving the goals that EU member states set these missions, while
their impact on the actual conflicts has in some cases been limited because of the narrow
mandates with which they were equipped.

The story that can be told of EU civilian crisis management operations is rather different.
While ambition here has been significantly greater, it has also exposed capability gaps: it
does not bode well for mission success if there are long delays in reaching full operability,
as in the case of EULEX Kosovo and EUPOL Afghanistan. Less ambitious missions, such
as EULEX Georgia or the police mission in Macedonia, Proxima, however, experienced
fewer difficulties in reaching operability and delivering on their mandates.

Where weaknesses of military and civilian crisis management operations meet, however,
is in the often limited, or unsustainable, impact on the conflict. This is a dual problem for the
EU: limited mandates can be more easily accomplished with existing capabilities but they
have, from the outset, a lower likelihood of long-term positive impact on the conflict in question; more ambitious mandates, on the other hand, face serious capability problems (especially in terms of hardware and personnel, and the maintenance of an EU-internal consensus,
i.e. political will) and are thus likely to have a limited impact on the conflict.

How does context matter?

The cross-section of cases that have been considered in the preceding parts of our book all
point out that context is obviously important in assessing the EU's performance in conflict
management. On the one hand, it shapes the mandate that the EU gives itself: the short-term,
relatively limited military crisis management missions that the Union has undertaken in
Africa, for example, reflect an appreciation of what the EU can do in complex situations
such as in the DRC. In other words, context assessment shapes EU decisions with a view to
making sure that whatever missions the organisation takes on can be completed successfully.
On the other hand, and closely related, looking at the contexts in which the EU has acted to
date, and with what mandates, reflects back on the capabilities it possesses and is willing to
deploy. For the context of the Western Balkans, over the past decade, EU capabilities were
and are sufficient to manage the actual and latent conflicts there through a combination of its
own capabilities and close cooperation with its allies, especially NATO. In the Western
Balkans, the EU has eventually risen to the challenge of conflict management, and framed
its efforts very much in these terms. In contrast, in Moldova and the South Caucasus, it has
not – or only reluctantly – done so, partly because of a lack of opportunity, partly because of
its own timidity about taking on more specifically political tasks, rather than acting within its
traditional comfort zone of institutional reform and economic development with the aim of
creating an environment in which conflict management (and even settlement) might become
possible. The Union's commitment to, and long-term engagement with, Moldova, a gradually more conducive regional and international context, and the fact that the EU, at long last

in the spring of 2011, has commissioned a strategic needs and conflict assessment for Moldova indicate that this approach might eventually bear fruit in this case. The lack of most of these positive factors in the context of Georgia and Afghanistan, on the other hand, explains the Union's relatively uninspiring performance in these two cases, in the same way in which it helps us understand the limited impact on the ground that the EU has made in Africa and in the Israeli–Palestinian conflict.

The capabilities – context nexus

Capabilities clearly matter, and so does context. Yet to understand fully how they both do, and what lessons we can learn from this, requires us to look at the capabilities – context nexus. This is nowhere more obvious than in the case of Cyprus where the EU provided the essential conditions for what was the most promising settlement plan for decades – the Annan Plan. The initial link between conflict settlement and EU accession injected crucial momentum into the negotiation process and provided real incentives for Turkey and the Turkish Cypriots to engage constructively in the settlement negotiations. Yet, at the same time, the EU failed to create the same incentives for Greece and Greek Cypriots, thus turning a very promising effort at finally settling the decades-old Cyprus conflict and overcoming the partition of the island into yet another failed settlement attempt. Crucially, this was primarily a home-made failure, attributable to a lack of strategic coordination within the EU. Looking at the way in which accession as an important policy failed in the case of Cyprus holds important lessons for the EU's use of conditionality as a whole, as well as having more immediate implications for conflict management in the Western Balkans, and potentially in Moldova, where the carrot of membership is supposed to move local conflict parties closer to burying their hatchets.

The questions that Cyprus raises about the EU's ability for a strategic approach to conflict management are profound. At one level, they are specific to this case, but in a more abstract sense, they can be asked of all the other cases in our book and more broadly of EU conflict management efforts in the past and, perhaps more importantly, the future. They relate to the compatibility of its various policies and their associated goals and how to prioritise them. They are about a realistic assessment of what the EU can achieve in which conflict (context) with the capabilities it possesses. They concern questions of whether the Union is willing to develop capabilities it currently misses, or enhance those that must be deemed insufficient at present. In other words, if we look at the larger picture of the EU as an international security actor, the most profound question that the Union has yet to answer is how its various institutions and policies for conflict management fit into the broader set of aspirations that it has articulated in its Security Strategy.

The institutional limitations of the EU

Based on the cross-examination of our case studies in the preceding section of the concluding chapter, it is clear that there are a number of institutional limitations that inhibited EU conflict management performance prior to the ratification of the Lisbon Treaty. In that era, there was an abundance of EU institutions that at least theoretically had a mandate in the area of conflict management, including the Presidency, the Political and Security Committee and the High Representative on the Council side, and on the Commission side the various Directorates General concerned with foreign affairs, above all DG External Relations, as well as EU Delegations on the ground. The European Parliament had a relatively limited impact as an institution, even though a number of MEPs tended to play a more active role in particular conflicts or specific aspects of EU conflict resolution, such as human rights. The bulk of the EU's conflict management work, however, tended to happen between Council and Commission. Commission officials generally saw their institution's role as confined to providing aid and offering financial and technical assistance, all aimed at creating conditions conducive to conflict settlement, and acknowledge that Council bodies have a greater role to play in political aspects of conflict management. Council officials accepted this more political role, but were hesitant to define clearly what it entails in relation to specific conflicts or more generally. Crucially, there was an absence of a commonly agreed strategy of conflict management across EU institutions. This left much to chance, or, to put it more positively, to the activism, skill, determination and vision of particular individuals, as exemplified in the role played by different Special Representatives, such as Kalman Mizsei in Moldova, or individual Heads of State and Government, such as French President Nicolas Sarkozy during the crisis in Georgia in 2008 or German Chancellor Angela Merkel in the context of the Meseberg Declaration and the engagement with Russia over the conflict in Transnistria that followed from it.

Another issue limiting the effectiveness of EU conflict management in the pre-Lisbon era was the lack of an integrated EU foreign policy structure and service. As a result, officials in the institutions in Brussels, delegations in countries, the representatives of different EU bodies on the ground, and member states' embassies all participated in the EU foreign policy process, including in its conflict management efforts, but all with their own priorities and capabilities. Coordination between them differed sharply from case to case, but was often less than comprehensive. In addition, local EU representatives and embassy staff of member states and desk officers in Brussels and national capitals rarely, if ever, had any specialist training in conflict analysis and management, limiting the anyway underdeveloped early warning capacity of the EU. Nor did the EU have a dedicated, well-resourced, cross-institutional conflict management body that could have taken on the role of coordination between institutions and member states and local staff, and develop and implement effective conflict management policies. This has offered a significant opportunity for the European External Action Service (EEAS) and we shall return to this issue below.

The coming into force of the Lisbon Treaty has addressed some of these limitations just noted, and there is considerable scope for further improvement, reflected, among other things, in the close collaboration of late between HR Ashton and Commissioner Füle on the EU's response to the Arab Spring. A different constraint, and one that has remained in the post-Lisbon era, is the complex relationship between EU institutions and member states: now a Union of 27 states whose institutional set-up at present still requires unanimous agreement within the Foreign Affairs Council on substantive foreign affairs decisions and makes reaching common positions very difficult in cases where national interests and domestic sensitivities are present. The very different historical and contemporary relationships of individual EU member states with Russia, for example, shaped by diverse social, political and economic links, has complicated the process of making and implementing effective decisions when it comes to conflict management in the Eastern Neighbourhood, dividing the EU at times sharply between member states with dominant pro- and anti-Russian sentiment. Similarly, divisions were obvious within the EU in relation to the response to various crises in the Middle East and North Africa throughout the first half of 2011, most notably Germany's abstention from supporting UN Security Council Resolution 1973 (2011) that authorised the subsequent NATO military operation against Colonel Gadhafi's regime. At other times, divisions are less pronounced or less openly articulated. For example, the EU, by and large, now speaks with one voice in relation to the Western Balkans, albeit with the notable exception of Kosovo; and other operations further afield, such as in the DRC, Chad or the EU Monitoring Mission in Aceh, Indonesia, are relatively uncontroversial once consensus has been reached on the mandate that the EU will seek to fulfil.

The policy limitations of the EU

Similarly to the abundance of institutions, and partly a result of it, the EU possesses a range of policy instruments for conflict management, including Joint Statements, Joint Actions, Common Positions, EU Special Representatives, economic sanctions, CSDP civilian, police and military operations, and support for civil society and other democratisation projects (under the framework of EIDHR).

Policies like the ENP, moreover, allow the EU to use the principle of conditionality in its conflict management efforts, albeit with a mixed track record. For example, the Action Plans, where they do make specific reference to conflict settlement, are often vague and lack the kind of specificity necessary to tie them credibly to incentives that are only conditionally available to partner countries. Moreover, Action Plans have to be based on a consensus between the EU, and thus among all of its 27 member states, and the partner country. In addition, the fact that ENP theoretically lends itself to the application of conditionality does not mean that it is in practice deployed in this way when it comes to conflict management efforts. The stronger emphasis on conditionality in the 2011 ENP Review is more than just an implicit acknowledgement of previous shortcomings in using conditionality as an effective instrument for conflict management.

The case of Georgia has shown that the EU more often than not does not engage in 'traditional' conflict management activities, such as confidence-building, mediation, etc., but rather focuses its efforts on what are basically infrastructure projects or institutional reform projects that are deemed to establish conditions conducive to conflict management but are not in themselves actual conflict management tools. Especially in projects of this kind in Abkhazia and South Ossetia the EU did not, either alone or in cooperation with the OSCE or UN, make its grants conditional on progress in settlement negotiations. Much the same can be said for the EU's engagement in Moldova and the Arab–Israeli conflict. More dramatically even, the EU completely eliminated any potential for using conditionality in the case of Cyprus where, enlargement being at stake, the opportunity to do so successfully was clearly there. Cyprus, at the same time, highlights the above-noted internal coordination problems: a single member state, in this case Greece, can effectively block vital tools for potentially successful EU conflict management. Also, and again with Greece at the centre, the EU itself is unable to force individual member states to abandon foreign policies that are counter-productive: Greece's continuing dispute with Macedonia over the latter country's constitutional name is less than conducive to EU policy *vis-à-vis* the Western Balkans.

The appointment of EU Special Representatives was a widely used tool for conflict management in the pre-Lisbon era. In the early days of the implementation of the Lisbon Treaty, it seemed as if there was, at best, little room for EUSRs, and the mandate for a number of high-profile posts, including for the South Caucasus and Moldova, was not renewed. At the time of writing (July 2011), the EU has eight special representatives: for Afghanistan, the African Great Lakes Region, the African Union, Bosnia and Herzegovina, Central Asia, Crisis in Georgia, Kosovo and Sudan. Perhaps crucially lacking are similar offices for the Middle East, Armenia/Azerbaijan and Moldova – especially at a time when the EU seeks to become more actively involved in efforts to manage these conflicts. At the same time, the very instrument of EUSRs has not always been effectively used, notably in the case of Georgia. Prior to 2008, Georgia was covered in the vast mandate of the EUSR for the South Caucasus, covering all three countries of the region and all three conflicts there (Abkhazia and South Ossetia in Georgia, as well as the Nagorno–Karabakh conflict between Armenia and Azerbaijan) and a multitude of other issues from democratisation to rule of law, organised crime, energy security, etc. At the same time, the EUSR's staff and resources were limited. What was perhaps more important for the effectiveness of the office, though, was the appointment of another EUSR to take charge of the crisis in Georgia in 2008 which seriously undermined the credibility of the EUSR across the South Caucasus, and especially in Georgia, and in the eyes of major regional players, while simultaneously creating overlaps of mandates and competences, stretching existing resources and complicating operations on the ground in terms of internal and external cooperation and coordination. Moreover, it was the EUSR for the Crisis in Georgia who represented the EU in the Geneva talks, rather than the EUSR for the South Caucasus who would have benefitted in this role from his much longer engagement with the region and its major players. This indicated a lack of coherence in the EU's approach to conflict management and the loss of an opportunity to maximise the impact of existing knowledge and understanding. It was also, from this perspective, questionable whether any lessons learned from previous, if marginal, EUSR involvement in conflict management initiatives in Georgia could be properly utilised. Similarly, in the case of Moldova, not renewing the mandate of the EUSR there had a negative impact on the EU's ability to manage the conflict in Transnistria – there is a crucial difference between a Delegation, which has a multitude of simultaneous tasks on its agenda, and a high-profile, seasoned diplomat who is exclusively focused on a specific conflict.

Limiting the use of EUSRs as conflict management tools, however, not only limits the external effectiveness of EU conflict management policy but also deprives the Union of opportunities to enhance internal coordination horizontally across institutions and among member states, and vertically between them and between Brussels and the Delegations. For example, recent initiatives by HR Ashton in the Middle East peace process lacked sufficient coordination with member states. In the case of Moldova, several parallel initiatives – the German–Russian Meseberg process, the German–French–Russian Deauville process, the previously informal and now again official 5+2 talks, as well as a number of individual programmes funded by Germany and the UK – are at best loosely coordinated and clearly lack a common strategic vision for an endgame in the Transnistria settlement process.

Future prospects for the EU as a global conflict manager

In the pre-Lisbon era, two key issues, in our view, have prevented the European Union living up to its aspirations of becoming a globally significant and impactful conflict manager. The first of these was structural – the lack of a permanent External Action Service – and the second substantive and conceptual – the lack of a coherent and comprehensive conflict management strategy.

The European External Action Service

With the ratification of the Lisbon Treaty, a permanent European Union External Action Service has become a reality, even though the service, two years since its inception, remains in many ways in its infancy, with turf wars between and among institutions and member states over its mandate, capacities, resources, personalities, etc. still ongoing. Ideally, what it would contribute to conflict management is a greater level of policy coherence through joined-up thinking between delegations on the ground and EU headquarters in Brussels, offering consistency and continuity of personnel over time, enhancing the role of the High Representative as a single voice of EU foreign policy, combining more effectively the range of policy tools available for conflict management, developing as yet non-existent capabilities (such as in the area of mediation and mediation support), ensuring that there is a greater level of policy learning and establishing best practices across the range of EU conflict management operations, thereby also enhancing the reputation of the EU as an effective conflict manager on a more global scale. This requires a high-profile, skilled, experienced and well-regarded personality in the role of the High Representative, who needs to enjoy unconditional backing from at least the 'Big Three' and ample room for initiative and manoeuvre – criteria on which the current HR, Baroness Ashton, at least in part falls short.

The political leadership of the EEAS will need to continue to establish a core team of officials to support them in the range of conflict management tasks; people selected because of the experience, expertise and/or training they have, rather than on the basis of national quota allocations. Equally importantly, the Union needs to invest greater care in the appointment of its representatives on the ground in Delegations and equip them with proper resources. They need to be incorporated into developing case-specific conflict management strategies and coordinate their implementation closely with Brussels. Given the complexity of contemporary conflict management, especially the range of actors and interests involved, it will also be key to future EU success that the role of Heads of Delegation in the capitals of the Union's strategic partners is strengthened.

In Brussels, the much-criticised crisis management organisation needs rethinking. It has civilian and military elements working side by side in a structure in which reporting lines and responsibilities are not entirely clear. It remains entirely separate from the regional and thematic directorates. The newly established Directorate for Conflict Prevention and Security Policy, which could potentially serve as a focal point for conflict analysis and management, is not put on an equal footing with other directorates and not adequately resourced for policy programming. The various Council Working Groups work in isolation from each other and technical and procedural details tend to gain priority over political analysis and problem-solving.

There is a need to review the crisis management structure, to broaden the focus from crisis management to conflict management (in the broad sense of also being aimed at prevention and settlement) and to streamline reporting and coordination structures. This should also include a 'mainstreaming' of conflict impact assessments into EU policies and programmes to ensure that EU engagement with (potentially) conflict-affected states does not lead to an unintended worsening of a particular situation on the ground. The crisis management board should become a crisis response and conflict management board focusing not only on crisis response but also on EU strategy *vis-à-vis* such states. Without this, it seems likely that the short-termism that has characterised EU action on many issues will continue.

However, it is the absence of a coherent and comprehensive conflict management strategy to which all the Union's institutions and member states subscribe, that is integrated and mainstreamed into all aspects of external relations with the relevant countries, and is implemented effectively in the EU's dealings with other players involved in each conflict that remains the most fundamental conceptual obstacle on the path of the EU towards a more effective conflict management role. The fact that the Union is too often merely reacting to developments rather than developing a clear strategic vision of, and will for, proactive and effective conflict management is partly a cause and partly an indication of this lack of a conflict management strategy.

A conflict management strategy

If the Union is serious about playing an active role in contributing to conflict management – as stated in numerous documents and statements by high-ranking officials – it needs not only to build a core human capacity in the European External Action Service but also to develop a proper conflict management strategy.[1] The formulation and subsequent implementation of such a strategy needs to rest on three pillars:

- a clear definition of EU interests and goals in the area of conflict management;
- an assessment of EU strengths and weaknesses in conflict management; and
- a feasible approach as to how these strengths can be best leveraged and weaknesses be overcome.

Within such a framework, EU officials need to develop a conflict management road map for specific conflicts. These road maps need to detail how the EU will contribute to the settlement of each conflict, including establishing what local conflict parties and other third parties need (or must not) do for the EU to become involved. This should also include contingencies for different scenarios regarding the impact of different local state, regional and global factors beyond the direct control of the Union, and define exit points for the EU in cases of both success and failure. The road maps would not as such suggest concrete solutions for each conflict but identify what the EU considers to be an appropriate process that can lead to a just and equitable, as well as attainable, settlement in an EU-led or co-led format. At the same time, the EU should set out the benefits that would accrue to the conflict parties (and where applicable third parties) as a result of their constructive engagement, or alternatively what sanctions the EU would apply in the case of non-conformity. In other words, in order to ensure the credibility and viability of these road maps, the EU, for each conflict, needs:

- to determine the relevant players and analyse in detail their interests and capabilities, and on this basis begin to build as broad a coalition as possible in support of an outcome-oriented settlement process;
- to develop a conflict-specific, that is context-sensitive, strategy for each conflict determining the incentives and sanctions the Union will bring to bear on these actors during the settlement process and the conditions that will trigger their application; and
- to define its own exit points from the settlement process if progress towards success becomes impossible or costs of succeeding outweigh the benefits.[2]

In addition, five substantive principles need to guide the EU's thinking about the process and outcome of its engagement in each individual conflict, bearing in mind that these conflicts are linked at different levels and that each individual road map has to be based on the three pillars on which the Union's overall conflict management strategy is based.

- *Primacy of negotiated solutions over imposed settlements.* The eventual outcomes of settlement negotiations must not be prejudged, but reflect what is practical and feasible given the interests of the immediate conflict parties and other relevant players. In order to attain such outcomes, the EU needs to stand ready to provide adequate resources for potentially protracted negotiations, as well as leadership and technical expertise as necessary to assist in crafting a sustainable settlement.

- *Inclusiveness of negotiations.* Comparative experience of conflict management indicates the need for negotiations to include all relevant parties if whatever settlement is obtained is to have a chance of being fully implemented and sustainably operated. Such inclusion need not be unconditional, but conditions need to be determined and enforced with care. While a commitment by all parties to non-violence is essential, the non-prejudicial approach to negotiation outcomes outlined above suggests that demanding prior acceptance of certain parameters of a settlement, such as continued territorial integrity or the permanence of demographic changes, might be counter-productive by undercutting the support that negotiators need from their constituencies.

- *Comprehensiveness of agreements.* In order to achieve comprehensive and thus sustainable agreements, a proper understanding of each relevant conflict is indispensable. This means to look beyond the often simplistic, but convenient labels that are given to contemporary conflicts. Conflict in the DRC, for example, is often equated with so-called resource conflicts, the conflict in Afghanistan is variably seen as part of the 'global war on terrorism' or as a counter-insurgency, the Israeli–Palestinian conflict is characterised as one of self-determination, and conflicts in the Western Balkans, Moldova and Georgia are considered secessionist. While these labels capture significant features of each of these conflicts, they also leave other, equally important dimensions to one side. The conflicts in the Western Balkans, Moldova and Georgia, for example, are indeed primarily secessionist in nature; yet, a mere compromise about who is to control which stretch of territory will be insufficient for any settlement to be sustainable. Experience indicates that, apart from accommodating territorial claims, security, economic and cultural concerns too need to be addressed. This will require the parties to make concessions and settle for compromises. As this is an often painful and risky process for the negotiators personally and the parties they represent, mediators need to be acutely aware of 'red lines' and carefully tease out the space for compromise between them, tabling proposals at key moments. Such proposals can be specific to address a particular impasse during negotiations, but they may also be broader, considering the interests of external parties whose support will be needed for settlement implementation and operation.

- *Building broad coalitions of support for negotiated settlements.* Difficult as it may be to reach a settlement at the negotiation table, the process of securing its implementation is often even more fraught with dangers of failure. The EU will need to put significant effort into securing the support of a particular settlement from key constituencies of those represented in negotiations, external stakeholders and interested parties, as well as manage potential spoilers and limit their ability to undermine a settlement agreement once it has been negotiated. Such a broad coalition of support would need to include civil society and media, diaspora networks, regional and international organisations, neighbouring states, and relevant great powers to offer the political elites who negotiated a settlement the necessary backing and give them the room for manoeuvre to accept compromises and make concessions.

- *Need for long-term external assistance.* Achieving a negotiated settlement in any conflict is a difficult enough task on its own. Its subsequent implementation and operation, moreover, will be long-term projects of state and nation-building that would, without external assistance, lack necessary human and material resources to be completed successfully. The EU has significant experience – of success and failure – in this from its engagement in the Western Balkans over the past almost two decades, and it will increase the likelihood of its success in conflict management if it commits to long-term, post-settlement engagement with the former conflict zones by providing security guarantees, development aid and institutional capacity-building and training.

The EU has gradually expanded its conflict management efforts since the end of the Cold War and assumed a growing responsibility as a global security provider. From the Western Balkans to the Eastern Neighbourhood, from the Middle East to Africa, and as far as the Aceh region of Indonesia, some of these efforts were successful while others were not (or are not yet). Many of the EU's efforts were *ad hoc*: while often carefully conceived in individual cases, an overarching strategy of conflict management has yet to be developed by the Union. Building on its successes, learning from its arguable failures, and using the opportunities offered in the Lisbon Treaty, the EU now has a real opportunity to translate these into an institutionalised, well-resourced, global conflict management strategy. Failing to do so would be a loss for the Union and a loss for the international community at large.

Notes

1   Such a strategy would need to go well beyond the 2001 Communication on Conflict Prevention, which offered a useful starting point for the Union's thinking about conflict management, but has not seen any major revision or update over the past ten years. See Commission of the European Communities, 'Communication from the Commission on Conflict Prevention', Brussels, 11 April 2001.
2   It might also be appropriate as part of this analysis to determine 'entry conditions', i.e. whether EU involvement in a particular case is likely to lead to positive outcomes.

Bibliography

Abuza, Z. (2003) *Militant Islam in Southeast Asia: Crucible of Terror* (Boulder, CO: Lynne Rienner).

Adamson, F. B. (2005) 'Globalisation, Transnational Political Mobilisation, and Networks of Violence', *Cambridge Review of International Affairs,*18 (1): 31–49.

Adebahr, C. (2009) *Learning and Change in European Foreign Policy: The Case of the EU Special Representatives* (Baden-Baden: Nomos).

Adebahr, C. and Grevi, G. (2007) 'The EU Special Representatives: what lessons for the EEAS?', *EPC Working Paper,* 28: 56–64.

Aggestam, L. (2008) 'Introduction: ethical power Europe?', *International Affairs*, 84 (1): 1–11.

Akçakoca, A., Vanhauwaert, T., Whitman, R. G. and Wolff, S. (2009) *After Georgia: Conflict Resolution in the EU's Eastern Neighbourhood* (Brussels: European Policy Centre).

Allen, D. and Smith, M. E. (1990) 'Western Europe's presence in the contemporary international arena', *Review of International Studies*, 16 (1): 19–37.

Almeida, D. G. de (2008) *The Darfur Conflict: Beyond 'Ethnic Hatred' explanations* (thesis, University of Stellenbosch).

Altunisik, M. B. (2008) 'EU foreign policy and the Israeli–Palestinian conflict: how much of an actor?', *European Security,* 17 (1): 105–21.

Asmussen, J. (2008) *Cyprus at War: Diplomacy and Conflict During the 1974 Crisis* (London: I. B. Tauris).

Asseburg, M. (2003a) 'From declarations to implementation? The three dimensions of European policy towards the conflict', in M. Ortega (ed.) *The European Union and the Crisis in the Middle East,* Chaillot Paper 62 (Paris: European Union Institute for Security Studies).

Asseburg, M. (2003b) 'The EU and the Middle East Conflict: Tackling the Main Obstacle to Euro-Mediterranean Partnership', *Mediterranean Politics,* 8 (2): 174–93.

Astill, J. and Norton-Taylor, R. (2003) 'News roundup: Africa: 100 British troops to go to Congo', *The Guardian,* 11 June: 13.

Augustin, P. (2005) *Operation Concordia/Altaïr: Lessons learnt* (online), available at: www.cdef. terre.defense.gouv.fr/publications/doctrine/doctrine06/version_us/retex/art_22.pdf (accessed 1 June 2009).

Averre, D. (2005) 'Russia and the European Union: convergence or divergence?', *European Security,* 14 (2): 175–202.

Averre, D. (2009) 'Competing rationalities: Russia, the EU and the "shared neighbourhood".' *Europe–Asia Studies,* 61 (10): 1689–713.

Avery, G. (2007) 'The new architecture for EU foreign policy', *Challenge Europe,* 17: 17–25.

Aybet, G. (2000) *A European Security Architecture After the Cold War: Questions of Legitimacy* (New York: St Martin's Press).

Ayub, F. and Kouvo, S. (2008) 'Afghanistan: intervention and the War on Terror', *International Affairs,* 84 (4): 641–58.

Bagoyoko, N. and Gibert, M. V. (2009) 'The linkage between security, governance and development: the European Union in Africa', *Journal of Development Studies,* 45 (5): 789–814.

Baracani, E. (2004) 'The European Union and democracy promotion: a strategy of democratization in the framework of Neighbourhood Policy', in F. Attinà and R. Rossi (eds) *European Neighbourhood Policy: Political, Economic and Social Issues* (Catania: The Jean Monnet Centre 'Euro-Med').

Barbe, E. and Johannson-Nogues, E. (2008) 'The EU as a modest "force for good": The European Neighbourhood Policy', *International Affairs*, 84 (1): 81–96.

Bassuener, K. and Ferhatovic, E. (2008) 'The ESDP in action: The view from the consumer side', in M. Merlingen and R. Ostrauskaite (eds) *European Security and Defence Policy: An Implementation Perspective* (Oxon: Routledge).

BBC (2007) *New force to head to Chad and CAR* (online), 25 September, available at: news.bbc.co.uk/1/hi/7011766.stm (accessed 21 July 2010).

BBC (2008) *Sudan troops clash with EU force* (online), 4 March, available at: news.bbc.co.uk/1/hi/world/africa/7276288.stm (accessed 23 July 2009).

Beatty, A. (2003) 'Israel waters down tough stance in face of EU criticism', *EUobserver.com*, 17 November.

Berg, P. (2008) *The dynamics of conflict in the tri-border region of the Sudan, Chad and the Central African Republic* (Berlin: Friedrich Ebert Stiftung).

Birand, M. A. (1985) *30 Hot Days* (Nicosia: K. Rustem).

Bird, T. (2007) 'The European Union and counter-insurgency: capability, credibility, and political will', *Contemporary Security Policy,* 28 (1): 182–96.

Biscop, S. (2005) *The European Security Strategy: A Global Agenda for Positive Power* (Aldershot: Ashgate).

Black, I. (2003) 'Ashdown backs creation of EU Bosnia force', *The Guardian* (online), 8 October, available at: www.guardian.co.uk/world/2003/oct/08/eu.warcrimes (accessed 8 April 2009).

Blair, S. (2009) 'Towards integration? Unifying military and civilian ESDP Operations', *European Security Review*, no. 44.

Blair, T. (1999) *Doctrine of the International Community* (Chicago), available at: www.number-10.gov

Blockmans, S. and Wessel, R. A. (2009) 'The European Union and crisis management: will the Lisbon Treaty make the EU more effective?' *Journal of Conflict and Security Law,* 14 (2): 265–308.

Boggero, M. (2009) 'Darfur and Chad: A fragmented ethnic mosaic', *Journal of Contemporary African Studies*, 27 (1): 21–35.

Bretherton, C. and Vogler, J. (1999) *The European Union as a Global Actor* (London: Routledge).

British Prime Minister's Office (2010) Declaration signed by the UK and France following the UK–France Summit 2010 in London 2 November 2010. Available at: www.number10.gov.uk/news/uk%E2%80%93france-summit-2010-declaration-on-defence-and-security-co-operation/ (accessed 27 April 2012).

Brok, E. (1999) *Statement on European security and defence identity after the EU summit in Cologne and the transatlantic link*, Hearing before the Committee on International Relations, US House of Representatives.

Brosig, M. (2010) 'The multi-actor game of peacekeeping in Africa', *International Peacekeeping,* 17 (3): 327–42.

Brown, M. E. (ed.) (1996) *The International Dimensions of Internal Conflict* (Cambridge, MA: The MIT Press).

Brubaker, R. (1996) *Nationalism Reframed: Nationhood and the National Question in the New Europe* (Cambridge: Cambridge University Press).

Buckley, J. (2010) 'Can the EU be more effective in Afghanistan?', *CER Policy Brief,* April (London: Centre for European Reform).

Budin, M. (2006) Public opinion and the Althea Mission one year on. Assembly of the Western European Union: the Interparliament European Security and Defence Assembly. Document A/1936, 20 June. Available at: www.assemblyweu.org/en/documents/sessions_ordinaires/rpt/2006/1936.pdf (accessed 23 January 2012).

Buscaneanu, S. (2006) *How far is the European Neighbourhood Policy a substantial offer for Moldova* (online), August, available at: pdc.ceu.hu/archive/00003073/01/how_far_is_the_EU_neighbour hood_policy.pdf (accessed 26 July 2010).

Buzan, B. and Wæver, O. (2003) *Regions and Powers: The Structure of International Security* (Cambridge: Cambridge University Press).

Calic, M.-J. (2008) 'Das ewige Laboratorium. Die Politik der Europäischen Union auf dem Balkan: Eine Evaluierung', *Internationale Politik*, 63 (6): 26–31.

Cameron, F. (2002) 'The European Union's growing international role: closing the capability—expectations gap?', paper presented at the conference on *The European Union in International Affairs*, National Europe Centre, Australian National University, July.

Cameron, F. (2006) 'The European Union's role in the Balkans', in B. Blitz (ed.) *War and Change in the Balkans* (Cambridge: Cambridge University Press).

Cannizzaro, E. (ed.) (2002) *The European Union as an Actor in International Relations* (The Hague: Kluwer International Law).

Carr, F. and Callan, T. (2002) *Managing Conflict in the New Europe: The Role of International Institutions* (Basingstoke: Palgrave).

Cascone, G. (2008) 'ESDP operations and NATO: Co-operation, rivalry or muddling-through?', in M. Merlingen and R. Ostrauskaite (eds) *European Security and Defence Policy: An Implementation Perspective* (Oxon: Routledge).

Centre for European Policy Studies (2010) *European Neighbourhood Watch*, 58, March, available at: www.ceps.eu/system/files/simplenews/2009/09/NWatch58.pdf (accessed 27 July 2010).

Cerny, P. G. (2000) 'The new security dilemma: divisibility, defection and disorder in the global era', *Review of International Studies*, 26: 623–46.

Chafer, T. (2002) 'France–African Relations: No longer so exceptional?' *African Affairs*, 101: 343–63.

Chafer, T. and Cumming, G (2010) 'Beyond Fashoda: Anglo-French security cooperation in Africa since Saint-Malo', *International Affairs*, 86(5): 1129–47.

Chandler, D. (2000) *Bosnia: Faking Democracy after Dayton* (London: Pluto Press).

Chappell, L. (2009) 'Differing member state approaches to the development of the EU Battlegroup Concept: implications for CSDP', *European Security*, 18(4): 417–39.

Charbonneau, B. (2007) *Dreams of Empire: France, Europe and the New Interventionism in Africa*, Paper presented at the *UACES Annual Conference*, 3–5 September, Portsmouth.

Charbonneau, B. (2008) *France and the New Imperialism. Security Policy in Sub-Saharan Africa* (Aldershot: Ashgate).

Charbonneau, B. (2009) 'What is so special about the European Union? EU–UN cooperation in crisis management in Africa', *International Peacekeeping*, 16 (4): 546–61.

Checkel, J. T. (2005) 'International Institutions and Socialization in Europe: Introduction and Framework', *International Organization*, 59 (4): 801–26.

Chilosi, A. (2006) 'The European Union and its neighbours: "Everything but Institutions"', *Munich Personal RePEc Archive Paper* no. 925: 2–8. Available at: mpra.ub.unitmuenchen.de/925/ (accessed 26 July 2010).

Chilton, S., Schiewek, E. and Bremmer, T. (2009) 'Evaluation of the appropriate size of the Afghan National Police Manning List (Tashkil)', *Final Report: European Commission Contract no. 2009/207401 – Version 1, Kabul, 15 July*.

Chivvis, C. S. (2007) 'Preserving hope in the Democratic Republic of the Congo', *Survival*, 49 (2): 21–42.

CIDSE (2009) *Policy Note: The EU's Aid to the Occupied Palestinian Territory (II), the Deepening Crisis in Gaza*, June.

Cilliers, J. (2008) 'The African Standby Force. An update on progress', *ISS Paper* 160, March.

Clark, J. F. (2001) 'Explaining Ugandan intervention in Congo: evidence and interpretations', *The Journal of Modern African Studies*, 39 (2): 261–87.

CNN (2000) 'Albright calls for end to "Africa's first world war". Congo's Kabila says cease-fire "deadlocked"', *CNN.com*, 24 January.

Cobham, A. (2005) 'Causes of conflict in Sudan: testing the Black Book', *The European Journal of Development Research,* 17 (3): 462–80.

Cohen, J. (2002) *Southern Caucasus: Struggling to Find Peace* (London: Conciliation Resources).

Collier, P. (2001) 'Economic causes of civil conflict and their implications for policy', in C. A. Crocker, F. O. Hampson and P. Aall (eds) *Turbulent Peace. The Challenges of Managing International Conflict* (Washington, DC : United States Institute of Peace Press).

Collier, P. and Hoeffler, A. (1998) 'On economic causes of civil war', *Oxford Economic Papers,* 50 (4): 563–73.

Collier, P. and Hoeffler, A. (2005) 'Resource rents, governance, and conflict', *Journal of Conflict Resolution,* 49 (4): 625–33.

Collier, P. and Sambanis, N. (2002) 'Understanding civil war', *Journal of Conflict Resolution,* 46 (1):3–12.

Coppieters, B. (2007) *The EU and Georgia: Time Perspectives in Conflict Resolution* (Paris: EU Institute for Security Studies).

Coppieters, B., Emerson, M., Huysseune, M., Kovziridze, T., Noutcheva, G., Tocci, N. and Vahl, M. (eds) (2004) *Europeanization and Conflict Resolution: Case Studies from the European Periphery* (Flensburg: European Centre for Minority Issues).

Coppieters, B., Emerson, M. and Tocci, N. (2004) *Europeanization and Conflict Resolution: Case Studies from the European Periphery* (Gent: Academia Press).

Cordell, K. and Wolff, S. (2009) *Ethnic Conflict: Causes—Consequences—Responses* (Polity: Cambridge).

Cornell, S. E. (2002) Autonomy as a source of conflict: Caucasian conflicts in theoretical perspective', *World Politics,* 54(2): 245–76.

Cornish, P. and Edwards, G. (2001) 'Beyond the EU/NATO dichotomy: the beginnings of a European strategic culture', *International Affairs,* 77 (3): 587–603.

Cornish, P. and Edwards, G. (2005) 'The strategic culture of the European Union: a progress report', *International Affairs,* 81 (4): 801–20.

Council of the EU (1995) *Council Decision 95/403/CFSP of 25 September 1995* (Brussels: European Union).

Council of the EU (1996a) *Council Joint Action 96/250/CFSP of 25 March 1996* (Brussels: European Union).

Council of the EU (1996b) *Council Joint Action 96/676/CFSP of 25 November 1996* (Brussels: European Union).

Council of the EU (1998) *Council Decision 98/608/CFSP of 26 October 1998* (Brussels: European Union).

Council of the EU (1999) *3–4 June 1999: Presidency Conclusions* (Cologne: Council of the European Union).

Council of the EU (2000a) *Conflict Prevention: Report by the High Representative and Commission,* Brussels.

Council of the EU (2000b) *Presidency Conclusions, Santa Maria de Feira European Council, 19 and 20 June* (online), available at: www.consilium.europa.eu/ueDocs/cms_Data/docs/pressData/en/ec/00200-r1.en0.htm (accessed 3 August 2010).

Council of the EU (2001a) *Council Joint Action 2001/492/CFSP of 29 June 2001* (Brussels: European Union).

Council of the EU (2001b) *Council Joint Action 2001/760/CFSP of 29 October 2001* (Brussels: European Union).

Council of the EU (2001c) *EU Programme for the Prevention of Violent Conflicts* (Gothenburg).

Council of the EU (2002a) *Council Joint Action 2002/832/CFSP of 21 October 2002* (Brussels: European Union).

Council of the EU (2002b) *Council Joint Action 2002/965/CFSP of 10 December 2002* (Brussels: European Union).

Council of the EU (2002c) *Implementation of the EU Programme for the Prevention of Violent Conflicts* (Seville).

Council of the EU (2003a) *Council Joint Action 2003/92/CFSP of 27 January 2003* (Brussels: European Union).

Council of the EU (2003b) *Council Joint Action 2003/537/CFSP of 21 July 2003* (Brussels: European Union).

Council of the EU (2003c) *Council Joint Action 2003/681/CFSP of 29 September 2003* (Brussels: European Union).

Council of the EU (2003d) *EU Special Representatives: Guidelines on appointment, mandate and financing,* Doc. 13833/03 (Brussels).

Council of the EU (2003e) *Civil–Military Coordination (CMCO)* (Brussels).

Council of the EU (2003f) *Council Decision 2003/563/CFSP of 29 July 2003 on the extension of the European Union military operation in the Former Yugoslav Republic of Macedonia* (Brussels: European Union).

Council of the EU (2003g) *Council Decision relating to the launch of the EU Military Operation in the former Yugoslav Republic of Macedonia. Official Journal* LO76, 22/03/2003 pp. 43–44.

Council of the EU (2004a) *Civilian Capabilities Commitment Conference: Ministerial Declaration,* Brussels, 22 November, available at: www.consilium.europa.eu/uedocs/cmsUpload/COMMITME NT%20CONFERENCE%20MINISTERIAL%20DECLARATION%2022.11.04.pdf (accessed 3 August 2010).

Council of the EU (2004b) *Civilian Headline Goal 2008,* 15863/04 (online), Brussels, 7 December, available at: register.consilium.eu.int/pdf/en/04/st15/st15863.en04.pdf (accessed 3 August 2010).

Council of the EU (2004c) *Presidency Conclusions–Brussels 25/26 March 2004,* 9048/04, Brussels, 19 May.

Council of the EU (2004d) *Action Plan for Civilian Aspects of ESDP: Adopted by the European Council, (17–18 June 2004),* available at: www.consilium.europa.eu/uedocs/cmsUpload/Action%2 0Plan%20for%20Civilian%20Aspects%20of%20ESDP.pdf (accessed 3 August 2010).

Council of the EU (2005a) *Multifunctional Civilian Crisis Management,* (Brussels).

Council of the EU (2005b) *EU–Afghanistan Joint Declaration. Committing to a new EU–Afghan Partnership* (online) Strasbourg, 16 November, available at: register.consilium.europa.eu/pdf/en/ 05/st14/st14519.en05.pdf (accessed 24 July 2010).

Council of the EU (2005c) *Council Joint Action 2005/586/CFSP of 28 July 2005* (Brussels: European Union).

Council of the EU (2005d) *Council Joint Action 2005/724/CFSP of 17 October 2005* (Brussels: European Union).

Council of the EU (2005e) *Council Joint Action 2005/796/CFSP of 14 November 2005* (Brussels: European Union).

Council of the EU (2005f) *Council Joint Action 2005/826/CFSP of 24 November 2005* (Brussels: European Union).

Council of the EU (2005g) *Follow-up on Hampton Court discussions regarding certain CFSP aspects, by EU HR Javier Solana,* S416/05 (online) 14 December, available at: www.consilium.europa.eu/ ueDocs/cms_Data/docs/pressdata/EN/reports/87644.pdf (accessed 3 August 2010).

Council of the EU (2006a) *Capability Improvement Chart I/2006* (Brussels).

Council of the EU (2006b) *Council Joint Action 2006/319/CFSP of 27 April 2006 on the European Union military operation in support of the United Nations Organisation Mission in the Democratic republic of Congo (MONUC) during the election process* (Brussels: European Union).

Council of the EU (2006c) *Press statement on EU military operation in support of the MONUC during the election process in DR Congo: Council adopts Joint Action, appoints Operation and Force Commanders* (online), 27 April, available at: www.consilium.europa.eu/ueDocs/cms_Data/docs/ pressData/en/misc/89347.pdf (accessed 26 January 2009).

Council of the EU (2006d) 'Council Joint Action 2006/121/CFSP of 20 February 2006 appointing the European Union Special Representative for the South Caucasus', *Official Journal of the European Union,* L 49/14, 21 February, available at: www.consilium.europa.eu/uedocs/cmsUpload/ l_04920060221en00140016.pdf (accessed 3 August 2010).

Council of the EU (2006e) 'Council Joint Action 2006/304/CFSP of 10 April 2006 on the establishment of an EU Planning Team (EUPT Kosovo) regarding a possible EU crisis management operation in the field of rule of law and possible other areas in Kosovo', *Official Journal of the European Union*, L 112/19, 26 April, available at: eur-lex.europa.eu/LexUriServ/LexUriServ.do?uri=OJ:L:2006:112:0019:0023:EN:PDF (accessed 3 August 2010).

Council of the EU (2006f) *Presidency conclusions. Brussels European Council, 15/16 December 2005,* 15914/1/05 REV 1 (online), Brussels, 30 January, available at: www.consilium.europa.eu/ueDocs/cms_Data/docs/pressData/en/ec/87642.pdf (accessed 3 August 2010).

Council of the EU (2006g) *Background DRC Elections 2006: EU Support to the DRC during the election process.* Available at: www.consilium.europa.eu/uedocs/cms_data/docs/pressdata/en/esdp/90508.pdf (accessed 27 April 2012).

Council of the EU (2007a), *Civilian Headline Goal 2010* (Brussels).

Council of the EU (2007b), *Final report on the Civilian Headline Goal 2008* (Brussels).

Council of the EU (2007c) *Council Joint Action 2007/369/CFSP of 30 May 2007 on establishment of the European Union Police Mission in Afghanistan (EUPOL AFGHANISTAN)*, OJ L 139/33 (Brussels, 30 May).

Council of the EU (2007d) *Annual report from the Council to the European Parliament on the main aspects and basic choices of CFSP, including the financial implications for the general budget of the European Communities – 2006*, Doc. 6992/1/07 (Brussels, 30 April).

Council of the EU (2007e) *Council Joint Action 2007/112/CFSP of 15 February 2007* (Brussels: European Union).

Council of the EU (2007f) *Guidelines on appointment, mandate and financing of EU Special Representatives,* Doc. 11328/1/07 (Brussels, 24 July).

Council of the EU (2007g) *Council Joint Action 2007/677/CFSP of 15/10/2007 on the European Union military operation in the Republic of Chad and in the Central African Republic* (Brussels: European Union).

Council of the EU (2007h) *New Civilian Headline Goal 2010*, 14823/07 (online), Brussels, 9 November, available at: register.consilium.europa.eu/pdf/en/07/st14/st14823.en07.pdf (accessed 3 August 2010).

Council of the EU (2008a) *Declaration on Strengthening Capabilities* (Brussels).

Council of the EU (2008b) *Civilian Headline Goal 2010: Progress report 2008* (Brussels).

Council of the EU (2008c) 'Council Joint Action 2008/124/CFSP of 4 February 2008 on the European Union Rule of Law Mission in Kosovo', *Official Journal of the European Union*, L 42/92, 16 February, available at: eur-lex.europa.eu/LexUriServ/LexUriServ.do?uri=OJ:L:2008:042:0092:0098:EN:PDF (accessed 3 August 2010).

Council of the EU (2008d) 'Council Joint Action 2008/736/CFSP of 15 September 2008 on the European Union Mission in Georgia, EUMM Georgia', *Official Journal of the European Union*, L 248/26, 17 September, available at: eur-lex.europa.eu/LexUriServ/LexUriServ.do?uri=OJ:L:2008:248:0026:0031:EN:PDF (accessed 3 August 2010).

Council of the EU (2008e) 'Council Conclusions on Civilian Capabilities', *Extract from the 2903rd External Relations Council meeting*, Brussels, 10 and 11 November 2008, available at: www.consilium.europa.eu/uedocs/cmsUpload/PESD_EN-civilian_capabilities.pdf (accessed 3 August 2010).

Council of the EU (2008f) Extraordinary European Council, Brussels, 1 September 2008: *Presidency Conclusions* (Brussels: Council of the European Union).

Council of the EU (2008g) *Presidency Conclusions of the Brussels European Council* (11 and 12 December), Annex 2: Declaration by the European Council on the Enhancement of the European Security and Defence Policy (ESDP).

Council of the EU (2009a) *ESDP operations* (online), available at: www.consilium.europa.eu/showPage.aspx?id=268&lang=EN (accessed 7 July 2009).

Council of the EU (2009b) *EU military operation in Bosnia and Herzegovina (EUFOR-Althea)* (online), available at: consilium.europa.eu/cms3_fo/showPage.asp?id=745&lang=en (accessed 26 January 2009).

Council of the EU (2009c) *EUFOR Chad/CAR* (online), available at: consilium.europa.eu/cms3_fo/showPage.asp?id=1366&lang=en&mode=g (accessed 26 January 2009).

Council of the EU (2009d) *EU Concept for civil–military co-operation (CIMIC) for EU-led military operations* (Brussels).

Council of the EU (2009e) *Civilian Headline Goal 2010: Outline of Goalkeeper software environment*, 8096/09 (online), Brussels, 2 April, available at: register.consilium.europa.eu/pdf/en/09/st08/st08096.en09.pdf (accessed 3 August 2010).

Council of the EU (2009f) *Civilian Headline Goal 2010: Civilian Capability Improvement Plan 2009*, 5602/09 (online), Brussels, 22 January, available at: register.consilium.europa.eu/pdf/en/09/st05/st05602.en09.pdf (accessed 3 August 2010).

Council of the EU(2009g) *EU Military Operation in Eastern Chad and North Eastern Central African Republic* (EUFOR Tchad/RCA. Available at: www.consilum.europaeu/uedocs/cmsUpload/Final_FACTSHEET_EUFOR_TCHAD-RCA-version9_EN.pdf (accessed 27 April 2012).

Council of the EU (2010) 'Council Decision of 26 July 2010 establishing the organisation and functioning of the European External Action Service'. (2010/427/EU). *Official Journal of the European Union*, 3 August 2010, L201/30.

Council of the EU (2011) 'Council conclusions on conflict prevention. 3101st Foreign Affairs Council meeting (20 June 2011)' (Luxembourg: Council of the European Union).

Crawford, T. and Kuperman, A. (eds) (2006) *Gambling on Humanitarian Intervention* (London: Routledge).

Crawshaw, N. (1978) *Cyprus Revolt: Origins, Development and Aftermath of an International Dispute* (London: Allen and Unwin).

Cumming, G. D. (2005) 'From Realpolitik to the third way: British Africa policy in the new world order', in U. Engel and G. R. Olsen (eds) *Africa and the North: Between Globalization and Marginalization* (London: Routledge).

Cyprus Mail (2004) *Money pledged to reunify Cyprus*, 16 April.

D'Alancon, F. (1994) 'The EC looks to a new Middle East', *Journal of Palestine Studies*, 23 (2): 44–51.

Daley, P. (2006) 'Challenges to peace: conflict resolution in the Great Lakes region in Africa', *Third World Quarterly*, 27 (2): 303–19.

Dannreuther, R. (2002) 'Europe and the Middle East: towards a substantive role in the peace process?', *Geneva Centre for Security Policy Occasional Paper Series* 39, Chapter 11.

Dannreuther, R. (2004a) 'The Middle East: towards a substantive European role in the peace process?', in R. Dannreuther (ed.) *European Union Foreign and Security Policy: Towards a Neighbourhood Strategy* (London: Routledge).

Dannreuther, R. (ed.) (2004b) *European Union Foreign and Security Policy: Towards a Neighbourhood Strategy* (London: Routledge).

Declaration on Strengthening European Cooperation in Security and Defence (2003) (Le Touquet).

Delcour, L. (2010) 'The European Union, a security provider in the eastern neighbourhood?', *European Security*, 19(4): 535–49.

Deletroz, A. (2010) 'The Spoils of EU Reform', available at: blogs.reuters.com/great-debate-uk/2010/02/19/the-spoils-of-eu-reform/ (accessed 29 July 2010).

De Maio, J.L. (2010) 'Is war contagious? The transnationalization of conflict in Darfur', *African Studies Quarterly*, 11(4): 25–44.

De Schoutheete de Tervarent, P. (1980) *La Coopération Politique Européenne* (Brussels: F. Nathan Editions Labor).

De Vasconcelos, A. (2009) *What Ambitions for European Defence in 2020?* (Paris: European Union Institute for Security Studies).

Devine, K. (2009) 'Irish political parties' attitudes towards neutrality and the evolution of the EU's foreign, security and defence policies,' *Irish Political Studies*, 24 (4): 467–90.

Deutsche Welle (2008a) *France pledges more troops to EU force in Chad, CAR* (online), 11 January, available at: www.dw-world.de/dw/article/0,3053474,00.html (accessed 21 July 2010).

Deutsche Welle (2008b) *EU soldiers accused of torturing civilians in Congo* (online), 29 March, available at: www.dw-world.de/dw/article/0,2144,3223692,00.html (accessed 16 March 2009).

De Waal, A. (2005) 'Who are the Darfurian? Arab and African identities, violence and external engagement', *African Affairs*, 104 (415): 181–205.

De Waal, A. (2007) 'Darfur and the failure of the responsibility to protect', *International Affairs*, 83 (6): 1039–1054.

De Waal, A. (2008) 'Making sense of Chad', *Hunger Notes,* 7 February, available at: www. worldhunger.org/articles/08/editorials/de_waal.htm (accessed 21 July 2010).

Drent, M. and Zandee, D. (2010) *Breaking Pillars: Towards a Civil–Military Security Approach for the European Union* (The Hague: Netherlands Institute of International Relations Clingendael).

DG Relex (2007) 'Human Rights and Frozen Conflicts in the Eastern Neighbourhood', *Briefing Paper prepared for European Parliament.*

Diehl, P. F. and Lepgold, J. (eds) (2003) *Regional Conflict Management* (Lanham: Rowman and Littlefield).

Dietl, E. (2005) *Ausbau der Konfliktmanagementfähigkeiten der EU durch den Sonderbotschafter für den Nahen Osten* (Frankfurt am Main: Peter Lang).

Diez, T. (ed.) (2002) *Enlargement and Reconciliation: EU Accession and the Division of Cyprus* (Flensburg: European Centre for Minority Issues).

Diez, T., Manners, I. and Whitman, R. G. (2011) 'The changing nature of international institutions in Europe: the challenge of the European Union', *Journal of European Integration,* 33 (2): 117–38.

Diez, T., Stetter, S. and Albert, M. (2006) 'The European Union and border conflicts: the transformative power of integration', *International Organization,* 60 (3): 563–93.

Dijkstra, H. (2010) 'The military operation of the EU in Chad and the Central African Republic: good policy, bad politics', *International Peacekeeping,* 17(3): 395–407.

Dobbins, J. (2008) *After the Taliban: Nation-Building in Afghanistan* (Washington DC: Potomac Books).

Dobbins, J., Jones, S. G., Crane, K., Chivvis, C. S., Radin, A., Larrabee, F. S., Bensahel, N., Lawson, B. S. and Goldsmith, B. W. (2008) *Europe's Role in Nation-Building: From the Balkans to the Congo* (Arlington: RAND).

Doyle, M. (1998) 'Africa's "First World War" to dominate summit', *BBC News*, 17 December.

Drousiotis, M. (2006) *Cyprus 1974: Greek Coup and Turkish Invasion* (Mannheim: Bibliopolis).

Duchêne, F. (1972) 'Europe's role in world peace', in R. J. Mayne (ed.) *Europe Tomorrow: Sixteen Europeans Look Ahead* (London: Fontana).

Duchêne, F. (1973) 'The European Community and the uncertainties of interdependence', in M. Kohnstamm and W. Hager (eds) *A Nation Writ Large? Foreign-Policy Problems before the European Community* (London: Macmillan).

Duke, Simon (2003) 'Regional organisations and conflict prevention: CFSP and ESDI in Europe', in D. Carment and A. Schnabel (eds) *Conflict Prevention: Path to Peace or Grand Illusion?* (Tokyo: United Nations University Press).

Duke, Simon (2008) 'The future of EU–NATO relations: a case of mutual irrelevance through competition?', *Journal of European Integration,* 30 (1): 27–43.

ECDPM (2006) *Mid Term Evaluation of the African Peace Facility Framework-Contract (9ACP RPR22) 250 M Euro. Final Report*, Maastricht, 16 January.

EEAS (2012a) Althea/BiH. Available at: consilium.europa.eu/eeas/security-defence/eu-operations/althea?/lang=en/(accessed 23 January 2012).

EEAS (2012b) EUPM/BiH. Available at: consilium.europa.eu/eeas/security-defence/eu-operations/eupm?/lang=en/(accessed 23 January 2012).

Ehrhart, H. G. (2002) 'What model for CFSP?', *Chaillot Paper*, no. 55 (Paris, EU Institute for Security Studies), available at: www.iss.europa.eu/uploads/media/ESDP_10-web.pdf (accessed 3 August 2010).

Ehrhart, H. G. (2007) *Civil–Military Co-operation and Co-ordination in the EU and in Selected Member States* (Brussels: European Parliament Policy Department External Policies).

Ehrhart, H. G. (2008) 'Assessing EUFOR Chad/CAR', *European Security Review*, no. 41 (online), ISIS Europe, available at: www.isis-europe.org/pdf/2008_artrel_231_esr42-euforchad.pdf (accessed 3 August 2010).

Embassy of the Republic of Cyprus in Washington DC (2010a) *The European Union and the Cyprus Question* (online), available at: www.cyprusembassy.net/home/index.php?module=page&cid=33 (accessed 13 July 2010).

Embassy of the Republic of Cyprus in Washington DC (2010b) *Application for membership – pre-accession strategy* (online), available at: www.cyprusembassy.net/home/index.php?module= page&cid=31 (accessed 13 July 2010).

Emerson, M. (2004) 'European Neighbourhood Policy: Strategy or Placebo?', *CEPS Working Document*, no. 215.

Emerson, M. and Gross, E. (eds) (2007) *Evaluating the EU's Crisis Missions in the Balkans* (Brussels: CEPS).

Emerson, M., Vahl, M., Coppieters, B., Huysseune, M., Kovziridze, T., Noutcheva, G. and Tocci, N. (2004) 'Elements of comparison and synthesis', *Journal on Ethnopolitics and Minority Issues in Europe,* 5 (1).

Emerson, M., Noutcheva, G. and Popescu, N. (2007) *European Neighbourhood Policy Two Years on: Time indeed for an 'ENP plus'*, (Brussels: Centre for European Policy Studies).

EU–Africa (2007) *The Africa–EU Strategic Partnership. A Joint Africa–EU Strategy*, adopted at the Second EU–Africa Summit, Lisbon, December 9.

EU Council Secretariat (2005) 'EU Special Representatives (EUSRs). A voice and face of the EU in crucial areas' (Factsheet) (Brussels)

EU Council Secretariat (2006a) *Factsheet: EU Battlegroups* (Brussels).

EU Council Secretariat (2006b) *Development of European Military Capabilities: the Force Catalogue 2006* (Brussels).

EU Council Secretariat (2006c) *European Union Police Mission for the Palestinian Territories (EUPOL-COPPS),* EUPOL-COPPS/02, 9 February, available at: www.consilium.europa.eu/ uedocs/cmsUpload/051222-EUPOL-COPPS.pdf (accessed 22 July 2010).

EU Council Secretariat (2008a) *EU Support to the African Union Mission in Darfur – AMIS* (Brussels).

EU Council Secretariat (2008b) *European Union Police Mission for the Palestinian Territories (EUPOL COPPS)* (online), January, available at: www.consilium.europa.eu/uedocs/cmsUpload/ 080107EUPOLCOPPS.pdf (accessed 22 July 2010).

EU Council Secretariat (2009a) *EU Police Mission in Afghanistan* (Brussels).

EU Council Secretariat (2009b) *EULEX Kosovo: EU Rule of Law Mission in Kosovo* (Brussels).

EU Council Secretariat (2010a) *EULEX Kosovo: EU Rule of Law Mission in Kosovo* (Brussels).

EU Council Secretariat (2010b) *EU Police Mission in Afghanistan* (*EUPOL Afghanistan*) (Brussels).

EU CSDP (2009) *EU Border Assistance Mission at Rafah Crossing Point (EUBAM Rafah)* (online), Rafah/11, November, available at: www.consilium.europa.eu/uedocs/cms_data/docs/mission Press/files/100204%20FACTSHEET%20EUBAM%20Rafah%20-%20version%2011_EN01.pdf (accessed 21 July 2010).

EU CSDP (2010) *EU Police Mission for the Palestinian Territories (EUPOL COPPS)* (online), COPPS/15, January, available at: www.consilium.europa.eu/uedocs/cms_data/docs/mission Press/files/100121%20FACTSHEET%20EUPOL%20COPPS%20-%20version%2015_EN03.pdf (accessed 21 July 2010).

EU Election Observation Mission (2006) *Statement of Preliminary Conclusions and Findings* (online), 26 January, available at: ec.europa.eu/external_relations/human_rights/eu_election_ass_observ/ westbank/legislative/statement_260106.pdf (accessed 4 December 2009).

EU Institute for Security Studies (2005) *EU Security and Defence: core documents 2004* (Paris: EUISS).

EU/Moldova Action Plan (n.d.) available at: ec.europa.eu/world/enp/pdf/action_plans/moldova_enp_ ap_final_en.pdf (accessed 27 July 2010).

EU/Ukraine Action Plan (n.d.) available at: ec.europa.eu/world/enp/pdf/action_plans/moldova_enp_ ap_final_en.pdf (accessed 26 July 2010).

EU@UN (2008) *EU Military Operation in Eastern Chad and North Eastern Central African Republic (EUFOR Tchad/RCA)* (online), 28 January, available at: www.europa-eu-un.org/articles/en/ article_7689_en.htm (accessed 21 July 2010).

EUFOR Chad/CAR (2008a) *EUFOR suffers its first fatality* (online), 10 March, available at: www.consilium.europa.eu/uedocs/cmsUpload/080310EUFORsuffersfirstfatality.pdf (accessed 1 April 2009).

EUFOR Chad/CAR (2008b) *EUFOR action under fire protect IDP's Refugees* (online), 14 June, available at: www.consilium.europa.eu/uedocs/cmsUpload/RezzouGozBeida.pdf (accessed 1 April 2009).

EUFOR Chad/CAR (2008c) *EUFOR challenge and disperse ambushers* (online), 19 August, available at: www.consilium.europa.eu/uedocs/cmsUpload/Press_Release_19_august_2008.pdf (accessed 1 April 2009).

EULEX Programme Report (2010) *Building sustainable change together* (online), pp.13–23, available at: www.eulex-kosovo.eu/docs/tracking/EULEX%20Programme%20Report%202010%20.pdf (accessed 3 August 2010).

EUPOL (2009) *EUPOL – Serving Afghanistan: Newsletter of the European Police Mission in Afghanistan,* issue 26/09, Kabul, 16 December.

EUPOL (2010) *EUPOL – Serving Afghanistan: Newsletter of the European Police Mission in Afghanistan*, issue 09/10, Kabul, 27 May.

Eur-Lex (1997) '21997A0716(01) Euro-Mediterranean Interim Association Agreement', *Official Journal L 187,* 16 July, available at: eur-lex.europa.eu/LexUriServ/LexUriServ.do?uri=CELEX:21997A0716%2801%29:EN:HTML (accessed 22 July 2010).

Europa (2007) 'A strong European neighbourhood policy – further efforts are needed', *Press releases RAPID* (online), 5 December, available at: europa.eu/rapid/pressReleasesAction.do?reference=IP/07/1843&format=HTML&aged=0&language=EN&guiLanguage=en (accessed 27 July 2010).

Europa (2008) 'Institution Building', *Press Releases RAPID* (online), 28 January, available at: europa.eu/rapid/pressReleasesAction.do?reference=MEMO/08/50&format=HTML&aged=0&language=EN&guiLanguage=en (accessed 21 July 2010).

Europa (2010a) *Europa – the official website of the European Union* (online), available at: europa.eu/

Europa (2010b) *Delegation of the European Union to Israel* (online), available at: www.delisr.ec.europa.eu/english/content/eu_and_country/asso_agree_en.pdf (accessed 22 July 2010).

European Commission (1993) 'Commission opinion on the application by the Republic of Cyprus for Membership (AVIS)', May, *Bulletin of the European Communities*, Supplement 5/93 (Brussels: European Commission).

European Commission (2001) *Communication from the Commission on Conflict Prevention* (Brussels).

European Commission (2001a) *Country Strategy Paper 2000–2006 and National Indicative Programme 2002–2003 Georgia* (Brussels: European Commission).

European Commission (2002a) *New Neighbours Initiative – Council conclusions, doc. 14078/02* (online), 18 November, available at: ec.europa.eu/world/enp/news/16062003_en.htm#6 (accessed 27 July)

European Commission (2002b) *Information Note: The Rapid Reaction Mechanism Supporting the European Union's Policy Objectives in Conflict Prevention and Crisis Management* (online), available at: www.europa.eu.int/comm/external_relations/cfsp/doc/ rrm.pdf

European Commission (2003a) *Country Strategy Paper (CSP) Afghanistan, 2003-2006* (online), available at: europa.eu.int/comm/external_relations/afghanistan/csp/03-06.pdf (Chapter 8).

European Commission (2003b) 'Wider Europe – Neighbourhood: A New Framework for Relations with our Eastern and Southern Neighbours', *Communication from the Commission to the Council and the European Parliament,* COM(2003) 104 final, 11 March. Available at: ec.europa.eu/world/enp/pdf/com03_104_en.pdf (accessed 26 July 2010).

European Commission (2003c) *Country Strategy Paper 2003–2006 and National Indicative Programme 2004–2006 Georgia* (Brussels: European Commission).

European Commission (2004a) 'European Neighbourhood Policy Country Report: Palestinian Authority of the West Bank and Gaza Strip', *Commission Staff Working Paper,* COM(2004) 373 final (online), available at: ec.europa.eu/world/enp/pdf/country/pa_enp_country_report_2004_en.pdf (accessed 22 July 2010).

European Commission (2004b) 'European Neighbourhood Policy Strategy Paper', *Communication from the Commission*, COM(2004) 373 final, 12 May. Available at: ec.europa.eu/world/enp/pdf/strategy/strategy_paper_en.pdf (accessed 26 July 2010).

European Commission (2004c) *Taking Europe to the world: 50 years of the European Commission's External Service* (Brussels: European Communities, External Relations).

European Commission (2005a) *Communication from the Commission: EU-Palestinian cooperation beyond disengagement - towards a two-state solution*, COM(2005) 458 final, 5 October.

European Commission (2005b) 'Road Map for the Common Space of External Security', Annex 3 to the 2005 Moscow Summit Declaration.

European Commission (2006) 'On Strengthening the European Neighbourhood Policy', *Communication from the Commission to the Council and the European Parliament*, COM(2006) 726 final.

European Commission (2006a) *EU/Georgia Action Plan* (Brussels: European Commission).

European Commission (2006b) Speech by EU Commissioner Ferrero-Waldner: 'Political Reform and Sustainable Reform in the South Caucasus'. Bled Strategic Forum, Slovenia, 28 August. 2006 (Brussels: European Commission).

European Commission (2007a) *Georgia Country Strategy Paper 2007–2013* (Brussels: European Commission).

European Commission (2007b) 'European Commission's Support to the Republic of Moldova', *Country Level Evaluation*, November.

European Commission (2008a) *Definitions and categorisation used by the European Commission* (online), available at: ec.europa.eu/development/policies/9interventionsareas/conflictprev_en.cfm, (accessed 16 February 2008).

European Commission (2008b) *Communication from the Commission to the Council: Review of EU-Russia Relations* (Brussels: European Commission).

European Commission (2009a) *Afghanistan: State of Play July 2009* (online), available at: www.delafg.ec.europa.eu/en/downloadable_documents/Nov_2008/reports/StateofPlay%20AFG2009-II.pdf (accessed 24 July 2010).

European Commission (2009b) *Initial Concept Note Potential Priority Areas for ENPI National Indicative Programme (NIP) 2011–2013 Georgia* (Brussels: European Commission).

European Commission (2009c) Commission Staff Working Document Accompanying the Communication from the Commission to the European Parliament and Council: Implementation of the European Neighbourhood Policy in 2008, Progress Report Georgia (Brussels: European Commission).

European Commission Trade (2010) *Countries: Israel* (online), available at: ec.europa.eu/trade/creating-opportunities/bilateral-relations/countries/israel/ (accessed 21 July 2010).

European Commission (2011) *A new response to a changing Neighbourhood* (Brussels: European Commission).

European Communities (2005) *EU Strategy for Africa: Towards a Euro-African pact to accelerate Africa's development*, COM (2005), 489 final (Brussels).

European Convention (2002) 'Final Report of Working Group VIII on Defense, Chaired by Michael Barnier', *Barnier Report* (Brussels, 16 December).

European Council (1999a) *Declaration of the European Council on Strengthening the Common European Policy on Security and Defence* (Cologne).

European Council (1999b) *Presidency Conclusions: Helsinki European Council* (Helsinki).

European Council (1999c) *Presidency Progress Report to the Helsinki European Council on Strengthening the Common European Policy on Security and Defence* (Helsinki).

European Council (1999d) *Presidency Report on Non-Military Crisis Management of the European Union* (Helsinki).

European Council (1999e) *Presidency Conclusions*, European Council Meeting in Cologne, 3–4 June, SN 300/1/101 REV 1.

European Council (1999f) *Presidency Conclusions*, Berlin, 24 and 25 March.

European Council (2000a) *Presidency Report on Strengthening the Common European Policy on Security and Defence* (Feira).

European Council (2000b) *Council Joint Action of 22 December 2000 on the European Union Monitoring Mission,* 2000/811/CFSP.

European Council (2001a) *Presidency Report to the Goteborg European Council on European Security and Defence Policy* (Gothenburg).

European Council (2001b) *Council Regulation (EC) no: 381/2001 of February 26 2001 Creating a Rapid Reaction Mechanism.*

European Council (2001c) *Presidency Conclusions*, European Council Meeting in Laeken, 14–15 December, SN 300/1/101 REV 1.

European Council (2002a) *Council Joint Action of 11 March 2002 on the European Union Police Mission,* 2002/210/CFSP.

European Council (2002b) *Presidency Conclusions*, European Council Meeting in Copenhagen, 12–13 December, SN 400/02.

European Council (2003a) *Council Joint Action of 27 January 2003 on the European Union Military Operation in the Former Yugoslav Republic of Macedonia,* 2003/92/CFSP.

European Council (2003b) *Council Joint Action of 27 January 2003 on the European Union Military Operation in the Democratic Republic of Congo,* 2003/423/CFSP.

European Council (2003c) *Council Joint Action of 29 September 2003 on the European Union Police Mission in the Former Yugoslav Republic of Macedonia,* 2003/681/CFSP.

European Council (2003d) *European Security Strategy: A Secure Europe in a Better World* (online), 12 December, available at: www.consilium.europa.eu/uedocs/cmsUpload/78367.pdf (accessed 26 July 2010).

European Council (2003e) *Presidency Conclusions*, European Council Meeting in Brussels, 28–30 September, 12294/03 (Presse 252).

European Council (2004a) *Presidency Report on ESDP* (Brussels).

European Council (2004b) *Council Decision of 25 November 2004 on the Launching of the European Union Military Operation in Bosnia and Herzegovina,* 2004/803/CFSP.

European Council (2004c) *Council Joint Action of 12 July 2004 on the European Union Military Operation in Bosnia and Herzegovina,* 2004/570/CFSP.

European Council (2004d) *Council Joint Action of 22 November 2004 on the Extension of the European Union Police Mission in the Former Yugoslav Republic of Macedonia,* 2004/789/CFSP.

European Council (2005) *Presidency Conclusions* (Brussels, 15 and 16 December).

European Council (2008a) *Report on the Implementation of the European Security Strategy* (Brussels).

European Council (2008b) *Presidency Conclusions Annex 2 Declaration by the European Council on the Enhancement of the European Security and Defence Policy* (Brussels).

European Council (2008c) 'European Union Police Mission in Bosnia and Herzegovina', *Official Website of the Council of the European Union* (online), available at: www.consilium.europa.eu/cms3_fo/showPage.asp?id=585&lang=EN&mode=g (accessed 9 March 2008).

European Council (2008d) 'Council Joint Action of 25 September 2008 on appointing the European Union Special Representative for the crisis in Georgia, 2008/760/CFSP', *Official Journal of the European Union*, L 259/16, 27 September, available at: eur-lex.europa.eu/LexUriServ/LexUriServ.do?uri=OJ:L:2008:259:0016:0018:EN:PDF (accessed 3 August 2010).

European Economic Community (1986) *Single European Act.*

European Neighbourhood and Partnership Instrument (n.d.–a) *Funding 2007–2013* (online), available at: ec.europa.eu/world/enp/pdf/country/0703_enpi_figures_en.pdf (accessed 22 July 2010).

European Neighbourhood and Partnership Instrument (n.d.–b) 'Israel', *Strategy Paper 2007–2013 and Indicative Programme 2007–2010* (online), available at: ec.europa.eu/world/enp/pdf/country/enpi_csp_nip_israel_en.pdf (accessed 22 July 2010).

European Parliament (1995) *Resolution on Cyprus's Application for Membership of the European Union*, A4-0156/1995.

European Parliament Committee on Foreign Affairs (2008) *Draft Report on the Implementation of the European Security Strategy and the ESDP* (Brussels).

European Union (1992) *Treaty on European Union*, 92/C191/01.

European Union (1997) *Treaty of Amsterdam (Consolidated Version of the Treaty on European Union)*, 97/C340/02.

European Union (2001) *Treaty of Nice (Amending the Treaty on European Union, the Treaties Establishing the European Communities and Certain Related Acts)*, 2001/C 80/01.

European Union (2004) 'Treaty Establishing a Constitution for Europe', *Official Journal of the European Union*, English Edition, C 310, 47 (16), December. Available at: europa.eu.int/eur-lex/lex/JOHtml.do?uri=OJ:C:2004:310:SOM:EN:HTML (accessed 30 March 2005).

European Union (2007) 'Treaty of Lisbon amending the Treaty on European Union and the Treaty establishing the European Community', *Official Journal of the European Union*, English Edition, C 306, 50 (17), December. Available at: bookshop.europa.eu/eubookshop/FileCache/PUBPDF/FXAC07306ENC/FXAC07306ENC_002.pdf (accessed 3 April 2008).

European Union (2009) *European Commission Delegation to Afghanistan: Overview of EU Assistance to Afghanistan* (online), available at: www.delafg.ec.europa.eu/Pa/downloadable_documents/report/Overview_of_EU_Assistance_to_Afghanistan_English.pdf (accessed 24 July 2010).

European Union (2010) *Africa–EU relations: key facts and figures*. Available at: europa.eu/rapid/pressReleasesAction.do?reference=MEMO/10/234&format=HTML&aged=O&language=EN&guiLanguage=en. (accessed 27 April 2012).

European Union Monitoring Mission in Georgia (2008) *Press Conference: Head of Mission, Mr. Hansjorg Haber* (online) 24 October, available at: consilium.europa.eu/uedocs/cmsUpload/081024-Press_Conference_HoM_Haber-transcript.ed.pdf (accessed 28 July 2010).

European Voice (2010). *EU Names New Afghanistan Special Envoy* (Brussels, 22 February).

Evans-Pitchard, A. (2009) 'Airbus admits it may scrap A400M military transport aircraft project', *Daily Telegraph*, 29 March.

Factsheet (2005) *EU Support for Peace and Security in Africa* (European Union: Council Secretariat).

Factsheet (2008) *EU support to the African Union Mission in Darfur – AMIS* (European Union: Council Secretariat).

Faria, F. (2004a) *Crisis Management in Sub-Saharan Africa: The Role of the European Union* (Paris: The European Union Institute for Security Studies).

Faria, F. (2004b) 'La gestion des crises en Afrique subsaharienne–Le rôle de l'union européenne', *Occasional Paper* 55 (Paris: European Union Institute for Security Studies).

Faucompret, E. (2001) *The Dismemberment of Yugoslavia and the European Union* (Antwerp: University of Antwerp).

Federal Foreign Office (2007) *Funding for Police Assistance in Afghanistan Tripled* (Berlin, 18 November).

Feith, P. (2007) 'The Aceh Peace Process: Nothing Less than Success', *US Institute of Peace Special Report*, 184.

Ferreira-Pereira, L. C. (2007). 'Between Scylla and Charybdis: Assessing Portugal's approach to the Common Foreign and Security Policy,' *Journal of European Integration*, 29(2): 209–28.

Ferrero-Waldner, B. (2007) 'The European Union and the World: A Hard Look at Soft Power', *Speech by EU Commissioner Ferrero-Waldner* (Ref: SP07-410EN) Columbia University, New York, 24 September.

Fiedler, A. (2004) 'The Great Lakes Region: testing ground for a European Union Foreign Policy', in D. Mahncke, A. Ambos and C. Reynolds (eds) *European Foreign Policy: From Rhetoric to Reality?* (Brussels: PIE–Peter Lang).

Finn, P. (2001) 'Peace deal signed in Macedonia; pact opens way for NATO troops', *The Washington Post*, 14 August.

Fischer, S. (2009) 'EUMM Georgia', in G. Grevi, D. Helly, and D. Keohane (eds) *ESDP: The First 10 Years (1999–2009)* (Paris: European Institute for Security Studies), available at: www.iss.europa.eu/uploads/media/ESDP_10-web.pdf (accessed 3 August 2010).

Fletcher, P. (2008) 'Interview: Chad rebel attack aimed to spoil EU mission', *Reuters* (online), 4 February, available at: www.alertnet.org/thenews/newsdesk/L0458937.htm (accessed 30 July 2009).

Fowkes, B. (2001) *Ethnicity and Ethnic Conflict in the Post-Communist World* (Basingstoke: Palgrave).

Framework Agreement (2001) (online), Ohrid, available at: faq.macedonia.org/politics/framework_agreement.pdf (accessed 3 February 2009).

Franciosi, M.-L. and Boulat, A. (n.d.) *Occupied Palestinian Territory: Support of Palestinian–Israeli negotiations towards a peace agreement* (online), available at: ec.europa.eu/external_relations/ifs/publications/articles/rep1/reportage%20vol1_chapter7_occupied%20palestinian%20territory%20-%20support%20of%20palestinian-israeli%20negotiations%20towards%20a%20peace%20agreement.pdf (accessed 22 July 2010).

Friesendorf, C. and Penska, S. E. (2008) 'Militarized law enforcement in peace operations: EUFOR in Bosnia and Herzegovina', *International Peacekeeping*, 15 (5): 677–94.

Frost, F., Rann, A. and Chin, A. (2003) *Terrorism in Southeast Asia* (Canberra: Parliament of Australia).

Garden, T. (2002) 'EU Crisis Management: A British View', *Paper presented to a Colloquy held at the Ecole Militaire*, Paris, 31 May, available at: www.tgarden.demon.co.uk/writings/articles/2002/020531eu.html (accessed 27 July 2010).

Gauttier, P. (2004) 'Horizontal coherence and the external competences of the European Union', *European Law Journal*, 10 (1): 23–41.

Gebhard, C. (2009) 'The Crisis Management and Planning Directorate: Recalibrating ESDP Planning and Conduct Capacities', *CFSP Forum*, 7 (4): 8–14.

Gebhard, C. and Norheim-Martinsen, P. M. (2011) 'Making sense of EU comprehensive security: towards conceptual and analytical clarity', *European Security*, 20 (2): 27–43.

Gegout, C. (2005) 'Causes and Consequences of the EU's Military Intervention in the Democratic Republic of Congo: A Realist Explanation', *European Foreign Affairs Review*, 10: 427–43.

Gegout, C. (2007) 'The EU and security in the Democratic Republic of Congo in 2006: Unfinished business', *CFSP Forum*, 4 (6): 5–9.

Gegout, C. (2009) 'EU conflict management in Africa: the limits of an international actor', *Ethnopolitics*, 8 (3): 403–15.

George, A. (2000) 'Peace will herald new Middle East Marshall Plan', *Evening Standard*, 13 September.

GFAP *(General Framework Agreement for Peace in Bosnia and Herzegovina)* (1995) (online), Paris, 15 December, available at: www.ohr.int/dpa/default.asp?content_id=379 (accessed 8 April 2009).

Giegerich, B. (2008a) 'EU Crisis Management: ambitions and achievements', *The Adelphi Papers*, 48 (397): 15–34.

Giegerich, B. (2008b) 'European Military Crisis Management: Connecting ambition and reality', *Adelphi Paper No. 397* (London: IISS/Routledge).

Giegerich, B. (2010) 'Military and Civilian Capabilities for EU-led Crisis-Management Operations', *Adelphi Series*, 50 (414): 41–58.

Ginsberg, R. H. (2001) *The European Union in International Politics: Baptism by Fire* (Oxford: Rowman and Littlefield).

Ginsberg, R. H. and Smith, M. E. (2007) 'Understanding the European Union as a global political actor: theory, practice, and impact', in S. Meunier and M. R. McNamara (eds) *Making History. European Integration and Institutional Change at Fifty* (Oxford: Oxford University Press).

Gleditsch, K. S. (2007) 'Transnational dimensions of civil war', *Journal of Peace Research*, 44(3): 293–309.

Glenny, M. (2001) *The Balkans: Nationalism, War and the Great Powers, 1804–1999* (London: Penguin Books).

Goodhand, J. (2004) 'Afghanistan in Central Asia,' in M. Pugh, N. Cooper and J. Goodhand (eds), *War Economies in a Regional Context: Challenges for Transformation* (Boulder CO: Lynne Rienner).

Gordon, C. (2009) 'The stabilization and association process in the Western Balkans: an effective instrument of post-conflict management?', *Ethnopolitics,* 8 (3): 325–40.

Gordon, S. (2006) 'Exploring the civil–military interface and its impact on European strategic and operational personalities: "Civilianisation" and limiting military roles in stabilisation operations?', *European Security,* 15 (3): 339–61.

Gordon, C., Rodt, A. P. and Wolff, S. (2008) 'Elements of successful EU interventions in conflict regions', *MIRICO, EU* Framework VI WP4 report.

Gordon C. and Sasse, G. (2008) 'The European Neighbourhood Policy: Effective Instrument for Conflict-Management and Democratic Change in the Union's Neighbourhood?', EU FP 6 (MIRICO), Working Paper, EURAC, August 2008, available at: www.eurac.edu/NR/rdonlyress/11B31AB2-FC47-42C1-9168-84E4D4026318/0/Web_del29ENp.pdf

Gordon, C., Sasse, G. and Sebastian, S. (2008) 'EU Policies and the Stabilisation Process', *MIRICO,* EU Framework VI WP4 report.

Gourlay, C. (2004) 'European Union procedures and resources for crisis management', *International Peacekeeping,* 11 (3): 404–21.

Gourlay, C. (2006a) 'Civil–Civil Coordination in EU crisis management', in A. Nowak (ed.) *Civilian Crisis Management: the EU Way* (Paris: EU Institute for Security Studies), pp. 103–22, available at: www.iss.europa.eu/uploads/media/cp090.pdf (accessed 3 August 2010).

Gourlay, C. (2006b), *Lessons Learned Study: Rosters for the Deployment of Civilian Experts in Peace Operations* (Geneva: United Nations Institute for Disarmament Research, UNIDIR), available at: www.crs.state.gov/index.cfm?fuseaction=public.display&shortcut=44FW (accessed 3 August 2010).

Government of Georgia (2010) *State Strategy on Occupied Territories: Engagement through Cooperation* (online), 27 January, available at: www.smr.gov.ge/uploads/file/SMR-Strategy-en.pdf (accessed 3 August 2010).

Gowan, R. (2007) 'The EU's multiple strategic identities: European security after Lebanon and the Congo', *Studia Diplomatica,* LX (1): 59–80.

Grabbe, H. (2006) *The EU's Transformative Power: Europeanization through Conditionality in Central and Eastern Europe* (Basingstoke: Palgrave Macmillan).

Grawert, E. (2008) 'Cross-border dynamics of violent conflict: the case of Sudan and Chad', *Journal of Asian and African Studies,* 43 (6): 595–614.

Grevi, G. (2007) 'Pioneering foreign policy: the EU Special Representatives', *Chaillot Paper 106* (Paris: European Union Institute for Security Studies).

Grevi, G., Helly, D. and Keohane, D. (2009) *ESDP: The first 10 years (1999–2009)* (Paris: EU Institute for Security Studies), available at: www.iss.europa.eu/uploads/media/ESDP_10-web.pdf (accessed 3 August 2010).

Gross, E. (2007) 'Germany and European security and defence cooperation: the Europeanization of national crisis management policies?', *Security Dialogue,* 38 (4): 501–20.

Gross, E. (2008) *EU and the Comprehensive Approach* (Copenhagen: DISS).

Gross, E. (2009) 'Security Sector Reform in Afghanistan: the EU's Contribution', *Occasional Paper no. 78* (Paris: EUISS).

Guthrie, C. and Quinlan, M. (2007) *Just War: The Just War Tradition: Ethics in Modern Warfare* (London: Bloomsbury).

Haaretz, 28 September 2008.

Hadden, T. (ed.) (2009) *A Responsibility to Assist: Human Rights Policy and Practice in European Union Crisis Management Operations* (Oxford: Hart Publishing).

Haine, J.-Y. and Giegerich, B. (2006) 'In Congo, a cosmetic operation', *Herald Tribune* (online) 12 June, available at: www.iiss.org/whats-new/iiss-in-the-press/press-coverage-2006/june-2006/in-congo-a-cosmetic-eu-operation/ (accessed 26 May 2009).

Hannay, D. (2000) 'Europe's common foreign and security policy: Year 1', *European Foreign Affairs Review,* 5 (3): 275–80.

Hannay, D. (2005) *Cyprus: The Search for a Solution* (London: I.B. Tauris).

Hansen, A. S. (2006) *Against All Odds – The Evolution of Planning for ESDP Operations. Civilian Crisis Management from EUPM Onwards* (Berlin: Zentrum für Internationale Friedenseinsätze).

Hardt, H. (2009) 'Rapid response or evasive action? Regional organization responses to peace operation demands', *European Security*, 18 (4): 383–415.

Harton, N. (2004) 'EU troops prepare for Bosnia swap', *BBC news* (online) 23 October, available at: news.bbc.co.uk/1/hi/world/europe/3944191.stm (accessed 8 April 2009).

Hatzivassiliou, E. (1997) *Britain and the International Status of Cyprus, 1955–59* (Minnesota: University of Minnesota).

Hazelzet, Hadewych (2006) 'Human rights aspects of EU crisis management operations: from nuisance to necessity', *International Peacekeeping*, 13 (4): 564–81.

Herrera, J. (2008) First Secretary of the French Embassy in Beirut, spoke at the Carnegie Middle East Center's roundtable on 'European Policies toward Lebanon, Syria and the Palestinian Territories: Challenges and Opportunities', 11 September. Reported in *the Daily Star*, 12 September 2008.

Hill, C. (1993) 'The capability—expectations gap, or conceptualising Europe's international role', *Journal of Common Market Studies*, 31 (3): 305–28.

Hill, C. (2001) 'The EU's capacity for conflict prevention', *European Foreign Affairs Review*, 6 (3): 315–333.

Hills, A. (2001) 'The inherent limits of military forces in policing peace operations', *International Peacekeeping*, 8 (3): 79–98.

Hoebeke, H., Carette, S. and Vlassenroot, K. (2007) *EU Support to the Democratic Republic of Congo* (Brussels: IRRI-KIIB).

Hofmann, A. and Wessels, W. (2008) 'Der Vertrag von Lissabon – eine tragfähige and abschließende Antwort auf konstitutionelle Grundfragen?', *Integration*, 1: 3–20.

Holbrooke, R. (1999) *To End a War* (New York: Random House).

Holland, R. (1998) *Britain and the Revolt in Cyprus, 1954–59* (Oxford: Clarendon Press).

Holliday, G. (ed.) (2004) *EU Enlargement and Minority Rights* (Flensburg: European Centre for Minority Issues).

Holzgrefe, J. L. and Keohane, R. O. (2003) *Humanitarian Intervention: Ethical, Legal and Political Dilemmas* (Cambridge: Cambridge University Press).

Homan, K. (2007) 'Operation Artemis in the Democratic Republic of Congo', in A. Ricci and E. Kytoemaa (eds) *Faster and More United? The Debate about Europe's Crisis Response Capacity* (Brussels: European Communities Commission, Directorate General for External Relations).

Horewitz, D. (1985) *Ethnic Groups in Conflict* (Berkeley, CA: University of California Press).

House of Commons Defence Committee (2008) *The Future of NATO and European Defence* (London: HMSO).

House of Lords (European Union Committee) (2007) *The EU and the Middle East Peace Process*, Volume I: Report (London: House of Lords).

House of Lords European Union Committee (2009) *Civil Protection and Crisis Management in the European Union* (London: HMSO).

Howorth, J. (2000) 'Britain, NATO and CESDP: fixed strategy, changing tactics', *European Foreign Affairs Review*, 5 (3): 377–96.

Howorth, J., (2003) 'France, Britain and the Euro-Atlantic crisis', *Survival: Global Politics and Strategy*, 45 (4): 173 – 92.

Howorth, J. (2003b) 'ESDP and NATO', *Cooperation and Conflict*, 38 (3): 235–54.

Howorth, J. (2007) *Security and Defence Policy in the EU* (Basingstoke: Palgrave).

Howorth, J. and Le Gloannec, A.M. (2007) 'The Institutional Logic behind the EEAS', in *EPC Working Paper*, 28.

Howorth, J., and Menon, A. (2009) 'Still not pushing back.' *Journal of Conflict Resolution*, 53 (5): 727–44.

Hughes, J., Sasse, G. and Gordon, C. (2004) *Europeanization and Regionalization in the EU's Enlargement to Central and Eastern Europe: The Myth of Conditionality* (Basingstoke: Palgrave).

Ilievski, Z., and Taleski, D. (2009) 'Was the EU's role in conflict management in Macedonia a success?' *Ethnopolitics,* 8 (3): 355–67.

Independent International Fact-Finding Mission on the Conflict in Georgia (2009) Report (Brussels).

International Crisis Group (2000) *Scramble for the Congo: Anatomy of an Ugly War* (Brussels, 20 December).

International Crisis Group (2001) *EU Crisis Response Capability: Institutions and Processes for Conflict Prevention and Management* (Brussels, 26 June).

International Crisis Group (2004) 'EUFOR-IA: Changing Bosnia's security arrangements', *Europe Briefing,* 31 (online), available at: www.crisisgroup.org/home/index.cfm?id=2833&l=1 (accessed 8 April 2009).

International Crisis Group (2005a) *Conflict history: Macedonia* (online), available at: www. crisisgroup.org/home/index.cfm?action=conflict_search&l=1&t=1&c_country=66 (accessed 29 February 2008).

International Crisis Group (2005b) 'EU crisis response revisited', *Europe Report,* 160 (online), available at: www.crisisgroup.org/home/index.cfm?id=3220 (accessed 1 June 2009).

International Crisis Group (2005c) *EU Crisis Response Capability Revisited,* (Brussels, 17 January).

International Crisis Group (2006) 'Conflict resolution in the South Caucasus: The EU's Role,' in *Europe Report* No. 173 (Brussels, 20 March).

International Crisis Group (2007) 'Reforming Afghanistan's Police', *Asia Report no. 138* (Brussels/ Kabul, August).

International Crisis Group (2008a) 'Afghanistan: The Need for International Resolve', *Asia Report no. 145* (Brussels/Kabul, February).

International Crisis Group (2008b) 'Central African Republic: Untangling the political dialogue', *Africa Briefing,* 155 (online), available at: www.crisisgroup.org/home/index.cfm?id=5800&l=1 (accessed 8 April 2009).

International Crisis Group (2008c) 'Chad: A new conflict resolution framework', *Africa Report,* 144 (online), available at: www.crisisgroup.org/home/index.cfm?id=5994&l=1 (accessed 8 April 2009).

International Crisis Group (2008d) 'Georgia: The Risks of Winter', *Europe Briefing no. 51,* 26 November.

International Crisis Group (2008e) *Conflict history: Chad* (online), available at: www.crisisgroup.org/ home/index.cfm?action=conflict_search&l=1&t=1&c_country=25 (accessed 29 January 2009).

International Crisis Group (2008f) *Conflict history: Democratic Republic of Congo* (online), available at: www.crisisgroup.org/home/index.cfm?action=conflict_search&l=1&t=1&c_country= 37 (accessed 29 January 2009).

International Crisis Group (2008g) *Conflict history: Kosovo* (online) February, available at: www. crisisgroup.org/home/index.cfm?action=conflict_search&l=1&t=1&c_country=58 (accessed 17 April 2009).

International Crisis Group (2008h) 'Russia vs. Georgia: The Fallout,' *Europe Report* no. 195, (Brussels, 22 August).

International Crisis Group (2009a) *Central African Republic* (online), available at: www.crisisgroup. org/home/index.cfm?id=5256&l=1 (accessed 29 January 2009).

International Crisis Group (2009b) 'Chad: Powder keg in the East', *Africa Report,* 149 (online), available at: www.crisisgroup.org/home/index.cfm?id=6055&l=1 (accessed 16 April 2009).

International Crisis Group (2009c) *Crisis in Darfur* (online), March, available at: www.crisisgroup. org/home/index.cfm?id=3060&l=1 (accessed 14 April 2009).

International Crisis Group (2009d) 'Macedonia's name: breaking the deadlock', *Europe Briefing,* 52 (online), Brussels, available at: www.crisisgroup.org/home/index.cfm?id=5862 (accessed 13 July 2009).

International Crisis Group (2009e) 'Bosnia's incomplete transition: Between Dayton and Europe', *Europe Report,* 189, Brussels, available at: www.crisisgroup.org/home/index.cfm?id=5978&1=1

International Crisis Group (2010) 'Reforming Afghanistan's Broken Judiciary', *Asia Report* No. 195 (Brussels: International Crisis Group).

Ioannides, I. (2007) 'Police mission in Macedonia' in M. Emerson and E. Gross (eds) *Evaluating the EU's Crisis Missions in the Balkans* (Brussels: Centre for European Policy Studies).

Irondelle, B. and Mérand, F. (2010) 'France's return to NATO: the death knell for ESDP?', *European Security,* 19 (1): 29–43.

ISAF (2009a) *COMISAF's Initial Assessment* (Kabul, 30 August).

ISAF (2009b) *ISAF Commander's Counterinsurgency Guidance* (online), available at: www.nato.int/isaf/docu/official_texts/counterinsurgency_guidance.pdf (accessed 24 July 2010).

ISAF (2010) *International Security and Assistance Force (ISAF): Facts and Figures* (online) 1 February, available at: www.nato.int/isaf/docu/epub/pdf/placemat.pdf (accessed 24 July 2010).

ISIS (International Security Information Service) (2003) *'Operation Concordia and Berlin Plus: NATO and the EU take stock',* NATO notes, 5 (8).

Jaanson, L. (2008) *Learning by doing. EU-Sonderbeauftragte in der Region des Westlichen Balkans* (Berlin: Stiftung Wissenschaft und Politik).

Jacoby, W. and Jones, C. (2008) 'The EU Battle Groups in Sweden and the Czech Republic: What national defense reforms tell us about European rapid reaction capabilities', *European Security,* 17 (2): 315–38.

Jakobsen, P. V. (2006) 'The ESDP and civilian rapid reaction: adding value is harder than expected', *European Security,* 15 (4): 299–321.

Jakobsen, P. V. (2008) 'NATO's Comprehensive Approach to Crisis Response Operations: A Work in Slow Progress', *DIIS Report 2008: 15* (Copenhagen: Danish Institute for International Studies).

Jerusalem Post, 5 January 2009.

Joint Declaration on European Defence (1998) (St. Malo, 4 December).

Jones, R. (2001) *The Politics and Economics of the European Union* (Cheltenham: Edward Elgar Publishing Ltd).

Juncos, A. (2007) 'Police Mission in Bosnia and Herzegovina', in M. Emerson and E. Gross (eds) *Evaluating the EU's Crisis Missions in the Balkans* (Brussels: Centre for European Policy Studies).

Juncos, A. E. and Reynolds, C. (2007) 'The Political and Security Committee: governing in the shadow', *European Foreign Affairs Review,* 12 (2): 127–47.

Kaufman, S. J. (2001) *Modern Hatreds: The Symbolic Politics of Ethnic War* (Ithaka, NY: Cornell University Press).

Keinon, H., Hoffman, G. and Radler, M. (2003) 'Seven days', *The Jerusalem Post,* 31 October, p. 5.

Kemp, W. A. (2004) 'The business of ethnic conflict', *Security Dialogue,* 35 (1): 43–59.

Kemp, W. A. (2005) 'Selfish determination: the questionable ownership of autonomy movements', *Ethnopolitics,* 4 (1): 85–99.

Ker-Lindsay, J. (2004) *Britain and the Cyprus Crisis, 1963–64* (Mannheim: Bibliopolis).

Keukeleire, S. and MacNaughtan, J. (2008) *The Foreign Policy of the European Union* (Basingstoke: Palgrave Macmillan).

Khatib, K. (2009) *'How Promotion of Political Reform by the European Union is Perceived in the Arab World: The Cases of Lebanon and the Palestinian Territories'*, International Institute for Democracy and Electoral Assistance, Stockholm.

King, C. (1999) *The Moldovans: Romania, Russia and the Politics of Culture* (Stanford, CA: Hoover Institution).

Kintis, A. G. (1997) 'The EU's foreign policy and the war in former Yugoslavia', in M. Holland (ed.) *Common Foreign and Security Policy* (London: Pinter).

Knutsen, B. O. (2009) 'The EU's security and defense policy (ESDP) and the challenges of civil–military coordination (CMCO): the case of the Democratic Republic of Congo (DRC).' *European Security*: 441 – 59.

Kohl, R. (2006) 'Civil military co-ordination in EU crisis management', in A. Nowak (ed.) *Civilian Crisis Management: the EU Way* (Paris: European Union Institute for Security Studies).

Korski, D. and Gowan, R. (2009) *Can the EU Rebuild Failing States? A Review of Europe's Civilian Capacities* (Brussels: European Council on Foreign Relations).

Krause, A. (2003) 'Die EU als friedenspolitischer Akteur in Afrikas Region der Großen Seen–eine Bilanz', in Bonn International Centre for Conversion (*et al.*) (ed.) *Friedensgutachten 2003* (Münster: LIT Verlag).

Krause, A. and Schlotter, P. (2007) 'Die Kommission als "Politikunternehmer" - Die Europäische Union als außen- und sicherheitspolitischer Akteur im Kongo', in M. Jopp and P. Schlotter (eds) *Kollektive Außenpolitik–Die Europäische Union als internationaler Akteur* (Baden-Baden: Nomos).

Kronenberger, V. and Wouters, J. (eds) (2004) *The EU and Conflict Prevention* (The Hague: TMC Asser Press).

Kronenberger, V. and Wouters, J. (eds) (2005) *The EU and Conflict Prevention: Policy and Legal Aspects* (The Hague: Asser Press).

Kuchler, F. (2008) *The Role of the European Union in Moldova's Transnistria Conflict* (Stuttgart: Ibidem-Verlag).

Lake, D. A. and Morgan, P. M. (1997) *Regional Orders: Building Security in a New World* (State College: Pennsylvania State University Press).

Lake, D. A. and Rothchild, D. (1996) 'Containing fear: the origins and management of ethnic conflict', *International Security,* 21 (2): 41–75.

Landgraf, M. (1998) 'Peace-building and conflict prevention in Africa: a view from the European Commission', in U. Engel and A. Mehler (eds) *Gewaltsame Konflikte und ihre Prävention in Afrika* (Hamburg: Institut für Afrika-Kunde).

Larsen, H., (2002) 'The EU: A Global Military Actor?' *Cooperation and Conflict,* 37 (3): 283–302.

Law, D. M. (2007) 'Intergovernmental organisations and their role in security sector reform', in D. M. Law (ed.) *Intergovernmental Organisations and Security Sector Reform* (Zürich: LIT Verlag).

Le More, A. (2005) 'Killing with kindness: funding the demise of a Palestinian State', *International Affairs,* 81 (5): 983–1001.

Lemer, J. (2009) 'Sarkozy and Merkel call for further six months on A400M project', *Financial Times,* 11 June.

Leonard, M. and Popescu, N. (2008). *A Power Audit of EU-Russia Relations* (London: European Council on Foreign Relations).

Levy, J. S. (2001) 'Theories of interstate and intrastate war: a levels-of-analysis approach,' in C. A. Crocker, F. O. (eds) Hampson and P. Aall, *Turbulent Peace: The Challenges of Managing International Conflict* (Washington, DC: United States Institute of Peace Press).

Lewis, J. (2003) 'Institutional environments and everyday EU decision-making: rationalist or constructivist?' *Comparative Political Studies*, 36 (1/2): 97–124.

Lindstrom, G. (2007) *Enter the EU Battlegroups* (Paris: European Union Institute for Security Studies).

Lintonen, R., (2004) 'Understanding EU crisis decision-making: the case of Chechnya and the Finnish Presidency,' *Journal of Contingencies and Crisis Management,* 12 (1): 29–38.

Lippert, B. (2007) 'Beefing up the ENP: toward a modernisation and stability partnership,' in J. Varwick and K. O. Lang (eds) *European Neighbourhood Policy: Challenges for the EU–Policy Towards the New Neighbours* (Opladen: Budrich).

Lobell, S. E. and Mauceri, P. (2004) *Ethnic Conflict and International Politics* (Basingstoke: Palgrave Macmillan).

Lobjakas, A. (2010) 'EU Plans to Scrap South Caucasus, Moldova Envoys', *Radio Free Europe Radio Liberty* (online) 31 May, available at: www.rferl.org/content/EU_Plans_To_Scrap_South_Caucasus_Moldova_Envoys/2057672.html (accessed 27 July 2010).

Longhurst, K., and Miskimmon, A. (2007) 'Same challenges, diverging responses: Germany, the UK and European security', *German Politics,* 16 (1): 79 – 94.

Lucarelli, S. (2006) 'Introduction', in S. Lucarelli and I. Manners (eds) *Values and Principles of European Union Foreign Policy* (London: Routledge).

Ludlow, D. J. (2003) 'Preventative peacemaking in Macedonia: An assessment of UN good offices diplomacy', *Brigham Young Law Review* (online), available at: www.law2.byu.edu/lawreview/archives/2003/2/LUD.pdf (accessed 27 July 2009).

Lutterbeck, D. (2004) 'Between Police and Military: The new security agenda and the rise of Gendarmeries', *Cooperation and Conflict*, 39 (1): 45–68.

Lynch, D. (2004) *Engaging Eurasia's Separatist States—Unresolved Conflicts and De Facto States* (Washington, DC: United States Institute of Peace Press).

Maas, C. (2007) 'Afghanistan: Staatsaufbau ohne Staat', *SWP Studie 2007/S04* (Berlin: Stiftung Wissenschaft und Politik).

Mace, C. (2004) 'Operation Concordia: developing a "European" approach to crisis management?', *International Peacekeeping*, 11 (3): 474–90.

McLoughlin, M. (1998) 'The role of a Special Envoy in the development of the CFSP: case of the Special Envoy for the Great Lakes region Brussels', *Working Document of the European Commission*.

Magen, A. (2006) *The Shadow of Enlargement: Can the European Neighbourhood Policy Achieve Compliance?*, European Legal Studies Center, Columbia University.

Mahncke, D., Ambos, A. and Reynolds, C. (eds) (2004.) *European Foreign Policy: From Rhetoric to Reality* (Frankfurt: Peter Lang).

Makovsky, D. (1997) 'EU wrote letter of Hebron assurance to Arafat', *The Jerusalem Post*, 10 February.

Manners, I. (2002) 'Normative power Europe: a contradiction in terms?', *Journal of Common Market Studies*, 40 (2): 235–58.

Marchal, R. (2008) 'The roots of the Darfur conflict and the Chadian civil war', *Public Culture*, 20 (3): 429–36.

Markides, D. W. (2001) *Cyprus 1957–1963: From Colonial Conflict to Constitutional Crisis: The Key Role of the Municipal Issue* (Minnesota: University of Minnesota).

Marsh, S. and Mackenstein, H. (2005) *The International Relations of the European Union* (Harlow: Longman).

Mattelaer, A. (2008) 'The strategic planning of EU military operations: the case of EUFOR Chad/CAR', *IES working paper*, 5/2008 (online), Brussels, available at: www.ies.be/files/repo/IES%20working%20paper%205_Alexander%20Mattelaer.pdf (accessed 1 June 2009).

Médard, J.-F. (2005) 'France and sub-Saharan Africa: A privileged relationship', in U. Engel and G. R. Olsen (eds) *Africa and the North. Between Globalization and Marginalization* (London: Routledge).

Meier, V. (1999) *Yugoslavia* (London: Routledge).

Menon, A. (2005) 'From crisis to carthasis: ESDP after Iraq', *International Affairs*, 80 (4): 631–48.

Menon, A. (2009) 'Empowering paradise? The ESDP at ten', *International Affairs*, 85 (2): 227–46.

Menon, A. and Sedelmeier, U. (2010) 'Instruments and intentionality: civilian crisis management and enlargement conditionality in EU security policy.' *West European Politics*, 33 (1): 75–92.

Mérand, F., Bonneu, M. and Faure, S. (2009) 'What do ESDP actors want? An exploratory analysis', *European Security*, 18 (3): 327–44.

Merlingen, M. and Ostrauskaite, R. (2005) 'ESDP Police Missions, meaning, context and operational challenges', *European Foreign Affairs Review*, 10 (1): 215–35.

Merlingen, M. and Ostrauskaite, R. (eds) (2008) *European Security and Defence Policy: An Implementation Perspective* (Oxon: Routledge).

Mideast Mirror (1998) 'Jerusalem "not keen" on EU peace-brokering role', 12 (17), 27 January.

Miliband, D. (2010) 'How to end the war in Afghanistan', *New York Review of Books*, 29 April.

Mirimanova, N. (2010) 'Civil Society Building Peace in the European Neighbourhood: towards a new framework for joining forces with the EU', *MICROCON Policy Working Paper* 10, March.

Missiroli, A. (2001) 'European security policy: the challenge of coherence', *European Foreign Affairs Review*, 6 (2): 177–96.

Missiroli, A. (2007) 'Introduction: a tale of two pillars – and an arch', *EPC Working Paper*, 28, 9–27.

Missiroli, A. (2008). *The Impact of the Lisbon Treaty on ESDP* (Brussels: European Parliament Policy Department External Policies).

Moller, B. (2002) 'Europe and the crises in the Great Lakes region', *Strategic Review for Southern Africa (Pretoria)*, 24 (1): 27–62.

Moratinos, M. A. (2002) 'Account of the Taba talks of January 2001', *Haaretz*, 14 February.

Morris, N. (2004) 'Humanitarian intervention in the Balkans', in J. Welsh (ed.) *Humanitarian Intervention and International Relations* (Oxford: Oxford University Press).

Morsut, C. (2009) 'Effective multilateralism? EU–UN cooperation in the DRC, 2003–2006', *International Peacekeeping*, 16 (2): 261–72

Müller-Brandeck-Bocquet, G. (2002) 'The new CFSP and ESDP decision-making system of the European Union', *European Foreign Affairs Review*, 7 (3): 257–82.

Muguruza, C. A. (2003) 'The European Union and humanitarian intervention in Kosovo: a test for the Common Foreign Policy', in F. Bieber and Z. Daskalovaki (eds) *Understanding the War in Kosovo* (London: Frank Cass).

Murithi, T. (2008) 'The African Union's evolving role in peace operations: the African Union Mission in Burundi, the African Union Mission in Sudan and the African Union Mission in Somalia', *African Security Review*, 17 (1): 70–82.

Nash, P. (2008) *EUFOR Chad/CAR Press Conference* (online), available at: www.military.ie/overseas/ops/africa/chad/index.htm (accessed 8 April 2009).

NATO (2004) *NATO's future role in Bosnia and Herzegovina* (online), available at: www.nato.int/docu/update/2004/12-december/e1202b.htm (accessed 29 January 2009).

NATO (2005) *SFOR* (online), available at: www.nato.int/sfor/index.htm (accessed 29 January 2009).

NATO (2006a) 'Strategic airlift agreement enters into force', *NATO Update*.

NATO (2006b) 'Building on Success: The London Conference on Afghanistan', *The Afghanistan Compact* (online), London, January, available at: www.nato.int/isaf/docu/epub/pdf/afghanistan_compact.pdf (accessed 24 July 2010).

NATO (2006c) *NATO Handbook* (Brussels: NATO Public Diplomacy Division).

NATO (2008) 'Bucharest Summit Declaration', *Press Release (2008) 049* (online), 3 April, available at: www.nato.int/cps/en/natolive/official_texts_8443.htm (accessed 24 July 2010).

NATO (2009) *ISAF mandate* (online), 29 April, available at: www.nato.int/isaf/topics/mandate/index.html (accessed 24 July 2010).

NATO (n.d.–a) 'EU–NATO Declaration on ESDP', available at: nids.hq.nato.int/docu/pr/2002/p02-142e.htm

NATO (n.d.–b) 'NATO–EU: A strategic partnership', available at: www.nato.int/issues/nato-eu/evolution.html

Nest, M. (2001) 'Ambitions, profits and loss: Zimbabwean economic involvement in the Democratic Republic of Congo', *African Affairs*, 100: 469–90.

Neugart, F. (2003) 'Nahost- und Mittelmeerpolitik', in W. Weidenfeld and W. Wessels (eds) *Jahrbuch der Europäischen Integration 2002/2003* (Bonn: Europa Union Verlag).

Neugart, F. (2006) 'Nahost- und Mittelmeerpolitik', in W. Weidenfeld and W. Wessels (eds) *Jahrbuch der Europäischen Integration 2006* (Baden-Baden: Nomos).

New York Times (2010) *U.S. Envoy's Cables Show Worries on Afghan Plans* (New York, 26 January).

Nolan, S. (1997) 'Optimistic talk of progress on peace proved premature', *The Independent*, 31 July.

Nonneman, G. (2003) 'A European view of the US role in the Israeli–Palestinian conflict' in M. Ortega (ed.) *The European Union and the Crisis in the Middle East*, Chaillot Paper 62 (Paris: European Union Institute for Security Studies).

Norheim-Martinsen, P. M. (2009) *Matching Ambition with Institutional Innovation: The EU's Comprehensive Approach and Civil–Military Organisation* (Oslo: Norwegian Defence Research Establishment).

Nowak, A. (ed.) (2006) *Civilian Crisis Management: the EU Way* (Paris: European Union Institute for Security Studies), available at: www.iss.europa.eu/uploads/media/ESDP_10-web.pdf (accessed 3 August 2010).

Nuttall, S. (2001) '"Consistency" and the CFSP: A Categorization and its Consequences', EFPU Working Paper 2001/3 (London: LSE).

Nuttall, S. J. (1992) *European Political Cooperation* (Oxford: Clarendon Press).

Nye, J. S. (1990) 'Soft power', *Foreign Policy*, 80: 153–71.

Office of the High Representative (2009) *Office of the High Representative and European Union Special Representative* (online), available at: www.ohr.int/ (accessed 26 January 2009).

Oguzlu, T. (2001) 'A confederal Cyprus as a member of the European Union', *The International Spectator: Italian Journal of International Affairs*, 36 (4): 89–100.

Olsen, G. R. (2002) 'The EU and conflict management in African emergencies', *International Peacekeeping* 9 (3): 87–102.

Olsen, G. R. (2006) 'The Africa-Europe (Cairo summit) process. An expression of "symbolic politics"', in H. Hänggi, R. Roloff and J. Rüland (eds) *Interregionalism and International Relations* (New York: Routledge).

Olsen, G. R. (2008) 'Coherence, consistency and political will in foreign policy: The European Union's policy towards Africa', *Perspectives on European Politics and Society,* 9 (2): 157–71.

Olsen, G. R. (2009) "The EU and military conflict management in Africa: for the good of Africa or Europe?" *International Peacekeeping* 16 (2): 245–60.

Olsen, G. R. and Pilegaard, J. (2005) 'The costs of Non-Europe? Denmark and the Common Security and Defence Policy', *European Security,* 14 (3): 339–60.

Ortega, M. (2003) 'Conclusion: peace lies in their hands', in M. Ortega (ed.) *The European Union and the Crisis in the Middle East,* Chaillot Paper 62 (Paris: European Union Institute for Security Studies).

OSCE Mission to Moldova (2010) *Conflict resolution and negotiation* (online), available at: www.osce.org/moldova/13426.html (accessed 27 July 2010).

Otunnu, O. A. and Doyle, M. W. (1998) *Peacemaking and Peacekeeping for the New Century* (Lanham, MD: Rowman and Littlefield).

Oxfam International (2008) 'Mission incomplete: why civilians remain at risk in eastern Chad', *Oxfam Briefing Paper*, September.

Pace, M. (2007) 'The construction of EU normative power', *Journal of Common Market Studies*, 45 (4): 1041–64.

Pace, R. (2002) 'A small state and the European Union: Malta's EU accession experience', *South European Society and Politics*, 7 (1): 24–42.

Partnership and Cooperation Agreement (1994) signed by the European Union and the Republic of Moldova, 28 November, available at: www.eubam.org/files/0-99/73/pca-moldova-eng.pdf (accessed 27 July 2010).

Patrick, S. (2009) 'Out of Area, Out of Business?', *National Interest online*, 25 March.

Peace Agreement (2008) *Submitted by M. Nicolas Sarkozy to President of Georgia Mikhaïl Saakachvili and President of Russia Dmitri Medvedev*, Paris, 14 August 2008, available at: www.ambafrance-us.org/IMG/pdf/accord6points.pdf (accessed 3 August 2010).

Peace Implementation Council (2009a) *Statement by the Ambassadors of the Peace Implementation Council's Steering Board: Ambassador Valentin Inzko appointed as the next High Representative* (online), 13 March, available at: www.ohr.int/pic/default.asp?content_id=43178 (accessed 14 April 2009).

Peace Implementation Council (2009b) *Communiqué of the Steering Board of the Peace Implementation Council* (online), 26 March, available at: www.ohr.int/pic/default.asp?content_id=43264 (accessed 14 April 2009).

Peace Implementation Council (2009c) *Communiqué of the Steering Board of the Peace Implementation Council* (online), 30 June. Available at: www.ohr.int/pic/default.asp?content_id=43665 (accessed 10 July 2009).

Peck, C. (2004) 'Special Representatives of the Secretary General', in D. M. Malone (ed.) *The UN Security Council. From the Cold War to the 21st Century (*Boulder, CO: Lynne Rienner).

Pelletreau, R. H. (1998) 'The US, Britain and Europe: Prospects for a joint approach to the Middle East', *Mideast Mirror*, 12: 55.

Pentland, P. C. (2003) 'The EU and Southeastern Europe after Dayton', *Europe–Russia Working Chapters,* January (Ottowa: Carleton University).

Peral, L. (2009) 'EUPOL Afghanistan', in G. Grevi, D. Keohane and D. Helly (eds) *European Security and Defense Policy: The First 10 Years (1999–2009)* (Paris: EU Institute for Security Studies).

Piana, C. (2002) 'The EU's decision-making process in the Common Foreign and Security Policy: the case of the Former Yugoslav Republic of Macedonia', *European Foreign Affairs Review*, 7 (2): 209–26.

Piiparinen, T. (2008) 'Pushing the boundaries of the possible at the margins of peacekeeping: the promises of ESDP–Russia co-operation for humanitarian intervention', *Global Society,* 22 (2): 277–95.

Pineau, E. (2008) 'Sarkozy condemns Sudan over French EU soldier death', *Reuters* (online), 7 March, available at: www.alertnet.org/thenews/newsdesk/L07840405.htm (accessed 24 July 2009).

Pirozzi, N. (2009) *EU support to African security architecture: funding and training components* (Paris: European Institute for Security Studies, Occasional paper, no. 76).

Pop, V. (2009a) 'EU–Moldova relations linked to electoral conduct', *EU Observer* (online), 28 July, available at: euobserver.com/15/28497 (accessed 27 July 2010).

Pop, V. (2009b) 'EU mission in Chad ends amid tensions', *EU Observer* (online), 12 March, available at: euobserver.com/9/27766?print=1 (accessed 13 March 2009).

Popescu, N. (2005) *'The EU in Moldova – Settling Conflict in the Neighbourhood'*, Occasional Paper 60, European Union Institute for Security Studies, Paris, October. Available at: www.iss.europa.eu/uploads/media/occ60.pdf (accessed 27 July 2010).

Popescu, N. (2006a) *The EU and South Caucasus: Learning Lessons from Moldova and Ukraine,* CPS International Policy Fellowships Programme.

Popescu, N. (2006b) *The EU and Transnistria,* CPS International Policy Fellowships Programme.

Popescu, N. (2009) 'EU and the Eastern Neighbourhood: reluctant involvement in conflict resolution', *European Foreign Affairs Review*, 14: 457–77.

Posen, B. R. 2006. 'European Union Security and Defense Policy: response to unipolarity?' *Security Studies,* 15 (2): 149–86.

Pottier, J. (2008) 'Displacement and ethnic reintegration in Ituri, DR Congo: challenges ahead', *The Journal of Modern African Studies*, 46 (3): 427–50.

Protsyk, O. (2006) 'Moldova's Dilemmas in Democratizing and Reintegrating Transnistria', *European Centre for Minority Issues* (online), available at: www.ecmimoldova.org/fileadmin/ecmimoldova.org/docs/ProtsykMolDilemmainTransnistriaApril06.pdf (accessed 27 July 2010).

Prunier, G. (2009) *Africa's World War: Congo, The Rwandan Genocide, and The Making of a Continental Catastrophe* (Oxford: Oxford University Press).

Pugh, Michael, and Singh Sidhu, W.P. (2003) *The United Nations and Regional Security: Europe and Beyond* (Boulder, CO: Lynne Rienner).

Putnam, R. (1988) 'Diplomacy and domestic politics: the logic of two-level games', *International Organization*, 42 (3): 427–60.

Quille, G. (2010) 'The European External Action Service and the Common Security and Defence Policy (CSDP)' in E. Greco, N. Pirozzi and S. Silvestri (eds) *EU Crisis Management: Institutions and Capabilities in the Making*, IAI Quaderni. English Series, No. 19, available at: www.iai,it/content.asp?langid=1&contentid=619

Quille, G, Gasparini, G., Menotti, R. and Pirozzi, N. (2006) *Developing EU Civil–Military Coordination: The Role of the New Civilian Military Cell* (Brussels: ISIS Europe/CeMiSS).

Radio Free Europe (2008) 'EU Mission Head Explains Monitors' Role in Georgia', *Interview with Hansjorg Haber* (online), 4 November, available at: www.rferl.org/content/EU_Mission_Head_Explains_Monitors_Role_In_Georgia/1338281.html (accessed 27 July 2010).

Radio Free Europe (2009) *Moldovan Leader Lauds Russia Over Rebel Region* (online), 19 March, available at: www.rferl.org/content/Moldovan_Leader_Lauds_Russia_Over_Rebel_Region/1513368. html (accessed 27 July 2010).

Ramsbotham, O., Woodhouse, T. and Miall, H. (2005) *Contemporary Conflict Resolution* (Cambridge: Polity).

Ramsbotham, A., Bah, A. M. S. and Calder, F. (2005) 'Enhancing African peace and security capacity: a useful role for the UK and the G8?', *International Affairs*, 81 (2): 325–39.

Rashid, A. (2002) *Taliban: Islam, Oil and the New Great Game in Central Asia* (London: I. B. Tauris Publishers).

Rashid, A. (2008) *Descent into Chaos: How the War Against Islamic Extremism is Being Lost in Pakistan, Afghanistan and Central Asia* (London: Allen Lane).

Regelsberger, E. (1997) 'Gemeinsame Außen– und Sicherheitspolitik', in W. Weidenfeld and W. Wessels (eds) *Jahrbuch der Europäischen Integration 1996/97* (Bonn: Europa Union Verlag).

Reichwein, A. and Schlotter, P. (2007) 'Auf dem Weg zu einem kollektiven Akteur? Die EU-Politik gegenüber Mazedonien', in M. Jopp and P. Schlotter (eds) *Kollektive Außenpolitik - Die Europäische Union als internationaler Akteur* (Baden-Baden: Nomos).

Relief Web (2009) *EU-funded pickups to help Palestinian Civil Police deliver better service* (online) 19 August, available at: wwww.reliefweb.int/rw/rwb.nsf/db900sid/JBRN-7V3DW2?OpenDocument (accessed 22 July 2010).

Research and Documentation Centre Sarajevo (2007) *Human Losses in Bosnia–Herzegovina 1991– 1995: Research findings* (online), available at: www.idc.org.ba/presentation/research_results.htm (accessed 4 April 2009).

Reuters (2004) *Greek Cypriots May Pay Price if They Thwart UN Plan*, 15 April.

Ricci, A. and Kytoemaa, E. (2007) *Faster and More United? The Debate about Europe's Crisis Response Capacity* (Brussels: European Communities Commission, Directorate General for External Relations).

Rieker, P. (2009) 'The EU — a capable security actor? Developing administrative capabilities', *Journal of European Integration,* 31 (6): 703–19.

Rijks, D. and Whitman, R. (2007) 'European diplomatic representation in third countries: trends and options', *EPC Working Paper*, 28, 35–47.

Robertson, G. (2003) *Speech at the EU welcoming ceremony* (online), Skopje, 31 March, available at: consilium.europa.eu/uedocs/cmsUpload/Speech%20of%20NATO%20SG%20Robert son.pdf (accessed 29 January 2009).

Rodt, A. P., and Wolff, S. (2010) 'The reactive crisis management of the European Union in the Western Balkans: policy objectives, capabilities and effectiveness' in U. Rabi (ed.) *International Intervention in Local Conflicts: Crisis Management and Conflict Resolution since the Cold War* (London: I. B. Taurus).

Roper, S. D. (2002) 'Regionalism in Moldova: the case of Transnistria and Gagauzia', in J. Hughes and G. Sasse (eds) *Ethnicity and Territory in the Former Soviet Union: Regions in Conflict* (London: Frank Cass).

Rotberg, R. I. (ed.) (2004) *When States Fail: Causes and Consequences* (Princeton: Princeton University Press).

Roy, O. (2004) 'Afghanistan: la difficile reconstuction d'un Etat', *Chaillot Paper no. 73*, (Paris: European Union Institute for Security Studies).

Rubin, B. (2001) 'Conceptual overview of the origin, structure, and dynamics of regional conflict formations', in *Conference on Regional Conflict Formation in the Great Lakes Region of Central Africa: Structure, Dynamics and Challenges for Policy*. Safari Park Hotel, Nairobi, Kenya.

Salmon, T. (2005) 'The European Security and Defence Policy: built on rock or sand?', *European Foreign Affairs Review,* 10: 359–79.

Salmon, T. and Shepherd, A. (2003) *Toward a European Army: A Military Power in the Making?* (Boulder: Lynne Rienner).

Sasse, G. (2008) 'The European Neighbourhood Policy: conditionality revisited for the EU's Eastern Neighbours', *Europe–Asia Studies,* 60 (2), 295–316.

Sasse, G., Hughes, J. and Gordon, C. (2004) *Europeanization and Regionalization in EU's Enlargement to Central and Eastern Europe: The Myth of Conditionality* (Basingstoke: Palgrave).

Scherrer, C. P. (2003) *Structural Prevention of Ethnic Violence* (Basingstoke: Palgrave).

Schneckener, U. (2001) 'EU crisis management in Macedonia', *Transatlantic Internationale Politik,* 2 (3): 90–94.

Schneckener, U. (2002) 'Developing and Applying EU Crisis Management: Test Case Macedonia', *ECMI Working Paper no. 14* (Flensburg: European Centre for Minority Issues).

Schulze, K. (2007) *Mission Not So Impossible: The Aceh Monitoring Mission and Lessons Learned for the EU* (Friedrich Ebert Stiftung, July).

Schuwirth, R. (2002) 'Hitting the Helsinki Headline Goal', *NATO Review* (online), Autumn, available at: www.nato.int/docu/review/2002/issue3/english/art4.html (accessed 27 July 2010).

Schuyer, J. (2008) 'The Civilian Headline Goal 2008: developing civilian crisis management capabilities in the EU?', in S. Blockmans (ed.) *The European Union and Crisis Management: Policy and Legal Aspects* (The Hague: TMC Asser Press).

Sebastian, S. (2009) 'The Role of the EU in the Reform of Dayton in Bosnia-Herzegovina', *Ethnopolitics,* 8 (3): 341–54.

SDA (2007) *The EU's Africa Strategy: What are the lessons of the Congo Mission?* Security and Defence Agenda, Brussels.

Sedelmeier, U. (2003) *EU Enlargement, Identity and the Analysis of European Foreign Policy: Identity Formation through Policy Practice Fiesole* (San Domenico: European University Institute).

Sepos, A. (2008) *The Europeanization of Cyprus: Polity, Policies and Politics* (Basingstoke: Palgrave Macmillan).

SHAPE (2004a) *SHAPE-EU Cooperation: Background Information* (online), available at: www.nato.int/shape/issues/shape_eu/background.htm (accessed 27 July 2010).

SHAPE (2004b) *Operation Althea* (online), available at: www.nato.int/shape/issues/shape_eu/althea.htm (accessed 27 July 2010).

Sheffer, G., (2003) *Diaspora Politics: At Home Abroad* (Cambridge: Cambridge University Press).

Shepherd, A. (2003) 'The European Union's Security and Defence Policy: a policy without substance?' *European Security,* 12 (1): 39–63.

Sheriff, A. *et al.* (2010) 'Between the Summits: background paper', in *Beyond Development Aid. EU-Africa Political Dialogue on Global Issues of Common Concern* (Portugal: Europe Africa Policy Research Network).

Silber, L. and Little, A. (1996) *The Death of Yugoslavia* (London: Penguin Books).

Singer, J. D., (1961) 'The level-of-analysis problem in international relations', *World Politics,* 14 (1): 77–92.

Siradag, A. (2009) *Cooperation between the African Union (AU) and the European Union (EU) with regard to peacemaking and peacekeeping in Africa*, MA dissertation, University of Johannesburg.

Sjursen, H. (2003) 'Understanding the Common Foreign and Security Policy: analytical building blocs', in M. Knodt and S. Princen (eds), *Understanding the European Union's External Relations* (London: Routledge).

Smith, D. (2002a) 'Framing the national question in Central and Eastern Europe: a quadratic nexus?' *Ethnopolitics,* 2 (1): 3–16.

Smith, H. (2002b) *European Union Foreign Policy: What It Is and What It Does* (London: Pluto Press).

Smith, K. (2005) 'The outsiders: the European Neighbourhood Policy', *International Affairs,* 81 (4): 757–73.

Smith, K. E. (2003) *European Foreign Policy in a Changing World* (Cambridge: Polity).

Smith, M. E. (2001) 'Diplomacy by degree: the legalisation of EU foreign policy', *Journal of Common Market Studies,* 39 (1): 79–104.

Smith, M. J. (2004) *Europe's Foreign and Security Policy: The Institutionalization of Cooperation,* (Cambridge: Cambridge University Press).

Smith, P.J. (2005) *Terrorism and Violence in Southeast Asia: Transnational Challenges to States and Regional Stability* (Armonk, NY: M.E. Sharpe).

Soetendorp, B. (2002) 'The EU's involvement in the Israeli–Palestinian peace process: the building of a visible international identity', *European Foreign Affairs Review*, 7 (2): 283–95.

Solana, J. (2000) *Report on the Western Balkans Presented to the Lisbon European Council by the Secretary-General/High Representative together with the Commission*, SN 2032/2/00/REV2, Brussels, 21 March.

Solana, J. (2003) 'A Secure Europe in a Better World', *Report to the European Council Meeting*, Thessaloniki, 20 June.

Solana, J. (2005) Opening remarks, *Seminar with EU Special Representatives* (S239/05) Brussels, 29 June.

Solana, J. (2008) 'Europe in the World: The Next Steps', Cyril Foster Lecture, Oxford, February 28. Available at: www.consillium.europa.eu/ueDocs/cms_Data/docs/pressdata/EN/discours/99116.pdf

Solana, J. (2009a) *Remarks By EU High Representative at the ESDP@10: What Lessons for the Future?* Conference, Brussels.

Solana, J. (2009b) *Remarks on the occasion of the informal meeting of EU defence ministers (online)*, Prague, 12 March, available at: www.consilium.europa.eu/uedocs/cms_data/docs/pressdata/en/esdp/106634.pdf (accessed 16 March 2009).

Spruds, A., Danelsons, R. and Konenko, V. (2008) *Analysis of the EU's assistance to Moldova*. Briefing for the Foreign Affairs Committee of the European Parliament.

Steele, J. (2009) 'Saakashvili's sideshow', *Guardian* (online) 3 August, available at: www.guardian.co.uk/commentisfree/2009/aug/03/georgia-russia-saakashvili-us (accessed 27 July 2010).

Stewart, Emma J. (2008) 'Restoring EU–OSCE cooperation for pan-European conflict prevention', *Contemporary Security Policy*, 29 (2): 266–84.

SVT (2008) *Prisoner tortured at a Swedish military base in Congo* (online), available at: svt.se/2.90352/1.1101022/prisoner_tortured_at_a_swedish_military_base_in_the_congo (accessed 16 March 2009).

Talmon, S. (2001) 'The Cyprus Question before the European Court of Justice', *European Journal of International Law*, 12 (4): 727–50.

Taylor, I. and Williams, P. (2001), 'South African foreign policy and the great Lakes Crisis: African renaissance meets "Vagabondage politique"?', *African Affairs*, 100: 265–86.

Tellis, A. J. (1997) *Anticipating Ethnic Conflict* (Santa Monica, CA: Rand).

Thakur, R. and Schnabel, A. (2001) *United Nations Peacekeeping Operations: Ad Hoc Missions, Permanent Engagement* (Tokyo: United Nations University Press).

The Economist (1997) 'Israel intransigent', *The Economist*, 28 June, Leaders, p. 17.

The Economist (2009) 28 November–4 December.

The Independent (2009) 2 December.

Thier, A. (2004) 'Reestablishing the Judicial System in Afghanistan', *CDDRL Working Paper no. 19*, Stanford University, 1 September.

Tocci, N. (2005) 'Conflict resolution in the neighbourhood: comparing EU involvement in Turkey's Kurdish question and in the Israeli–Palestinian conflict.' *Mediterranean Politics*, 10 (2): 125–46.

Tocci, N. (2005b) 'The Widening Gap between Rhetoric and Reality in EU Policy Towards the Israeli–Palestinian Conflict', *CEPS Working Document No. 217* (Brussels: Centre for European Policy Studies).

Tocci, N. (2006) 'Has the EU promoted democracy in Palestine … and does it still?', *CFSP Forum*, 4 (2): 7–10.

Tocci, N. (2007a) *The EU's Role in Conflict Resolution: Promoting Peace in the European Neighbourhood* (London: Routledge).

Tocci, N. (2007b) *The EU and Conflict Resolution: Promoting Peace in the Backyard* (London: Routledge).

Tocci, N. (2009) 'Firm in rhetoric, compromising in reality: the EU in the Israeli–Palestinian conflict', *Ethnopolitics*, 8 (3): 387–401.

Toggenburg, G. von (ed.) (2005) *Minority Protection and the EU: The Way Forward* (Budapest: LGI).

Tonra, B. (2001) *The Europeanisation of National Foreign Policy. Dutch, Danish and Irish Foreign Policy in the European Union* (Aldershot: Ashgate).

Tovias, A. (2003) 'Israeli policy perspectives on the Euro-Mediterranean partnership in the context of EU enlargement', *Mediterranean Politics*, 8 (2): 214–32.

Trajkovski, B. (2003) Speech at the ceremony marking the ending of NATO's Operation Allied Harmony and transfer of authority to EU (Brussels: NATO) (online). Available at: www.nato.int/docu/speech/2003/s030331d.htm (accessed 1 June 2009).

Treaty Establishing the European Gendarmerie Force (2007) (Den Haag: Asser Institute).

Tull, D. M. (2009) 'Peacekeeping in the Democratic Republic of Congo: waging peace and fighting war', *International Peacekeeping*, 16 (2): 215–30.

Turkish Daily News (2001) *Turkey signals defiance to EU over Cyprus*, 7 November.

Turkish Daily News (2004) *Greek Cypriots face rancor for 'no'*, 26 April.

Ulriksen, S., Gourlay, C., and Mace, C. (2004) 'Operation Artemis: The shape of things to come?', *International Peacekeeping*, 11 (3): 508–35

UN Secretary–General (2009) *Report on the UN Mission in the DR Congo* (online), 27 March, available at: allafrica.com/peaceafrica/resources/00011770.html (accessed 10 April 2008).

UNHCR (UN High Commissioner for Refugees) (2005) *Refugee Statistics: Afghanistan* (online), available at: www.unhcr.ch/cgibin/texis/vtx/afghan?page=background, Chapter 8.

UNICEF (2006) 'Child Alert: Democratic Republic of Congo' (online). Available at: unicef.org/childalert/drc/content/Child Alert DRC en.pdf

UNISPAL (2009) *EU funded vans for Palestinian Civilian Police* (online) 17 March, available at: unispal.un.org/UNISPAL.NSF/0/C462CA96A1E9C52D8525757F004B3A77 (accessed 22 July 2010).

United Nations (1992) *An Agenda for Peace: Preventative Diplomacy, Peacemaking and Peace-keeping* (online), 17 June, available at: www.un.org/docs/SG/agpeace.html (accessed 13 July 2010).

United Nations (2001) *Agreement on Provisional Arrangements in Afghanistan Pending the Re-establishment of Permanent Government Institutions (Bonn Agreement)* (online), 7 December, available at: www.un.org/News/dh/latest/afghan/afghan-agree.htm (accessed 24 July 2010).

United Nations (2009a) *Human Development Report – Afghanistan* (online), available at: hdrstats.undp.org/en/countries/country_fact_sheets/cty_fs_AFG.html (accessed 24 July 2010).

United Nations (2009b) *MONUC* (online), available at: www.monuc.org/Home.aspx?lang=en (accessed 7 February 2009).

United Nations (2010) MONUSCO: *United Nations Organisation Stabilisation Mission in the Democratic Republic of Congo* (online). Available at: monusco.unmissions.org/

United Nations Security Council (2001) *Resolution 1371*, S/RES/1371.

United Nations Security Council (2002) *Resolution 1396*, S/RES/1396.

United Nations Security Council (2003) *Resolution 1484*, S/RES/1484.

United Nations Security Council (2004) *Resolution 1575*, S/RES/1575.

US Department of State (2003) 'A Performance-Based Roadmap to a Permanent Two-State Solution to the Israeli-Palestinian Conflict', Press Statement, 30 April, available at: www.state.gov/r/pa/prs/ps/2003/20062.htm (accessed 4 December 2008).

Vankovska, B. (2002) *Current Perspectives on Macedonia: The Struggle for Peace, Democracy and Security* (Berlin: Heinrich Böll Foundation).

Van Meurs, W. (2004) *Moldova ante portas: the EU Agendas of Conflict Management and 'Wider Europe'*, CAP, LMU München.

Varwick, J. and Lang, K. O. (eds) (2007) *European Neighbourhood Policy: Challenges for the EU-Policy Towards the New Neighbours* (Opladen: Budrich).

Venice Declaration (1980) 13 June, available at: ec.europa.eu/external_relations/mepp/docs/venice_declaration_1980_en.pdf (accessed 21 July 2010).

Vines, A. (2010) 'Rhetoric from Brussels and reality on the ground: the EU and security in Africa', *International Affairs*, 85(5): 1091–1108.

Vlassenroot, K. and Raeymaekers, T. (2004) 'The politics of rebellion and intervention in Ituri: the emergence of a new political complex?', *African Affairs*, 103 (412): 385–412.

Wagnsson, C. (2010) 'Divided power Europe: normative divergences among the EU "big three"', *Journal of European Public Policy,* 17 (8): 1089–105.

Wallace, H. (2007) *The Impact of the Reform Treaty on the Institutions of the EU. Corrected Oral Evidence*, House of Lords, 6 December.

Waltz, K. N., (1959) *Man, the State and War* (New York, NY: Columbia University Press).

Washington Post (2004) *Turkey Asks UN's Annan to Restart Cyprus Talks*, 25 January.

Whitman, R. G. (1998) *From Civilian Power to Superpower? The International Identity of the European Union* (London: Macmillan).

Whitman, R. G. and Wolff, S. (2010a) 'The EU as a conflict manager? The case of Georgia and its implications', *International Affairs,* 87 (1): 87–107.

Whitman, R. G. and Wolff, S. (eds.) (2010b) *The European Neighbourhood Policy in Perspective: Context, Implementation, and Impact* (Basingstoke: Palgrave).

Whitney, N. (2008) *Re-energising Europe's Security and Defence Policy* (Brussels: European Council on Foreign Relations).

Williams, M.J. (2011) 'Empire lite revisited: NATO, the comprehensive approach and state-building in Afghanistan', *International Peacekeeping*, 18(1): 64–78.

Williams, P. (2001) 'Transnational criminal enterprises, conflict and instability.' in C. A. Crocker, F. O. Hampson and P. Aall (eds) *Turbulent Peace. The Challenges of Managing International Conflict* (Washington, DC: United States Institute of Peace Press).

Williams, P. (2009) 'Into the Mogadishu maelstrom: the African Union mission in Somalia', *International Peacekeeping*, 16(4): 514–30.

Wilson, A. (2009) 'New blow for EADS as France considers cut to A400M order', *Daily Telegraph,* 17 March.

Wilson, A., and Popescu, N. (2009) 'Russian and European neighbourhood policies compared.', *Southeast European and Black Sea Studies* 9 (3): 317–31.

Wolff, S. (2001) 'Context and content: Sunningdale and Belfast compared.' in R. Wilford (ed.) *Aspects of the Belfast Agreement* (Oxford: Oxford University Press).

Wolff, S. (2003a) *Disputed Territories: The Transnational Dynamics of Ethnic Conflict Settlement* (New York, NY: Berghahn).

Wolff, S. (2003b) 'Positionspapier zum Fallbeispiel ehemaliges Jugoslawien', in J. Calließ (ed.) *Zivile Konfliktbearbeitung im Schatten des Terrors* (Rehburg-Loccum: Evangelische Akademie Loccum).

Wolff, S. (2003c) 'The limits of non-military intervention: a case study of the Kosovo conflict', in F. Bieber and Z. Daskalovski (eds) *Understanding the War in Kosovo* (London: Frank Cass).

Wolff, S. (2008) 'Learning the lessons of ethnic conflict management? Conditional recognition and international administration in the Western Balkans since the 1990s.' *Nationalities Papers,* 36 (3): 553–71.

Wolff, S. (2011a) 'The regional dimensions of state failure', *Review of International Studies,* 37 (3): 951–72.

Wolff, S. (2011b) 'A resolvable frozen conflict? Designing a Settlement for Transnistria', *Nationalities Papers*, 6 (39): 863–70.

Yacobi, H. and Newman, D. (2007) 'The EU and the Israel–Palestine conflict', in T. Diez, M. Albert and S. Stetter (eds) *The European Union and Border Conflicts: The Power of Integration and Association* (Cambridge: Cambridge University Press).

Yakinthou, C. (2009) 'The EU's role in the Cyprus conflict: system failure or structural metamorphosis?', *Ethnopolitics,* 8 (3): 307–23.

Youngs, R. (2008) 'Fusing security and development: just another Euro-platitude?' *Journal of European Integration,* 30 (3): 419–37.

Zartman, I. W. (2001) 'The timing of peace initiatives: hurting stalemates and ripe moments', *The Global Review of Ethnopolitics,* 1 (1), 8–18.

Zartman, I.W. (1985) *Ripe for Resolution* (New York: Oxford University Press).

Index